ORGANIZED LABOUR
IN THE 21ST CENTURY

Organized labour
in the 21ˢᵗ century

Edited by A. V. Jose

International Institute for Labour Studies Geneva

ISBN 92-9014-642-7

First published 2002

Cover photocredit: Federation of Korean Trade Unions (FKTU), Seoul.

Copies can be ordered directly from: ILO Publications, International Labour Office, CH-1211 Geneva 22 (Switzerland)

Preface

The last quarter of the twentieth century was a period of profound social and economic transformation which has far-reaching implications for organized labour. In many countries, the numerical strength of unions declined, and the viability of labour market institutions, which unions helped establish, has been called into question. Globalization and its ramifications present a formidable challenge which requires new approaches and strategies on the part of the labour movement if it is to remain a major actor influencing social policy.

The International Labour Organization has an obvious interest in these developments. It is especially concerned with the ways in which trade unions, a pillar of the Organization, have responded to challenges arising from globalization. Early in 1998, the International Institute for Labour Studies launched a project entitled "Organized Labour in the 21st Century", designed to highlight the role of the trade union movement in contributing to dynamic social policy and equitable growth. The project addressed three major issues: the changing environment of labour and unions; trade union responses to these changes; and future perspectives for labour in society and in the global economy.

The project was launched in collaboration with major international trade union organizations and the ILO Bureau for Workers' Activities. Activities were organized on two tracks: an electronic network linking trade union practitioners with academics and the ILO; and comparative research on union responses and strategies in different countries.

The electronic network was originally established to elicit views from both union practitioners and labour specialists and to provide a forum for dialogue between the ILO, working people and the academic community. The network developed into an on-line conference, a unique experiment which enabled its members to build links with each other and exchange ideas on the future of the labour movement. This process revealed widespread concern and interest in revitalizing the labour movement. The Institute has prepared a number of reports based on the themes and proceedings of the on-line conference. These reports, along with an anthology of the main contributions by the conference participants, have been posted on the Institute web-site (www.ilo.org/public/english/bureau/inst/project/labns.htm).

Comparative research was also organized within the framework of structured case studies on "Trade union responses to globalization". The studies were conducted by noted academics in 15 countries: Brazil, Canada, Chile, Ghana, India, Israel, Japan, Republic of Korea, Lithuania, Niger, South

Africa, Spain, Sweden, Tunisia and USA. The studies have been published in different languages as Discussion Papers of the Institute and posted on the Institute web-site.

The on-line conference and the case studies together have yielded several significant findings. They highlight the importance of organizational strategies to enable unions to exercise voice and influence policy. They reveal that the major challenge for unions in all countries, notably in developing countries, is the representation of non-traditional constituents and the provision of new services. They show that changes in the world of work and in social attitudes are leading to union alliances and coalitions with other civil society actors for common goals.

This volume presents a representative sample of the comparative research undertaken by the Institute. It includes selected country case studies on the theme "Trade union responses to globalization", edited and abridged to illustrate experiences drawn from three broad groups of countries: industrialized economies; middle-income countries; and developing nations.

It is our hope that these studies will generate wider understanding of the role and changing priorities of organized labour in countries at varying stages of development. More specifically, by stimulating greater reflection and analysis, we hope they will contribute to the formulation of effective policies and strategies for labour movements in the years ahead.

Padmanabha Gopinath
Director, International Institute for Labour Studies

Contents

PART 3

About the authors

Souley Adji studied in Bordeaux, France, where he received his Ph. D. in 1991. He is currently a Professor at the University of Niamey in Niger. His research interests are chiefly in the field of social movements, democratization and civil society in Africa.

Kwasi Anyemedu taught economics at the University of Ghana and has also had extensive experience in the public services of Ghana. Among positions held by him are Director, Policy Analysis Division, Ministry of Finance; Executive Chairman, State Gold Mining Corp. He has also spent a year with the Trades Union Congress of Ghana as Director of Research. His areas of specialization are economic policy analysis and international trade and economic development.

Andries Bezuidenhout is a researcher at the Sociology of Work Unit at the University of the Witwatersrand in Johannesburg, South Africa. Apart from a research interest in union responses to globalization and regionalization, he is currently working on projects analysing union involvement in industrial policy formulation in southern Africa, and the impact of global processes of industrial restructuring on local manufacturing economies.

Debashish Bhattacherjee is a Professor at the Human Resources Group of the Indian Institute of Management at Calcutta. He holds a Ph. D. in labour economics and industrial relations from the University of Illinois in the United States. His particular research and teaching interests are the economics and political economy of labour markets and labour movements, discrimination, corporate compensation and applied econometrics.

Guillermo Campero, sociologist, studied at the Catholic University of Chile and spent two years in advanced studies in social science in Paris. He is currently a member of the Cabinet of Consultants to the Chilean President. When he carried out this study he was an advisor to the Ministry of Labour and Social Security.

Roma Dovydeniene is Deputy Secretary of the largest national trade union centre in Lithuania and a Member of Parliament, representing the Social Democrats. By training she is a labour lawyer and spokesperson for the trade unions and Social Democrats on labour legislation.

Reinhold Fahlbeck is Professor of labour law at Lund University and head of the Department of Labour Law and Associate Professor at the Stockholm School of Economics. He has been visiting Professor at universities in the United States, Poland and Japan. His main interests within the field of labour law and industrial relations are (i) comparative studies, in particular comparative industrial relations, (ii) Catholic social thinking, (iii) the law of collective agreements and (iv) trade secrets, restrictive covenants and freedom of speech.

Stephen A. Herzenberg is Executive Director of the Keystone Research Center, an economic policy "think and do" tank in Harrisburg, Pennsylvania, USA. He served as assistant to the chief US negotiator of the labour side agreement to the North American Free Trade Agreement. He holds a Ph. D. in economics from the Massachusetts Institute of Technology.

Sadahiko Inoue majored in economics and philosophy and graduated from Tokyo University of Education (Tsukuba University) in 1964. He has been the Deputy Director-General of the JTUC Research Institute for the Advancement of Living Standards (RIALS) since February 1990.

A. V. Jose headed the Labour and Society Programme in the International Institute for Labour Studies, ILO, Geneva. An economist with specialization in labour markets, he did postgraduate studies at Delhi University; worked and pursued doctoral studies at the Centre for Development Studies Thiruvananthapuram (India); and joined the ILO in 1980. At the ILO he managed the Programme on "Organized labour in the 21st century".

Roby Nathanson is currently Chairman of the Israeli Institute for Economic and Social Research. He studied at the University of Cologne, Germany, gaining a Ph. D. in economics in 1982. He has lectured in industrial relations and on economics at the Universities of Haifa and Tel Aviv, and at the Hebrew University of Jerusalem. From 1989 to 1995 he was Director of the Institute for Economic and Social Research of the Histadrut.

Ho Keun Song, Sociology Professor of Seoul National University in the Republic of Korea, is currently interested in research on welfare and labour politics and their consequences during two democratic governments of the 1990s. He has worked on democratization and globalization in the Republic of Korea with a focus on the politics of crisis management. He is also a Director of the Institute of Social Development and Policy Research.

Organized labour in the 21ˢᵗ century – Some lessons for developing countries

A. V. Jose[1]

This introductory chapter is organized in two parts. Part I gives an assessment of the findings from various studies and activities carried out under the project "Organized Labour in the 21ˢᵗ Century".[2] The main focus here is on the lessons learned from the approaches and strategies of trade unions in terms of promising responses to the social and economic changes that came along with globalization. First, we make some observations on changes in the environment due to globalization and its impact on some labour market institutions. Then we look at how the unions have responded to the changing environment by making suitable adaptations to the labour institutions and also the structures for organizing and representing the interests of workers.

The main theme advanced in Part I is that trade unions over the past several decades have constantly adapted themselves to changes in the world of work; in the process they emerged as major partners in development contributing to the growth of markets and democratic institutions. Unions blended strategies for converting labour into non-competing groups, as a result of which they have come to occupy a unique position as purveyors of social cohesion in all societies. We argue further that in recent times the political fall-out of globalization has cast a shadow on the cohesive role and

---

[1] The author alone is responsible for the views expressed here. He would like to acknowledge the valuable advice and support received from Jean-Michel Servais and Padmanabha Gopinath in the preparation of this paper.

[2] The studies are the following: Nathanson et al. (1999), Bhattacherjee (1999), Inoue (1999), Song (1999), Fahlbeck (1999), Dovydeniene (2000), Campero (2000), Ojeda-Aviles (2000), Bezuidenhout (2000), Adji (2000), Anyemedu (2000), Ennaceur (2000), Herzenberg (2000), Jose (2000), Matteso and Pochmann (2001), Murray (2001) and Wong (2000). The study on Singapore by Wong was prepared for an Asian regional meeting on Organized Labour held in Seoul. Most of these studies in their original version have been published as Discussion Papers and posted on the Institute web-site: http://www.ilo.org/public/english/bureau/inst/project/labns.htm. The present chapter has also drawn from several reports of the Institute based on the themes and proceedings of the on-line conference, referred to in the preface to this volume. These reports: Murray (2000), Hermann (2001) Mozdzer (2001), and Tan (2001), along with an anthology of the main contributions by the conference participants, are on the Institute web-site.

that unions need to configure new strategies if they are to resume their role as guardians of social cohesion.

Based on the above findings, Part II of this chapter discusses some conclusions about the priorities and strategies of the labour movement in developing countries.

Part I

1. The changing environment

Trade unions came of age during the second and third quarters of the twentieth century when they became significant forces influencing the course and content of economic progress among the industrial economies of the West. During that period, the unions built strong organizations to represent the interests of workers and they guided the development of numerous social institutions governing labour markets. In the process they delivered major outcomes through improved living standards, equity and justice to workers all over the world.

The benefits which unions have gained for labour are embodied in the regulatory instruments and institutions of the industrial relations system that governs labour markets. Salient features of the system in the industrialized countries are: (a) full-time employment, governed by an open-ended contract; (b) collectively negotiated wage structure; (c) social benefits to workers and their dependents distributed through the main income earner; (d) control over working time and safety standards; and (e) job security for a majority of workers.

The institution of industrial relations has not been limited to the developed countries. Some variants emerged in the developing countries too, where industrial workers in their capacity as pioneers among the ranks of an economically powerful middle class could claim numerous benefits including higher wages, better working conditions, civic amenities and social security benefits. They were politically important allies of the state, and were represented through unions active in regulated industries and public sector enterprises. The benefits they derived from employment were embedded in a "social pact" which set the terms of compromise between capital, organized labour and the state in sharing the national product.

Until the 1970s trade unions functioned in industrial societies within a framework mainly marked by the following features: stable employment relations, a significant public sector, organized social actors, and common values shared by all the social partners. Following globalization, the above features underwent significant alteration during the closing decades of the twentieth century. Some contributory factors that have added to the pace of change may be listed as follows: (i) technological progress and accompanying changes in the composition of the workforce; (ii) an increased supply of new entrants into labour markets, particularly women; (iii) the adoption of liberal economic policies by governments; and (iv) the practice of flexible labour market policies.

Technological changes made it possible to reshape production through new forms of industrial organization and the relocation of production platforms. They led to the disintegration of large work places and the rise of small, geographically dispersed units of production. The changes also set in motion a polarization of the workforce into two distinct categories, traditionally less represented by the unions. At the higher end of the scale, workers tend to be better educated, career minded, individualistic and less motivated by class interests and solidarity. At the lower end are workers with fewer skills, who are marginalized, scattered and prone to exploitation.

There has also been a significant increase in the supply of workers in urban labour markets, mostly on account of demographic changes. A large proportion of the new incumbents are women or migrants. The influx of women workers has mostly been into insecure and poorly paid work on export platforms and production chains, thereby accentuating inequalities within labour markets.

Competitive pressures generated by globalization have led to a decline in the capacity of the state for resource mobilization, an increased reliance on austerity measures and a government retreat from Keynesian approaches to full employment and expansionary economic policies. Besides, the historical alliance between the labour movement and social democratic regimes seems to have weakened over time. The new emphasis is on privatization and downsizing of public sector enterprises and on liberal economic policies to encourage private enterprises in areas traditionally reserved for the public sector.

Liberal economic policies coupled with supply side pressures have resulted in a widespread adoption of flexible labour market policies. Practices such as subcontracting, outsourcing and the hiring of temporary and part-time workers, long considered as atypical work, are becoming more common especially at the lower end of the labour market.

The changes in the composition of the workforce and the adoption of flexible labour market policies have called into question the viability of several labour institutions upon which the unions have always relied. In the past, labour legislation and collective agreements embodying job security, wages and non-wage benefits have taken into account the requirements of a relatively homogeneous workforce that conformed to the post-war construct of a "normal employment pattern" characterized by full-time jobs and stable

career trajectories. It became increasingly difficult for unions to defend these
institutions as they came under attack by market forces.

New entrants at the higher end of the labour market are not necessarily
inclined to support the normal employment pattern espoused by unions. At
the lower end of the market, excess supply is reflected in the widespread use
of non-standard employment relations including subcontracting, part-time,
temporary and home-based work. The end result may have been rising wage
inequality, eroding job-ladders, and in some countries, falling rates of health
care coverage and declining value of social security benefits.[3]

2. The modification of labour institutions

Unions in some industrialized countries and also emerging economies
have been remarkably successful in adapting to globalization, maintaining
their strength, influence and visibility. This is because they anticipated change
and modified their institutions and structures for strategic engagement with
the constituents. Sweden, Canada and Singapore stand out among the
countries that followed new approaches with positive results.[4]

It has been noted that in Sweden and Singapore the unions accepted the
need for flexibility and prepared themselves to live in a era of profound
technological changes. They opted for a shift in emphasis towards ensuring
the employability of workers; they mobilized resources along with the state
and business to create facilities for continuous training and skill upgrading.
The training facilities especially addressed the needs of less-skilled workers
who were at risk of exclusion from employment. The unions also took
responsibility for assisting the state in providing a variety of services —
educational, social, cultural and recreational— that enriched the personal and
professional lives of members and their families.

There is, however, a notable difference between developed and
developing countries with regard to the current situation of unions and labour
institutions. In the industrial economies, trade unions are in most cases well
past the stage of having had to struggle to improve the basic conditions of
work and living standards of their constituents. Economic growth during the
post-war decades has led to a conspicuous decline in the number of workers
exposed to exploitative conditions. As the industrial economies advanced to
higher levels of income and productivity, the traditional membership base
of unions shifted towards skilled work. The unions also moved into new fora

---

[3] These issues have been highlighted by Herzenberg (2000) as major problems facing labour
in the United States.
[4] The repertoire of union responses is discussed in Fahlbeck (2000), Murray (2001) and Wong
(2000).

for collaboration with employers, ostensibly for the creation of a new industrial relations regime based on the management of human resources.

The outlook and approach of the unions in industrialized countries have been influenced by the fact that the emerging industrial workforce in these countries is employed in companies or enterprises at the very frontier of technological progress and global economic leadership. Increasingly they are inclined to view industrial society through a supply side optic and to work with business and government for the development of human resources. Besides, the maturing of representative institutions during the "golden age" of industrial society has effectively guaranteed workers a voice in the making of social policy.

The situation is quite different in the developing countries where labour institutions have been unable to achieve a secure income for the majority of workers. The ascent of flexible labour market policies seems to have reduced the influence of unions over the development of institutions for labour market governance. The "language of flexibility" is more widely used; it has become a critique of the legitimacy and position of the labour movement in developing societies.[5] Nonetheless, among the developing countries there has been a discernible shift away from an earlier phase when unions resisted globalization towards a readiness to accommodate the demands of market forces. The results produced during the early years of confrontation were not very encouraging either.[6] The new thrust is to develop a broad support base for unions through addressing the needs of multiple constituencies, backed by innovative schemes for job creation and active involvement in human resource development.[7]

3. Adaptation of union structures

Two observations stand out: first, the unions have adapted their representative structures in accordance with changes in the composition of the workforce; and second, they have embraced new approaches to providing services for their constituents.

When technological changes and liberal economic policies together undermined the social basis of unionization, two related factors emerged

---

[5] This observation made by Bezuidenhout (2000) in the context of South Africa is applicable to all developing countries.

[6] For instance, in countries like India where unions strongly defended workers in predominantly labour intensive industries, the net outcome was a long-term decline in employment and wages. The industries closed down and the regions that harboured them became industrial wastelands. The textile mills of western India and the jute mills of eastern India are cases in point (Sherlock, 1996).

[7] The new approaches being tried out are discussed in the studies on Ghana (Anyemedu, 2000), India (Bhattacherjee, 1999), Korea (Song, 1999) and Chile (Campero, 2000).

restricting any further growth of unions. First, industrial employment gradually shifted towards small and geographically dispersed units that were more adept at flexible work practices. Second, the civil service and the public sector enterprises that have always been the main citadel of unions were faced with a significant reduction in size.

In terms of size and location decentralized units of production are not necessarily viable for the purpose of organizing.[8] The inverse relationship found to exist between the cost of organizing and the size of enterprises has compelled the unions to create new representative structures that can maximize the benefits of unionization.[9] Another notable development, observed in several countries, has been the rise of enterprise-based company unions, akin to business unionism, representing workers at the higher end of the skill spectrum, but insulating them from a sense of collective identity or solidarity among workers. The new structures offered efficient solutions, better wages and more fringe benefits compared to earlier ones that catered to large numbers in an environment of militancy and solidarity.[10]

In the changing environment unions created new structures at different levels for organizing workers and representing their interests. Even in countries where collective bargaining traditionally took place at the plant level, there was a move towards centralized structures for negotiation. In continental Europe enterprise unionism became an important forum for complementing negotiations at the higher level. The Works Councils which started in countries like Germany, where labour and business practise mutually beneficial consultation, are now being adopted all over Europe.

The changes also forced the unions to address the concerns of new constituents, notably women workers, who were traditionally not represented through union structures. A commendable achievement in Sweden is that almost all the women entering the workforce have been brought into the union fold. In the industrialized countries, unions have increasingly been campaigning for better community services for children and dependents,

---

[8] Herzenberg (2000) draws attention to a significant increase in the cost of unionizing in the United States. This topic also figured in the on-line debates on the future of *Organized Labour* (Murray, 2000).

[9] In the United States, unions have laid emphasis on organizing less-skilled workers, women and minority groups in the service industries (Bronfenbrenner et al., 1998). There have also been innovative approaches to organizing low-skilled workers in small enterprises under the aegis of area-specific organizations.

[10] The rise of enterprise unions, generally independent and non-affiliated to apex bodies or political parties has been reported in a number of studies, for instance: Bhattacherjee (1999), Inoue (1999), Song (1999), Campero (2000), Adji (2000), Anyemedu (2000), and Murray (2001). In India, the rise of such unions has also been associated with an increase of regional disparities in income distribution (Jose, 2000; Sherlock,1996).

parental leave for working parents, training facilities for working women and an increased number of women in leadership positions within unions. These concerns are just beginning to surface in union strategies in the developing world.[11]

More important is the fact that the unions have been on the lookout for new constituents; they have broadened their definition of collectivity through fresh recruitment and mergers with other unions. The unions also secured the support and loyalty of another rising category—temporary and part-time workers—through concluding special agreements on their behalf. These experiences indicate that a strong fraternity of workers built through the provision of specialized services can make the unions a force to be reckoned with for many years to come.

The competitive forces generated through globalization seem to have undermined the unique status of unions in some countries as the exclusive providers of services. They have been compelled to adapt their structures to make them efficient and far more responsive to the changing needs of workers and society in general.[12] Unions have learned the hard way that the provision of services is a necessary but not sufficient condition for building strength and that equal attention needs to be directed to the provision of competitive services.[13]

Unions also encountered new problems arising from mismatches between their traditional platforms for representation and the new employer structures appearing as the result of mergers, acquisitions and corporate restructuring.[14] The rise of macro-regional markets such as the EU, NAFTA and ASEAN has also prompted the unions to consolidate their representative structures at regional level.[15]

---

[11] The need for unions to address gender-specific problems such as pay equity, child care, sexual harassment, etc. and also the needs of multiple constituencies based on gender, race, ethnicity and age were raised in several studies and also during the on-line conference. See Network Report (1999), Murray (2000), Fahlbeck (2000), Spalter-Roth et al.(1994), and Milkman (1992).

[12] For instance, the traditional structures that provided union services became dysfunctional among the former planned economies such as Lithuania in Eastern Europe. It became necessary for unions to cooperate with the state and business for the development of new institutions concerned with social insurance and social assistance (Dovydeniene, 2000).

[13] The experience of Histadrut, the apex union of Israel, is a case in point. The emergence of competitive providers of heath care following the enactment of the National Health Insurance Law in 1994 severed the links between trade unions and the provision of universal health care and resulted in a 60 per cent fall in union membership (Nathanson et al., 1999).

[14] This problem has been discussed by Herzenberg (2000) in the US context.

[15] The acronyms respectively stand for European Union, North Atlantic Free Trade Area and Association of South East Asian Nations. The consolidation of markets is referred to in a report on network activities under the project on *Organized Labour* (Network Report, 1999).

A general observation arising from the studies and on-line discussions held under the project is that over the years, unions in all countries have grown from a predominantly bargaining role to a broader one in representing the voice and interests of labour. Unions responded to the challenge of meeting the changing requirements of the industrial workforce, established themselves as credible partners and provided a variety of services to members and non-members, including mutual aid, credit, insurance, housing and consumer services. In many countries the preeminent position which unions enjoyed in terms of membership and influence over government policy was anchored in the services which they provided to their members.[16]

Perhaps the most significant outcome of unions taking on a broad range of responsibilities is that they created an enduring platform for workers' participation and partnership in the development of industrial economies. Unions contributed to building a unique set of institutions that helped sustain workers' involvement in the development of markets. More important, they made use of such institutions to develop the political space for democratic institutions. Union experience in these areas provides some valuable lessons for their counterparts in developing countries.

4. Unions as partners in development

An important lesson arising from industrialization in the West is that large numbers of workers were absorbed as partners in the development of markets. Growth and accumulation in industrial economies made it possible for workers to secure higher wages, better living standards and more opportunities for wealth creation. Workers played the dual role of mass producers and mass consumers, thus contributing to a continuous expansion of the economy.[17] The institutions embodying the partnership between workers were crucially important to the development of markets. This partnership had three main aspects: (i) participating directly in the production of goods and services; (ii) strengthening markets through raising or sustaining the general level of consumption; and (iii) promoting the professional mobility of workers.

---

[16] See for instance studies on Israel (Nathanson et al., 1999) Japan (Inoue, 1999) Sweden (Fahlbeck, 1999), South Africa (Bezuidenhout, 2000), Singapore (Wong, 2000) and Canada (Murray, 2001). Workers' perception of unions as effective providers of services was a crucial factor underlying high union density in Scandinavia. The Histadrut of Israel grew in strength until the early 1990s with an impressive membership based on the provision of services, notably health care, that covered almost the entire population.

[17] This theme figures prominently in the works of Landes (1998) and Hobsbawm (1994).

Participation in production often came through initiatives organized by cooperatives in fields such as housing, transportation, retail distribution, food and catering, health care, financial and personal services. These ventures mobilized the capital and skills of numerous small-scale producers as well as workers, and provided them with technical services which helped them organize production and distribution. The goods and services they produced had a moderating influence on prices; they helped consumers stretch their income and derive greater benefits from limited resources. Besides, the enterprises created a range of income-earning opportunities to labour-market entrants in urban areas and facilitated their long-term mobility into secure jobs.

Organized labour also participated in the creation of different institutions that strengthened the markets. The institutions for wage determination, in particular minimum wages and solidarity wages, ensured a solid and rising wage floor for workers, boosted their purchasing power and raised aggregate demand in society. A second category of institutions aimed at reducing workers' vulnerability to cyclical fluctuations in the market and other contingencies beyond the workers' control. Numerous insurance-based schemes, either privately funded or socially financed, have been organized to guard against contingencies such as unemployment, morbidity and disability.[18] They are seen as an important element underlying the stability of market economies.

A third area for union collaboration has been in creating opportunities for workers' mobility in terms of income, skills and employment status. This involved the design and development of institutions to impart skills, especially premium skills, also ensuring that skill acquisition becomes affordable to workers.[19]

5. Development of democratic institutions

In the past, organized labour has served as a potent social actor creating a political space for the ascent of democracy. The post-war decades, known as the "golden age" of industrialization in Europe, created a favourable climate for sharing the fruits of economic growth. Organized labour, by virtue of its vantage position as a partner in production, helped establish several institutions for a broad-based sharing of prosperity. The presence of an activist

---

[18] For a detailed discussion of the types, context and purpose of these institutions, see Piore and Sabel (1984), Ch.4.

[19] The partnership of unions in development through cooperatives and special institutions for skill development, as it evolved in the context of Singapore has been discussed by Wong (2000).

state involved in the allocation, stabilization and redistribution functions of modern governments, encouraged the unions to consolidate their position and contribute to social policy making in the framework of democratic institutions.[20]

Unions were an important vehicle for the transition to social democracy; they converted the economic space of the industrial workforce into a political space and made it possible for the whole of society to gain access to civil and political liberties.[21] Historically, the most important contribution of unions has been to broaden the base of a workers' constituency that has attained entry into industrial market economies and in turn, gained access to civil and political liberties through democratic institutions. As a result, Western industrial societies have become near synonyms for democratic societies. A new challenge before the labour movement today is to take democracy and human rights beyond the portals of industrial societies and make them accessible to all workers in the developing world.

In developing countries, globalization seems to have yielded an indirect and unexpected result in that it has strengthened democratic institutions. The earlier "social pact" created to prop up the compromise between the state, capital and labour failed to withstand the tide of market forces; it rendered the economy fragile and the labour force vulnerable. What followed was a shift away from inward-looking industrialization strategies and a decline in the protection of domestic industry. Labour became more militant and there was a disruption of the social accord which sustained the early phase of paternalistic industrial relations. In many developing countries, labour organized huge protests which were not simply a response to the decline in income and employment opportunities, but also a moral struggle against the "breach of trust" implicit in the break-up of the pact. They culminated in a powerful movement demanding democratic accountability by the regime in power.[22]

---

[20] The rise of a welfare state and workers' involvement in the development of social democratic institutions in the context of Western Europe are discussed by Crouch and Dore (1990) and Esping-Anderson (1996).

[21] A number of case studies held under the *Organized Labour* project-Fahlbeck (1999), Ojeda-Avilés (2000), Song (1999), Campero (2000), Bezuidenhout (2000) and Adji (2000)–highlight the positive contribution of organized labour to the development of democratic institutions.

[22] Webster and Adler (1998) explain this breach of trust as an aftermath of the stabilization and structural adjustment programmes inspired by the Bretton Woods Institutions. They argue that the struggle against the violation of the pact discredited several state corporatist regimes and fuelled pro-democracy movements in the 1980s and the 1990s. The latter observation is supported by several studies under the project: Song (1999), Adji (2000), Anyemedu (2000), and Campero (2000).

In many countries the protests were met with repression and also the arrest and intimidation of union leaders.[23] As it happened, adversity and repression brought out the best in trade unions. They campaigned against authoritarian regimes, broadened their social base beyond organized labour, developed solidarity with progressive forces in society and led a sustained struggle to establish or restore democracy. Among the countries studied under the project, the Republic of Korea and Chile stand out as cases where organized labour consolidated its political space and accelerated the pace of change to multi-party democracy. The studies also indicate that a union-led process of democratic transformation is well under way in a number of developing countries.[24] Evidence from these countries shows that democracy enhances the potential of trade unions to act as counterweights to the power of state and capital.

6. The cohesive role of unions

Unions nurtured social cohesion by involving themselves in the design of institutions that minimized income disparities, guaranteed a secure income and improved living standards in industrial society as a whole. Firstly, unions aimed at correcting imbalances in income distribution through maintaining "solidarity wages" that minimized differentials between workers. Secondly, they adopted an inclusive approach to workers outside the union, and provided a variety of services which made them non-competing groups in the world of work.[25] The latter role brought them to new fora for collaboration with other actors representing different interest groups in society.

It appears that in recent times the cohesive role of unions has become less important. This may be attributed to a decline in the commonalities that defined the collective identity of workers in industrial societies. The conventional model of unionism, built on a collective identity of workers, is not necessarily appropriate to address the needs of a heterogeneous workforce, differentiated in terms of skills and living standards.[26] The studies

---

[23] The story is recalled in several studies listed in footnote 21.

[24] Studies in Africa: Bezuidenhout (2000), Adji (2000), and Anyemedu (2000) draw attention to the current union thrust towards building democratic institutions.

[25] The union strategy of creating non-competing groups is discussed in Western (1997). The cohesive role of unions based on the provision of services to workers and non-workers figured prominently in the discussions during the on-line conference on *Organized Labour*. See Murray (2000).

[26] This point is argued by Murray (2001) in the setting of trade unions in Canada. Valkenburg (1996) has pointed out that collective frames of reference for industrial society, from which people in the past derived part of their individual and social identity, are losing significance.

point to some contributory factors that have aggravated the divergence of interests between workers in all countries, both developed and developing.

Firstly, the rise of the information society seems to have sharpened skill differences between workers.[27] Knowledge or human capital is becoming a prized resource that operates in a sellers' market, without frontiers and independent of union involvement. If all the emerging categories of knowledge workers and managers were to join trade unions, they would go for independent unions of professional workers. There is greater mobility among such workers and they are less likely to identify with the unions of the firm or enterprise they work for.

If the unions were to focus exclusively on the concerns of workers at the high end of the market, there is a risk of their influence becoming circumscribed and of interest to a dwindling proportion of the workforce. Large numbers of workers who do not possess improved skills or belong to competitive enterprises are likely to be excluded from the benefits of new industrial relations being adopted worldwide.[28] The crucial question is whether the labour movement can rise to the challenge of simultaneously addressing the concerns of all sections of the workforce.

The emergence of larger regional markets such as the EU, NAFTA and ASEAN also exacerbates the differences between workers, within and between the regions, in terms of employment, income and access to markets. The above development seems to cast a shadow on the transnational solidarity platform of workers nurtured by the international trade union organizations. Globalization has added to the insecurity of workers, making them compete even within the same region for highly mobile international capital. The competition appears to be fiercer against workers outside the region, to whom production is likely to be outsourced or subcontracted.[29] This points to the need for strategies that minimize competition between workers in different countries and at the same time raise their access to global markets.

The findings from the *Organized Labour* project suggest that there are two major problems which epitomize the main tasks ahead for the labour

---

[27] Taylor (2001) has reported that between 1992 and 1999 total employment in the European Union and the USA increased by 19.8 million. More than 50 per cent of the increase was made up of knowledge workers (5.4 m) and managerial staff (4.7m). The rest was shared by service workers (7.6m) and data workers (2.1m). During the same period employment in manufacturing declined by 0.7m.

[28] Campero (2000) argues that this problem needs priority attention by unions in Latin America.

[29] The question of workers from developed and developing countries having to compete for the same jobs and the possible impact on the transnational solidarity of unions came up for discussion at a meeting of the Research Committee on Labour Movements of the International Sociological Association in Johannesburg (RC 44, 1999).

movement. First is the rise in income inequalities between workers, especially in developing countries; second, an obverse of the above problem, is the entry of numerous people working under flexible employment relations which fall outside the reach of any institutional safeguards. If unions resume their traditional role as guardians of social cohesion, they need to find solutions to the above problems in terms of arresting any further deterioration in income distribution and developing institutional safeguards for vulnerable workers.

Part II

In the rest of this chapter we make some observations concerning the problems, priorities and strategies of the labour movement with special reference to the situation in developing countries. It is also argued that currently the labour movement is better placed to address and solve these problems than at any time in history, since it is poised to gain strength and support due to the rise of politically open regimes all over the world.

1. Correcting inequalities: Focus on developing countries

At this juncture there is need for a concerted attempt to turn the workers crowding into the lower end of labour markets into non-competing groups within and between countries. Three objectives require special attention: (i) raising the level of minimum social wages as a long-term solution to low-wage strategies; (ii) creating new institutional safeguards for people working under flexible market relations; and (iii) facilitating equal opportunities for access to and mobility within labour markets. The three goals together correspond to an absolute floor in terms of social wages, safety nets and opportunities for all in the global economy. They also constitute an agenda for sustainable development, based on "intra-generational equity" for pursuance by the labour movement.[30]

A minimum social wage can serve as a powerful instrument for taking wages out of competition in overcrowded labour markets. Experience in developing countries suggests that social spending determines the level of minimum wages which can be set in relation to a basket of entitlements including elementary education, primary health care, shelter, civic amenities and a safe environment made available to all citizens through social spending programmes. These transfers would in turn determine a minimum "reserve

---

[30] Anand and Sen (2000) make a persuasive case for sustainable development strategy based on intra-generational equity through enhancing the capabilities of people, particularly the poor, to live in better conditions.

price" below which labour would not be undersold on account of supply side pressures. It might be noted in this context that some regions in the developing world which have moved in the direction of carefully planned public expenditure have attained significant increases in the real earnings of workers in rural areas.[31]

Another area for attention is the creation of new institutions to safeguard the long-term interests of low-skilled workers in terms of benefits such as health care, insurance cover and old age pensions. It is probable that most labour-market entrants, particularly the low-skilled workers, will remain without regular full-time jobs, and therefore outside the protective umbrella of labour institutions cherished by the union movement. This indicates a pressing need for new institutional safeguards that can guarantee portable entitlements to all workers—casual, migrant, piece workers and subcontractors—irrespective of the location or duration of their job. The possibility of many developing countries having to receive a large influx of mid-career return migrants makes this an urgent task.

A third area for trade union involvement is in the establishment of suitable and affordable facilities for skill development so that workers at the lower end of the market can be helped to overcome the barriers of gender, ethnicity and race that hamper their mobility in terms of income and professional advancement. Such facilities can raise the supply price of labour, equip workers to respond to expanding economic opportunities and help them emerge as equal partners in the development of markets.

It needs to be emphasized that social wages, new institutions for social protection and training facilities for workers at the lower end of markets are relatively unexplored areas in the context of developing countries. Nonetheless, they represent major challenges calling for innovative approaches, leadership and guidance by the labour movement, which has the capacity and resources to mobilize political support for the above agenda.

2. Accent on human rights and democratic institutions

Enhancing the entitlements of workers essentially means that the labour movement should be in a position to demand increased social spending on a political platform. To this end, the movement could build on a "rights-based agenda for development", making basic human rights i.e., civil and political liberties, accessible to a broad spectrum of the polity. An important lesson

---

[31] There is some evidence that in recent years, the Indian State of Kerala has attained progress on the wages front through raising the level of social consumption based on an impressive array of social spending programmes. This point has been elaborated in relation to the observed increase in real wages of rural workers in Kerala (Jose, 1994).

that follows from the experience of unions in industrialized countries is that civil and political liberties are essential preconditions for converting the economic interests of workers into rights and entitlements, and that only liberal democracy provides the institutional environment for deriving such rights.

Experience has also shown that the social pacts of trade unions in developing countries were too fragile because they were not underpinned by democratic institutions. Democracy can provide the labour movement with the political space required for negotiating social wages, income security and skill mobility within the framework of social pacts. Democracy will also ensure that negotiated compromises work towards equity and justice for all in the world of work.[32] One positive feature is that the developing countries today are closer to the goal of democratic governance than at any time in history.

Many developing countries have begun to evolve democratic institutions; they are closer than ever to establishing a liberal democracy for two reasons. First, there is a universal trend towards the liberalization of political regimes as a side-effect of globalization. Second, the unions have been instrumental in accelerating the pace of transformation through their sustained support and solidarity with the struggle for democracy. The labour movement offers the best prospects for leading the way to a constitutionally liberal society in which civil and political liberties, including the right to life, property and freedom of expression, become accessible to all citizens. Only in a democratic setting can the rights and entitlements of workers derive synergy from each other.

3. Configuring the strategies

The priorities identified in the previous section point to the need for organized labour to emerge as a politically important actor in a broad sense of the term, influencing the content and direction of social spending. This goal warrants some modifications to the strategies of the labour movement at both national and international levels. We will conclude this paper by drawing attention to three elements for consideration: (i) forging alliances with other actors in society who share the values and objectives of the labour movement; (ii) building on existing initiatives for strengthening the rights and entitlements of people; and (iii) collaborating with other national and international labour movements to strengthen democratic institutions.

---

[32] The instrumental importance of democratic institutions for the drawing of social pacts is highlighted by Webster and Adler (1998).

Organized interest groups who share the values and concerns of the labour movement exist in all societies. They are embedded in communities, religious organizations, ethnic groups and neighbourhood associations that generally operate outside the workplace. An alliance with the above interest groups makes good political sense, for it would help the labour movement reach out to a larger collectivity, enhance its legitimacy and gain political support for programmes addressed to sustainable development, equity and justice.[33] In a world of divisive forces based on race, religion, gender and ethnicity, the labour movement can emerge as a powerful secular force binding all who share common values and aspirations. The destiny of the labour movement is inextricably tied up with its cohesive role in society.

There are numerous instances of initiatives launched by activist groups at local level aimed at securing different rights and entitlements such as civil liberties, land rights, gender equality, education, health, shelter and a safe environment. Organized under the aegis of non-governmental organizations, cooperatives and development agencies these interest groups have a rich repertoire of means to pursue the goals they have set for themselves. The labour movement is ideally placed to build on such pro-people initiatives, and consolidate them into a common platform for collective action. Political pressure emanating from coalitions of interest groups offers the best prospects for realizing the minimal goal of the labour movement —a *social floor* in terms of human rights, minimum wages, safety nets and skill formation— for all in the world of work.

A first step in this direction would be to initiate a dialogue between the labour movement and other civil society organizations with a view to understanding the economic and political environment in which the interest groups articulate their demands; identifying the common ground that they share; and discussing the modalities for pooling resources in search of common objectives.

Finally, the creation of a *social floor* based on the rights and entitlements of workers in all countries is an area for greater transnational collaboration between the labour movements. It would be worthwhile pursuing the idea of a global coalition of movements that could stimulate the provision of support and assistance to fraternal organizations in individual countries, thus helping to realize the basic goals of the movement.[34] Ideally the main thrust

---

[33] The transparency and representative character of these organizations are important issues to be addressed in the context of launching joint activities. The problems and prospects of alliances among like-minded actors, pursuing common goals, are discussed in the *World Labour Report* 1997. See I LO (1997), Ch. 2.

[34] The case studies included in this volume point to a number of initiatives in the above direction launched by trade unions of industrialized countries, for instance, the programme of assistance and training by the Swedish unions in support of campaigns for democracy in African countries (Fahlbeck, 1999) and the support for building strong labour institutions in South East Asia by the Japanese unions (Inoue, 1999).

of such inter-regional collaboration should be to generate a momentum for political action leading to the adoption of social policies. A political commitment to the *social floor* can come only through endogenous processes involving the beneficiaries in individual countries. At best, the solidarity and support of fraternal organizations can help activate the political processes and sustain the labour movement in its demand for change.

4. Summing up

Throughout the twentieth century, trade unions have functioned in an environment marked by dynamic changes in the world of work. During the period they built organizational strength and a capacity to mobilize their constituents; constantly improvised strategies to represent workers' interests, broadened their agenda to combine the multiple functions of bargaining, voice and service provision, and created appropriate structures to implement the agenda. At the same time unions influenced social policy and assisted the development of institutions to regulate markets.

The positive role of unions in society has had two distinct features. Firstly, unions transcended their role of defending special interest groups to became major partners in the development of markets; in the process they matured into a powerful engine driving economic growth in industrial economies. Secondly, unions converted their organizational space into a political space and contributed to the development of democratic institutions. Through pursuing the above goals unions came to occupy a unique position as the purveyors of social cohesion in all societies.

Globalization and the increased integration of markets during the closing decades of the twentieth century entailed two inter-related developments: a trend towards greater economic liberalization of markets and a movement towards the democratization of governments in all regions. These two developments together have posed challenges as well as opportunities to the labour movement.

The changes in the social and economic environment along with the evolution of new technologies have led to distinct changes in the size and composition of the industrial workforce. They have affected union structures and called into question the viability of the regulatory instruments and labour market institutions which the unions helped create and administer in the past. In a number of countries unions have responded to the challenge and gained or regained considerable ground in terms of organizational strength and political influence. The strategies developed and the experience gained offer interesting lessons for their counterparts in other countries.

Developing countries offer a vast array of opportunities to the labour movement. Rising inequalities among workers in those countries points to a need for unions to strengthen their role as guardians of social cohesion. A coordinated global strategy is required for raising the floor price of labour and protecting the workers who crowd into the lower end of markets; it should be complemented with support programmes for the development of democratic institutions. The historical role of the labour movement is to serve as a secular force guaranteeing equity and opportunity for all in the world of work. This role is just as valid today as it was a century ago.

Bibliography

Adji Souley. 2000. *Globalization and union strategies in Niger*, Discussion Paper 122. Labour and Society Programme, (Geneva, International Institute for Labour Studies).

Anand, Sudhir; Sen, Amartya. 2000. "Human development and economic sustainability" in *World Development*, Vol 28, No. 12, pp. 2029-2049.

Anyemedu, Kwasi. 2000. *Trade union responses to globalization: Case study on Ghana*, Discussion Paper 121, Labour and Society Programme, (Geneva, International Institute for Labour Studies).

Bezuidenhout, Andries. 2000. *Towards global social movement unionism? Trade union responses to globalization in South Africa* , Discussion Paper 115. Labour and Society Programme, (Geneva, International Institute for Labour Studies).

Bhattacherjee, Debashish. 1999. *Organized labour and economic liberalization. India: Past, present and future*, Discussion Paper 105, Labour and Society Programme, (Geneva, International Institute for Labour Studies).

Bronfenbrenner, K.; Friedman, S.; Hurd, R.; Oswald, R.; Seeber, R. (eds.). 1998. *Organizing to win, New research on union strategies* (Ithaca and London ILR Press, Cornell University Press).

Campero, Guillermo. 2000. *Respuestas del sindicalismo ante la mundialización: El caso de Chile*, Discussion Paper 113. Labour and Society Programme, (Geneva, International Institute for Labour Studies).

Crouch, C.; Dore, R. 1990. "Whatever happened to corporatism?" in *Corporatism and accountability* (Oxford, Clarendon Press).

Dovydeniene, Roma. 2000. *Trade union responses to globalization in Lithuania*, Discussion Paper 111, Labour and Society Programme, (Geneva, International Institute for Labour Studies).

Ennaceur, Mohamed. 2000. *Les syndicats et la mondialisation: le cas de la Tunisie* Discussion Paper 120, Labour and Society Programme, (Geneva, International Institute for Labour Studies).

Esping-Anderson, G. 1996. "After the golden age? Welfare state dilemmas in a global economy" in Esping-Anderson (ed.). *Welfare states in transition, national adaptations in global economies* (London, Sage).

Fahlbeck, Reinhold. 1999. *Trade unionism in Sweden*, Discussion Paper 108, Labour and Society Programme, (Geneva, International Institute for Labour Studies).

Hermann, Michael. 2001. Trade unions and labour standards, Summary of the Discussion, Interactive conference on "Organized Labour in the 21st Century", ILO-Institute web-site.

Herzenberg, Stephen. 2000. *Reinventing the US labour movement, Inventing post-industrial prosperity: A progress report*, Discussion Paper 119, Labour and Society Programme, (Geneva, International Institute for Labour Studies).

Hobsbawm, Eric. 1994. *The age of extremes - The short twentieth century 1914-1991* (Michel Joseph).

ILO. 1997. *World Labour Report 1997-98: Industrial relations, democracy and social stability* (Geneva, International Labour Office).

Inoue, Sadahiko. 1999. *Japanese trade unions and their future: Opportunities and challenges in an era of globalization*, Discussion Paper 106, Labour and Society Programme, (Geneva, International Institute for Labour Studies).

Jose, A. V. 1994. "Social policy towards wage determination: Some lessons from the Indian States", Abstracts of the International Congress on Kerala Studies, AKG Centre for Research and Studies, Thiruvananthapuram.

— . 2000. *The future of the labour movement: Some observations on developing countries*, Discussion Paper 112, Labour and Society Programme, (Geneva, International Institute for Labour Studies).

Matteso, Jorge; Pochmann, Marcio. 2001. *Respostas sindicasis à globalizacao: o caso brasilero* - Forthcoming Discussion Paper, Labour and Society Programme, (Geneva, International Institute for Labour Studies).

Landes, David. 1998. *The wealth and poverty of nations* (Abacus).

Milkman, Ruth. 1992. "Union response to workforce feminisations in the United States" in Jenson and Mahon. (1993) (ed.). *The challenge of restructuring, North American labor movements respond* (Temple University Press, Philadelphia).

Mozdzer, Mariana. 2001. "Trade unions and the challenge of globalization", Summary of the Discussion, Interactive conference on "Organized Labour in the 21st Century", ILO-Institute web-site.

Murray, Gregor. 2001. *Trade union responses in Canada*, Forthcoming Discussion Paper, Labour and Society Programme, (Geneva, International Institute for Labour Studies).

Murray, Jill. 2000. *The ILO's on-line conference on organized labour in the 21st century*, Discussion Paper 125, Labour and Society Programme, (Geneva, International Institute for Labour Studies)

Nathanson, Roby et al. 1999. *Union responses to a changing environment: The New Histadrut - The General Federation of Labour in Israel*, Discussion Paper 104, Labour and Society Programme, (Geneva, International Institute for Labour Studies).

Network Report. 1999. *Network on Organized Labour in the 21st Century: Progress Report*, Discussion Paper 101, Labour and Society Programme, (Geneva, International Institute for Labour Studies).

Ojeda-Aviles, Antonio. 2000. *Respuestas sindicales a la mundialización: El caso español,* Discussion Paper 114. Labour and Society Programme, (Geneva, International Institute for Labour Studies).

Piore, Michael. J.; Sabel, Charles F. 1984. *The second industrial divide: Possibilities for prosperity* (Basic Books).

RC44. 1999. *Report of a workshop on Labour Movement Studies in the 21st Century* (Johannesburg, South Africa, 29-30 October, Research Committee on Labour Movements (RC44) of the International Sociological Association).

Sherlock, S. 1996. "Class re-formation in Mumbai: Has organized labour risen to the challenge?" in *Economic and Political Weekly,* Review of Labour, pp. L 34-L38, December 28 (Bombay).

Song, Ho Keun. 1999. *Labour unions in the Republic of Korea: Challenge and choice,* Discussion Paper 107, Labour and Society Programme, (Geneva, International Institute for Labour Studies).

Spalter-Roth, R. et al. 1994. "What do unions do for women?" in Sheldon Friedman et al. (eds.). *Restoring the promise of American labour law,* pp. 193-206 (Ithaca: ILR Press, Cornell University).

Tan, Ern-Ser. 2001. *Trade unions and organizing strategies,* Summary of the Discussion, Interactive conference on "Organized Labour in the 21st Century", ILO-Institute web-site.

Taylor, Robert. 2001. "Bridging the digital divide" Column based on OECD Studies in *Financial Times, 23 Feb.*

Valkenburg, B. 1996. "Individualization and solidarity: The challenge of modernization" in Leisink, P et al. (eds.). *The challenge of trade unions in Europe: Innovation or adaptation* (Cheltenham, Brookfield, Edward Elgar).

Webster, E.; Adler, G. 1998. *Towards a class compromise in South Africa's double transition: Bargained liberalization and consolidation of democracy,* Paper presented at 14th World Congress of Sociology, Montreal, 26 July - 1 August.

Western, Bruce. 1997. *Between class and market, Post war unionization in capitalist democracies* (New Jersey, Princeton University Press).

Wong, Evelyn, S. 2000. *Partnership of trade unions in national development programmes and in promotion of labour mobility in Singapore,* Discussion Paper 117, Labour and Society Programme, (Geneva, International Institute for Labour Studies).

Part 1

Studies on Japan, Sweden and the United States

Japanese trade unions and their future: Opportunities and challenges in an era of globalization

Sadahiko Inoue

Introduction

This report provides an overview of the Japanese trade union movement in the 1990s, a decade which saw the continued integration of Japan into the global economy. The paper also makes a brief reference to trade union movements at the international level today.

The Japanese trade union movement, which suffered divisions during most of the post-war period, was at last unified in the fall of 1989 when Rengo (the Japanese Trade Union Confederation) was formed as a national centre of trade unions representing the overwhelming majority of unionized workers. Two crucial developments in the 1990s were the end of superpower dominance following the collapse of the Berlin Wall, and globalization of the world economy. Faced with the new international context, Rengo has been seeking to promote a flexible trade union movement which still draws on the traditions and historical evolution of Japanese trade unionism until the 1980s.

Chapter 1 of this report presents the major changes which have taken place in the 1990s, i.e. the economic, social and political context of the trade union movement. Japan had extraordinarily high economic growth compared to other major industrialized economies in the past. However, in the last ten years or so, the country has been suffering very low growth, behind the United States and the major European economies. This economic stagnation is likened to American experiences during the Great Depression from 1929 through the early 1930s, rather than to recent experiences of economic slowdown in Europe. The Japanese model of labour/management relations represented by lifetime employment and the seniority-oriented wage system, has been considered possible only in a fast-growing economy. Can it survive the low-growth economy of the 1990s? The situation has changed so drastically that it is reasonable to ask this question. Meanwhile, the Japanese political party system, which remained stable for years, has been exposed to frequent disruptions in the post-Cold War era.

Chapter 2 examines the major challenges to the Japanese trade union movement. Wage negotiation practices feature talks at company level in the spring every year (the spring offensive), with similar demands for pay increases. They take the form of separate talks, but they result in almost the same rate of wage increase. The paper describes the extent to which this centralized mechanism of wage increases has changed over the 1990s, and to what extent lifetime employment is threatened by low economic growth during the decade. Remarkable progress in the reduction of working hours is another feature of the 1990s. Worker participation is also discussed in Chapter 2, together with improvements in policy and schemes to help ensure that workers have a role in decision making. On the other hand, in spite of the creation of the new national centre of trade unions, the ratio of unionized labour has been declining gradually in Japan. A growing sense of anxiety about this began to emerge among trade unions in the second half of the 1990s, and Rengo launched a systematic effort to increase union membership in 1997.

Chapter 3 looks at new areas of union activity, including support for international trade union movements and development assistance overseas, efforts to address global environmental issues, and collaboration with non-profit organizations. The report concludes with a preliminary evaluation of Japanese labour/management relations and the typical corporate model. Characteristics such as long-term employment, seniority-oriented wages, human resources development within the company, and enterprise-based labour/management talks have often been cited as typical of industrial relations in the developing world, or as only sustainable in a fast-growing economy. But these views have been proved incorrect. Rather, the Japanese labour/management system has provided flexibility during the substantial changes in industrial structure and the period of economic stagnation which the country has experienced. However, as globalization of the financial sector continues and many more Japanese corporations are growing into multinationals, the traditional Japanese corporate system and its labour relations model are exposed to new challenges. Among the prevailing social and political trends, the emergence of neo-liberalism is significant. Against this new background, the Japanese trade union movement is attempting to establish much better social and labour/management models on the basis of worker solidarity.

1. Changes in the trade union context in the 1990s

1.1 Economic and social changes

During the 1990s, Japan was exposed to one of the most difficult structural transition periods in its post-war history, in terms of social and economic conditions. There have been two major changes: one is a substantial decline in economic growth in real terms, and the other is a changing social structure characterized by the declining birth rate and the ageing population.

The effects of recession on the employment system

The decline in real economic growth during the 1990s makes a stark contrast to the period of high growth from the 1960s until 1990. Japan's average GDP growth between1991 and 1998 was only 1.6 per cent per annum, lower than the 2.5 per cent achieved in the United States over the same period and the 1.9 per cent average in the major European countries. For the Japanese economy, the 1990s are the "lost decade", and the principal causes of stagnation have now become apparent. Basically, the prices of stock and land were inflated in the late 1980s and early 1990s, and then the bubble burst. Government and industry failed to solve the problems caused by this financial collapse. "The collapse of bubbles in asset prices has resulted in cumulative losses in book value of Yen 1,000 trillion, or capital loss amounted to $7 trillion" (OECD: Economic Survey: Japan 1997-1998, p.3.) These huge losses are equivalent to Japan's GDP for two years. The vicious spiral of asset price deflation and the downturn of business that came after is the basic cause of the current prolonged recession.

The dramatic shift from high economic growth to lower growth, and then protracted low growth have posed several problems for the Japanese labour market and labour/management relations. They include mounting unemployment, which caused little concern in the past, challenges to the seniority-oriented wage system, and a re-examination of problems caused by stringent fiscal restraints, especially social policy measures which have belatedly begun to be introduced in Japan.

There have been some unexpected developments in demand and supply in the labour market under a low-growth economy. In spite of protracted low GDP growth the jobless rate has stayed at 4.3 per cent as of January 1999, rather than rising to a two-figure rate. (Nevertheless, a steady increase in unemployment seems inevitable as a result of negative GDP growth over the last two consecutive years, i.e. 1997 and 1998.) Also, in contrast to the United States, where the shift to an information-intensive society and changes in job structure have been remarkable, in Japan there is little evidence of the widening wage discrepancies typical of the United States labour market.

It is difficult to explain these phenomena without referring to the Japanese employment system, which features adaptability in terms of incomes and employment, and the spring labour offensive which provides a mechanism for reaching a social consensus on incomes at national level. The Japanese employment system is characterized by very rigid restrictions on dismissal and high flexibility on job relocation within the internal labour market. As such, the system allows greater freedom for employment adjustment and job relocation within the company and its affiliates, instead of resorting to layoff or dismissal. Also, because the determination of working conditions through the spring offensive allows both industry and labour to adapt to changes in economic growth every year, and because wage levels refer to those in the manufacturing industries which are exposed to international competition, pay increases are commensurate with productivity gains. The moderation of wage increases is also established in the Japanese labour market. The spring labour offensive has an important influence over all wage levels because it reflects a social consensus and it works as an information-disseminating mechanism for all industrial sectors. This socially reached wage level influences not only trade unions but unorganized labour, too. The social standards established through the spring labour offensive are not entirely dependent on the short-term business results of individual enterprises or of specific industrial sectors, even though the wage negotiation system is decentralized, Hence, it can be said that the system retains a social equalization function for wages and other working conditions.

The argument that the Japanese employment system is too rigid, and that the spring labour offensive is outdated, has been reiterated again and again. This was particularly true in 1975 after the first oil crisis, and also in 1986 when the sharp yen appreciation to the dollar caused a recession. Likewise, it has often been said that the Japanese employment system has already collapsed. But this is not the case. The fact is that the employment and labour system known as the Japanese model has gradually changed while retaining its main characteristics, and it will continue to change.

An ageing population, declining birth rate and the welfare state

Japan has an ageing population with a low birth rate. Already by the 1980s, the average life expectancy of the Japanese was the highest among OECD countries, and this factor alone means an ageing population. In addition, smaller families have become the norm in an urban society, with fewer people supported by the self-employed, including farmers. More and more families depend on employed workers. This tendency is further augmented by rising educational levels, increased female labour force participation, the trend towards later marriage and/or the decision to remain single: all of these factors contribute to the phenomenon of a declining birth rate. Total fertility has declined from 1.7 children in 1986 to 1.43 in 1996, and a further decline is anticipated. In 1995, the number of new graduates entering the labour force began to decrease for the first time, and it is expected that the total workforce and then the total population will begin to decline by 2005 and 2010, respectively. In other words, national institutions have to cope with the transition to an ageing society with a declining birth rate within a period of about 20 years. Western European countries have been making this adaptation over the past 50 to 100 years. Moreover, the much increased labour force participation of women has meant that the social functions traditionally assumed by families and communities (often cited as Asian characteristics) have waned. Thus, there is an urgent need for childcare, nursing for the sick and elderly, and pension schemes for retired workers.

Therefore, Japan has to become a welfare state in the context of stringent budget constraints due to the significant decline in economic growth. While the need to develop welfare schemes at a faster tempo is widely recognized by the Japanese public, there is a parallel debate on the crisis of the welfare state, as was experienced in Western European countries some time ago.

On the other hand, the opening up of wider job opportunities for women and older workers, and the trend towards partial labour liquidity among younger workers, have led to a gradual increase in the number of employees working less than full time. The ratio of part-time workers, mostly women, to total workers rose from nearly 10 per cent in 1980 to around 20 per cent in 1995. The increase in labour turnover is insignificant among employees working standard regular hours, while sections of the workforce featuring higher labour liquidity, mostly part-time workers, are on the rise.

Hence, Japan is now required to integrate segments of the workforce with higher labour liquidity into the framework of employment and social policies. It is also necessary to re-invent existing welfare programmes, including public pension schemes, unemployment benefits, sickness benefits and health care, into sustainable social welfare systems which correspond to changes in social structure. Labour is increasingly in conflict with government and business circles on the direction that social welfare reforms should take.

There is confusion about what should be done in response to the challenges facing trade unions. The different approaches can be broadly divided into an emphasis on the supply side in the sense of the new market doctrine, and an emphasis on the demand side, attaching importance to consumers and improved living standards for workers. Until the first half of the 1990s, these two basic approaches were confused by other elements, rather than being clearly polarized. In the summer of 1993, the Liberal Democratic Party's one-party government, which had dominated post-war politics in Japan, collapsed to open the way for a non-LDP coalition government. Since that time, successive coalition governments have been in power, consisting of various combinations of the major political parties.

During 1997 to 1998, the Ministry of Health and Welfare presented a plan to reduce public pensions, and the Ministry of Labour began to push for amendments to the Labour Standards Law in order to ease limitations on temporary employment and expand the services offered by private job-placement agencies. Rengo, the national centre of trade unions, opposes these initiatives.

Coping with globalization

Corporate efforts to cope with economic integration began as early as the 1960s in the manufacturing industry, which was exposed to international competition. These efforts accelerated in the 1980s, and in the 1990s they spread to the automotive, electric and other key industries. Imports of manufactured goods from the emerging Asian economies increased sharply in the first half of the 1990s, to cause concern about a possible hollowing out of the entire Japanese manufacturing industry. There were numerous closures of small businesses and cottage industries, as well as a significant deterioration in the local industries in some areas. Nevertheless, from a macroeconomic viewpoint, big Japanese corporations have either become multinationals, or have globalized their corporate management, including sourcing of inexpensive products and components from vendors overseas. These big corporations have successfully adapted to globalization through "habitat segregation" between domestic production and overseas production, whereby new models and upmarket items are produced in Japan while inexpensive, versatile items are produced offshore. In other cases, manufactured goods for the domestic market are produced in Japan, while goods for overseas markets are produced in local bases overseas. While Japan has increased its imports of manufactured goods from Asian countries, it has shifted its industries to the manufacture of capital goods and high value-added items. Total employment has declined in domestic manufacturing, but it is not a drastic decline.

The stagnation observed in Japanese manufacturing industry in the wake of the Asian economic crisis threw into relief the complementarity between Japan and other countries of the region, rather than the competition. Japan's huge current account surplus is mainly generated by its manufacturing industry, which may indicate the continuing soundness of this sector, even though it is forced to undergo severe adjustments in a period of negative economic growth.

Structural reform and unemployment

The collapse of the economic bubble in the first half of the 1990s and the protracted financial crisis in the aftermath of the collapse have obliged the Japanese financial system to carry out a thorough reorganization. It became clear that the system needed fundamental reform in the domestic market, and that its efforts to adapt had lagged behind changes in global financial markets. The tempo of liberalization, which began in the middle of the 1980s, remained slow, and it became increasingly apparent that the system was out of date in an era of financial globalization. Since the Financial Systems Law was passed in June 1997, the financial system has been in turmoil as it attempts to overcome the after-effects of the bubbles and adapt to global change, while avoiding possible system risks. As part of these developments, restructuring and retrenchment are taking place in banking, insurance and securities trading. But the most serious employment problems are in construction and civil engineering, which employ 6 million workers at present. As public capital expenditure has gradually been reduced in these sectors, there are fears that retrenchment will contribute to the mounting threat of serious unemployment.

1.2 Political climates

Socioeconomic conditions in the late 1990s seemed very unfavourable for the Japanese trade union movement. Until the mid-1990s, the labour movement was in an extremely favourable situation. From the second half of the 1980s through the first half of the 1990s, the Japanese public were well aware that their living standards, including working hours and the environment, lagged behind the economic success enjoyed by Japanese industry. It was generally believed that improvements should be facilitated as the utmost priority.

Throughout most of the post-war period, Japanese trade unions were divided between several national centres; they were finally united in November 1989. Although its organized ratio of trade unions remained at 24 per cent or so, Rengo was established with some 8 million members representing the majority of organized workers, mostly in manufacturing. Rengo received nationwide worker support for improvements in living standards. Rengo's slogan in its earliest days was "Leisure, prosperity and social justice", representing a protest against long working hours and demonstrating a will to improve the conditions of employment generally. Trade union demands for reduced working hours and better living conditions were gradually accepted by the public, since the business establishment moved away from its former opposition to such improvements.

During the first half of the 1990s, for the first time in post-war history, economic and industrial development as a national priority was increasingly eroded by the importance attached to improving   living standards for the working public, and both the government and opposition parties showed their acceptance of this way of thinking. Concurrently, a significant change took place in the political scene: the single party dominance of the conservative Liberal Democratic Party over most of the post-war period collapsed in 1993, and a non-LDP coalition government was inaugurated. In 1994 the non-LDP government was succeeded by an LDP-Socialist Party coalition which stayed in power until the middle of 1998.

From the late 1980s through the 1990s, some progress was made in reducing working hours: net annual hours in manufacturing for male production workers amounted to 2,189 hours in 1988, longer than any country in Europe or the United States. In 1995, seven years later, this was reduced to 1,975 hours, comparable to the United Kingdom and the United States.

During the economic setback, the policy of improving living standards continued, and in 1992 the government's medium-term economic plan was published under the title "Five-Year Plan toward a Major Economic Power with Advanced Living and Welfare Standards". The plan introduced policy changes directed to the supply side. In December 1994, the government announced the "New Gold Plan", a seven-year programme aimed at strengthening improvements in the social security system by addressing problems arising from the declining birth rate and the ageing population. Health care for elderly people and childcare services were introduced to complement the existing public pension and health insurance schemes. Until the 1980s, the policy on public welfare programmes was to restrict these services to the very poor, while the Council for Social Welfare Systems, responsible for determining the basic direction of government social welfare policies, proposed "universalism in social welfare" in its third "recommendation" since the war. A law to provide nursing care for the aged has been enacted, and came into effect in April 2000. The concept of equal opportunity in employment has gradually been accepted by the public, and preparation for the "UN Women's Action Plan" is in progress.

In retrospect, the changes which took place during the 1990s were not limited to a shift in policy. Other changes occurred which ought to be seen in a broader historical context. The new orientation amounted to an extensive review of the national identity and its social system. Since the Meiji Restoration (1868) when Japan began to steer a course towards a modern state, the nation has retained more or less "development-oriented" policies. Institutional distortions and other anomalies inevitably accompany such policies when a country tries to catch up quickly on the economic levels of advanced nations. The ongoing review is an effort to correct the effects of these development-oriented policies and related institutional distortions. Specifically, long-term structural reforms have been initiated, which represent efforts to transform relations between market and state, between central government and local governments and municipalities, and between regulatory agencies and industry, making them more modern, fair and transparent. This process requires a sweeping review of the financial reforms imposed by budgetary constraints arising from lower economic growth, and also regulatory reform and deregulation.

These developments have led to the establishment of various means to promote reform and deregulation, the creation of new systems and institutions to facilitate decentralization, and the enactment of laws on regulatory procedures, product liability, consumer contract, environmental protection and environmental impact assessment, as well as information disclosure.

Position of trade unions in Japanese society during the 1990s

In the course of social and political developments during the 1990s, it can be said that trade unions have become more influential than in the past. The successive coalition governments have traded partners among the major political parties, and these parties have consulted Rengo as the national centre of trade unions. Rengo has been able to influence regulatory matters and policies through representations to government advisory commissions. Rengo and Nikkeiren, an influential employers' organization dedicated to industrial relations, have been continuing their labour/management partnership. This partnership was reflected in the joint Rengo/Nikkeiren "One Million Job Creation Plan" made public in December 1998, and the tripartite Government/Nikkeiren/Rengo "Government, Labour and Management Congress on Employment" held shortly after. Also, primarily in manufacturing, there are regular talks at labour/management conferences in the various sectors, which discuss desirable industry policies and issues related to employment. Some salient features of labour/management relations are the exchange of information among companies and the consultation system; these two features have remained basically unchanged since the 1980s. Despite the challenges it faces, this Japanese neo-corporatism still retains its fundamental characteristics.

Nevertheless, an awareness of redundant labour in corporations and the increased labour costs due to an ageing workforce have led corporate management to begin restructuring employment. Alterations in wage schemes include management efforts to introduce performance-based pay and annual salary schemes, to loan middle-aged workers to affiliate companies which provide poorer working conditions, and to raise the proportion of temporary and part-time workers on the payroll while curbing recruitment of new graduates. The role of unions and the extent of worker involvement in managing these situations vary between unions. Several unions have been tackling the issue of part-time and temporary workers, but they have been generally unsuccessful, notably in their efforts to organize such workers.

Another feature which has emerged during the 1990s is the remarkable social activity of non-profit organizations: Rengo promoted enactment of the Basic NPO Law (1997) recognizing an NPO as a legal person. NPOs are still generally weak in the social field but they were very active in rescue work after the Hanshin-Awaji Great Earthquake of 1995, and it is expected that they will play a greater role in society in the future. Rengo's many community-based organizations have formed good relations with these non-profit organizations.

1.3 Seeking a new model

As stated earlier, until the mid-1990s, organized labour enjoyed considerable latitude in union activities, partly because of the social position acquired by trade unions, and partly because their practices were based on corporatism. However, since mid-1997 the situation has begun to change. One reason for the change is the deepening recession with negative economic growth for two or three consecutive years. Besides this, the LDP is reviving as the single government party, and a tendency towards supply side policies is gaining momentum. The pendulum is swinging away from policies emphasizing the advancement of living standards. The Congress on Economic Strategy, an advisory body to the Prime Minister, has published its view of Japan's medium- and long-term challenges. The Congress argues: "the Japanese-specific social system that attaches too much importance to equality and fairness must be revised", and that "Japan must seek to structure a competitive society". Rengo is rebutting these moves, and it is unlikely that such a way of thinking could prevail. However, as the recession continues, conflicting views on the direction for structuring Japanese society will undoubtedly be expressed more fiercely.

Regarding the practice of long-term employment, some writers argue for adopting American-type management practices and short-term employment contracts; Rengo sharply criticized these tendencies in its "Rengo White Paper" published in December 1998. The paper defends the rationale for long-term employment and other corporate decisions based on long-term interests.

In an effort to promote a successful labour movement in the 21st century, Rengo has set up a working committee including independent experts, to prepare an initiative called "Challenges to Rengo in the 21st Century". This will be made public at Rengo's annual convention in the fall of 2001. This process is modelled on AFL-CIO's "Committee on the Future of Labour" and on Germany's Dresden Basic Platform.

2. Developments in the Japanese trade union movement

2.1 Towards justice and job security

2.1.1 Developments in wage formation

Wage determination

In the wage bargaining process, the "spring labour offensive" has played an important role since 1955. Typically, unions and employers conduct negotiations in the spring every year, setting strategic schedules. For labour, the objective of the spring offensive is twofold: to help raise the general level of wage hikes by referring to the leading "market price" of labour in prosperous industries in order to influence talks in other industries; and to narrow wage discrepancies between large and smaller businesses by holding talks at smaller enterprises after the completion of negotiations with big corporations.

In the spring offensive, labour/management negotiations are conducted primarily between individual companies and their company-based unions, and talks between industrial unions and employers' organizations are limited to a few exceptional cases. In this sense, wage talks in Japan are "decentralized" negotiations, but almost the same level of wage hikes is agreed in a particular industry, and similar rates are achieved in almost all industries. The process can be regarded as "centralized" in that intensive adjustment functions are working: a "centralized" result is brought about in spite of "decentralized" talks. This is explained by a kind of information dissemination mechanism. The labour side collects information on company-level talks and makes adjustments, if necessary, at industry level, based on the average rate of increase demanded, counter-offers from employers and wage hikes agreed. The target wage increase set by the national centre is reflected in the standard level of wage demand filed by any industrial union. An intensive coordinating function works on the employer side, too. Major companies in the same industry coordinate their responses and hold informal labour/management negotiations at many levels before the spring labour offensive begins. In the electrical machinery industry, for example, between the late 1980s and the early 1990s, discrepancies in wage increases were narrowed in spite of the widening gap in business performance between individual companies. This demonstrated the continuous working of the adjustment mechanism.

Some notable changes in the 1990s are as follows: in the spring labour offensive, now led by Rengo, some emphasis is given to reducing working hours rather than increasing wages. Attention is also given to harmonizing worker demands with labour initiatives for a new policy orientation and institutional change. Other changes include the introduction of a multiple-year labour contract by the Japan Federation of Steel Workers Unions in 1998. Under a business slump and continuing zero growth, labour and management in the steel industry agreed on new wage levels for two years starting from 1998 through a single round of wage talks. Finally, in 1997 major private railways discontinued the central labour/management collective bargaining process which had lasted over 30 years because of widening discrepancies in business performance between individual railway companies. It is not clear whether these changes have been caused by the recession, or if they represent a structural change in industrial relations.

Wage increases during the 1990s

Between 1990 and 1998 the highest average wage increase granted by major corporations was 5.94 per cent in 1990. The rate then declined year after year to 2.66 per cent in 1998. The wage increase rate ranged between 3.56 per cent and 7.68 per cent in the 1980s, and slowed significantly in the 1990s. The decline in real economic growth and the slower increase in general price levels in the 1990s were reflected in the lower wage increases during the decade.

In Japan, the "automatic annual pay raise" system is widely adopted. Wages rise according to years of service, which serve as an indicator for skills. The wage increase includes this regular component, and the average regular pay raise was over 2 per cent in the 1980s and 2 per cent or slightly less in the 1990s. On the other hand, consumer prices rose slightly faster in 1980 and 1981 in the wake of the second oil crisis, while they rose by only 0.1 per cent to 2.8 per cent through the rest of the 1980s, and at -0.1 per cent to +3.3 per cent in the 1990s. Since 1994 consumer prices have stabilized partly because of the serious recession. Wholesale prices have fallen during the decade, so it can be said that Japan has entered into a deflationary period after the inflationary trend in earlier decades.

In terms of real wages, unions have gained marginal improvements during the 1990s. However in 1998, as consumer prices increased marginally (0.7 per cent over the previous year) due to the higher consumption tax, real wages declined slightly. The wage position in 1998 for regular workers was severe indeed: actual take-home pay declined for the first time from the preceding year. This is attributed to the fact that the wage increase negotiated in 1998 remained at almost the same level as in 1997, but bonuses and payments other than the regular wage decreased in the midst of the severest recession of the 1990s. In addition, some full-time workers were replaced by part-timers who received a relatively lower wage. These developments reflected the extremely tough situation in the labour market. Fiscal year 1998 (ending March 1999) is likely to be the third consecutive year of negative GDP growth.

Generally speaking, during the inflationary period of the 1980s wage increases served to restrict inflation, while in the 1990s when deflationary pressure built up, the spring wage increase helped to mitigate deflation.

Wage structure: Earnings inequality and wage disparity

Earnings inequalities over all employed workers are smaller in Japan than in other major economies. Over the past 20 years, inequalities have been less significant than in the United States and other major countries (OECD, Employment Outlook, 1996, pp. 64-65.)

On the other hand, there is greater wage disparity between big corporations and smaller businesses. In an attempt to correct this, Rengo has explicitly included the same amount of wage increase, in addition to the same rate of wage increase in its national standards for wage demands. Since 1997, in order to correct discrepancies between individual workers, Rengo has emphasized "individual wage levels". The national centre has determined wage levels for workers at age 18, 30 and 35, in addition to the wage increase demanded.

However, a business slump, changing industrial structure and widening discrepancies in performance between industries or individual companies have all contributed to widening wage discrepancies between business corporations of different sizes. As the recent recession has hit small enterprises much harder in financing and other operations, discrepancies in the rate of wage increases between big corporations and smaller ones have begun to expand, though only slightly. In 1998, under the financial crisis, variations in wage increases at major corporations were smaller than those in the second half of the 1980s, while for all enterprises, including small and non-unionized companies, variations reached a record high.

For wage discrepancies between industries, in terms of take-home pay for the regular workforce including part-time workers, the best paid industries were electricity/gas/thermal energy supply, water supply and finance/insurance, while the low-wage sectors included wholesale and retail businesses, catering and various services. This wage discrepancy between industries corresponds to the discrepancy between big corporations and smaller businesses, where industries made up of big companies show the higher wage level, while those made up of many smaller businesses show the lower wage level.

The wage discrepancy between men and women is wider. This can be explained by the differences in type of job, educational level, age, seniority and ratio of part-time workers to total workforce, availability of the family allowance paid to the head of household (mostly men), and restrictions on late night shift for women workers. For regular workers except part-timers, earnings for female employees compared to men (= 100) stood at 59 in 1980, narrowing slightly to 60 in 1990 and 63 in 1997. The narrowing discrepancy is primarily attributed to the rising educational level of female workers, and to the Equal Employment Opportunity Law enacted in 1986.

Japanese wage system: Change and continuity

The system whereby workers' pay increases as they grow older exists among white-collar workers in the United States and Europe, while in Japan this seniority-oriented wage profile also applies to blue-collar workers up to the age of 40.

The wage profile generally has been showing a steeper gradient due to rising educational levels, the increasing proportion of white-collar workers in the labour force and the extended years of service. The wage profile for male white-collar workers in manufacturing showed a slightly steeper gradient in the 1980s, and flattened out in the 1990s. This may be attributed to the soaring wage level of younger workers, including entry level pay, due to a tight labour market in the economic bubble period, and to the fact that "baby boomers" reached the top of the wage profile in their forties. On the other hand, the wage profile of the standard workforce (the newly employed) rose more slowly in the 1990s, and the components of the wage increase which reflect age and seniority have been getting smaller. But their wage profile gradient is by no means gentle, probably because of reduced job mobility due to low economic growth, and because of the longer years of service due to the raised retirement age.

One recent development is the introduction of annual salary structures and other wage schemes based on performance-oriented pay. Such an individualized approach is limited, at least at present, to managerial staff. Nevertheless, some blue-collar workers are subject to performance-based corrections in their pay schemes. The unions no longer totally refuse this practice, and some unions have begun to accept performance-based corrections on condition that transparency in the system is assured.

On the other hand, wage discrepancies within the same age groups have changed little through the 1980s and 1990s. These and other revisions in the Japanese wage system have not taken place suddenly: they have been in progress since the 1960s, although the tempo of change accelerated slightly in the 1990s. Nevertheless, the basic format of the system which is characterized by: 1) the seniority-oriented wage profile; 2) the institutionalized lump-sum payment scheme (seasonal bonus); and 3) huge lump-sum payments for retiring workers (retirement allowance) has not been changing as rapidly as some analysts claim.

2.1.2 Reduction in working hours

Reductions in working hours showed significant progress from 1955 through the first half of the 1970s. But during the next 15 years or so little progress was made due to the deteriorating economic conditions, including the two oil crises. Efforts to reduce long working hours then showed remarkable progress from the late 1980s, when Rengo was formed, through the middle of the 1990s. The improvement was brought about not only by the efforts of organized labour, but also because of criticism from overseas in the 1980s. Competing economies perceived the long working hours in Japan as a threat to the equilibrium of international trade among major trading partners, and the Japanese government changed its trade policy in response to such criticism. The government showed a positive attitude towards reducing working hours. For example, in a report entitled "Workshop on Economic Structural Adjustment for International Cooperation (Maekawa Report)" published in 1986, and in the "Five-Year Plan for a Major Nation Respecting Advanced National Life" (from 1992 to 1996), the government specified a target of 1,800 hours annually by fiscal year 2000.

Rengo presented a tripartite demand consisting of wage hikes, reductions in working hours and adoption of policies favouring labour; specifically, Rengo sought the introduction of a five-day week. In 1993 Rengo adopted the policy delineated in the "New Medium-Term Working Hour Reduction Plan" with the target of fiscal year 1996, and in 1997 it initiated fresh activities to achieve an annual total of 1,800 working hours by fiscal year 2000, the new target. Rengo's effort in this area continues.

With amendments to the Labour Standards Law in 1987, effective April 1988, mandatory working hours were reduced to 40 hours per week from the previous 48 hours. However, actual working hours were reduced in phases by government decrees, which resulted in the full implementation of the 40-hour week in April 1997.

The annual total working hours of a regular employee in an enterprise employing 30 workers or more was reduced slightly to 2,052 hours in 1990. Then, through amendments to government decrees, working hours were reduced at an accelerated tempo between 1991 and 1994, when the economic bubbles collapsed. Partly because of reductions in overtime due to the prolonged recession, total working hours were later reduced to 1,800 hours with 1,879 hours in 1998.

Over the ten-year period between 1988, when the Labour Standards Law was amended, and 1998, annual working time was reduced by 232 hours or 11 per cent, and the number of working days was reduced by 24 days or 9.2 per cent. These reductions were achieved primarily through an increase in holidays, including the shift to a five-day week, rather than through shorter working days. Moreover, the increase in the ratio of part-timers during the same period meant a reduction in the average number of working days and working hours per employee.

The 11 per cent reduction in hours achieved between 1988 and 1998 had the potential to create 11 per cent more new jobs through the work-sharing effect. This would amount to some 4.4 million jobs or it would lower the unemployment rate by as much as 6.5 per cent in 1998.

In the years ahead, there will be many obstacles to further reductions in working hours. One of these obstacles is the perception among employers that they have reached a deadlock. Hence, the trade union role has become critical. Unions must aim at 1,800 working hours per annum in all industries, and prevent any possible increase in hours which might result from the expanded use of atypical forms of employment.

2.1.3 *Job security during recession*

During the 1990s Japan experienced a prolonged recession and stagnant employment. Enterprises have been fighting desperately to restructure their operations and adjust their workforce. Nonetheless, long-term employment practices remain intact, at least at present, although many commentators anticipate the collapse of the traditional system. On the contrary, there is a tacit agreement between labour and management to avoid massive layoffs as far as possible. This agreement is manifest in employment adjustment practices during the recession in the 1990s.

This section discusses the attempts of company-based unions to save the jobs of their members, employment adjustments during recession, union efforts to counter adjustments, and new policy challenges on employment.

Long-term employment

For Japanese trade unions, safeguarding their members from any threat of unemployment has a special importance. For employees in big corporations, who constitute the core of organized labour, the cost of leaving the internal labour market in which they have participated is prohibitively high. In big corporations the practice is to recruit new graduates and train them in the skills required. Pay and promotion offered to workers hired in mid-career are usually much less favourable than for career workers who joined the company when they started work. Workers who have left the internal labour market find it difficult to get jobs in mid-career.

In general, Japanese trade unions do not accept layoffs. During the 1950s and1960s there were many protracted labour disputes caused by threatened dismissal. Trade unions lost most of these big disputes, but the losses incurred by the companies were also enormous. The costs for companies included bad labour/management relations, low morale on the shopfloor and damaged public image, in addition to huge financial losses. In other words, the cost to the company of having its workers leave the internal labour market was very high, too.

Such experiences led to a tacit understanding between labour and management that it was in the interest of both to avoid layoffs as far as possible. Thus, company-based unions which represent the internal labour market tend to perpetuate this system.

Markets for goods and services fluctuate constantly, and any substantial change in demand or supply inevitably causes some employment adjustments. It is important to recognize that a mechanism for circumventing adjustment in the form of layoffs is built into the Japanese system. On the other hand, trade unions have made flexible decisions in response to the economic situation of the time during the annual wage talks. Another important element is the relocation of workers within the company. When an operation becomes redundant, the workers are transferred to other operations as a way of ensuring job security. Workers must therefore be highly adaptable. Multiskilling through in-house job training programmes is thus an essential prerequisite for relocation.

Besides collective bargaining, a joint consultation system is common, i.e. a standing body between labour and management to talk about corporate management, especially employment and working conditions. The "voice" raised by a trade union at this forum covers very diverse topics, including working conditions and personnel management, and also basic management policy, the introduction of new technologies and plant, and equipment investment projects. Apart from this forum, there are many occasions for informal talks between labour and management, including meetings between senior officials and disclosure of secret management information to top union officials. Through these multiple channels of communication, Japanese trade unions have been able to take the measures necessary to ensure stable employment for their members.

These and other approaches have resulted in the labour/management practice whereby the company retains a newly recruited worker until retirement age, unless the worker commits any grave misconduct. The practice of long-continuing employment was established in this way.

Employment adjustments during the 1990s

The tacit agreement to avoid layoffs as far as possible has generally been observed during the 1990s. The current unemployment rate is 4 per cent, the worst in post-war history. This adverse situation continues and more enterprises are adjusting their workforce. Nonetheless, the ratio of enterprises resorting to employment adjustment between July and September 1998 remained at 38 per cent, far lower than the 71 per cent recorded after the first oil crisis (April to June 1975), and lower than the 40 per cent during the recession in the wake of the Plaza Accord (October to December 1986).

Before any employment adjustment, protracted negotiations usually take place between the trade union and company management. In some cases, union involvement extends to issues which are usually a management prerogative, including personnel matters. Recent studies indicate that the "voice" raised by trade unions has become more influential since the mid-1980s.

Since the mid-1980s, significant growth has been observed in relocation and loaning, a form of adjustment which transfers employees to other jobs within the same company or to its subsidiaries or affiliates. In particular, use of the "loaning system" for a certain period of time (typically three years) is on the rise. This means that the internal labour market has been expanding to the quasi-internal labour market, including all the companies of a group. Japanese trade unions adhere to job security, while they are very flexible about relocation. Regarding recent increases in "loaning", unions have accepted this measure provided that the affected workers consent and that their working conditions at the host company are not unfavourable.

However, trade union efforts to address employment adjustment remain insufficient. The "Employment Check-up Questionnaire Survey", conducted by Rengo among its company-based unions in June 1995, indicated that nearly 40 per cent of the respondent unions did not have rules on labour/ management talks about voluntary retirement and layoff or job relocation and loaning, and 16.3 per cent of them did not enter collective bargaining or labour/management consultation on employment adjustment. These figures are regarded as unsatisfactory and Rengo has started a campaign to facilitate labour contracts on employment, and has urged its unions to establish rules on employment adjustment.

Challenges for the future

Under the pressure of changes in the economic environment caused by globalization and innovations in information technology, Japanese business corporations are forced to adapt to the new situation. Companies faced with fierce international competition have implemented survival measures such as reorganizing management and restructuring the corporation. To cut labour costs many corporate managers press for changes in personnel administration to further enhance flexibility; they select/weed out individual workers according to their capabilities and performance.

Rengo points out that in order to promote the development of capable staff and stable employment, corporate management should not sacrifice lifetime employment to a flexible labour market. Rengo also insists that in evaluating individual workers' capabilities and performance, the fairness of evaluation criteria should be ensured and workers' consent should be given. At the same time Rengo proposes that wage schemes should incorporate both a fair price for labour and the assurance of a stable cost of living. Furthermore, at the industrial union level, specific wage policy initiatives have been proposed, taking into account the situation of the individual industries, in an effort to match the revitalization of industries with improvements in employment and living conditions. Furthermore, at the level of the individual company-based union, the need for effective ways of promoting counter-proposals to management plans is an important task.

In this picture of strained industrial relations, a strategic choice will have to be made. In order to revitalize industry, with stable employment and improved conditions of work, trade unions are expected to exercise the power of organized labour and exert their intellectual and ethical capabilities.

2.2 Participation in industry and society

2.2.1 Trade union activities in political decision making

Tax systems, employment insurance schemes and pension programmes

Japanese trade unions have achieved improvements through collective bargaining on pay, working hours, fringe benefits and in-house welfare programmes. With regard to unemployment insurance, job training benefits, public pension programmes, health insurance, taxation, consumer prices and economic policy, trade unions draw up their demands, submit proposals to the government and political parties, and ask the Diet and local assemblies to legislate or revise the laws in order to implement labour's policy initiatives.

Union efforts are based on the belief that workers' well-being is linked with unemployment benefits, pensions, fair prices and reasonable levels of taxation. Unions must speak out on issues affecting workers' lives and assume responsibility for improvements. Union efforts have become more important in recent years as higher economic growth and substantial improvements in income have become unlikely. Behind these developments is the fact that Japan is faced with the need to cope with an ageing population and to cooperate with the international economy, which requires innovative policy initiatives. Economic growth declined from 10 per cent per annum in the 1960s to about 4 per cent after the mid-1970s and about 1 per cent in the 1990s. Under these circumstances, the rate of improvement in wages has been declining, too, so that working conditions other than wages have become more important. Older people now account for a substantial proportion of the population. This demographic change is affecting social welfare schemes, including medical expenses and income for the aged, raising the question of how to tackle problems related to an ageing population.

Furthermore, as there has been remarkable progress in women's participation in social activities, and a substantial change in their lifestyle, it has become necessary for society to establish fair labour standards and ensure equal opportunity in employment. Trade unions have launched intensive campaigns to achieve these aims.

The effort to influence policies affecting the working public is primarily assumed by the national centre, i.e. the central body of trade unions. The Japanese Trade Union Confederation (Rengo), considers this to be one of its important roles. Every year, many working groups discuss policy issues and draw up proposals. A national meeting is then convened to formally adopt Rengo demands. Rengo then starts activities to realize these demands through petitioning and negotiating with the government, major political parties and public agencies.

Rengo's position with regard to policy issues

In its basic document of association, Rengo states that: industrial trade union organizations assume responsibility for improving the working conditions of their members, and Rengo assumes the role of coordinator in support of industrial unions in this area ..... labour's effort to improve public policies and systems affecting the working public is represented by Rengo and its industrial organizations participate in this process. Rengo's role in facilitating improvements in public policies and systems is expressly stated in this document.

Rengo states that its effort should be made in light of a vision of a future society that trade unions ought to strive for. In 1993 Rengo adopted eight targets for the society of the future (stated in "Japan's Future Course"):

(i)   to continue environmentally sustainable economic growth and achieve full employment;

(ii)   to realize better living standards commensurate with Japan's economic power;

(iii)   to develop a society where freedom, human rights and democracy are observed and social justice is carried through;

(iv)   to create an open society where unfair discrepancies and discrimination are eliminated;

(v)   to assure the well-being and security of older people;

(vi)   to develop a society in which work and personal life are balanced and individuals develop their own capacities and interests;

(vii)   to promote peace and prosperity all over the world, and respect for freedom, human rights and democracy in all nations;

(viii) to establish a just society which is open to the rest of the world.

Every year Rengo works on several hundred issues which are grouped into 16 areas of policy initiatives. These include economic and fiscal policy, tax reforms, comprehensive industrial policy, employment and labour issues, social security, equal opportunity, environmental protection, land development and housing, regulatory reform, reform in politics and foreign affairs. Rengo adopts these initiatives at its Central Committee and then petitions the government and major political parties.

For example, the government and the Diet are discussing unemployment benefits, health care and other issues related to the reform of the social security systems. Rengo urges implementation of its policy measures, including: (i) recovery of business through income tax cuts; (ii) reductions in jobless workers through the one million job creation initiative; (iii) reform of public pension schemes and health care programmes to provide security for the working public; and (iv) restrictions on overtime and establishment of fair work rules, including equal opportunity, through amendments to the Labour Standards Law.

Mechanism for trade union participation

There is an institutional mechanism that requires the government to hold discussions with trade unions on planned changes in matters directly affecting workers. When any change is planned in minimum standards such as working hours, the government is obliged to convene meetings of the Central Labour Standards Council which has representatives from trade unions and employers' organizations, as well as members representing the public interest such as academic experts. When changes are planned in pension schemes, health care programmes, and public insurance programmes, the law requires the government to convene advisory commissions representing labour/ management and the parties involved, as well as researchers in each policy area. In both cases the government is obliged to take account of the views expressed by all parties.

Rengo is entitled to recommend the members representing workers' interests on these advisory commissions. Through this participatory mechanism, Rengo has been successful in amending the Labour Standards Law to a 40-hour week (enacted in fiscal year 1994). Rengo has also made efforts to improve labour standards and equal opportunities through the Child-Care Leave Law (fiscal year 1990) and nursing care leave (incorporated into amendments to the Child-Care Leave/Nursing Care Leave Law in fiscal year 1997). Concerning revisions in the minimum wage requirement, too, a tripartite advisory commission of representatives from public bodies, labour and management meets every year and makes recommendations to the government.

Advisory commissions also take part in policy decisions on reform of public pension schemes and health care systems, changes in economic policies and tax systems, and a total of 323 labour representatives have sat on these and other commissions (as of 1999). But the influence that labour representatives exert varies from commission to commission. Almost all commissions dealing with employment regulation employ the tripartite structure, while labour representation is rather weak in other advisory bodies.

Currently, the Liberal Democratic Party, which tends to represent mostly employers' interests, is in power, which makes it rather difficult for Rengo to achieve its political objectives. Therefore, Rengo is organizing popular campaigns such as petitions to the Diet, public speeches and distribution of bills on the street. In the Diet, Rengo has been obliged to make compromises with political parties on its major policy initiatives. For example, the government introduced substantial income tax cuts in its fiscal year 1994 and 1998 budgets, which contained measures favouring high-income groups, in contrast to those proposed by Rengo.

Establishment of the minimum level of social security

Japanese trade unions have been trying to establish satisfactory social security systems which assure the working public of employment opportunities for those willing to work, adequate medical care when necessary, and a tolerable standard of living after retirement. Unions argue that social security schemes must provide unemployment benefits, health care and retirement pensions. Unions have sought to develop policy measures and systems to meet these requirements, as well as lobbying the government.

Presently, Japan provides: (i) employment insurance and accident compensation schemes covering all workers; (ii) health insurance schemes covering all residents; and (iii) pension programmes covering all Japanese citizens. Furthermore, a national scheme to provide nursing care for the aged came into effect in April 2000. Compulsory schooling up to the age of 15 assures all Japanese citizens of the right to a basic education.

However, there are many areas for improvement. The existing employment insurance scheme assures a jobless worker of up to 300 days of unemployment benefits, but in the protracted recession over recent years many people have been unemployed for more than one year, and many of them are no longer covered by unemployment benefits.

With regard to pensions, some self-employed workers have not paid the insurance premium and are thus excluded from the national pension scheme, and workers in small enterprises employing less than five people are not eligible for the scheme. Moreover, as the population is ageing, the financial base of the national pension scheme is expected to weaken in the next 10 or 20 years, so that employers and the government have proposed a reduction in pension benefits. Rengo is opposing this move.

Promoting regulatory and financial reforms

It is often said that Japanese regulatory agencies, not political parties or the Diet, have de facto discretionary power in policy making. An overwhelming majority of bills are based on ideas from administrators or politicians. Within the structure of regulatory agencies, advisory commissions and other participatory systems, worker representation is rather fragile. Therefore, Rengo has strongly urged such agencies to disclose information, include the parties concerned in their policy-making process, and conduct prior- and post-assessment of their policies. Rengo has proposed that the Diet should strengthen its supervision and evaluation of regulatory agencies, and also enhance lawmakers' capacity to legislate by themselves. Regarding fiscal policy, Rengo has urged the government to provide a stable financial base under a medium-term budgetary plan to fund social security programmes, education, housing and other items of social infrastructure, rather than simply cutting public expenditure in order to balance the budget.

As well as acting at the central level, unions scrutinize the policy position of regulatory agencies, the Diet and local governments, and take action, when necessary, to press for improvements. Rengo favours decentralizing government action to local government level as much as possible. This is because unions believe that decisions on issues directly affecting workers should be taken with the participation of citizens at community level.

Rengo runs local offices in each of the 47 prefectures, and brings together union leaders in these districts to develop local labour movements. Rengo's unions have been petitioning local governments on local employment policies, welfare programmes and community development projects as Rengo does at national government level.

2.2.2 Towards equal employment

Equal rights for men and women workers

Women account for 40 per cent of all employed workers. Of women aged 15 and over, about half hold jobs, of whom 80 per cent are salaried workers. Women account for 28 per cent of organized labour. The overall ratio of unionized workers to the total workforce is 23 per cent, but organized women workers account for only 16 per cent of all women workers. This is attributed to the fact that many women are employed in small enterprises or as part-time workers.

It can be said that men and women have been able to work without discrimination in terms of law since 1945 when the New Constitution stipulated equal rights between men and women and gave suffrage to women. Before that time discrimination against women was enshrined in the law. The Labour Standards Law expressly prohibits discrimination against women at work and the New Civil Code stipulates equal rights of inheritance between men and women.

Despite these changes in the law, until the 1970s the generally accepted idea was that men earn an income to keep their family and women stay at home to look after the children. Except in a few professions such as teaching and nursing, women were expected to stop working when they married or had a child. This meant that women were not offered responsible positions.

There have been long and sustained efforts to make equal rights a reality for women. In order to have children and a job, working women and labour movements had to press for childcare facilities in the face of prejudice against working mothers. The 1960s and 1970s saw many campaigns to force management to retain women employees when they married, as well as campaigns for day nurseries. These were succeeded by pressure for childcare holidays (leaves of absence) and demands for non-discriminatory employment terms and working conditions.

Those movements have been fairly successful, and equal opportunities for both sexes have now begun to prevail in society. In 1986 the "Equal Employment Opportunities Law" was enacted, which prohibits discrimination by gender in education, training, retirement and layoff. In 1997 the Law was amended to ban discrimination on recruitment, hiring, posting and promotion. Further, in 1990 the Law on Child-Care Leave was enacted, which provides for options of either one year's leave without pay for either working parent of a child under 12 months, or shorter working hours.

Between 1987 and 1993, several amendments were made to the Labour Standards Law, which provided for a 40-hour week (in 1997) and an increase in paid holidays. The law requires parents to share responsibility for taking care of their family, and extended maternity leave to improve the protection of maternity.

Wage discrepancies

In spite of union efforts to improve employment and working conditions for working women, wage discrepancies between men and women are still a serious problem. The average wage of female workers remains at about 60 per cent that of male workers, and the wage gap has hardly been reduced. This is because there are few women in better paid jobs, their years of service are shorter than male workers, and they are less likely to be promoted. Women have to serve more years before they are appointed to responsible positions and this contributes to the wage gap. Unions have been pressing for equal treatment in education and training for women workers, and for equitable promotion and retraining when they return to work after childcare leave.

Apart from childcare, women are expected to look after their elderly relatives. Realizing equality between men and women in domestic matters is, therefore, very important. The Japanese legal system assures women of equal participation in politics, volunteer and other social activities, but in practice they have to choose part-time jobs or stay at home because of their family responsibilities. They also have very little time for political and social activities. One of the challenges for unions is to improve conditions for women so that they can participate in social activities on equal terms with men. In the late 1980s and early 1990s, the government initiated policy measures to make equal treatment a reality, including adoption of the "Social Programme for Equal Participation".

2.2.3 Mutual benefit activities

Japanese trade unions participate in workers' mutual aid cooperatives, credit cooperatives and consumers' housing cooperatives. Credit cooperatives once existed in all 47 prefectures, but they were merged and 22 are now in operation. A regional credit cooperative collects deposits from union members and offers loans. Workers' mutual aid co-ops operate in all 47 prefectures, and they offer personal and group life insurance plans as well as fire insurance for local union members. Local trade unions provide support to their workers' mutual aid co-ops. Consumers' housing cooperatives are building societies which are mainly for union members; they operate in several prefectures. Their central organization, the Workers' Housing Society, is incorporated by law. This society builds living accommodation in the Tokyo Metropolitan area.

Trade unions in the regions cooperate with mutual aid activities, and trade union organizations make these services available for members of unions at small and middle-sized enterprises.

2.2.4 Social dialogue with employers

Workers' organizations hold talks with employers' organizations on wages and other working conditions; many company-based unions routinely hold talks with management in their labour/management councils. Some industrial labour organizations and their employer counterparts have consultations on industrial policy and other policy measures. This occurs mainly in the electrical machinery, chemical and shipbuilding industries. In other industrial sectors, labour/management talks are mostly on working conditions and consultations on industrial policy are rare. In these industries, employers' organizations are not well-established and employers are not ready for labour/management talks at industry level. Even if individual employers are happy about consultation within their company, they are reluctant to talk with the corresponding industrial organization of unions.

The Japan Federation of Employers' Associations (Nikkeiren) is the central employer body concerned with industrial relations. Over the past five years, Rengo has held regular talks with Nikkeiren, and they have filed joint petitions to the government on economic policies and job creation initiatives; they have conducted joint studies and presented joint proposals on job creation. Both Rengo and Nikkeiren strongly press for business-stimulating economic policies against the current recession. On employment, Nikkeiren has persistently argued that the basis of Japanese management rests on the stability of employment, which has provided a background for Nikkeiren to accept Rengo's proposal for a joint study on the stability of employment and joint initiatives for job creation.

Through these and other developments in relations between the two organizations, Rengo and Nikkeiren published "A Joint Study on Job Creation" in 1996, "A Joint Report on the Second Study on Job Creation" in 1997, jointly petitioned the government to "Fortify Job Creation Measures" based on the joint report in the same year, and jointly filed a petition on "A Specific Initiative for One Million Job Creation" in 1998. In the fall of 1998, the government studied this labour/management joint petition and incorporated the "Yen1 Trillion Budget for 1 Million Job Creation" into its emergency economic policy package. This item was included in the government's supplementary budget for the fiscal year 1998 and its budget bill for 1999.

In conjunction with labour/management joint action at central level, several local employers' associations and Rengo's regional organizations have begun to hold joint workshops and announce joint proposals on local job creation programmes.

2.3 Towards solidarity

2.3.1 Unification of labour's umbrella organizations

The Japanese trade union movement, revived immediately after the end of the Second World War, began to launch aggressive social movements and became a powerful force in post-war society and politics. But their national centres were divided into four apex bodies – the General Council of Trade Unions of Japan (Sohyo), the Japanese Confederation of Labour (Domei), the Federation of Independent Unions (Churitsuroren) and the National Federation of Industrial Organizations (Shinsanbetsu). The division of national centres, affiliated primarily either to the Japan Socialist Party or to the Democratic Socialist Party, lasted over most of the post-war period. Earlier efforts to unite them had failed because of their differing politics and ideologies. Finally, in November 1987, the All Japan Federation of Trade Unions in the Private Sector was formed. In November 1989, unions in the government and public sector decided to join the new national centre and the Japan Trade Union Confederation (Rengo) was inaugurated. As of 1998, Rengo represented 7,580,000 workers, the overwhelming majority of organized labour. (Other than Rengo, the National Confederation of Trade Unions (Zenroren) under the influence of the Japan Communist Party organizes 840,000 workers, and the National Trade Union Council (Zenrokyo), an independent leftist labour organization, organizes 270,000 workers).

The significance of Rengo can be summarized in three points. First, Rengo represents labour organizations that respect free collective bargaining based on market forces, social solidarity and protection for the vulnerable segments of society. Second, Rengo, in its role as advocate for all employees, not only organized labour, is in a position to influence the government, as it is one of the key social groups. Third, Rengo defines the achievement of its declared objectives as one of its major activities, and tries to work through a participatory approach. Rengo intervenes in the policy-making process so that tangible results are gained. To this end, Rengo attaches importance to dialogue with the Federation of Economic Organizations (Keidanren), Nikkeiren and other employer/management organizations. Rengo communicates through regular consultation with government agencies and major political parties, and meets the Prime Minister for regular government/labour talks.

2.3.2 Organizational reform of unions

The Ministry of Labour conducts an annual survey on the ratio of organized labour to the total workforce. In June 1998 the ratio stood at 22.4 per cent, confirming a declining trend since 1975. In less than a year after the war, the ratio of organized labour exceeded 40 per cent and reached 55.8 per cent in 1949. By the 1970s, however, the Japanese economy had matured, and unions were recognized as a social entity and a prerequisite to firmly established labour/management relations. Ironically unions then lost their power to attract and mobilize workers with the objectives of the immediate post-war period. Thus, trade unions had to find a new raison d'etre.

Union identity (UI) campaign

A campaign called "Union Identity (UI)" was launched in the 1980s, mainly by private sector unions. The abbreviation "UI" was used as the trade union version of "Corporate Identity" (CI) for business corporations.

The UI campaign aims to revitalize union organization and activities. Any organization tends to remain conservative by its very nature, and trade unions are no exception. During the earliest phase of the labour movement, unions needed strong leadership as they faced the challenge of overcoming poverty. There was also keen confrontation between leftist and right factions in the union movement. But by the 1970s trade unions had already solved this problem; a new generation of leaders had taken over, and a new generation of union members, too. Union organization needed revitalization measures, and the UI campaign surfaced through the daily activities of unions. The campaign began with an extensive review of the visual aspect of traditional activities, such as union songs and flags, the style of reports and proposals submitted to meetings, and the proceedings of Conventions. Then, union officials and members re-examined the way that unions should respond to changes in the economic and social environment. This led to a reconsideration of the vision of the union organization and the direction that the labour movement should take. Before the UI campaign, unions had reviewed the movement on several occasions, but with a focus on doctrine and political stance, so that for younger workers who had little interest in politics, unions became less appealing. The UI campaign changed the image of unions and introduced a new style in events, proposals, communication and community activities.

Union initiatives for lifelong welfare

In parallel with the UI campaign, the scope of union activities was expanded into several new areas to link the unions more closely to the personal life of their members. Many company-based unions formulated a comprehensive initiative for lifelong welfare, covering major life events such as marriage, childbirth, education for children, housing, health management and retirement. The objectives of these comprehensive initiatives were grouped into those for government action, those to be gained through collective bargaining, and those that individual workers must achieve through their personal efforts.

The major industrial unions have been organizing industry-wide private pension plans and health care schemes since the late 1980s. They have developed these schemes in partnership with life insurance companies and other financial institutions, and invited their members to subscribe to them.

Unions are also beginning to offer consultancy services for members with personal problems. These include lifestyle counselling and stress management. This represents an extension of union activities, and indicates an effort to become more attractive and to encourage members' sense of participation and involvement.

2.3.3 Organizing the unorganized

Article 28 of the Constitution of Japan recognizes the right to organize as an essential right. But the percentage of Japanese people who are aware of this right is declining. A continuous decline in the national consciousness of the right to unionize and take assertive action at work is indicated by surveys organized every five years by the Research Institute for Broadcasting Culture. This may not be independent from the declining ratio of organized workers in the total workforce.

Ten million Rengo members

It is important for unions to halt the decline in the proportion of workers who are organized. At the fourth central committee held in November 1990, one year after its foundation, Rengo confirmed its aim of a "10 million strong Rengo". However, no significant progress has yet been made in increasing the number of union members organized under Rengo. In June 1996, Rengo adopted an immediate policy to expand organized labour, targeting:

- workers in small enterprises, major affiliates of big corporations, and major non-union companies;
- workers in atypical forms of employment and services, including part-time and temporary workers; and
- independent workers who cannot be organized through a company.

However, as of June 1998, unionists organized under Rengo totalled 7,476,000 workers, according to a survey of the Ministry of Labour; this represented a decrease of 97,000 from 1997. The direct causes for declining unionization are: a) business corporations have been retrenching, which means fewer members in existing company-based unions; b) the dissolution of unions due to permanent and temporary closures exceeds the formation of new trade unions; c) unionization of part-time and temporary workers is slow because of the wide range of types of employment.

Moves towards integrating industrial unions

Rengo is made up of individual industrial unions. These range from unions which organize workers at a majority of the companies in a particular sector to aggregations of unions related to company groups, and to trade organizations in certain regions. A total of 72 industrial unions belong to Rengo, with membership ranging from a few thousand to nearly a million.

This situation in Japan is quite different from that in Germany where industrial unions have been integrated since the earliest years and are concentrated into a very few entities. To improve organization in Japan, some argue for the integration of the many dispersed industrial unions. Thus, there have been mergers of several industrial unions, for example the Japanese Federation of Chemical, Service and General Trade Unions (the CSG Federation) was formed in 1995, and in 1998 the Japanese Federation of Chemical Workers' Union (Chemical League 21) was formed. In the summer of 1999, the two major unions in the metal and machinery sector were expected to amalgamate. In view of the prolonged recession and reductions in membership, other mergers may also take place.

Unionization campaigns at industry level

Despite the general decline in unionization, the Japanese Federation of Textile, Garment, Chemical, Mercantile, Food and Allied Industries Workers' Unions (Zensen Domei) has increased its membership, and its efforts are attracting attention. Zensen Domei was formed in July 1946 as a textile workers' union. This industry has swung between prosperity and depression, and hence many union members leave the industry. Zensen Domei has actively organized workers at smaller enterprises, and at the same time it has expanded the trades covered, from manufacturing to distribution and services, thus increasing its membership.

According to a survey of the Ministry of Labour in the 1990s, Zensen Domei membership declined between 1994 and 1996, and rose again after 1997. During a comparable period, other Rengo unions have lost members, and Rengo as a whole has been unable to halt the fall in membership since 1995. Zensen Domei alone has been successful in attracting new members in spite of retrenchment.

There are several reasons for the success of Zensen Domei. First, the union persuades managers of non-union companies of the need for trade unions, concentrating on the distribution and service industries which have a lower proportion of organized workers. Some managers are hostile to trade unions, and in such cases Zensen Domei intensifies its efforts, giving personal attention to all potential members.

Second, Zensen Domei has been focusing its organizing effort on part-time workers. A Ministry of Labour survey indicates that there are 240,000 unionized part-time workers, which is only 2 per cent of total organized labour. Most unions make little effort to recruit part-time workers, but Zensen Domei had organized a total of 95,000 part-timers as of September 1998.

Third, in order to recruit workers in small enterprises with a lower unionized ratio, Zensen Domei is collectively unionizing workers in particular communities, and running federations of smaller company-based unions. These activities are well-organized and systematic.

2.3.4 Political activities of trade unions

Political activities are an important way for unions to achieve their aims. Structuring relations between political parties and trade unions has been a big problem for the consolidation of national centres. When four national centres existed, the question of union support for a particular party was an obstacle to unification.

When Rengo was formed in 1989, it avoided supporting a single party, leaving the question of political affiliation to the judgement of individual unions. Rengo accepted that it would be difficult to liquidate the traditional relations of cooperation and support with particular parties which had been developed by the individual labour organizations over the years.

In its policy statement "Rengo's Political Line" adopted in November 1993, Rengo summarized its basic position as follows: (i) trade unions and political parties differ in their nature and functions and are completely independent of each other, so that the principle of mutual non-intervention must be observed; (ii) trade unions seek to realize their political objectives in cooperation with political parties and politicians whose objectives, policies and demands coincide; and (iii) based on the principles described above, trade unions provide assistance in election campaigns for the parties and politicians that they support in order to strengthen their political influence.

The Liberal Democratic Party, established through the amalgamation of conservative parties, stayed in power from 1955 until 1993. In July 1993, LDP split over the question of political reform, and lost its single party majority in the Diet: it was replaced by a coalition government of non-LDP parties. The rest of the decade saw a succession of governments and Rengo is still waiting for one that truly stands for the interest of the working public.

3. New frontiers for trade unions

3.1 International activities

Rengo is the third largest member of the International Confederation of Free Trade Unions (ICFTU); in the Asia-Pacific region Rengo is the largest labour organization among ICFTU affiliates.

Rengo maintains observation of the Constitution of Japan and the doctrine of UN-centred diplomacy as its ideal. It emphasizes the creation of a new security mechanism based on arms reduction, social justice, respect for human rights and democracy, fair competition, reduced economic discrepancies among nations and environmental conservation. Rengo urges the government to help strengthen the role of international organizations, provide more development assistance and encourage private aid, serve international policing activities, and promote peace in the Asia-Pacific region.

Rengo believes that without social development in Asia, including the elimination of poverty, the introduction of social security systems, the establishment of human rights and recognition of basic labour rights, economic development, peace and stability in the region are not attainable. In this context, it is essential to give effect to the "Asian Social Charter", which was drawn up by Rengo in 1994 and adopted by ICFTU-APRO.

The Charter confirms the importance of social progress and cooperation in Asia, and aims to establish basic labour rights in each country of the region. Chapter 1of the Charter promotes ratification of relevant ILO Conventions, and proposes a tripartite consultation mechanism in Asia. It states that ICFTU-APRO has requested WTO and ILO to promote cooperation between the two organizations in matters related to international trade in order to encourage the observation of social standards on basic labour rights. Chapter 2 of the Charter asserts that full employment should be a priority objective in economic development, together with the principle of equitable distribution, and social dialogue in every area of activities. This approach was reinforced through the UN Summit on Social Development in 1995, and campaigns promoting the Charter continued with petitions to the host countries of the APEC summits and the ASEM conference.

Rengo's international policy for fiscal year 1998

Rengo's "Policy Initiatives and Proposals for Fiscal Year 1998" included the following international policy initiatives:

(i) Rengo encourages international organizations and agencies to strengthen, revitalize and improve their efficiency.

Rengo urges the Japanese government to continue contributing to international organizations and their activities by providing human resources and funds. Japan should help enhance the position of these organizations and the country itself in international society. Rengo also requests the government to include trade union representatives in delegations to the conferences organized by international organizations.

ii) Rengo asks IMF and the World Bank to encourage borrowing countries to observe human rights and basic labour rights and to ensure that their citizens have a means of livelihood.

Rengo, as the national trade union of a major funding country to IMF, urges the Fund to consult trade unions in the borrowing countries, and to take account of their views. In this context, Rengo congratulates the World Bank on launching sincere talks with trade unions, and urges the IMF to make similar efforts in hearing from trade unions.

(iii) Rengo appeals to governments to develop a consensus on the ratification and application of the core labour standards which are recognized worldwide. These standards are incorporated in the ILO Declaration on Fundamental Principles and Rights at Work, 1998.

Japan itself has not yet ratified Conventions No. 105 (Abolition of forced labour), No. 111 (Equal treatment in employment and occupation) and No. 138 (Minimum age for employment) . Rengo calls for early ratification of these Conventions by the Japanese government, and at the same time urges other governments in Asia to ratify and apply the core standards.

iv) Rengo encourages the parties concerned to strengthen the provisions on labour and the environment in the multilateral agreement on investment (MAI).

As the MAI now being considered in the OECD is directly related to production and employment, Rengo believes that it should observe basic labour rights and environmental standards, and that these should be included in the text of the MAI, together with procedures in case of violation.

(v) Rengo asks the Japanese government to make further efforts towards consolidation and retrenchment of the US military bases deployed in Okinawa.

Rengo has been requesting the Japanese government to make a strenuous effort for closure of US military bases. Upon the return of these bases, Rengo requests the removal of pollutants from the land to prepare the area for the development of Okinawa and for job creation.

(vi) Rengo appeals for improvements in the quality and efficiency of Japan's overseas development aid and seeks the enactment of a basic law on ODA.

It is necessary for ODA to emphasize projects that meet basic needs, including the fight against poverty, education, sanitation and protection of the environment. To this end, Rengo believes it is necessary to promote cooperation between trade unions, NGOs and international organizations. In particular, Rengo solicits the government to strengthen its support for the International Labour Foundation, a Rengo-affiliated organization.

(vii) Rengo makes efforts to strengthen environmental protection and occupational safety in the Asian region, and recommends incorporating into ODA projects an exchange of experience and technology in these fields at union level.

Japanese trade unions have played an important role in improving environmental conservation and occupational safety programmes. As part of its technical cooperation activities Japan agreed on the occasion of the Kyoto Conference to help developing countries in these fields. Rengo asks the government to allow the participation of Japanese and local trade unions as well as NGOs in technical cooperation projects financed by ODA.

(viii) Rengo pushes for fair labour/management relations in Japanese multinational corporations.

In general, labour/management relations in multinational corporations with headquarters in Japan remain favourable. However, there have been some problems in the management of industrial disputes. Rengo has put pressure on their Japanese parent company and the Japanese government to correct any misconduct. Rengo has also been pushing Japanese multinationals to adopt codes of conduct.

(ix) Rengo urges early ratification of the Japan-Germany Pension Agreement, and encourages similar agreements with the United States and European countries.

With globalization, the number of Japanese nationals working in foreign countries has been increasing, and vice versa. Reciprocity between pension programmes in different countries is essential to eliminate duplicate payments for premiums and to provide a secure retirement. With the Japan/Germany scheme as the starting point, Rengo urges the government to conclude similar agreements with other countries. In particular, Rengo is encouraging an extensive review of possible schemes with the United States, where the system is very different from that in Japan. This matter should receive early attention as many Japanese work in the United States.

Japanese multinationals and their labour/management relations

During the 1960s many Japanese companies in textiles, food processing and electrical machinery began to advance into foreign markets, centred on the Asian region. IMF-JC was formed as a branch of the International Metalworkers' Federation at about this time.

During the 1970s, labour disputes occurred frequently in Japanese-controlled companies operating in Asia, and local workers and their unions turned to Japanese trade unions for support and assistance. In response IMF-JC, acting as the core union organization, took the first steps to inaugurate the Trade Union Committee on Multinationals (TCM) which operates across the various national centres. Since that time, TCM has taken a central role in negotiating with parent companies whose local subsidiaries are experiencing labour problems. It also exerts an influence on employers' organizations and government agencies. Through these efforts TCM assumed responsibility for monitoring the conduct of Japanese multinationals in cooperation with local trade unions.

When Rengo was formed, the TCM office was transferred to Rengo's International Bureau. According to a questionnaire survey conducted by TCM in 1997 on Rengo trade unions, a total of 496 companies own one or more subsidiaries overseas, i.e. 4,258 corporate entities with 944,000 employees. In a separate survey conducted by the Japanese Electrical, Electronic and Information Union (Denki Rengo), 92 companies in this sector own foreign subsidiaries, i.e. 1,393 firms with 478,000 employees. Japanese corporations running overseas operations provide some 1.5 million jobs in different countries.

In recognition of the important role of Japanese trade unions based in the home country in improving working conditions and facilitating regulatory measures, Rengo is active in this particular area. Japanese unions contribute to international industrial forums and organizations, and exert an influence on the 24 world councils formed for each major international corporation within the IMF, of which six are Japanese multinationals (Toyota, Nissan, Honda Motor, Mitsubishi Motor Industry, Mazda and Matsushita). These councils exchange information between their operations in various parts of the world and discuss questions on their management practices. During the turmoil caused by the Asian currency crisis, Rengo appealed for the economic reconstruction of Asian economies and security for Asian workers.

Rengo activities in development cooperation

Rengo established the Japanese International Labour Foundation (JILAF) in 1989 as a specialized body devoted to international exchange and development cooperation. JILAF activities cover three main areas.

First, the Foundation invites trade union activists in developing countries to Japan and provides them with opportunities for training. Every year some 20 teams or about 100 unionists from developing countries in Africa, Asia and Latin America (50 countries in all) participate in these training programmes. Between 1989 to 1997, a total of 985 persons visited Japan; 23 per cent were from Africa, 52 per cent from Asia, and 17 per cent from Latin America. The remaining 8 per cent were from rest of the world.

Second, JILAF runs "local projects" which support trade union activities in developing countries addressed to their members and local people. These projects started in 1994 and they cover labour/management relations, unionizing workers, occupational health and safety, family planning and educational projects to combat child labour. From 1994 to 1997, a total of 425 seminars were held in the context of local projects, with 13,169 participants. In carrying out these activities, Rengo and JILAF emphasize an exchange of information with the regional organizations of ICFTU, particularly with ICFTU-APRO.

Third, JILAF organizes equipment supply programmes to support trade union activities in developing countries (audio/visual/educational equipment, printers, etc.). Over nine years, more than 100 equipment grants were extended to 50 organizations in some 40 countries.

The annual JILAF budget amounts to about Yen 500 million (US$4.2 million) raised from JILAF's own revenues from government contracts and donations, together with funding from Rengo.

Other Rengo activities in international development cooperation include financial support to disaster victims, refugees and displaced persons. Such assistance is financed by fund-raising campaigns and from Rengo's International Solidarity Fund.

Finally, the Rengo International Development Cooperation Centre (FAN), jointly established by some of Rengo's industrial unions, provides assistance to disabled persons in Thailand, sponsors sports events for the handicapped, and hosts seminars on international cooperation for union members.

International cooperation at union level

International activities organized by individual industrial unions and company-based unions are becoming more common. These efforts include assistance for social welfare facilities and equipment, and aids to human resources development in developing countries. In addition, Rengo unions provided cash donations and emergency relief for the victims of natural disasters in China, Indonesia and the Philippines. JILAF aims to contribute to social and economic development by supporting democratic and independent trade union movements in developing countries. As part of these activities, Rengo organizes exchange visits with members of foreign trade unions, arranges seminars in developing countries, and provides equipment and materials for union activities overseas.

3.2 Environmental problems

Before Rengo was established, trade unions were already active in environmental protection. They had been campaigning against water pollution, air pollution and deforestation since the 1960s. Rengo has expanded the scope of its environmental policy to include global issues since around 1992 when Rengo sent a delegation to the Global Environment Summit held in Rio de Janeiro.

Rengo's environmental policy

The pillars of Rengo's environmental policy are prevention of global warming, control over hazardous chemicals, and the promotion of waste management/recycling. It also advocates environmental standards for industry and respect for the natural environment. Rengo's approach is to structure a recycling society, and the organization has gradually developed a way of promoting environmentally sustainable business and industry, community living and personal lifestyle.

In 1994, Rengo formulated its Trade Union Guidelines on Environmental Issues, designed to orient union activities on environmental problems at each level (Rengo central, industrial union, local union association and company-based union levels).

Also, in response to the adoption of "Agenda 21" by the government, Rengo supported enactment of the Basic Law on the Environment and then the Basic Environmental Plan. Rengo took the lead in establishing the Japan Environmental Forum, a coalition of NGOs, including the World Wild Life Foundation-Japan Committee (WWF-Japan), and Earth Day Japan, to help draw public attention to environmental problems. Since that time, Rengo has sponsored symposia and study meetings on environmental issues in Japan. It also participates in international conferences on environmental issues.

Rengo makes proposals on environmental policy to the Environment Agency and the Ministry of International Trade and Industry, and its representatives sit on advisory commissions on the environment. Rengo has been strengthening its efforts in this area since 1998 in order to address global issues within the framework of the social movements in which it participates.

Rengo's Committee on the Environment

The Committee on the Environment was set up in 1998. The Committee is made up of senior union officials and specialists in environmental issues. In its first year, the Committee initiated the Rengo Eco-Life 21 campaign, which still continues. The campaign aims to alter the lifestyle of massive consumption/massive waste. The first phase was launched in union offices and workshops (Step 1). Three months after the Step 1 campaign began, it was reported that more than half of Rengo's union offices engaged in environmentally friendly union office practices. Step 2 started in April 1999 in the form of a massive campaign among company-based unions and in communities, involving union members and their families. Step 3, to be initiated in October 1999, takes the form of a nationwide campaign, involving NGOs as well as trade unions.

Rengo's Committee on the Environment reviewed the Trade Union Guidelines on Environmental Issues, and published a revised version in February 1999. The revised guidelines include: (i) case studies of company-based unions; (ii) tasks to be assumed in the flow of environmental efforts, starting from each workshop to its company-based union, and from its higher union organization to the Rengo central office; and (iii) a systematic analysis of the flow of environmental efforts. Since efforts at local level are becoming more and more important, the revised guidelines look seriously at the role of regional union organizations.

The guidelines are designed to be widely used at study meetings and in daily practice at workshops, local offices and headquarters of union organizations at each level. They are also expected to open the way to an active exchange of opinion on environmental issues at labour/management talks.

Many of Rengo's industrial unions have formulated their own environmental policy and initiatives, and they carry out their own industry campaigns, advocating good practice for environmental conservation. In some cases unions define their position and role in tackling environmental issues in their daily activities. For example, several unions in the chemical industry promote environmental protection based on occupational health and safety considerations. Topics of environmental concern are discussed between labour and management at their regular talks, and in some instances unions actively participate in health and safety inspections of factory premises.

Some local and regional union associations organize regional activities on the environment. Several of them conduct environmental studies in order to formulate policy proposals to submit to local assemblies and regulatory bodies such as prefectural commissions on the environment.

3.3 Trade unions in civil society

Local union activities and citizens

On the vertical axis, Rengo consists of its industrial unions and company-based unions, and on the horizontal axis it has regional associations at prefectural level (47 prefectures in all) and local union councils at municipal level (some 470 councils in cities, towns and villages). These organizations submit their demands to local government offices every year, in parallel with Rengo's central organization and the national government.

In drawing up their policy demands and proposals, unions generally consult citizens' organizations in their localities and carry out surveys in their communities. The All-Japan Prefectural and Municipal Workers' Union (Jichiro) plays the central role here, so that campaigns at local level are organized efficiently.

Local union organizations engaging in regional campaigns often have strong political influence in the election of councilors to local assemblies.

The volunteer movement, NPOs and NGOs

In response to the Kobe earthquake, Rengo initiated the "Citizens/Rengo Volunteer Network" in April 1995, in partnership with other citizens' groups and social welfare councils, and engaged in support activities to reconstruct

Kobe City. Rengo's union members had provided emergency relief immediately after the disaster, which occurred on 17 January of that year. Including those who participated in or cooperated with some forms of relief and support activities, as many as 6,460,000 Rengo members were involved in relief activities for the victims of the tremor.

Non-profit organizations had an uncertain position in Japan, in terms of their social standing and legal status. During the 1990s Rengo took an active role in promoting legislation recognizing such bodies as a legal entity. In January 1997, Rengo Rials and the "Citizens/Rengo Volunteer Network" co-sponsored a symposium to discuss relations between NPOs and trade unions, and cooperation between citizens' groups and Rengo.

In March 1998 the House of Representatives unanimously adopted the Law to Facilitate Designated Non-Profit Activities. The Law was achieved through partnership between Rengo and diverse citizens' organizations, and in the course of this collaboration Rengo expanded its scope of activities and exploited a new dimension by developing multiple communication channels with citizens' groups supporting Rengo activities.

In 1997 the Citizens/Rengo Volunteer Network became the Citizens Volunteer Bureau, a department in Rengo headquarters. The Citizens Volunteer Bureau served as an office for the solidarity movement promoting the NPO Law between Rengo, diverse citizens' groups, NGOs and NPOs.

In 1998 Rengo decided to encourage policy agreements with citizens' organizations, NGOs and NPOs, to collaborate in a broad spectrum of activities which contribute to society (including volunteer activities).

References

Inoue, S.; Suzuki, F. 1998. *The high road approach in the Japanese context: The stakeholders' agenda for the coming century*, in Rengo Research Institute Report No. 7.

Inoue, S. 1998. *Meaning and main points of the International Symposium by Rials*, Rengo Research Institute Report No. 8.

Ministry of Labour. 1986. *Workshop on economic structural adjustment for international cooperation* (Maekawa Report) (Tokyo).

— . 1992. *Five-year plan for a major nation respecting advanced national life* (Tokyo).

— . 1998. *Survey of employment trends* (Tokyo).

— . *Wage structure statistics* (Tokyo).

— . *Monthly labour statistics survey* (Tokyo).

OECD. 1996. *Employment outlook 1996* (Paris).

— . 1998. *Economic survey: Japan 1997-1998*.

Rengo/DGB. 1997. *Future of work, future of social welfare state, future of trade unions* (Tokyo).

Rengen/Nikkeiren. 1996. *Joint study on job creation* (Tokyo).

— ; — . 1997. *Joint report on the second study on job creation* (Tokyo).

Rials. 1996. *Future tense of happiness*, Rengo Research Institute Report No. 6.

— . 1998.*Towards a welfare society, market and social solidarity in 21ˢᵗ Century Japan*, Rengo Research Institute Report No.7.

Trade unionism in Sweden

Reinhold Fahlbeck

Introduction

The purpose of this text is to present Swedish unionism to a foreign readership in a succinct but analytical way. The emphasis is on attitudes, structures, trends and overall characteristics rather than minute factual information. Since the approach is analytical it is imperative to highlight the elements that set Swedish unionism apart from unionism in most other (non-Nordic) countries.

Sweden is a parliamentary democracy. Its present constitution is quite new – the 1974 Instrument of Government – but constitutional traditions stretch back several centuries. The Head of State is the King who, however, plays only a formal role. Power is divided between three independent bodies: the government, headed by the Prime Minister, the legislature (the single-chamber *Riksdag*) and the judiciary. Political representation is proportional, majority representation never having been part of the Swedish system. Since the mid-1930s the Social Democratic Party, SAP, has completely dominated political life. With few interruptions it has been in power since that time. SAP is close to the main union federation in Sweden, the LO.

Sweden is a unified country and legislation is under the exclusive authority of the *Riksdag*. However, the government enjoys a strong position vis-à-vis the legislature. This is demonstrated by the fact that government, rather than the legislature, is the main initiator and architect of new legislation. Provincial or local (municipal) regulations of a statutory type do not exist in labour questions.

Sweden has no equivalent to the NLRB (National Labor Relations Board) in the United States, nor is there a state labour inspectorate. The public authorities have a limited role in administering day-to-day labour relations. This is in sharp contrast to the role of public authorities in administering labour market policy schemes, e.g. full employment policies, employment exchanges, vocational training and retraining. Such policies, which are very important in Sweden, are administered by the Labour Market Board together with its provincial and local branches. Despite its name the Board is not concerned with labour and employment law or labour relations generally. The Industrial Safety Board and its local branches are responsible for health and safety at the workplace as well as the working environment.

Employers and workers play an important role in regulating the labour market. The collective agreement is the instrument primarily used and these exist in every sector of the Swedish economy. Employers accepted collective regulation early this century.

Strong elements of trust, cooperation and mutual understanding between employers and workers characterize the Swedish industrial relations system. Acceptance of trade unionism on the part of employers and appreciation of the trade union contribution to the daily running of the enterprise is matched by a pragmatic acceptance on the part of the union movement of employers' freedom to manage the business and make decisions on technological change. In most instances the relationship between an employer (or an employer organization) and the union is firm and of long standing. The parties live together in something like a "marriage of convenience" with no possibility of "divorce", as it were. Despite this rather cosy relationship there is little collusion between the parties and featherbedding is unknown. By and large the parties deal with each other at arms' length, while preserving their "marriage of convenience".

The population of Sweden was between 8.8 and 8.9 million in 1997.[1] The total labour force (including the unemployed) in the same year was around 5.5 million, i.e. a participation rate of about 77 per cent of the population between 15 and 64 years of age. The participation rate for men was slightly higher than for women, about 79 per cent versus 74.5 per cent. The overall participation rate has gone down from 84.5 per cent in 1990, mainly due to ageing of the population. The employed population stood at 3.9 million, of whom 11 per cent were self-employed or family members. Women accounted for 48 per cent of the total.

Women are strongly over-represented in atypical work such as fixed-term contracts and part-time employment. For example, the total percentage of fixed-term contracts stood at 14.5 per cent in 1997, nearly 17 per cent for women and 12 per cent for men. The difference is far more dramatic in part-time work, i.e. less than 35 hours per week. About 38 per cent of women work part-time, compared with only 9 per cent of men.

The primary sector (agriculture) accounted for only 2.8 per cent of the total labour force. Manufacturing and construction (the secondary sector) accounted for 26 per cent of the working population, down from the 1991 figure of 28.3 per cent. Public sector employment accounted for 37 per cent of total employment in 1997, primarily in local government, down from 40 per cent in 1990. Women dominate in the public sector, particularly in health and welfare.

---

[1] For statistical data see the *Statistisk Årsbok* (*Statistical Yearbook of Sweden*). Data are presented in Swedish and English. When not otherwise stated, figures (and percentages based on them) in the text are from this publication and refer to 1997.

In 1990 manual workers accounted for 44 per cent of all employees, 46 per cent of them being women. Salaried employees, white-collar workers as well as professionals, accounted for 41 per cent, of whom 53 per cent were women. The remaining 15 per cent were self-employed or unclassified.

1. Overall characteristics of Swedish unionism

Trade unionism in Sweden has a number of special features. To a great extent these are common to all five Nordic countries (Denmark, Finland, Iceland, Norway and Sweden). The most conspicuous are highlighted here: some of them distinguish Sweden from any other country.

The uniquely high rate of unionization is *the* single most outstanding point. Union density rates are well above 80 per cent of the employed population. In some sectors they are over 90 per cent and increasing, not declining. Between 1990 and 1996 the overall figure rose from 80 to 83 per cent (Kjellberg, 1997).

Another rather unusual phenomenon is that employers do not resist unions. Since a compromise was reached in 1906 between the then infant organizations on both sides, private sector employers belonging to the dominant Swedish Employers Federation, SAF, (*Svenska Arbetsgivareför-eningen*), have accepted unionism. A cooperative attitude on the part of employers has prevailed ever since, despite some bitter conflicts.

Unions have traditionally pursued a highly ideological agenda. The transfer of the means of production to society was long a stated goal of the dominant blue-collar federation of employees, the Swedish Federation of Trade Unions, LO (*Landsorganisationen i Sverige*). Although that goal was never pursued with much determination, the transformation of Sweden into a welfare state based on political and economic democracy and on equality has been relentlessly pursued. However, and this is *the* outstanding feature, LO and its member unions have always maintained good lines of communication with their employer counterparts. This has enabled them to sign traditional collective agreements on wages and other terms and conditions of employment. It has also enabled them to negotiate master agreements on employer/worker cooperation on a variety of issues, such as grievance procedures, limitation of industrial action, health and safety at work, and gender equality. In other words, one outstanding feature of Swedish unionism is its pragmatism in dealing with the employer community.

Yet another outstanding feature is that unions look upon themselves as organizations with a mission, a kind of secular religion. Unions also see themselves as the vanguard of a better society. The task of unions is to help create this society and to lead their constituents into it. Closely related to the last characteristic is that inter- and intra-union disputes have always been rare.

Continuity is yet another characteristic of trade unionism and industrial relations generally. Existing unions can look back on an unbroken history since their foundation: LO celebrated its centenary in 1998. It is much the same organization today as it was in 1898, only society has changed considerably. This continuity permeates unionism and imbues the movement with a feeling of tradition coupled with responsibility.

2. Background and structure

Labour market organizations are voluntary, non-profit associations. There is no general legislation governing such organizations in Sweden, and no specific regulations. The requirements for a legally recognized union are minimal, making it extremely easy to form one. No registration is necessary. Some general principles of law exist but unions enjoy a considerable degree of self-governance. There have been few allegations of abuse of this freedom and these have generally not been concerned with serious misconduct. Corruption or dictatorial practices are very rare. Calls for statutory regulation have been frequent but unions have consistently and adamantly opposed them. Given their strong position in Swedish life and the fact that union conduct has never caused truly serious concern, moves for legislation have never gained any significant momentum. Union recognition is not really an issue since they all enjoy basic union rights as bargaining agents for their members.

As already mentioned, the Swedish labour market is highly organized. A recent study put the overall rate of unionization at 77.7 per cent in 1980, 81.6 per cent in 1990 and 83.6 per cent in 1996 (Kjellberg, 1997). Unionization rates are somewhat higher among white-collar than blue-collar workers. Union membership is fairly evenly distributed among the three main sectors of the labour market: private, local government and central government (state), though it is higher in the public sector than in the private sector. The size of the company is not particularly relevant, nor is the branch of industry. Age and geographical location are reflected since unionization rates are higher among older workers and in small towns rather than big cities. Women are unionized to a slightly higher degree than men. The rate among part-time employees is slightly above average. About 70 per cent of employees on fixed-term contracts belong to a union. Temporary workers, i.e. people working for agencies that place their employees with third-party clients, are organized at about the average level. They are covered by a nationwide collective agreement which addresses the concerns of "temps".

The union movement is divided into three main federations: for blue-collar workers, white-collar employees, and professionals. This division is largely an anachronistic remnant of the more class-oriented society of the early twentieth century. Mergers between unions are quite common within federations, in particular LO. To a certain extent mergers are defensive, but the chief motivation is offensive. Small unions realize the need to join a bigger union or else to form a bigger union together with other small union(s) in order to represent their members better. Moreover, technological developments may have rendered an existing union structure obsolete. All these points were relevant when the three unions in the typography, printing and bookbinding industries merged some 25 years ago. Three proud craft unions with long-standing traditions decided to merge, but it was a painful process.

So far no major amalgamation has taken place between unions belonging to different federations. Historically transmitted traditions and attitudes still obstruct trans-federation mergers despite a growing awareness of the need for common platforms and programmes. To an increasing extent, the relevant distinctions between employees are more likely to be found within the industry-wide unions of the three separate federations than between them.

Employees tend to cooperate across traditional borderlines. In some sectors collective agreements on wages and other conditions of work now cover all employees, but this trend is still very much in its infancy. The 1995 industry-wide agreement in the pulp and paper industry is a pioneer, covering some 35,000 blue-collar workers, white-collar employees, professionals and supervisors belonging to unions affiliated with the three federations plus the independent union of supervisors.

Cooperation between unions belonging to different federations has resulted in several industry-wide bargaining bodies. The best known is the Cartel of Private Salaried Employees (*Privattjänstemannakartellen, PTK*), a federation of 27 industry-wide unions, 17 from *Sveriges Akademikers Centralorganisation* (SACO) and 10 from the Central Organization of Salaried Employees (*Tjästemännens Centralorganisation, TCO*). In the past PTK entered into binding collective agreements on wages and other conditions of work, but that mandate was removed some years ago. The central, industry-wide mandate for PTK today is limited to matters concerning retirement, insurance and employment security, retraining and adjustment. At enterprise level PTK usually represents all salaried employees and their local unions.

In the international field cooperation and common action between the three federations are becoming the norm. Some differences of opinion exist between LO and TCO on the one hand and SACO on the other hand about union aims and strategies in the international arena. In a broad perspective these differences are minimal.

The Swedish Federation of Trade Unions (LO) completely dominates blue-collar unionism. LO was founded in 1898, which makes it by far the oldest of the three employee federations. It is a federation of 20 (1998) industry-wide

unions.[2] LO organizes blue-collar workers (and some white-collar workers
as well, e.g. insurance company employees) over the whole labour market,
private sector as well as public. With 2.1 million members (1998) it represents
slightly more than half of the working population in Sweden. Membership
peaked in the mid-1980s and declined somewhat in the 1990s. The density
rate has gone up slightly, both phenomena reflecting the diminishing role of
blue-collar work in the economy generally. Women account for 45 per cent
of overall membership but they dominate the single biggest union in the LO
family, the Swedish Municipal Workers' Union. The overall unionization rate
of the blue-collar sector of the economy hovers slightly above 80 per cent
(1997).

LO has a close relationship with the main political party, the Swedish
Social Democratic Workers' Party, SAP. This alliance gives it a strong position.
LO also commands a very powerful position from another point of view in
that it represents slightly more than half the workforce, which in turn accounts
for half of the entire population. The membership figures alone mean that
LO speaks for one quarter of the entire population. Counting those who are
dependent on members, the percentage increases further. This means that LO
can speak to the government and public or private bodies on more or less
equal terms and with great confidence.

The combination of political affiliation and membership figures has given
LO a unique position in national life for most of this century. It has played
an important role in shaping Swedish society. Without exception LO
members are industry-wide unions organizing employees throughout the
entire country. Most are industrial unions, organizing all blue-collar
employees in a particular branch of the economy regardless of occupation,
skill or training. Historically, member unions were primarily craft based, i.e.
organizing employees according to their skills and training. However, the
number of craft unions has diminished during the century as they have
merged and formed industrial unions. Some craft unions still exist, mainly
in the construction industry.

Private sector unions have generally dominated the LO family. The
Swedish Metal Workers' Union was traditionally both the biggest and the
single most influential member. Strong growth in public sector employment
after 1945 meant a concomitant increase in public sector unionism. The private
sector still accounts for more than 50 per cent of total membership. However,
the single biggest member now is a public sector union, the Swedish
Municipal Workers' Union. No LO members are general unions, organizing
employees regardless of occupation, education or skill.

---

[2] For statistical data concerning LO and its member unions see Kjellberg, 1997. For more
detailed information see the Annual Reports of LO.

The number of LO member unions has declined steadily over several decades. Traditionally, many unions were quite small in terms of total membership. Mergers have reduced the number of unions while ensuring that total membership has increased. There were 25 member unions in 1988 and 20 in 1997. However, there are still some quite small unions, such as the tin-plate workers' union with 5,200 members and the musicians' union with 6,400 members (1997).

White-collar unionism is much more recent than blue-collar. Starting in the 1930s white-collar and professional employees began forming unions or turning existing associations into union-type organizations and demanding collective bargaining. Employers resisted. The government intervened and the 1936 Act on Freedom of Association and Collective Bargaining was passed. Building primarily on the experience gained by SAF and LO and copying most of the mechanisms that they had built, the statute extended collective bargaining rights to all private sector employees, guaranteeing them freedom of association in the process. Under the protection of the statute, white-collar and professional unionism expanded quickly, albeit along different organizational routes. By and large white-collar unionism is now federated into the Central Organization of Salaried Employees (Tjästemännens Centralorganisation, TCO), founded in 1944.[3] TCO is a federation of 18 industry-wide unions (1999) with a total membership (in 1998) of 1.2 million employees, 60 per cent of whom were women. TCO organizes employees in all sectors of the labour market: private, local government and central government, divided fairly equally between private and public employment. The unionization rate is about 90 per cent; it is particularly high in the public sector. Most members are industrial unions, many of which began as friendly associations for the promotion of professional standards and mutual assistance. Under its statutes TCO has no political affiliation or ties.

Professional employees are organized by unions federated into SACO, founded in 1947.[4] (SACO is an acronym for *Sveriges Akademikers Centralorganisation* but the acronym has been adopted as the official name of the federation.) The total membership of its 26 industry-wide unions (1998) is 460,000 employees. Women account for around 45 per cent of total membership. Some 30 per cent of working members are employed in the private sector, 65 per cent in the public sector and the remaining 5 per cent are self-employed.

The predominant role of public sector employment among SACO members distinguishes it from LO and TCO. Another distinguishing feature

---

[3] For detailed statistical data see the Annual Reports issued by TCO.
[4] For detailed statistical data see the Annual Reports issued by SACO.

is the predominance of craft unions within SACO. Membership in the various unions is usually based on education, a university degree being required to join most of the member unions. Another distinguishing feature is the large number of unions and the modest size of most of them. This is because the recruitment basis of quite a few member unions is limited, e.g. physiotherapists, pharmacists or merchant navy officers. The smallest member union is the Swedish Veterinary Association with only 2,200 members. Yet another distinguishing feature is that 14 per cent of members are students or self-employed (5 per cent on a full-time basis and 5 per cent part time). The self-employed can be found in a variety of professions: they are architects, dentists, lawyers, physicians, or other specialists.

One SACO member is a general union, organizing employees who do not belong elsewhere. It is the only such union in any of the three federations but it is small, with less than 10,000 members. Most SACO members have an important role as a professional association as well. More often than not they grew out of professional associations, some dating back to the nineteenth century. The biggest member is the Swedish Association of Civil Engineers with a membership accounting for nearly 17 per cent of all SACO members.

SACO has experienced rapid growth in the 1990s, increasing its membership by 40 per cent since 1990. This is in sharp contrast to the other two federations, with little (TCO) or negative (LO) membership growth during the same period. Obviously SACO is growing from a much lower level and it is benefiting from higher educational standards in the population. In 1998 SACO also saw a new union entering the federation, increasing the number of member unions. This is noteworthy in an era when the number of member unions is decreasing in LO and TCO, although this is due to mergers between members rather than to unions leaving the organization.

SACO has faced considerable difficulties in gaining recognition as a federation of equal standing with LO and TCO. It was only in 1997 that SAC0 was admitted as a member of the European Trade Union Confederation (ETUC) and the Council of Nordic Trade Unions (NSF). There are several reasons for this somewhat discriminatory treatment. One is that SACO often pursued policies in labour market matters that deviated from and angered not only LO and TCO but also the Social-Democratic Party. Another factor is that SACO competed with LO and TCO in some activities, such as trying to set up a European-wide employee organization other than ETUC (the CESI). A third reason, perhaps, is that SACO is strictly neutral in political matters. In addition, most of its members probably vote for the non-socialist bloc in Swedish politics!

Much of the acrimony between LO and TCO on the one hand and SACO on the other hand seems to have been overcome in the very recent past. The entry of Sweden into the EU seems to have united them into a common front vis-à-vis employers and the EU bureaucracy in labour and social matters. They have shared an office in Brussels since 1997. The strong membership growth that SACO has experienced is also a factor behind its growing acceptance as a player on equal terms.

Minority unionism should not occur within the three federations since jurisdictional rules aim at preventing two member unions from organizing the same employees.[5] These rules have generally prevented minority unionism from emerging inside the same federation. There are a certain number of jurisdictional agreements between unions belonging to separate federations but disputes are not all that uncommon. However, they have not led to any minority union situations since those involved in jurisdictional disputes are majority unions in their core field.

Independent unions, not affiliated with the three federations, are uncommon in Sweden, playing a very marginal role in the labour market. Independent unions are mostly minority unions, and independent unionism has never been a serious issue in Sweden. LO and its member unions aimed at organizing all (blue-collar) employees from the very start. The LO policy was strengthened by a corresponding policy on the part of SAF. Already in the early stages of modern industrial relations SAF preferred to deal with LO and its member unions (although there were instances where both SAF and individual employers promoted splinter unionism and independent unions). No Communist union movement was ever formed or even seriously considered; no truly important Communist party ever emerged in national politics. At the same time no religious union movement was formed either. Sweden was a firmly Protestant country so there was no ground for a union movement inspired by Catholic social thinking, as was the case in many European countries.

By and large the structure established in the first decades of this century of a unified labour movement rather than pluralistic unionism became the tradition of the land. The attitude that emerged is that multiple unions are ultimately detrimental to the employees concerned and to the country as a whole. This attitude partly reflects the strength of the larger unions. They dominate the field both in terms of actually unionizing employees in their various parts of the labour market and also in terms of creating an atmosphere in which union multiplicity is frowned upon. In other words, a classic example of the successful monopolist!

One consequence is that Sweden does not have an official system to establish majority status for unions. Some kind of border would have to be

---

[5] For extensive explorations of jurisdictional matters, both inter- and intra-union, see Government White Papers SOU 1988:49 – 50, Arbetsmarknadsstriden. Gränstvister. Stridsåtgärder mot småföretag. III - IV.

established to separate the employees represented by two (or more) unions from other employees and no such rules exist in Sweden. They are considered unnecessary because minority unions are very rare and they are unwanted because minority unions are considered undesirable. However, it usually poses no problem to ascertain which is the majority union since minority unions tend to be very small. If a problem arises it is usual to regard all associations in the business concerned as the "unit" for establishing majority status. Obviously this makes it very difficult for new unions or splinter unions ever to achieve majority status. An example will illustrate this point. In the ports longshoremen are traditionally organized by the Swedish Transport Workers' Union, a member of LO. This union organizes all workers in any job related to transport, e.g. trucking or bus driving. A splinter union was formed in the ports among longshoremen. This union achieved majority status in many ports, perhaps even among longshoremen in the entire country. However, it clearly did not have majority status if all transport work was to be included in establishing this. The fact that the entire transport business was taken into account evidently reflects the strength of the Transport Workers' Union. On the employer side the transport business is divided into several sectors, road hauling being separate from port handling of goods for example. Given the stern opposition of the powerful Transport Workers' Union and the entire LO federation, prospects for this splinter union were never very bright. The same is true for all unions that try to break into a field where there is already a union belonging to one of the three federations.

There are some independent unions that enjoy unchallenged majority status. The prime example is the union organizing supervisors. Now called "The Leaders" (formerly the Supervisors' Union of Sweden), this was formed as a professional association in 1905. In recent decades it has had a somewhat stormy history in terms of affiliation. It belonged to TCO for long periods of time but stayed outside at other times, as now (1999). Jurisdictional disputes are at the root of the friction between the two. The union organizes most supervisors in public and private employment. Supervisors enjoy the same basic rights of freedom of association and labour rights as other employees. Swedish law knows of (virtually) no exceptions for managerial employees. "The Leaders" is a very strong union and its position is unchallenged. The same is true of the Swedish Airline Pilots' Union. There are no other truly unchallenged and powerful independent unions apart from these two at the present time.

The syndicalism movement is federated into the Central Organization of Swedish Workers (SAC), which is a general union although most of its members are blue-collar workers. It was founded in 1910 as a splinter from LO. Today's total membership (1998) does not exceed 10,000 employees, i.e. less than 0.25 per cent of the employed population. Although it has been bigger than this at certain times it has always been small because the movement has been fought consistently and fiercely by LO, and SAF has never wanted anything to do with it. Despite its tiny size its influence on industrial relations in Sweden has not been quite negligible. It has served to challenge its mighty rival, LO. It sometimes manages to sign collective agreements with small, non-organized private employers. Problems usually ensue since the local branch of the LO-affiliated union will follow suit. By applying superior pressure it will obtain a collective agreement covering the same work, and a confrontation is inevitable.

How active are union members? In other words, how much active support can unions count upon from members? A study conducted by the Central Bureau of Statistics, published in 1996 but based on interviews carried out in 1992/93, provides the following information. Fifteen per cent of members actively participated in union work at that time. On average 40 per cent of members had attended a union meeting in the past year, with 53 per cent for SACO and 40 per cent for LO. A 1999 LO report on "Union Activity and Union Work" shows an increase in interest among women, particularly young women under 30, in union work and a concomitant increase in the number of women holding a union position of some kind (12 per cent in 1998 against 8 per cent in 1993). Corresponding figures for men reveal declining interest and also a decline in union positions held (16 per cent in 1998 against 19 per cent in 1993). Women held 40 per cent of voluntary union positions in 1998 against 27 per cent in 1993. Some 60 per cent of members affirm that they take an active interest in union matters. Women are still under-represented at the top of unions. Only two women are union presidents within the LO family of 20 unions. There are seven women presidents among the 18 member unions of TCO and the same number in the 26-member SACO family.

Inter-federation disputes between member unions are rare.[6] Agreements between unions belonging to the same federation are common and several also exist between unions belonging to different federations. Still, jurisdictional disputes are not unheard of. Since they have not caused any real concern, calls for legislation to curb them have gone unheard. In most instances a settlement is reached without open conflict between employers and employees. LO has authority to make a binding decision: TCO and SACO can do so only if authorized by the unions involved. No public agency has authority to intervene, much less to settle a bargaining issue. There is no exclusive representation for a majority union.

Disputes between unions and individual members are rare and lawsuits are extremely rare. The number of reported court cases in the entire country

---

[6] Cf. previous note.

is less than ten since 1945. Sweden has no rules on fair representation of union members but discriminatory treatment is unlawful.

3. Attitudes

What is a union? What are union attitudes and opinions regarding their work and their relations with members? One way of characterizing a union movement is to look at typical attitudes among members and officials to various aspects of unionism. Swedish unions display some very characteristic features in these respects (Fahlbeck, 1996).

Box 1.1 What is a union, its function?

(a)   A voice for those who have none.

(b)   An organization for those who prefer collective representation to individual representation.

(c)   An alter ego of the enterprise, i.e. the company's alternative personality.

Box 1.2 What is a union, its common bond?

(a)   An organization for people with a common attribute, e.g. skill or ideology.

(b)   An organization to take labour out of competition.

(c)   An organization for people with a common background, e.g. an enterprise.

Box 1.3 What is the relationship between unions and their members?

(a)   Unions take care of their members' best interests.

(b)   Unions present their members' views and wishes.

(c)   Unions harmonize members' views with management views.

Box 1.4 What attitudes do union officers have towards their union work?

(a)   Union work is a vocation, a kind of secular priesthood.

(b)   Union work is a job among others, offering a career in "the union business".

(c)   Union work is an exercise in cooperation with management, even training for management positions.

These boxes may be used to compare Japan, Sweden and the United States. Union members and officials in these countries – and in other countries as well – respond to all the alternatives in the four boxes. Several exceptions would have to be made in the case of Sweden. Swedish unions, their members and officers do not respond at all to alternative (c) in boxes 1.1 and 1.4 and alternative (b) in box 1.4.

A classification should focus on the features that characterize unions and their officers. Table 1 attempts to do this with regard to the three countries, by summarizing responses to the questions in the boxes above.

Table 1. Attitudes of Japanese, Swedish and US unions

	Box 1.1	Box 1.2	Box 1.3	Box 1.4
Japan	c	c	c	c
Sweden	a	a	a	a
USA	b	b	b	b

The differences are considerable, revealing important characteristics of the national union movements. Box 1.3 is of particular interest.

Swedish union officials, particularly in the blue-collar sector, see themselves as people with a mission. Their mission is to serve the employee community. Their gospel is the welfare of their members. Their mode of operation is that of a pastor leading his flock.

Some historical background will help to clarify the situation in Sweden. The blue-collar union movement was formed late in the nineteenth century. At that time blue-collar workers had lost contact with the established religion (i.e. the state-controlled Protestant church). They lived in a spiritual vacuum or void. The nascent socialist movement and the labour unions offered values such as solidarity, brotherly love and concern for others, equality and fair shares for all according to their needs. These principles closely resemble Christian ethics. Union campaigners and officials proclaimed them at that time and they still do. Unions were and still are communities of women and men inspired by these ideals and values: they are striving to better their lot in life by working together. There is an unbroken line of thinking between the early unionists and those of today. It is certainly true that the semi-religious fervour is less pronounced today, as poverty and exploitation no longer exist in Sweden and everyone, comparatively speaking, is affluent, but the spirit is still there. Unions are leaders but the purpose of leadership is to serve the community.

Describing the attitudes and values of the Swedish union movement as semi-religious reveals and explains certain aspects of the movement.

Alternative (a) in box 1.1 and box 1.3 means that union officials speak for their members, in the sense of formulating what is to be said and in actually saying it. The voice function (box 1.1) is much less important today than in the infancy of unionism, owing to vastly higher educational standards and workers' ability to speak for themselves, as well as the existence of many channels to express an opinion. But the voice function is still there because unions are supposed to represent rank-and-file workers and speak for them.

There is much less of a religious undertone in white-collar unionism. But unionism is still considered a noble activity, the unselfish pursuit of a fuller and more dignified life for members. Career thinking might be somewhat more prevalent but only marginally so. The doctrinal role of taking care of members' best interests is also less conspicuous today, but it is still very strong and permeates the actual functioning of unions.

Two examples to illustrate this point are votes on issues at hand, e.g. strike ballots or collective bargaining agendas, and votes on proposed agreements. If the role of unions is to present their members' views, votes and referenda are the order of the day: at each and every juncture the rank and file must be asked for its opinion. If, on the other hand, the task of the union is to formulate, obtain and take care of its members' best interests the opposite becomes true. Votes and referenda are not the order of the day. They might even seem to disrupt the orderly running of things. In Sweden membership votes are very rare. Most unions never organize votes on current issues. When a vote is taken it is virtually never mandatory and the results are practically never binding on union officials. Reflecting this, Swedish labour law has no provisions on membership votes or referenda within unions. This situation is in sharp contrast to detailed regulation in the United States where votes and referenda are common, usually mandatory and almost always binding.

This all means that alternative (a) in box 1.4 is very strong and elements of (b) certainly exist as well. Unions do provide a career ladder. Traditionally the most coveted position for a working class person is to become a senior official of LO, the federation of blue-collar employees. And it is a fact that all those who have achieved this rank have come from the anonymous masses of the rank and file. They have little formal training. They have not graduated from senior high school and certainly not attended college. They have risen because of their dedication and skill. Contacts or hard elbows count for little and so do intra-union infighting and intrigue. Once there, they belong to the innermost circles of power in Swedish society. However, at least until very recently, they have been very modestly paid and enjoyed few fringe benefits. Any tendency on their part to forget the people they represent is quickly and resolutely quelled. This is true of all senior officials in blue-collar unions as well (although the Transport Workers' Union traditionally presents a livelier picture). Rare, for example, is the union president of a blue-collar union who has attended college.

Obviously educational levels have increased considerably among top union office holders even in blue-collar unions. It is still true, however, that the vast majority have attended neither high school nor college. On the other hand they have always benefited from extensive in-union education and have often attended non-formal educational institutions for long periods of time. Once they reach the top they are certainly very knowledgeable about all matters of concern to the union. This means that the idea of union work as a vehicle for one's personal career is very remote indeed at the bottom of the hierarchy and is generally absent even among the higher echelons. The union is not a business and union work is not a job like others.

The above also applies to a great extent to white-collar unionism and – to a lesser extent – to professional unionism, for example SACO and its member unions. Obviously, educational levels are higher among union officials here since the border between the three different union federations is drawn along educational lines. Apart from that the picture is rather similar.

One illustration of the effect of this frame of mind is the length of tenure. The period in office tends to be quite short in Sweden, rarely exceeding ten years in the same post. This is in sharp contrast to some other countries, notably in the United States (where the (b) alternative in box 1.4 is very strong). Consider, for example, Samuel Gompers, who was president of the AFL for some 40 years until his death at age 74. Nothing similar is even conceivable in Sweden.

Another illustration of the importance of attitude (a) in box 1.4 (in particular when coupled with attitude (a) in box 1.2) concerns members' satisfaction with union leadership. All studies strongly indicate that the rank and file are satisfied with union leaders and trust them.[7] There is nothing surprising in that. If union officials consider themselves to be people with a mission, charged with a noble and honourable task, and if they behave in this spirit, it is probable that members will have great confidence in them. If, on the other hand, alternative (b) is strong, even prevalent, a built-in source of conflict exists between members and their representatives. The risk of a gap between members and their representatives is always possible and that seems to be the main reason why extensive legislation is needed in the United States to prevent such gaps from occurring. Sweden lives in blissful ignorance of such rules.

Another way to illustrate the effects of alternatives (a) and (b) in box 1.4 is to study intra-union strife. Obviously the more alternative (a) prevails

---

[7] A leading study is Lewin, 1997.

among union members and officials the less intra-union strife should be expected. The more alternative (b) prevails the more likely is intra-union strife. Sweden certainly illustrates this point. Intra-union strife is rare and when it does occur it is generally quickly eliminated (Fahlbeck, 1996). The situation in the United States is the opposite.

Yet another way to illustrate the effects of the various alternatives in boxes 1.1 to1.4 is to study the amount of legislation considered necessary to strike a balance between the interests of members and the interests of union office holders. Obviously a strong (a) attitude will reinforce the community of interests between members and their representatives, making statutory rules redundant. The absence of regulation in Sweden presumably reflects the strength of the (a) alternative.

The attitudes listed as alternative (c) in boxes 1.1 to1.4 are generally alien to Swedish unionism. Box 1.4 is perhaps the most important here. It is true that Swedish unions cooperate with management and that personal relations between union officials and managers are usually friendly. But this does not mean that union officials tend to be co-opted by management. Swedish employers have never seriously pursued a policy of trying to reduce or even eliminate the influence of union officials by co-opting them. In the second place, union representatives have never shown a tendency to forget their roots or their mission. Rare indeed is the union representative who has assumed a true management position (apart from becoming a supervisor). Those who do accept a management job receive little sympathy or understanding from the rank and file, to put it mildly.

4. Agenda

Swedish unions represent their members in all negotiations on employment issues. The bargaining agenda is the broadest possible. As far as working life is concerned unions offer a total package "from the cradle to the grave". In addition, the union platform has both a public, society-oriented, and a private, member-oriented side.

Unions maintain a very conspicuous presence in virtually every aspect of public life, although they are not political bodies per se. Still, LO proudly states that: "We even formed a political party in order to pursue our demands in Parliament, the Swedish Social Democratic Party, a party which proved to be the most successful of all Swedish political parties in the twentieth century" (Jonsson, 1998).

However, one of the characteristics of Swedish unions is that they do not pursue a strictly political course of action. It is true that LO and TCO have a strong ideology but they and their member unions pursue a pragmatic policy of not alienating themselves from the employer community.

Federations and their member unions work closely with employer organizations, and they cannot jeopardize that cooperation in the political arena.

It is also true that Swedish unions are social creatures. They take part in public debates and policy discussions on social and economic questions. They also maintain a high profile in all matters concerning education and international solidarity. No field of human endeavour totally escapes them, even matters of a more private nature (see below).

Unions routinely participate in the legislative process, which they often set in motion. They have an intimate knowledge of social realities which enables them to pinpoint social problems, and other matters that need attention. Once the legislative process has begun, unions are involved in virtually every step. Since the process is meticulous and lengthy this gives unions considerable influence.

The first step is to set up a government committee to investigate the issue at hand and submit proposals. Unions are routinely represented on such committees and union representatives often chair them. Once the committee has published its findings and recommendations in a White Paper, copies are routinely sent to the organizations, agencies and other bodies concerned for comment. Unions participate in this round of consultations. Internal union efforts during the consultations differ considerably according to the importance of the question. When crucial issues are at stake internal union procedures might involve extensive member discussion before an opinion is given to the government. Once the government takes over the process, the influence of unions diminishes but public debate continues. Unions have no further formal influence once a bill is submitted to Parliament, but several Members of Parliament are or were union officials.

The "private" part of the union agenda concerns members as individuals. By far the most important activities here are the extensive training and education programmes conducted by virtually all unions. LO, for example, has a wide range of educational programmes and runs several schools. Some 11 per cent of LO expenditure in fiscal year 1997 went on education (LO Annual Report 1997). Most of the programmes run by unions are directed at training members for union office, but some offer education of a more general nature. One LO school (Brunnsvik) plays an important role in Swedish cultural life, and it has trained many well-known writers. Vocational training proper is not usually part of union educational programmes.

Unions also provide services that have to do with the private lives of their members. Since unions can offer a huge number of customers to prospective business partners they are in an excellent position to secure a good price for their members. In most instances these services are optional but sometimes they are mandatory: the courts have accepted that unions have a wide margin of discretion here. Examples of union action include contracting insurance policies for their members, such as home and accident insurance. In addition, unions can arrange private bank loans or provide collateral for a loan ("If you need a new car, contact your union!"). Recently LO has entered the field of utilities. The electricity supply is being deregulated in Sweden, largely at the initiative of LO, which urged that competition should be introduced for the benefit of consumers. LO has made a deal with a big supplier, on behalf on 1.4 million households, giving them access to special rates if they so wish. LO also rents out computers to its members. Unions routinely assist members in realizing meaningful activities during time off, and also help in arranging vacations. One of the leading travel and tour operators in Sweden, which also runs hotels, is a creature of the LO movement (Reso).

Critics sometimes argue that unions meddle in things that are none of their business. Still, no restrictive legislation exists and courts found in favour of unions in one highly publicized case involving home insurance.

Swedish unions are very active in the international arena. Working either directly through international organizations, such as ILO, or indirectly through international union bodies, such as ETUC or professional associations, Swedish unions forcefully pursue an overall international agenda, looking upon themselves not just as participants but often as initiators as well. For example, LO takes the position that it was a main actor, if not *the* main actor, behind the creation of ETUC and TCO feels the same. LO has pushed hard to have its member unions enter European federations.

First on the international agenda are strenuous and unrelenting efforts to have basic human rights, including core workers' rights, accepted everywhere and to have these included in international instruments, e.g. the Treaty of Rome as amended by the 1997 Amsterdam Treaty. Swedish unions adamantly support the inclusion of social clauses in international instruments, such as the WTO charter. More will be said on this topic in section 7.

Another important aspect of international activities concerns education and training. Unions spend increasingly large amounts on these in developing countries. Countries in Eastern Europe also receive sizeable financial assistance.

5. The information society

In 1982, the labour market parties in the private sector (SAF, LO and PTK) signed a "Development Agreement", designed to promote cooperation, mutual understanding and business efficiency. It vibrates with the dynamism of change and also with the optimism of change. It stresses the need for business flexibility and adaptation, both for companies and for employees.

It underlines the need for continuous learning and skill formation but at the same time acknowledges the legitimacy of employee expectations of a rewarding and fulfilling life at work. The agreement proves that the union movement is prepared to look ahead and take an active part in a fast-changing work environment.

The years since the "Development Agreement" was signed have shown that the vision of the agreement was correct. There has been a period of stunning technological advance: information technology and tele-communication systems have revolutionized our way of perceiving human interaction. The era of standardized mass production in huge factories is being replaced by smaller and leaner facilities where the contribution of each individual is much more quantifiable and visible. The importance of each individual worker's knowledge and skill has grown considerably. Manufacturing is increasingly computerized, turning many blue-collar workers into highly specialized technicians. At the same time, the number of employees in manufacturing has gone down dramatically, and services are becoming the dominant economic sector. Work processes and employee quali-fications are much more individualized in services than in traditional manufacturing.

The structure of the labour force has changed as well, with a core staff working on a full-time basis. These are considered permanent employees in the sense that they are not likely to be dismissed. Surrounding them are people employed on different types of contract. Part-time and fixed-term employees form one group. Many work for long periods as part-timers or on successive fixed-term contracts and many turn into core employees, only to be replaced by others. Another group is composed of workers employed by independent contractors. Temporary workers are a third group. Temporary hiring has become much more common and has spread into new sectors, such as accountancy and research.

In the information society[8] personal contacts and closeness are based on what the parties agree at any given time. So is their interdependence, but typically there is a close professional relationship: this relationship is mutual and the seller often holds the trump cards. Traditional capital (i.e. money and equipment) becomes less important as a wealth factor. Knowledge and creativity are what count. Brain power increasingly replaces machine power and brain power is primarily individual like knowledge and creativity. The transition from an industrial society to an information society profoundly changes the role of capital. Since the relevant capital is knowledge, ownership moves from the buyers of work to the sellers, from capitalists/employers to

---

[8] For a more extensive discussion see Fahlbeck, 1998a, 1998b, 1998c.

employees/self-employed. Capital is disseminated to an increasingly wide section of the population so that everyone becomes a "capitalist". Possession and control of capital are increasingly atomized.

Elements of both the agrarian and the industrial society remain in the information society but their relative importance gradually diminishes. A multiplicity of activities with radically divergent structures is the hallmark of the information society. The evolution towards an information society also means a trend towards decentralization and flexibility as it is primarily individuals who possess knowledge.

The move towards an information society is a challenge to unionism. Knowledge and creativity are individual and have little to do with standardization and collectivization. The core idea of unions – to monopolize the labour supply and remove labour from competition – does not seem compatible with labour supply patterns in an information society. Due to the importance of individual knowledge and creativity, sellers of work will become increasingly independent and self-sufficient. Increased individualism is likely to follow. Unions will not benefit from this. They will not benefit from the increase in unemployment either, since unions do not represent workers who are jobless.

Yet another factor that will not benefit unions is anticipated change in the market place. Product output will become much more varied and adjusted to the needs and wishes of customers. This will result in less rigid price structures and businesses will focus on maximizing income rather than minimizing cost. This, in turn, will make unions less necessary to the sellers of labour.

An increasingly individualized demand for goods and services will enhance the trend towards an individualization of the labour supply. People will be more discerning and specific when they sell their labour if this is how they act as buyers of goods and services. Raised buyer expectations go hand-in-hand with raised seller expectations.

The paragraphs above reiterate some standard explanations for the recent decline in union density rates in highly developed countries. These can be summarized in four points. (1) Changes in industrial structure resulting in fewer big factories. (2) Relative increase in the number of atypical (non-permanent) workers. (3) Higher education and better living standards resulting in individualism and less interest in unions, combined with an increased emphasis on employee mobility and lower levels of employee identification with the enterprise. (4) Traditionally low unionization rates in medium and small companies because of employer resistance, little union interest and greater difficulty in organizing them.

However, there are at least some countervailing factors. First, the atypical workforce is more vulnerable than the core workforce. Many people on atypical contracts have working conditions that are far less favourable than those of core workers. It is a fact that the decline in unionization rates and the increase in the atypical workforce have happened simultaneously. The standard thesis is that the peripheral workforce is less inclined to join unions. In most countries unionization rates among atypical workers are lower than among traditional full-time employees. Unions in many countries show little interest in organizing atypical workers. Second, all those in agriculture and industry face harder times. Price competition will intensify and management will increasingly concentrate on cost cutting. Labour costs will not escape their attention.

Swedish unions are obviously aware of the potential in agriculture and traditional industry. There is nothing surprising here and that aspect needs no further comment. The important question is what they do with the new situation.

As indicated by the 1982 "Development Agreement", Swedish unions want to be partners in the ongoing process and they want to make a contribution. One way is to be instrumental in formulating rules for flexible work organizations, and unions take part in all approaches to increasing flexibility. This has been done while preserving the "Nordic model", i.e. the model that relies on collective bargaining and collective agreements. As far as possible the general standards in collective agreements also apply to atypical employees. Where this is not possible collective agreements often establish special standards for atypical employees. Statutes provide for bilateral flexibility since they allow room for derogation by means of collective agreements.

Atypical workers in Sweden are not unionized to a lesser degree than core workers. Indeed, the opposite is true in that part-timers are more often union members than people on fixed-term contracts. One explanation is that the unionization rate among women is slightly higher than among men, and women account for the overwhelming majority of part-time employees. Women also dominate among temporary workers and they – as well as their male colleagues - benefit from what the leading union has done for them.

How have unions responded to the changing work environment and avoided a declining unionization rate? There is no one simple answer to that question. A slogan might be "hard work". To elaborate, one might say that unions have shown tenacity and stubbornness in defending positions already won. Much more important, they have displayed considerable enthusiasm and inventiveness in opening up new vistas, greeting the changing work environment, adapting to new technology, and accepting that fear is always connected with change. Evidently their success has been greatly helped by a positive social context that supports them in a variety of ways. Perhaps even more important is that the employer community has not tried to exploit the new situation to get rid of unions.

One remarkable achievement is the fact that unions have managed to organize the temporary work business and negotiate collective agreements covering temporary workers. No business is more difficult to unionize than temporary work, but it has been done. The leading role was played by the Clerical Workers Union (*Tjänstemannaförbundet HTF*), which belongs to TCO. Starting from nothing only a few years ago it has negotiated a series of collective agreements covering the core sector of the temporary work business. As of September 1999 it is negotiating a new contract, having terminated an existing agreement early in 1999 despite that fact that this was spectacularly good from an international point of view. The focus of the HTF agreements is income security for temporary workers. Obviously, the employers – temporary work agencies – only want to pay their employees – the temps – for time actually worked and consequently billed by the agency. Just as obviously the temps want to be paid regardless of whether they work or not (as long as they are available to work, of course). Up to a point the HTF agreement provides for precisely that. The now terminated agreement guaranteed 75 per cent of full salary for the individually agreed working time of each employee/temp. In other words, the employer and the employee shared the risk for non-billable time but the employer carried the greater risk. HTF is now demanding that the employer assume full responsibility for non-billable time. This would offer full income security for employees/temps (provided, of course, that they are available to work as ordered and covered by their individual contract of hire).

How has this seemingly impossible feat been accomplished? No simple and clear-cut answer can be provided. Industrial action is conspicuous by its absence, so the answer does not lie there. Hard, imaginative and tenacious union work account for much, as does the employer response. It should be noted that temporary work was illegal in Sweden for some 50 years until deregulation in the early 1990s legalized it. However, legalization did not come easily and it was accompanied by strong expectations that temporary work agencies would see that fair standards and socially acceptable practices were observed; collective regulation of labour conditions is standard practice in Sweden. Another factor has probably helped the union despite the fact that it works against the temps and puts them in a weaker position. Established case law holds that temps are not entitled to unemployment benefit for time not worked (and not paid) by the employer/agency. The rationale is that temps are employed regardless of whether they are paid or not: in that sense they are not unemployed. This legal ruling means that temps are in fact deprived of pay altogether for the time not covered by the employer guarantee in the collective agreement. It has been made clear that no change in the law can be expected, so that the labour market partners have to find a solution. In a way society is helping the union in its quest for full compensation from employers. The need for full compensation becomes more obvious when unemployment benefits are unavailable. This means that the possibility of a full payment guarantee in a new collective agreement seems quite high.

This achievement would probably not have been possible if the union had not in the process rendered a service to the temporary work agencies. Incidentally, this is one of the fastest growing business sectors in the entire national economy. The union contribution is to make temporary work agencies an accepted feature of economic life. As indicated above temporary work was strictly prohibited in Sweden for decades. A general feeling of discomfort or even suspicion in many circles greeted the total lifting of the ban by a non-socialist government. The union movement campaigned against lifting the ban completely and advocated a return to the middle ground in force before total deregulation. A government commission proposed a partial retreat from deregulation. But the social democratic government, with the tacit support of the trade union movement, decided not to heed that proposal. Without the introduction of a collective regime by HTF things would probably have developed quite differently for the temporary work agencies.

Another union success is the organization of atypical employees. There is no hesitation in recruiting atypical workers as members and unions vigorously campaign for them. To give just one example: unions have campaigned hard for part-timers to have the right to increase their working time if they so wish. Rules to that effect have become rather common in collective agreements and a statutory rule was enacted in 1996. A final example concerns flexible working time and business cycle variations, where unions have helped shape socially acceptable schemes. The 1982 Working Time Act does not deal with flexitime as such, but it does not permit employers to introduce flexitime or business cycle variations unilaterally. The Act provides for collective agreements to that effect and the social partners have ensured that virtually all collective agreements include elaborate rules on flexitime. Rules on business cycle variations in the total number of working hours are closely related to flexitime arrangements. These can also be agreed by means of a collective agreement. A breakthrough 1995 blue-collar agreement introduced rules to that effect in engineering and metalworking. Proposals for lifetime flexisystems have attracted wide attention, as have proposals for regular sabbaticals. So far these have not produced any concrete results which are generally applicable, but at least one company (the insurance giant Skandia) has introduced a system of recurrent sabbaticals so that its employees can spend time studying. The unions wholeheartedly endorse the scheme.

Union efforts concerning atypical employment have been protective and offensive at the same time. In both respects they have served atypical employee groups well and it is not difficult to understand why union density rates are no lower than among other groups.

6. Structure and finance

The organizational structure of Swedish unions is fairly uniform despite the fact that their origins differ considerably. LO, the oldest union federation, has served as a model for the other two federations, TCO and SACO, and their member unions. However, since many SACO unions have a long history as professional associations they have often developed characteristics all their own. The by-laws of the various organizations spell out the exact structure of each union and its internal working.

Generally speaking union governance is highly centralized. LO in particular has a very strong position vis-à-vis its member organizations. The by-laws of LO parallell the corresponding by-laws of the member unions. LO has proposed model by-laws for its members, which are not binding but which establish certain standards as a recommendation. To gain membership in LO a union must meet certain mandatory standards.

The most striking feature is that LO controls industrial action by member unions to a considerable extent. Other provisions also confer power on LO: a) disputes between member unions are settled by a binding decision of LO; b) member unions have to await an opinion from LO before signing industry-wide collective agreements; c) LO must be consulted on all matters of major importance. Despite the power of LO, the member unions are truly independent organizations. They pursue diverging policies in many respects while at the same time striving for unity. Frequent meetings are held between the presidents of the member unions. Nevertheless, union officials are responsive to the rank-and-file members of that particular union. For example, member unions do not necessarily adopt master agreements entered into by LO. The 1938 Saltsjöbaden Agreement on collective bargaining, grievance handling and prevention of certain kinds of industrial action provides an illustration. This agreement is considered as a cornerstone of Swedish industrial relations. The rules laid down have served as a model for the entire labour market and also for legislation. The norms have achieved the status of principles of law. However, some private sector unions in construction and transport, which belong to LO, have never adopted the agreement.

The prime role of LO is to serve as the vanguard of blue-collar unionism, indeed unionism generally. According to its by-laws LO shall "perform the central governance of the efforts of the trade union movement to look after and protect the interests of employees on the labour market and within the economy and in this respect as in other respects to promote social development on the basis of political, social and economic democracy" (Article 1). The model by-laws adopted by LO for its member unions propose a similar wording.

Though using slightly less "leftist" language the by-laws of TCO and SACO state the same aim. However, the power of TCO and SACO vis-à-vis their member unions is significantly less than that of LO. Neither has any control over industrial action. Unless specifically authorized, neither has authority to settle disputes between member unions.

Industry-wide unions have regional and local branches. The local branches are bargaining agents, usually at enterprise or workplace level. Regional branches are usually not bargaining agents: they perform a variety of services for the industry-wide union and the local unions. Support to local unions is at the heart of their functions. Though employees are members of the industry-wide organization, union dues are levied at regional level. Regional and local branches are legally independent entities but since union by-laws contain detailed rules on their operations there is little room for manoeuvre. The number of regional unions has declined dramatically among LO members in recent decades as a result of a determined policy to streamline the organization and raise the professional level of each regional union. In 1952 there were 8,915 regional unions, and the number had dropped to 651 in 1997. In 1952 total membership was 1.3 million but had risen to 2.1 million in 1997, so the declining number of regional unions is not related to a decline in total membership (LO Annual Report 1997).

Local branches form the basis of unions and all but the smallest workplaces establish local branches. Since three federations and their member unions operate side by side and since the union of supervisors is also represented at most workplaces, it is common to find four local branches at any given place of work. Local branches negotiate with the employer. Given the recent trend towards a more decentralized collective bargaining structure, the importance of local collective agreements on wages and other conditions of work has increased. So, in its wake, has the role of local branches. Thanks to statutory rules on information and cooperation between employers and employees, local unions take part in virtually every aspect of workplace operations. In their dealings with employers concerning long-term planning and day-to-day operations, they have considerable room for manoeuvre. It is not the task of regional or industry-wide unions to quell local inventiveness and creativity in dealing with individual employers.

Local union officials are elected by direct membership vote. Office holders higher up in the hierarchy are nominated by the elected representatives of members rather than by direct vote. By and large unions are organizations of the one-party type in the sense that it is very uncommon for two or more factions to fight for control of a union. This is true at all levels of the hierarchy. When two or more candidates present themselves for office they virtually never represent diverging union platforms. They are distinguished by their personal history, character, age and professional background. Tenure is for specific periods, spelled out in union by-laws. For example, tenure as president of TCO is four years. Re-election is possible and no maximum period is specified, but in most unions elected office is held for a relatively short period.

In addition to their elected or nominated office holders, all union bodies except the local branches employ staff.[9] At federation level LO had a staff of 220 in 1997. SACO employed about 40 people. Employees range from office workers to highly specialized professionals, such as economic analysts. All three federations (LO, TCO and SACO) maintain research departments, particularly for economic matters. These are staffed by university graduates, many with PhDs, so speakers for LO and TCO play an important role in socioeconomic debate and analysis in Sweden. The various industry-wide unions also employ specialists. At regional level the core employees do most of the grassroots work. They are often appointed on the basis of a membership referendum, even though they are employees. Most of them have a background as elected local union officers. Despite the importance of employed personnel at various levels in the hierarchy, union governance is firmly in the hands of elected office holders.

Unions have far-reaching authority to represent their members. This authority is partly statutory, partly contractual, based on union by-laws. Unions conclude legally binding collective agreements, interpret them and represent employees in the grievance process and before the Labour Court. Unions have authority under most labour statutes to conclude collective agreements with employers derogating from the statute. Such agreements are binding on members and non-members alike. On the other hand, unions also have obligations towards their members, notably to support and represent them. However, the exact union obligations are far from clear. No statutory rules exist regarding the relationship between unions and their members and case law is practically non-existent. The same is true in situations where member interests clash, for example in agreeing to priority lists of employees in mass layoffs and terminations. Rules on union duty of fair representation are conspicuously absent.

The financial situation of Swedish unions is very good. They have three main sources of income: member dues, income from investments and contributions from employers. Member contributions are the foundation of

---

[9] For details see the Annual Reports of the trade union federations and individual unions.

union finances. Unions are free to decide the amount and, except in cases of discrimination, the courts have no jurisdiction. No reported case on discriminatory fee structures exists.

The dues that are levied differ considerably among unions,[10] and no pattern can be detected among the three federations. Union dues are often higher in absolute terms in LO member unions than in SACO members despite the fact that average incomes are higher among SACO members. Some unions charge a fixed percentage. A member of LO, the Swedish Metal Workers Union, charges 1.9 per cent whereas a leading member of TCO, the Union of Swedish Salaried Industry Workers (SIF), charges 1 per cent. Many unions have a ceiling. A survey of 23 major unions within the LO, TCO and SACO families, conducted by SIF, reported the following findings. In 1998 on a 24,000 kronor monthly income (approximately 2,750 euro) a high of 549 kronor (approximately 62 euro) was reported by the LO Swedish Food Workers Union (*Livsmedelsarbetareförbundet*) and a low of 218 kronor (approximately 25 euro) by the SACO Union for Civil Engineers (CF). However, unions differ in terms of what they offer in return for dues. They all offer standard union representation, of course, but in addition many provide members with other services, such as accident insurance or home insurance, or both. Some provide discounts for members using union recreational facilities. Others offer medical insurance as part of the package. Many also offer collateral-free bank loans. But, again, it is difficult to discern a pattern.

Unions are free to decide how to use member dues. Nothing prevents them from using the money for purposes other than strictly union business, e.g. political contributions. Employees cannot join a union on condition that their dues are not spent in such a way. There is no equivalent to an American type "agency shop".

Historically membership dues represented the main, if not sole, source of union income.[11] The situation is radically different today. In many unions, dues account for less than 50 per cent of income. Unions have accumulated wealth through the years, primarily by building strike funds. Today these funds are considerable, allowing unions to engage in protracted industrial action if need be. Many unions are in a position to fight not just one war, but two or more at the same time. Union assets are invested primarily in real

---

[10] No survey of an official or semi-official nature exists. The figures given are based on a survey of 23 major unions within the LO, TCO and SACO families undertaken by SIF and published in its membership magazine, SIF-tidningen 1998:17.

[11] Figures in the text are based on a survey published by the daily Svenska Dagbladet, 16 May 1998.

estate, stocks and bonds. The financial management of assets has become an important part of union management. For example, in fiscal year 1998 financial transactions accounted for some 65 per cent of total income in SIF, the biggest TCO-member union. Though this figure is probably higher than for most unions it still represents a common trend. Membership dues do not cover expenses. For example, in 1998 SIF recorded a 150 million kronor deficit (approximately 19 million euro). That equals 425 kronor (approximately 45 euro) per member in a union that charges an average of 2,400 kronor (approximately 265 euro) annual dues. Union wealth is primarily owned and administered by the industry-wide unions. Local unions do not dispose of any investment capital nor do the three federations to any significant degree.

Contributions from employers are either direct or indirect, although cash contributions are unusual. These occur only in a few blue-collar unions, primarily in the construction industry. Such contributions are really payment for services rendered by the union in measuring piece work and calculating pay for that work. Employer payments here are supposed to cover union costs, no more. Under some construction industry agreements employers cover union expenditure for supervising employer observance of pay provisions in the collective agreement. There is serious doubt about whether the money is actually spent on this purpose. No one asserts that the money represents featherbedding. Indeed the parties deal with each other at arms' length.

The overwhelming majority of employer payments are indirect, taking the form of time off for union work at full pay. Originally based solely on collective agreements, such indirect payments are now mandated in several statutes. The union does not actually receive any money. It is relieved of the expense of compensating its voluntary officers for union work at workplaces. It is not known how much the employer community pays for union work of this kind but it can safely be assumed that the total amount is considerable. Unions take the position that indirect payment of this kind is no different from other business costs since work performed by union representatives benefits the employer.

A hotly debated issue in recent years has been employee-union-controlled investment funds, financed by employer contributions. Such "wage earners' funds" were introduced by statute in the 1980s and employer payments were collected for some years; the funds were dissolved in the mid-1990s, as they were considered to disrupt the social balance between capital and labour. Not even the social democrats, who guided them through the legislative process in Parliament, were happy with them. They had become prisoners of their own propaganda to have them introduced. On the other hand, the "private" wealth accumulated by unions has attracted little attention and virtually no criticism. Unions are seen as one investor among many.

Doubts about union "fund capitalism" are of a radically different kind, being mostly concerned with the ethical aspects of union investment. Unions are supposed to pursue investment policies that do not conflict with socio-political agenda, e.g. they do not invest in companies using child labour. In 1998 TCO adopted ethical guidelines for investment. LO is actively promoting a common union front vis-à-vis multinational enterprises to make them respect human rights, including the core ILO Conventions. Fund capitalism is one way to exert pressure. So far union "fund power" has not been a factor of any particular importance in financial markets. The resources of the truly important actors in financial markets dwarf union wealth, however impressive.

Evidently, union expenditure is primarily aimed at maintaining the ability to represent members. Much money is also spent on education, information and public relations. Federations spend more on information and lobbying activities. In 1997, for example, LO devoted 38 per cent of total expenditure to policy and lobbying and 14 per cent to information. In the same year 11 per cent was spent on education and 9 per cent on supporting kindred organizations in Sweden or abroad (LO Annual Report, 1997).

7. Regional and global action [12]

As mentioned in Section 4, Swedish unions are very active in the inter-national arena. The three federations cooperate closely in this field, main-taining a common office in Brussels. There are some differences of opinion between them, mainly between LO and TCO on the one hand and SACO on the other hand, but in a wider perspective these are not significant.

Unions display apprehension but no real fear of Europeanization and globalization of the economy. Pointing at the risk of increasing opposition in a global arena, Swedish unions call for increased international union cooperation to meet globalized business. Strong union cooperation is necessary to tackle runaway capitalism and fast-moving investment.

Swedish unions believe that the present context is rather like the situation in Sweden at the beginning of the twentieth century. At that time and for most of the century, attention was focused on the domestic scene. Now the perspective has widened and the EU has become the domestic scene. Beyond the EU is the rest of the world.

LO and TCO are among the most ardent proponents of international cooperation. They pride themselves on being among the chief initiators of ETUC, in which the Swedish federations are very active. The Brussels office

---

[12] The text in this section is based on unpublished union material and informal interviews with union officials.

is the main centre for that work as well as EU activities. The prevailing attitude among LO, TCO and SACO is dynamism and openness to the changing work environment and the challenges of internationalization. The three are united in wanting ETUC to play a pivotal role in shaping the ever-changing realities.

In comments on the proposed "General trade union policy resolution" submitted to the 1999 ETUC congress, SACO strongly advocates:

> ...a policy programme that is proactive, outreaching, and marked by a desire to meet problems and challenges head-on. The resolution should not in any way be marked by defensive attitudes; the European trade union movement should take care of the new possibilities in the Amsterdam treaty and establish a high profile.

It goes on to state that economic growth is necessary for new jobs and sustained welfare for all. Significantly, it adds that "economic growth is nothing "others" create, it is a shared responsibility of governments, social partners, industry and other economic actors" and concludes that "ETUC should have a framework programme on this issue". In an ever-changing world, so the document tells us, "Swedish trade union experiences have taught us that trade unions must tackle these changes in a forward-looking way, trying to anticipate and prepare, and formulate union strategies and tactics even before the changes hit with full force". In line with Swedish trade union traditions it advocates that ETUC should demonstrate that "trade unions are active in favour of industrial change and development". The document also stresses the need for free trade and adds that "free trade must go hand-in-hand with the promotion and defence of core labour rights". All these statements reflect long-standing union opinions in Sweden.

Swedish unions want a European model of industrial relations. They see this model from the Nordic perspective, i.e. strong unions, heavy reliance on collective bargaining and collective agreements, strong tripartite cooperation between employers, unions and the government. They advocate European collective bargaining and European collective agreements but are not pressing for these at the present time. They feel that mechanisms for uniform enforcement and adjudication must first be created. However, LO pushed hard for European bargaining procedures and considers the social clause of the Maastricht Treaty a big victory. A revision of ETUC's by-laws to handle European-wide negotiations and European collective agreements has also been carried through with strong LO input. Important elements here were consultation with national unions and a well-defined mandate for ETUC prior to negotiations.

On the global front three issues are currently at the fore. First, promotion of human rights, including core union rights. Second, the struggle against social dumping and support for social clauses in international instruments, such as the WTO charter. Third, safeguarding of union rights to engage in international, cross-border sympathy action. Unions are making a strenuous effort to have basic human rights, including core union rights, accepted everywhere and to have these included in international instruments.

Swedish unions strongly advocate free trade. At the same time they insist that free trade should be coupled with respect for basic human rights, including union rights, and also minimum conditions of work. They strongly advocate the inclusion of the core conventions in the WTO charter or at least a mention of them. They also advocate close cooperation between ILO and WTO. The same policies are pursued with regard to other international institutions, such as IMF and the World Bank. Non-regulated export processing zones cannot count on support from Swedish unions!

The eight basic ILO Conventions – the eighth on child labour was added in June 1999 – are seen as vital for a sound and fair economic world order. Unions do not deny that their motives are not solely idealistic. "Solidarity and self-interest are two sides of the same coin", states a 1998 TCO discussion brochure ("Europe is Part of the World"). Swedish unions worked hard to achieve the 1998 ILO "Declaration on Fundamental Principles and Rights at Work". It certainly did not harm those efforts that one member of the ILO Governing Body is the LO staff official responsible for international union work. Also, Swedish unions, at least LO, strongly advocate wider authority for ILO to monitor observance of its Conventions.

Swedish unions strongly support the adoption of company codes of conduct and are staunch supporters of the 1976 OECD Code of Conduct of Multinational Enterprises. The 1997 unilateral decision by Renault to close its factory in Vilvoorde in Belgium demonstrated both the importance of the code and the need to strengthen it.

Finally, Swedish unions strongly favour multinational cooperation and rule making over regional or bilateral arrangements.

8. Collective action and institutional support

A characteristic of Swedish labour regulation and practice is collectivization. This comes to the fore in all aspects of labour market functioning. Swedish law and industrial relations practice have no rules like those in France or Germany, where the employee community is represented by an elected body separate from the union (*Comité d'entreprise* or *Betriebsrat*). Unions have monopolized employee representation in Sweden, as it were.

The predominant role of collective bargaining is the oldest and most conspicuous feature of the collectivist system. Historically, collective bargaining is *the* method for rule making on the Swedish labour market. Though statutory regulation has become quite common since the 1970s, collective agreements still retain their position as the prime regulatory instrument. In addition, statutes defer to collective regulation to a large extent. Anti-trust legislation does not apply to collective agreements proper.

The subject matter of collective bargaining covers all questions concerning the relationship between employers and employees (including unions). With very few exceptions there are no managerial exemptions. Collective agreements are comprehensive, covering the entire employment relationship and they are often very detailed, in particular when dealing with issues such as working time or vacations. Collective agreement regulation is more or less exclusive in some areas concerning the individual employment relationship, notably with regard to pay. Sweden has no legislation at all on pay, not even a minimum wage. Swedish unions (and the business community) adamantly oppose the introduction of anything like a mandatory income policy or minimum wage. Tentative proposals by ETUC for some kind of incomes policy or minimum wage in Europe have met with downright rejection by Swedish unions.

Collective bargaining is very centralized, adding to the collectivist structure. Few nations with a market economy and privately owned industry have equally centralized bargaining. In the 1990s SAF worked hard to decentralize the bargaining system and it met with some success, particularly in wage setting. The process will probably continue but it does not seem likely to bring about a profound change. Unions adamantly oppose a dismantling of the system with industry-wide bargaining as the nucleus of collective bargaining. The result of the power struggle is mixed. Industry-wide bargaining still commands the field but much of the fighting has been delegated to negotiations at local level.

The union federations are not bargaining agents per se but that does not rule out participation in negotiations or wage bargaining. Industrial relations are marked by a series of agreements between LO and SAF. Starting in 1906 with a compromise that is the foundation of industrial relations LO has taken upon itself to negotiate master agreements intended to cover the whole private blue-collar labour market. These master agreements are not legally binding on member unions but most members will subsequently adopt them as legally binding collective agreements in collaboration with their employer counterpart. The scope of LO involvement depends on the willingness of SAF to engage in negotiations. On the whole SAF agreed to negotiate with LO concerning matters of overriding interest. Agreements between SAF and LO have been common during most of this century on matters such as collective bargaining procedures and timetables, grievance procedures, prevention of industrial action, information and consultation, as well as safety and health at the workplace.

Another area where LO has been an active partner is in establishing basic norms for pay and pay increases. During "the golden age" of Swedish industrial relations in the decades after 1945 such negotiations were quite common. SAF and LO agreed on certain basic principles for pay and specified percentage increases, leaving the rest of pay bargaining to industry-wide unions and local branches.

Early in the 1990s SAF adopted a policy of decentralization and non-participation in direct negotiations. This brought an end to the periodic wage negotiations that had held Sweden in suspense for decades. SAF also took itself out of negotiating master agreements. It still negotiates on highly technical matters which require uniformity, e.g. private pension schemes, but otherwise SAF has delegated negotiation to its member organizations and even some master agreements previously entered into. The late 1990s saw some renewed interest on the part of SAF in negotiating directly with LO but so far no substantive result has been produced.

Legally binding collective agreements are concluded at all levels of bargaining, national, industry-wide and local (company or plant) level. Due to their by-laws the three national federations are not authorized to enter into collective agreements that are binding upon their member unions, but many agreements entered into by them are subsequently ratified by member organizations. The industry is the traditional focus of bargaining and there are comprehensive, industry-wide collective agreements for every sector of the labour market, private and public. Uniform standards apply to workplaces regardless of size or location. The overwhelming majority of employees are covered by a collective agreement, including management representatives from production lines and supervisors to senior executives in both the private and the public sector. Some agreements cover vast sections of the economy. For instance one single agreement for blue-collar employees covers the core of the engineering industry. The agreement dates back to 1905 and it has been renegotiated from time to time. It is obvious that the structure of collective agreements also adds to the collectivist nature of Swedish industrial relations.

The exact number of industry-wide agreements is not known and does not much matter since every sector of the economy is covered. There is usually just one leading agreement in every sector and the others are mostly adaptations of this. Most industry-wide agreements affect a large number of employees. For example, 20 agreements in the blue-collar municipal sector cover about 635,000 employees, or an average of 32,000 employees per agreement. LO reports that some 7,000 industry-wide agreements were in force in 1997. Excluding the Metal Workers Union with some 6,900 agreements, 269 agreements covered 1.2 million LO members (LO Annual Report, 1997). Extensive labour legislation in Sweden has not undermined unions or the pre-eminence of collective bargaining. In fact, in many respects it is the opposite.

Another very conspicuous example is in the legislation on employment protection. Such legislation can differ profoundly in the role assigned to unions: they are not necessarily given a role at all. This is a political decision. The interesting point is that Swedish legislation has not deprived unions of arguments to persuade employees to join them. Indeed the legislation is structured in such a way that it gives unions tremendous influence over employers and employees alike.

The 1982 Employment Protection Act (and its 1974 predecessor) is comprehensive and detailed. It can be implemented without additional regulation, e.g. collective agreements, work rules or individual employment contracts. In that sense the statute is self-sufficient. However, it is unsatisfactory from the employer standpoint for two main reasons: (i) It imposes significant restrictions on employers, limiting managerial flexibility in running the workplace and (ii) the rules are based on individual employee needs rather than employer or collective employee needs. For example, seniority is an important factor in the statute whereas business efficiency is not. For these reasons employers want to derogate from the statute in many instances. Collective employee interests may also point in that direction.

One point concerns redundancy. The statute accepts *bona fide* business considerations as just cause for termination of employment contracts. No substantive union participation is needed here. However, the statute regulates the sequence in which employees are to be dismissed in redundancy situations where not all employees have to be laid off. The statute does not permit managers to decide which employees to dismiss, but provides detailed, mandatory rules on priority rating. The rules are exclusively based on seniority, defined as aggregated time of employment. Ability is a factor only to the extent that those retained must be able perform the work. Superior ability is not considered above that minimum level nor are other factors such as qualification, training, motivation or past record generally. Employer interest in retaining only the best-qualified employees or in composing a workforce to meet some specific criterion is not considered either.

These statutory rules call for adaptations to meet specific needs and the 1982 Act authorizes broad derogation, except in cases involving abuse or discrimination. Employers cannot derogate at their own discretion, nor can a labour inspector or the like give permission. Further, the statute rules out agreements between employers and employees. The one and only route is by means of collective agreements and only unions can be parties to an agreement on the employee side. Consequently, unions effectively control derogation from the Act.

The combined facts that employers strongly want, and often need, to derogate from the 1982 Act and that unions are in control of such derogation give unions a very strong position indeed in the administration of the Act. But it does not stop at that. A further point is that collective agreements under the Act apply not only to union members but to all employees within reach of the agreement as well. Unionized employees can influence the content of collective agreements through the democratic decision-making structures of the union. Non-unionized employees have no similar channel of influence. Nor do they have recourse to the courts (or any administrative agency) other than in exceptional instances of abuse of statutory authority to derogate.

Obviously the Act is a powerful tool for unions and demonstrates that protective employment legislation does not necessarily affect union power negatively. It is perfectly feasible to construct statutes that strengthen unions vis-à-vis both employers and employees. The 1982 Employment Protection Act is just one of many statutes which have that effect.

The collectivist tradition, strongly supported by legislation, also permeates co-determination and procedural labour legislation, the basic law on co-determination being the 1976 Joint Regulation Act, MBL. The Act invites the employee side to participate at its discretion in the dynamic process of managing the company and handling day-to-day work operations. Again, unions exclusively represent the employee side. However, with just a few exceptions, only unions that have concluded a collective agreement on employment conditions with the employer are entitled to participate in management. No Works Councils or similar bodies exist. If, exceptionally, there is no collective agreement at the workplace the consequence is that the employee side has no right to information and co-determination as provided in the Act. Obviously the 1976 Act works in favour of unions. What is more it favours majority unions since they are generally the only ones that are strong enough to obtain a collective agreement.

With regard to administering labour market policies the position of unions is also strong, though not as strong as in the field of employment proper. State agencies carry the main responsibility for administering labour market policies but close cooperation with unions is a prerequisite for success in many instances. In one way or another unions are represented on the board of state labour market policy agencies.

One very important scheme is primarily administered by the unions, i.e. the unemployment benefit insurance scheme. Historically, unemployment benefits were exclusively for union members and financed by member contributions. This was replaced by a public insurance system. Today the system is 95 per cent funded by state grants, financed primarily by employer contributions. Employee contributions are marginal, if not symbolic, averaging

100 Swedish kronor per month (approximately 12 euro). Leaving technicalities aside, unions are in fact the exclusive administrators of the state scheme.

Union membership is not required (and never has been) for employees to receive benefits under this scheme. The fact that unions administer it has nevertheless given them tremendous influence. It takes courage on the part of an employee to stay outside the union but ask for assistance when in need. Despite this, non-membership is not uncommon, especially in white-collar employment where 15 to 20 per cent of members in the unemployment benefit associations do not belong to a union.

A 1997 statute changed the unemployment insurance system to some extent, slightly reducing union influence. Some of the responsibility for administration was transferred to a less union- dominated agent. Unions make no secret of the fact that power is at the heart of union administration of the state scheme. For example, in a 1998 interview a key LO official (Hans Larsson) bluntly stated: "Unions administer the unemployment scheme for egoistic and rational reasons. Union density rates are lower in countries where the unions are not in charge of unemployment schemes".[13] The connection between unions and the unemployment benefit system is often quoted as the best recruitment argument that unions have. If this is really the case it means that employees are either ignorant or timid since union membership is not a requirement for unemployment benefits. The employer community is highly critical of the system and advocates a complete transfer to the state social security administration. The non-socialist parties share that opinion but their terms of office in the late 1970s and early 1990s were not long enough to undertake the transfer. Such a move would have caused uproar among unions so perhaps the political cost was considered too high.

9. Collective action and social alliances

Unions maintain close contacts with a variety of organizations. This is especially true of LO, because the federation either started or initiated many of the organizations that surround it, including the Swedish Social Democratic Workers' Party, SAP. Other examples are the consumer cooperative movement, Folksam, the home and housing cooperatives, HSB, and the travel agent and hotel operator, Reso.

Nothing comes even close to the relationship between LO and SAP. These are the two (main) components of what is commonly referred as the "workers' movement". This "movement" is a socio-political concept, a non-

---

[13] Swedish monthly Sunt Förnuft 1998, p. 5.

organizational phenomenon. However, it has a very strong emotional and attitudinal substance indeed. It constitutes a frame of mind and a way of thinking that permeates Swedish society and that continues to play an enormous role in the social fabric. The ideological platform of these two organizations is basically the same. They have divided the work between themselves, SAP dealing with the "political" field and LO being responsible for the "professional" field. Since there is no clear demarcation between these fields the two organizations often find themselves on the same turf. But SAP implements policies through political channels (legislation and local rule making) while LO is at the bargaining table with employers. Strong economic ties have traditionally linked the two branches in the sense that contributions from LO members to SAP were the main source of income for the party. These ties still exist but they are much weaker than they used to be.

Membership in a union affiliated to LO used to mean automatic membership in SAP. Until 1987 it was common practice for LO-affiliated local unions to collectively enrol their members in the party. This is no longer done but financial contributions from unions to political parties have not stopped, in particular LO-union contributions to "its" party. This issue becomes more sensitive every year as many individual LO-union members vote for other political parties. This means that LO cannot promise to "deliver the union vote" to any party, not even "its own party".

Close personal bonds also hold the two organizations together. For example, the president of LO is usually a member of the select group that makes up the powerful steering committee of SAP. SAP routinely recruits people from the professional branch at all levels of the party hierarchy, including the top level. Since the central government in Sweden has been headed by SAP for most of the time since the mid-1930s, many top representatives of LO have become cabinet ministers or have taken up other senior political positions. Recruitment in the opposite direction is less common, perhaps because there is no real need for it.

LO is represented on the boards of numerous organizations, bodies and institutions: a September 1998 list contains no less than 453 agencies. Some of these are LO bodies proper but the vast majority are not. They range from organizations close to the heart of the "workers' movement", such as the insurance company Folksam, to bodies of little immediate concern to the core business of LO, for example the Criminal Detention Board, the Traffic Injuries Commission or the Central Bureau for Statistics. LO, of course, is also represented at the tripartite Labour Court.

TCO has no political affiliation or ties, although its leadership has leaned towards social democracy in the past decades. Significantly a former president of TCO is now (1999) a prominent member of the social-democrat government. The first female president of TCO has just been appointed to head a government industrial relations research organization close to the social-democrat establishment. SACO maintains strict political neutrality.

Has the new situation in economic life produced new alliances? Yes and no. Since many alliances have existed for long periods of time there has not been a great need for new ones. As new needs arise the organizations change their agenda to cover these as well. Nevertheless some noteworthy additions have been made.

In recent years unions have become increasingly involved in environmental ('green') issues. The thrust of their involvement here is social justice in international trade. Union campaigns focus on solidarity with growers in developing countries who are competing with big multinational companies. A variety of "fair trade" and "fair grown" symbols and products have hit the market. Another area where union cooperation with other organizations has increased considerably is in consumer goods other than food, notably clothing. Unions are at the forefront of campaigns to force multinationals to increase transparency in their operations in developing countries and also to impose strict conditions on subcontractors in these countries to respect human rights, including union rights, and to refrain from exploiting workers.

10. Parting words

The picture presented here of Swedish unionism might strike the reader as overly positive. Are unions really so strong? Do they really face the challenges of a new work environment and an internationalized economy with so much aplomb?

The picture is indeed a positive one in the sense that it depicts a strong and bold movement, afraid of no one and willing to meet the challenges that arise. The movement is capable of innovation and it is open to new developments; it does not only look back on past achievements but also – and primarily – faces the challenges of today and tomorrow.

Critics of Swedish unionism tend to say that it has become too strong. It has woven itself into every corner of the social fabric. It has monopolized labour output and labour conditions. It has in fact put Swedish society into a union straitjacket.

Unions say that human rights, the welfare state, equality and everything else that unions stand for has to be defended, indeed created, every day over and over again. Nothing can be taken for granted so a continuous struggle is necessary.

It is a fact that unions have largely monopolized labour conditions. It is a fact that union strength is awesome in the labour market. Those who stand up against it do so at their own risk and pay a high price, often a ruinous price. It is a fact that SAF often prefers to have the political process rule on labour and employment matters rather than have such questions decided at the negotiating table with unions. Political decision makers, so the reasoning goes, take issues into consideration in their entirety. They cannot concentrate solely on what is immediately beneficial for union members, so the outcome of the political process should be more balanced between workers and employers.

Sweden was at the top of the OECD wealth league about 20 years ago but now it has slipped to a position near the bottom of European OECD-member countries. Critics blame much of that on the suffocating influence of unions. Unions tend to look the other way but, if pressed, would answer that the welfare state and equality have high costs in financial terms but that the overall quality of life must also be taken into account.

It is a fact that unilateral flexibility on the part of employers has diminished considerably in the past 20 years. Critics here see one reason for comparatively poor economic performance. Unions do not deny that unilateral employer discretion has diminished. However, they point at the fact that employers can obtain virtually any kind of flexible solution when cooperating with unions. Critics retort that unions control most of the flexibility arrangements and that this has been achieved by cunning, indeed spurious, lawmaking more or less dominated by unions. Unions strongly reject the very idea that they control the lawmaking process, pointing out – quite rightly - that SAF turns to lawmakers rather than to collective bargaining in many instances.

Critics say that unionism is smug, even arrogant. Unions behave as if they owned not just industry but the country at large. Unions respond that they are built on membership support and approval. They point at the dedication of their voluntary officers and they insist that their prime goal is to serve.

Critics say that the union movement is self-congratulatory. Unions respond that they are proud. Some might add "gratefully so". Some might even say that they feel humbly proud.

And so the debate goes on. It is not for the present writer to pass judgement. It is certainly true that unionism in Sweden is strong. It is also true that employers, existing and prospective (entrepreneurs), are severely restricted in acting unilaterally. But does that justify the position taken by critics?

Suffice it to say that the union movement verifies an old saying: Nothing succeeds like success!

Bibliography

Works in English

No major texts in English are exclusively concerned with trade unionism in Sweden. The books listed are of a general nature but some devote important sections to trade unionism, in particular the book by Bruun et al.

Adlercreutz, A.1999. "Sweden", in *International encyclopaedia of law and social security* (Kluwer, Netherlands).

Bruun, N. et al. 1992. *The Nordic labour relations model: Labour law and trade unions in the Nordic countries – Today and tomorrow* (Dartmouth, UK).

Fahlbeck, R. 1996. "Reflections on industrial relations", in *International Journal of Comparative Labour Law and Industrial Relations*, Vol. 12, p. 289.

—. 1998a. "Flexiblisation of working life: Potentials and challenges for labour law: An international analysis", in *Acta Societatis Juridicae Lundensis*, ISBN, 91-544-2391-0.

—. 1998b. "Flexibility: Challenges and potentials for labour law", in *Comparative Labour Law and Policy* (formerly *Comparative Labour Law Journal*), Vol. 19, No. 4, Summer.

—. 1998c. "Towards a revolutionised working life: The information society and the transformation of the workplace", in *International Journal of Comparative Labour Law and Industrial Relations*, Vol. 14, No. 3.

—. 1998d. "Labour and employment law in Sweden", in *Acta Societatis Juridicae Lundensis*, ISBN 91–544-2301-5.

—; Sigeman, T. "Sweden", in *European employment and industrial relations glossary* (Office for Official Publications of the European Communities, forthcoming).

Jonsson, B. 1998. in *World Wide Workers*, a book to celebrate the centenary of LO (Stockholm, ISBN, 91-574-5395-0).

Kjellberg, A. 1998. "Sweden: Restoring the model?", in Ferner, A.; Hyman, R. (eds.): *Changing industrial relations in Europe* (Blackwell, UK).

Neal, A.; Victorin, A.(eds.) 1981-1983. *Law and the weaker party: An Anglo-Swedish comparative study*, Vols. I-III (Professional Books, UK).

Nordic Council. 1994. *The future of the Nordic model of labour relations: Three reports on internationalization and industrial relations* (Nord 1993, p. 36, Nordic Council, 1994, ISBN 92-9120-368-8).

Schmidt, F. 1977. *Law and industrial relations in Sweden* (New Jersey, Rothman).

World Wide Workers. A book to celebrate the centenary of LO. 1998. (Stockholm, ISBN 91-574-5395-0).

Works in Swedish

Books

Standard text books on labour and industrial relations in Sweden are not listed here. The books listed deal specifically with trade unionism.

Elvander, N. 1980. *Skandinavisk arbetarrörelse* (Liber).

—. 1988. *Den svenska modellen* (Allmänna förlaget).

Hadenius, A. 1976. *Facklig organizationsutveckling: En studie av Landsorganizationen i Sverige* (Rabén & Sjögren).

Kjellberg, A. 1977. *Fackliga organizationer och medlemmar i dagens Sverige* (Arkiv, 1997, ISBN 91-7924-105-09).

Lewin, L. 1977. *Hur styrs facket? Om demokratin inom fackföreningsrörelsen* (Rabén and Sjögren, Stockholm.

Nilsson, T. 1985. *Från kamratföreningar till facklig rörelse. De svenska tjänstemännens organisationsutveckling 1900-1980* (Arkiv, ISBN 91-85118-974).

Sandberg, P. 1969. *Tjänstemannarörelsen. Uppkomst och utveckling* (Stockholm, Tidens förlag).

Westerståhl, J. 1945. *Svensk fackföreningsrörelse* (Stockholm, Tidens förlag).

Reinventing the US labour movement, Inventing postindustrial prosperity: A progress report

Stephen Herzenberg

Introduction

Only 9.5 per cent of private sector workers in the United States now belong to labour unions. In the labour force as a whole, 14 per cent of workers are members of unions (Hirsch and MacPherson, 1999, pp. 11-12). This paper considers the response of the US labour movement to conditions that have brought union density down to the level recorded before the New Deal. The underlying issue is whether the labour movement could rebound in a way that would substantially raise union density and restore the movement's influence in US politics and society. The paper is premised on the idea that such a rebound is necessary to reverse the growth of economic inequality and to generate a higher quality of life for the majority of Americans.[1]

In addition to the sources and documents cited, the paper draws on interviews with six top-level staff members at the labour federation to which most US unions belong (the American Federation of Labour-Congress of Industrial Organizations or AFL-CIO); it also draws on interviews with top elected officers or staff members at three of the largest and healthiest US unions (the American Federation of State, County, and Municipal Employees, the Communication Workers of America, and the Service Employees International Union). The paper is also informed by the author's observations as director of a state-level public policy think tank connected to both the world of labour and the world of research. This think tank has been an instructive point from which to view the way in which the programme of the "New Voice" administration of the AFL-CIO has been implemented since John Sweeney became its President in 1995.[2]

---

[1] For an extended analysis of the basis for these premises, see Herzenberg, Alic and Wial, 1999a. For shorter treatments, see Herzenberg, Alic and Wial, 1998 and Herzenberg, Alic and Wial, 1999b.

[2] The think tank, the Keystone Research Center, was created in 1996 in Pennsylvania at the initiative of state-level union officials concerned that progressives were losing the battle of ideas. The Center receives support from the Pennsylvania AFL-CIO as well as from a half-dozen affiliated labour unions.

The body of the paper divides into four sections. The first reviews the decline of the US labour movement and the second examines changes implemented at the national AFL-CIO under John Sweeney. The third section analyses restructuring at the three leading US unions and looks at some common themes in the restructuring efforts of these unions. The final section identifies a series of overarching challenges and sketches how the labour movement might reposition itself to regain a more central place in American society.

1. The US labour movement in crisis

The basic dilemma faced by trade unions is the need to simultaneously serve the interests of their members and be seen to serve the interests of society as a whole. From the 1940s to the 1970s, the movement solved this dilemma by playing several key roles within the US manufacturing-based economy. The wage increases negotiated in collective bargaining ensured that purchasing power kept pace with the economy's capacity to produce, avoiding the kind of under-consumption problems thought to have caused the Great Depression. Union work rules and grievance procedures gave protection against arbitrary treatment from autocratic factory supervisors. In the political sphere, unions were at the centre of a political coalition that counterbalanced corporate power; they fought for legislation that benefited working people generally, including a higher minimum wage and social insurance.

In 1945 and again in 1955, unions represented 35 per cent of US workers. From this peak, union density declined gradually at first as the result of a shift in employment to less unionized industries. After 1973, density began to fall in virtually every industry, including large-scale manufacturing. Employers contributed to this trend by investing heavily in avoiding unions. While many other countries consider that the decision to join a union is for workers to make without interference from employers, US employers have extensive rights to persuade workers not to join unions. Charges against employers for illegally violating workers' rights to organize have increased over time. Unfair labour practice charges against employers increased by 750 per cent from 1957 to 1980, while the number of union certification elections rose by less than 50 per cent (Weiler, 1983). Morris (1998) estimated that by the late 1990s one out of every 18 workers involved in an organizing campaign suffered discrimination for union activity.

In 1977 and 1978, a Congressional proposal to stiffen penalties for employer violations of worker freedom to organize died in the US Senate. After the election of President Ronald Reagan in 1980, a deep recession and an overvalued dollar brought a flood of manufactured imports and further loss of union jobs. A wave of concession bargaining ensued in which unions gave up annual wage increases that had tied manufacturing workers' wages to the national rate of productivity growth since the late 1940s. In 1981, the Reagan Administration dismissed and replaced members of the striking union of air traffic controllers; this was seen as a sign that private employers would be given further leeway to challenge unions or become "union-free".

Thus by the 1980s, the post-war solution to the unions' basic dilemma had lost its power. Union density had fallen below a quarter of the workforce. In an economy with rising imports and lagging productivity growth, union wage increases and work rules were seen as contributing to inflation and making US products less competitive. As the economy shifted away from manufacturing, some people saw protection against arbitrary treatment on the job as less essential. And the post-war social democratic coalition had splintered, in part because of tensions between union members and the anti-war campaign and the civil rights movement. In its political activity as well as in bargaining situations, the labour movement was increasingly seen as just another special interest.

In response to these circumstances, some leading unions launched internal strategic planning exercises in the early 1980s. In 1984 the AFL-CIO as a whole formed a "Committee on the Evolution of Work" chaired by its Secretary Treasurer Thomas Donahue (AFL-CIO, 1985). In the labour federation, however, the report issued by the Committee did not generate major new initiatives. Energies refocused on representing current members, not on organizing new ones. While the number of workers voting in union representation elections exceeded 500,000 in every year but one from 1965 to 1979, the number fell to 200,000 in 1988 and 140,000 in 1995 (NLRB, 1998). The number of workers who voted in representation elections won by unions fell from 300,000 in the 1960s to 200,000 for most of the 1970s to 100,000 from 1985-95. Only those unions which win representation elections can negotiate or sign contracts with the employers. In many cases, moreover, workers in workplaces that voted for union representation often did not get a first contract.

After his 1992 election, President Clinton established a Commission on the Future of Labour- Management Relations, chaired by John Dunlop, a pro-labour Republican and former Ford Administration Secretary of Labour. The prospects that this Commission might broker meaningful changes in US labour law, however, quickly faded. Employers were in no mood to cut a deal. Nor were unions interested in trading away prohibitions on employer-sponsored consultative committees (so-called "company unions") in exchange for potentially ineffective increases in penalties for employer violations of workers' rights to organize unions. The Republican takeover of the US

Congress in 1994 dashed any lingering hopes that the Dunlop Commission would lead to changes in the law.

2. An accidentally radical change at the national AFL-CIO

President Clinton's successful campaign in support of the North American Free Trade Agreement (NAFTA) over the objections of the labour movement, and the Republican takeover of the US Congress in the 1994 national elections intensified the sense within the labour movement that it was time for a change. Leaders within affiliates that had continued to grow concluded that their long-term success depended on the movement as a whole regaining power. Islands of relative strength, such as the public sector and hospitals, would ultimately be swamped if the labour presence elsewhere in the economy continued its disappearing act.

A critical mass of leading affiliates seeking a change decided to run Sweeney against Kirkland in the October 1995 AFL-CIO presidential election. Sweeney, a New York labour leader with an Irish heritage, was then president of the Service Employees International Union (SEIU). SEIU is one of the few unions that has grown in membership since 1980.

Once it became clear to Kirkland that he would lose his bid for re-election, he agreed to step down in favour of Donahue. By now, however, it was too late for Donahue to be a consensus candidate. An energetic campaign then took place between Donahue and Sweeney–both originally from the same SEIU building services' local in New York.[3]

Sweeney's victory led to what one top staff person called an "accidentally radical" transition at the national AFL-CIO. The victory of an outside challenger led to new heads of virtually every major department within the reorganized AFL-CIO headquarters. According to an AFL-CIO staff member, a majority of current members of the AFL-CIO Executive Council have also come in since Sweeney took the reins. This is a consequence of an increase in the number of council seats approved after Sweeney took office and also of turnover among representatives from the Kirkland era.

2.1 Managing change

The AFL-CIO spans all industries. It was formed in 1955 by the merger of the craft-dominated AFL and the industrial union CIO. It is the only labour federation of any significance in the United States. Individual national unions (or "international" unions, to use the term common in the United States)

---

[3] For Sweeney's own perspective on the events leading up to becoming AFL-CIO president, see Sweeney with Kusnet, 1996, pp. 88-96.

affiliate with the AFL-CIO at their own discretion. The AFL-CIO is thus structurally a weak federation that derives its power from that of the affiliated unions.

To his tenure at the head of the AFL-CIO, Sweeney brought two critical interrelated traditions from his management of the Service Employees International Union.[4] The first was a tradition of hiring committed progressive staff members and allowing them to formulate innovative organizational strategies. While hiring staff remains a political balancing act at the national AFL-CIO, Sweeney's top two assistants and several other high-level staff members came over from SEIU. Several others were hired from the Amalgamated Clothing and Textile Workers' Union (since merged with the International Ladies Garment Workers Union), which had developed a reputation for effective organizing against difficult odds in southern textiles plants. In attracting staff to Washington, the Federation benefited initially from a perception that Sweeney's administration was the place to be – the nerve centre for an overdue attempt to revitalize the labour movement.

The second tradition brought over from SEIU is the use of strategic planning and other organizational development tools (such as membership surveys and focus groups) to develop organizational consensus around change. One of Sweeney's assistants asked: "How can any organization that is democratic build a consensus around change? How can it not find itself behind the pace of change, when the pace of change is so rapid at certain points in time?" Strategic planning has now become a basic tool of organizational management within the AFL-CIO as well as leading affiliates. Planning not only generates new ideas, but is also a vehicle for generating support for the strategies that emerge, the outlines of which may be clear at the outset.

> We have tried to...help organizations do strategic planning in a formal way to develop a clear mission statement, goals, and clearly defined objectives. The value of that is important in terms of the public strategy and direction we develop. The more important value is the political consensus that you build using that process by engaging all the stakeholders in the organization...

The approach to managing change at AFL-CIO today is grounded in the experience of Sweeney's top management team when it came together to lead the SEIU. In the early 1980s, a network of activists in top staff positions in Washington-based unions, including Sweeney's top assistants, was struggling with the problem of unions and looked "high and low for people in academia

---

[4] For an analysis of SEIU and its ability to respond more effectively than other unions to the pressures of the 1980s and 1990s, see Piore, 1994.

who thought about this". But most academics and consultants were unfamiliar with unions and unions were also reluctant to open up to outsiders.

With the help of a "pragmatic, low-key" labour educator, Wayne State's Hal Stack, who "got along with our leadership well", SEIU established a "Committee on the Future". Over several years, the committee polled SEIU members and conducted worksite visits. Out of this process, the SEIU reorganized into five industry divisions: building services (primarily janitorial workers), health care, public sector, manufacturing, and office work. Within these divisions, workers had common experiences that could serve as a basis for debate and decision making about union strategy. Within industry divisions natural leaders emerged more readily. These leaders were able to gather people around them and project a "vision" for the union; they were not representing a clique bound together by personal ties and loyalty.

Within the AFL-CIO, Sweeney has less power than he did as SEIU president to combine with persuasion and strategic planning in developing consensus. For example, Sweeney has little influence over the careers of affiliate officers, only a small amount of patronage in the form of AFL-CIO staff positions, and he cannot put affiliates in receivership. "You can get cooperation from affiliates through leadership or by moral suasion or by the brilliance of your arguments, but there's not a lot more you can do." In addition, since the federation spans all organized industries and occupations, no common experience is as readily available as that which sustains a common purpose within the industry divisions of SEIU. According to one source, the federation has been a place where unions protect their turf, not a place to define a common vision. To convey the difficulty of generating labour movement consensus, another staff member compared AFL-CIO to the United Nations. "A lot of what John Sweeney did in his first two years was sell the notion of a common destiny and the need to have a unity of focus and unity of purpose." This involves a battle against "a general belief that there wasn't really anything could be done. The normal formulation was that anything that could be done wasn't worth doing. Anything we can accomplish, won't change anything".

To jump start the political and the planning processes, AFL-CIO created a "Committee 2000," chaired by Sweeney, and consisting of 20 of the most powerful Executive Council members. With the support of Committee 2000, Sweeney and his staff have also reorganized and sought to make more effective use of other committees of the Executive Council.[5] In SEIU,

---

[5] The 1997 Convention expanded the authority of the AFL-CIO president, subject to Executive Council approval, to create new committees whose members are appointed by the president. See AFL-CIO, 1997, p. 95.

Sweeney's management team had often relied on committees as a more effective forum than the large and diverse Executive Board. Unlike SEIU's Executive Board, however, the full Executive Council is less inclined to trust the decisions of its committees. On major issues such as politics, organizing or AFL-CIO structure, getting consensus support at the Executive Council requires a painstaking process of vetting ideas with each member of the Council and with the staff of individual affiliates who deal with each subject.

One tool used by Committee 2000 to generate support for change has been a series of "union density exercises". AFL-CIO staff divided the US economy into "sectors" overlapping the jurisdictions of major unions (e.g. health care, hospitality, construction, durable manufacturing, education, etc.). By sector, AFL-CIO staff calculated total employment, union density, and the number of union and non-union workers at various points in time. They also documented the number of workers organized each year. Projections into the future showed that employment expansion would continue to be concentrated in sectors and geographical areas where union density is low. The union density exercises made an irrefutable case that business as usual would mean continued union density decline, in most sectors to below levels that enable unions to influence industry-wide standards, in some cases close to zero. The analysis also showed that huge numbers of non-union workers exist in every major sector of the US economy. There is no truth to the claim that manufacturing unions must organize public and service sector workers because there's no one left in their core jurisdiction to organize. Forced to confront reality at a gathering of their peers, many union leaders felt embarrassed. Generating such discomfort was one tactic for getting beyond business as usual.

2.2 Building power

A central message of the Sweeney administration is that, while the AFL-CIO headquarters in Washington had focused on "wielding power," the challenge now is to "build power". A major concern is to do this quickly, leveraging labour's current resources and economic and political power before they dwindle further.

As part of the effort to build power, the AFL-CIO has reorganized its internal departments and sought to coordinate different departments more effectively. All AFL-CIO field staff around the country are now part of the Field Mobilization Department (formerly Field Services). In the past, separate field operations dealt with Field Services and with election activity, the latter within the AFL-CIO's Committee on Political Education (COPE).

The AFL-CIO created a Corporate Affairs Department within national headquarters. The work of the Department is premised on the idea that bargaining alone is not enough, given current levels of union density and the imbalance of power between labour and management. Unions have to try to change corporate behaviour by exercising influence wherever they can – via sourcing arrangements that link union and non-union companies, in financial markets, through the use of union pension monies, in the regulatory sphere, in politics. Through such interventions, the Department seeks to make it harder for corporations to pursue low-wage (or "low road") strategies and make it easier for them to pursue higher- wage (or "high road") strategies that develop and utilize workers' capacities.

The activities of the Corporate Affairs Department include strategic analysis of corporations and industries. The analysis may be used in devising organizing plans or to find leverage points with particular corporations in the context of bargaining or organizing. The Corporate Affairs Department also oversees the activities of two independent, non-profit organizations supported by outside foundations and government funds in addition to dues dollars.

One of these organizations, the Working for America Institute (WFAI), coordinates labour's participation in efforts to strengthen the US skill development infrastructure and to promote work reorganization and industrial modernization consistent with a high road economic development path. The predecessor of WFAI, a Human Resources Development Institute founded in the late 1960s, operated fairly independently of the core activities of the Federation. Reinventing HRDI as the WFAI illustrates the attempt to address skill building and work organization as part of an overall AFL-CIO strategy to change the way American firms do business. At present, WFAI provides technical support to a growing number of efforts across the United States to build multi-employer labour/management training partnerships.[6] The WFAI also fosters the creation of a "high road network" that brings together labour leaders and researchers engaged at the grassroots with efforts to transform the development path of regional industries. Support for training partnerships is premised on the idea that individual firms, acting alone, under-invest in general skills because they cannot capture all the benefits of their investment. In addition, increased career mobility across firms creates a need for more inter-firm labour market coordination and transparency. Labour/management training partnerships can help solve coordination and under-investment problems. By providing employers with critical skills and relieving them of some responsibility for employment security, partnerships could also lessen employer antagonism to unions. The high road network

---

[6] For examples of such partnerships, see Herzenberg, Alic and Wial 1998a, Chapter 7; and Parker and Rogers, 1996.

could help meet the long-term need for a critical mass of leaders who see the "high road" as a real institutional alternative, not just a catch phrase.

The second non-profit organization linked with the Corporate Affairs Department is the Centre for Working Capital (CWC), which intervenes in financial markets to change corporate behaviour. The pension funds, employee stock ownership plans and savings plans of unionized workers amount to over $7 trillion, about a quarter of the net worth of publicly traded US corporations. The Centre for Working Capital seeks to ensure that this money works to raise living standards, not lower them. The Centre conducts training for pension fund trustees and uses pension funds to support shareholder activism to influence corporate management. Another strategy that is under consideration, drawing on experience in Quebec, is the establishment of regional "solidarity funds" that would invest workers' financial resources directly in high road strategies.

2.3 Reviving the federation at local level: Union Cities

Another major initiative of the New Voice Administration has been to energize central labour councils (CLCs). There are approximately 600 CLCs, which are the most local body of the AFL-CIO.[7] CLCs are funded through a per-member tax from unions in their geographic jurisdiction. The decision of area unions to affiliate with the local CLC is separate from the decision of the state level and national structures to affiliate with state federations of labour and the national AFL-CIO. (Thus, for example, the major trucking union, International Brotherhood of Teamsters, is an affiliate of the national AFL-CIO but not of the Pennsylvania AFL-CIO. The Teamsters are affiliates of some Pennsylvania CLCs but not others.) On average, AFL-CIO affiliates pay-per-member fees to CLCs on about 55 per cent of their membership. CLCs are constitutionally mandated to provide support for each union in organizing and bargaining, as well as to work collectively on politics.

Dating back to the 1890s American Federation of Labour, CLCs have had only a single vote within the AFL or AFL-CIO structure, while national unions have the same number of votes as they have (paying) members. In addition, CLCs were often moribund in the decades after 1945. Power in that prosperous era lay with the industrial unions and bargaining with major manufacturing firms was centralized at national level.

By the early 1990s, however, central labour councils in such places as Atlanta, Cincinnati, Ithaca, Milwaukee, San Jose and Seattle, had begun to

---

[7] The AFL-CIO web page reports that 614 Central Labour Councils existed as of 1996. The number is slightly smaller now because of mergers of some councils.

reinvent themselves in response to labour's decline. CLCs in these cities sought to rebuild the power of the local labour movement rather than just serve affiliated local unions and endorse political candidates. Activist CLCs built alliances between community and labour groups to protect both union and non-union workers. They sought funding from foundations (e.g. to create labour market intermediary organizations that provide training, career counselling, and job matching to workers), used ties with community and religious groups to pressure employers not to violate workers' organizing rights, and conditioned support for local political candidates on concrete commitments that facilitate organizing.[8] In 1994, before Sweeney's election, a group of activist councils met in Las Vegas. The experience of these councils suggested that CLCs might be a possible breeding ground for a new generation of activists (Ness, 1998). While CLCs had often been dominated by "old boy networks", CLCs' low profile might make it easier for a new, more demographically diverse generation to rise to leadership than it would be within individual affiliates. CLCs might also provide an arena for "acting locally" that would give the labour movement a more direct connection to the daily lives and concerns of its members and the community.

Economic research also suggests that metropolitan areas and regional economies are critical venues for the overall effort to "block the low road" and " pave the high road". According to this research, much of it rooted in analyses of manufacturing, egalitarian growth depends on creating a web of local and regional institutions. In non-mobile service industries, too, metropolitan and regional institutions – area-wide unions, training institutions, portable credentials and career ladders – appear essential to promoting good jobs and high quality and service (Herzenberg, Alic and Wial, 1998, especially Chapter 7). As of the mid-1990s, however, no regional political actor had emerged to develop a blueprint for the high road in local economies and start implementing the blueprint. Labour, and other elements of the more progressive half of the US political spectrum, had remained in a defensive posture. According to Bruce Colburn, President of the Milwaukee CLC, "We knew what we were opposed to in this economy, but we didn't always know what we were for" (Eimer, 1999, p. 73). University of Wisconsin Professor Joel Rogers argued that CLCs were natural vehicles for promoting the political alliances and institutional interventions in the economy necessary to reverse the growth of inequality (Rogers, 1994).

---

[8] For an analysis of some of the activities of "transformative" CLCs and how they differ from "conventional" CLCs, see Gapasin and Wial 1997. Before becoming a labour educator, Gapasin was secretary treasurer of the South Bay Labour Council in San Jose, the heart of California's Silicon Valley.

In January 1996, the Sweeney administration created a labour council advisory committee "with the goal of persuading an ambivalent labour movement of the potential for expanding union power through the councils" (Ness, 1998, p. 82). In June 1996, the first national meeting of CLCs in Denver provided an opportunity for an open-ended discussion – with "not too many talking heads"– of "what CLCs should be doing", informed by a presentation on what some of the most dynamic CLCs were already doing.[9] In the wake of the meeting, the AFL-CIO announced the "Union Cities" programme.

To become a Union City, CLCs must engage in strategic planning. AFL-CIO field mobilization staff help facilitate these planning sessions, often with the help of area labour educators. Central labour councils must then pledge to pursue eight strategies for rebuilding the labour movement: recruit half the local unions in their community into the Changing to Organize programme and develop local organizing plans; recruit at least one per cent of union members for "street heat" mobilization in support of organizing and first contract campaigns; organize grassroots lobbying and political action committees; organize the community in support of high road economic development; sponsor "common sense economics" programmes to educate a majority of area unions about why working families have experienced economic decline; generate support from local authorities and political candidates for the "right to organize"; work to make CLCs mirror the diversity of area union members; and reach an annual membership growth rate of 3 per cent by the year 2000.

As of early 1999, 150 central labour councils in areas with 8 million union members had become Union Cities. Efforts to create a "network" of effective CLCs and CLC activists included a newsletter on Union Cities and four regional CLC meetings in May and June 1999.

Union Cities generated frustration among some local activists. They saw the new national leadership as outlining grand plans for labour movement revival without providing resources or technical assistance for implementation (Ness, 1998 and author's observations in Pennsylvania). Efforts to expand the reach of central labour councils sometimes overstretched local leaders and unions who already bore the burden of activity not directly linked to individual unions' self-interest. Many CLCs that have gained Union City designation have done so in name only, because of the political influence of area leaders, not because they have really begun to implement the eight strategies.

Even so, pressure and encouragement from the national level have expanded openings for local union leaders and activists who want to use

---

[9] Fernando Gapasin facilitated a discussion based on Gapasin and Wial, 1977.

CLCs to transcend divisions between unions, raise the level of mobilization, and begin building CLCs into new centres of economic and political power within regional economies. The demand from CLCs for resources and support itself reflects their expanding ambitions. According to the Director of the AFL-CIO Field Mobilization Department:

> We're finding a need for what we're calling a second generation. The first generation was to get the overall strategy to build the labour movement in a community, and we had to go through each part of this to try to generate some ownership of the process locally. Once you get there, and the local labour movement passes the Union Cities resolution and puts a plan together, as they start moving it, a whole new set of questions comes up. We need to be able to provide support to tackle these pieces...It's not like there are any easy answers.

2.4 A new alliance between CLCs, state federations of labour and the national AFL-CIO

Following up on Union Cities, the AFL-CIO Committee 2000 has been studying how it can generate more support for CLCs, including from state federations of labour. State federations have been more active than CLCs since the Second World War, partly because US states have major responsibilities for funding and regulation in important policy areas (e.g. taxation, education, childcare, welfare, unemployment insurance, employment and training, economic development subsidies, regional "land-use" planning, transportation, and infrastructure spending). Nonetheless, outside the building and construction trades, regional and state policy and institutions were considered as of secondary importance from the 1940s to the 1990s. Most state federations continued to focus on "wielding" power, while declining union density reduced their influence. In addition, coordination between the three levels of AFL-CIO has been limited. As well as individual unions affiliating separately with the local, state, and national federation, no formal line of authority exists from the national to state federations or from the state federation to CLCs.

At its October 1999 convention, the national AFL-CIO ratified a resolution outlining a "New Alliance" between CLCs, state federations, and the national AFL-CIO. A central component of the New Alliance will be a process of strategic planning and the development of two-year budget cycles aligned with the two-year legislative cycle in US states. Additional training and education will be made available to state and CLC staff. National unions will be asked to guarantee per capita funding to "qualifying" state and local bodies whose strategic plans have been approved by the national AFL-CIO (Lazarovici, 1999).

2.5 Changing to organize

Historically, individual unions have jealously guarded their control over organizing, ceding no significant role in this area to the national AFL-CIO. The New Voice Administration came to power on a platform that stressed the need to "Change to Organize". It immediately established a new AFL-CIO Organizing Department by bringing in house the quasi-independent Organizing Institute (OI) established in 1989. The new administration also committed itself to devoting 30 per cent of its resources to organizing by the year 2000 and urged its affiliates to do the same (AFL-CIO, 1997, p. 2).

The federation's role in organizing is still evolving. The least controversial aspects of its role are its efforts at recruiting and training organizers. While the Organizing Institute emphasized recruiting and training college students, the Organizing Department trains more rank-and-file members of affiliates. A particular emphasis now is training lead organizers. The federation subsidizes individual campaigns using an organizing fund. Through the services of its Corporate Affairs Department, the AFL-CIO conducts strategic analysis of industries to identify potential organizing targets and individual employers from which affiliates are seeking recognition.

The AFL-CIO has also initiated a campaign to persuade the public to see workers' freedom to choose a union as a basic democratic and civil right. The campaign initially phrased the challenge as the "right to organize". Focus groups indicated that "freedom to choose a voice at work" would have a wider public appeal.

In 1998, more workers voted in union certification elections and unions organized more new members than at any point since the 1970s. Nonetheless, new organizing has not yet been rapid enough to overcome the loss of union members as a consequence of the rapid pace of economic restructuring.

2.6 Industry committees

A large number of US unions divide the low level of union density that exists in many industries (although in many cases one union has substantially more members than others). In health care, for example, the Service Employees International Union (SEIU) is the dominant union but large numbers of other unions have some members. The "conglomerate" tendency of US unions has increased because unions with declining memberships in their primary industry have often organized new members wherever and whenever they could (Piore, 1994, pp. 520-522).

Sweeney's successor as SEIU President, Andrew Stern, has argued that unions need to merge and form new alliances to keep up with dynamic shifts in corporate organization and industry boundaries (Stern, 1998). A complicating factor is that high levels of density within local and regional markets are important in many non-mobile service industries. The same union need not necessarily represent workers in different regional markets, although there may be economies of scale if it does.

In one major industry, health care, AFL-CIO has formed a committee of its Executive Council. The federation provides neutral ground to address sectoral issues of mutual interest, such as public policy, the strategies and vulnerabilities of industry players that may negotiate with unions in different markets, or joint organizing. Just as industry divisions proved effective within SEIU, industry committees could become a vehicle for cooperation across unions, possibly laying the foundations for mergers or membership exchanges that will bring the organization of the labour movement into better conformity with the economy. Even so, the political challenges of such restructuring should not be underestimated. At the October 1999 AFL-CIO convention, after the presentation of union density trends by sector, delegates ratified a resolution which stated that no union has exclusive jurisdiction over any sector.

3. Restructuring at individual US unions

This section outlines some common themes in the responses made by leading AFL-CIO affiliates to the pressure of the 1990s. It relies heavily on the experience of three leading unions: the Communications Workers of America (CWA), the SEIU, and the American Federation of State, County, and Municipal Employees (AFSCME). Top elected leaders or staff members of these unions were interviewed in April or May 1999. The unions are all based in service industries and are considered atypically effective. Their experience tells us something about approaches that are likely to become more widespread in the future if the US labour movement is to rebound.

The CWA represents over 600,000 workers, mostly in the telecommunications industry. The SEIU represents over 1.3 million workers, primarily in the health care, janitorial and public sectors. AFSCME represents about 2 million public sector workers.

3.1 Permeability to pragmatic, progressive activists

While the division between the unions and the ideological left that emerged after the Second World War is well known, this division does not appear important at national level within the CWA, AFSCME or SEIU. Whether as union leaders or staff members, left activists have been central partners in strategy development in these three unions. The non-bureaucratic "mission" and critical world view of these individuals may have helped bring basic questions – "what is to be done?"– quickly to the surface in the 1980s and 1990s. In the wake of the labour movement's sense of crisis and the loss of Soviet control of Eastern Europe, there are indications within some more conservative unions, including the building trades, of a new permeability to progressive activists.

3.2 A sense of crisis

At national level, all three of these unions share a sense that "business as usual" is not enough and that the labour movement may be in danger of extinction. For SEIU, this sense goes back to the early years of the Reagan era; it intensified during the 1980s when the janitorial industry was substantially deunionized in strong union cities such as Los Angeles and Pittsburgh. For CWA, the break-up of the telephone monopoly, AT&T, in 1984, ushered in a new era that threatened its survival. For AFSCME, which continued to grow rapidly in the 1980s, the 1994 election created a sense of urgency. After that election, in which the Republican Party won a Congressional majority, AFSCME:

> ...made a major decision to reevaluate its organizational strategy. We were provoked to do that by the [Republican speaker of the US House of Representatives Newt] Gingrich victory in 1994...We are in this precarious moment in the history of the United States when it can go either way. Easily it can go downhill. What happened in 1994 could be the beginning of a 40-year rule by a Gingrich and his acolytes. Thank God we are awake and recognizing this.

The leadership role that AFSCME president Gerald McEntee played in the transition from Kirkland to Sweeney was one direct consequence of AFSCME's view that the labour movement is in danger of extinction.

For CWA and SEIU, despite a range of activities launched to turn the tide, recent union density trends reinforce the sense of crisis. For example, while CWA has done what Batt, Katz and Keefe (1999) call "a masterful job broadening its vision and strategies", it has still suffered membership decline. At AT&T alone, membership fell from 117,000 to about 40,000 in 1996, according to the CWA research department. In its traditional core industry, telephone services, the union has maintained significant representation among residential service providers but has been unable to organize anti-union employers in the cable, cellular, internet service provider, and long distance sectors. Union density among technical workers in the telecommunications industry has fallen from 68 per cent in 1983 to 52 per cent in 1996; among clerical and sales workers, it has fallen from 63 per cent to 35 per cent (Batt, Katz and Keefe, 1999). For SEIU, union density in the janitorial and health care industries remains at 10-12 per cent nationally. Only in a few geographical markets does the union possess sufficient density to set area-wide wage and benefit standards.

3.3 Strategic planning and plan implementation

All these unions engage in formal processes of internal strategic planning. In SEIU, planning and internal reorganization began in the 1980s when "Sweeney took this very decentralized AFL-style organization and led a change process to bring more coordination and centralization". The reorganization into industry divisions in the 1980s was one result. Most recently, over a four-year period beginning in 1992, the SEIU Committee on the Future produced a series of five reports (on the state of the world, the state of the economy, leaders' views of the union, members' views of the union, and recommendations for the future) designed to outline the next set of strategic directions for the union. The recommendations highlighted the need to build "industry power" by raising the union's density in particular labour markets within SEIU's major industries. Organizing priorities over the next several years will be geared to raising industry power.

Within AFSCME, the planning launched after the 1994 elections has identified two new organizing strategies to complement the union's main strategy for the past four decades (which was to work relentlessly to pass state laws establishing workers' right to organize and bargain collectively and then to organize as many workers as possible immediately thereafter). The new strategies are to systematically organize public sector workers who have remained outside the union although they are protected by existing state bargaining laws; and to organize private sector providers that compete with public sector workers.

Within SEIU, the most recent strategic plan, completed after Andrew Stern succeeded Sweeney, has led to a major internal reorganization. According to Stern:

> We went through the whole headquarters and asked ourselves the question how would we change from...a smorgasbord union, in which locals got to choose which foods they ate, to a union structure that maximizes our ability to implement the Committee of the Future report. Rather than asking whether people were doing good work, which everybody was, we asked ourselves which functions matched the mission of the union and therefore should be maintained or expanded?

Seven SEIU departments were eliminated. The health and safety department has declined from 22 staff members to two. One hundred and forty out of 350 national union staff members now have different assignments.

Based on observations of restructuring within US unions generally, one AFL-CIO staff member observed a generational process at play. The four or five union leaders associated with the most rapid and dramatic internal restructuring tend to be younger; they were rising through the ranks in the difficult climate of the late 1970s and 1980s. Older leaders whose careers began during the years of post-war prosperity have had more difficulty coming to terms with the change in the economic and political climate. They may also have stronger ties to local leaders and staff members who perceive reorganization as threatening.

3.4 Keeping up with corporate structure – Union centralization and local autonomy

In the major industries where they represent workers, both CWA and SEIU confront dramatic changes in industry structure and business organization. For CWA, the definition of the industry which employs most of its members is in flux, with telecommunications (including wireless telephony) now converging with publishing, computing and entertainment into "information services" (CWA, no date, p. 2). Within the amorphous information services sector, firms are constantly merging and forming alliances in an effort to position themselves for the future. In health care, self-contained and independently managed hospitals are giving way to regional health care networks which link physicians' offices, hospitals, outpatient clinics and ancillary services. In janitorial services, building owners now routinely contract out to specialized cleaning services, which may be small local firms, national companies or international corporations.

As a result of corporate restructuring, unions often find that " the union structures don't match up with the employer's structures". In some cases, their traditional bargaining partner now has little authority. In one illustration, the president of the American Broadcasting Company (ABC) (one of the US television networks) recently excused himself from bargaining with CWA President Morton Bahr so that he could telephone Michael Eisner, CEO of the Disney Corporation. Since Disney now owns ABC, the ABC president no longer has the power to conclude a final agreement. According to SEIU president Stern:

> The person that is bargaining nursing home contracts in Pennsylvania is dealing with the same companies that are in California. The head of George Washington Hospital (in Washington, D.C.) now reports to a guy in King of Prussia, Pennsylvania, because he's part of a hospital chain. All of a sudden, hospitals are a thing of the past, now you deal with health care systems. You no longer deal exclusively with non-profit you deal with for-profits. So people have had to figure out how to maintain and control their density with an understanding of what is happening in the industry.

In today's economic climate, neither the centralized industrial union tradition nor the decentralized craft union tradition fits with industry and corporate structure. Both these traditions meshed with forms of business organization based on independent firms – industrial unions fit with vertically integrated giants, craft unions with small local firms. Now corporations are trying to network forms of organization that stand between the hierarchical, vertically integrated firm and independent businesses that operate at arms length (Herzenberg, Alic and Wial, 1998, particularly Chapter 6). Through networks firms hope to achieve the coordination possible through vertical integration with the entrepreneurial flexibility of independent business units. Unions need structures capable of tracking and responding to changing business networks.

3.5 Strategic coordination of union activity in different spheres

Another common theme in more successful unions is the strategic coordination of politics, bargaining and organizing. The need for such coordination and the potential benefits have grown as a result of corporate restructuring: more complex interconnections among corporations create the potential for unions to exercise leverage at a widening array of levels and venues. In the past, industrial unions tended to exercise strategic coordination only to win strikes. To rebuild power, according to Stern, they need to use their connections, financial resources and political leverage in organizing and increasing density. At CWA, strategic coordination has deep roots that go all the way back to the last large-scale organizing of the AT&T telephone monopoly, Bell, in the 1950s (Nissen and Rosen, 1999). A 1960s CWA internal educational programme labelled bargaining and representation, organizing, and community/political action the union's "triple threat". In the next two decades, CWA participation in national and state regulatory arenas helped sustain awareness of the connection between political action and union leverage in bargaining. CWA now refers to the "triple threat" as the "CWA triangle" and emphasizes that "if you break down one side, the other two will collapse".

Consistent with the philosophy of the triangle, the CWA has been perhaps the most active union practitioner of "bargaining to organize" – negotiating contractual clauses that prevent employers from fully exercising their extensive right under US labour law to campaign against unionization. The most common contractual clauses require employers to remain neutral in union certification elections, to expedite such elections, or to grant union recognition when more than 50 to 60 per cent of bargaining unit members sign union cards.

3.6 Stronger ties to the community

US labour unions and community-based organizations (e.g. religious organizations, minority groups, and organizations that help members of low-income communities to find housing and jobs, or access social services) are often suspicious of one another. Labour sees community groups as adding little to the unions' own efforts and seeking resources without offering credit. Unions are perceived as wanting to control joint efforts and expecting community groups to rally round labour in disputes with employers. More fundamentally, unions are seen as being narrowly self-interested. Some urban minority organizations are suspicious because craft unions are perceived to have kept minorities out of high-paying construction jobs in the past.

Both CWA and SEIU have invested in efforts to strengthen labour and community ties. The CWA helped found "Jobs with Justice", a national network of metropolitan chapters that bring the labour, religious, minority, and academic communities into coalition to protect workers' rights to organize. CWA and SEIU have also formed coalitions with consumer organizations in fights in the state regulatory or legislative arena. For example, in a ten-year campaign in California, a coalition with consumers was critical to the passage of state legislation that facilitates the formation of county-wide unions of home health workers who are employed by many different small provider organizations but whose services are paid for by the state. (The legislation accomplishes this by allowing counties to establish a county-wide authority that will bargain with a union of home health workers on behalf of all employers if a majority of workers vote for representation.) In Los Angeles County, the California law led to the organization of 75,000 home care workers. Unions have also supported community-based organizations in efforts to establish "living-wage" ordinances that require contractors to local government and corporate recipients of public subsidies to pay a living wage well above the minimum wage.

3.7 Strengthening of collective identities based on occupation

Both SEIU and CWA have strengthened their internal structures for promoting union-wide links among workers within particular occupations. In CWA, a high proportion of the membership falls into two major occupational groups, clerical workers (operators, customer service and, increasingly, sales workers) and "outside" crafts. A third group, computer programmers and software specialists, "inside crafts", has grown recently, although many members of this group have been classified as outside the bargaining unit. CWA has strengthened its occupational network of customer service and sales workers by organizing annual conferences which bring together 200-300 members of these groups from different companies (Batt,

Katz and Keefe, 1999). These gatherings focus on developing coordinated bargaining agendas and contract language as well as discussing workplace issues and mobilization strategies. This internal organizing has helped build a network of local leaders in customer service and sales that cuts across local unions and individual employers. Through this network, the union has sought to develop the professional identity of customer service workers, building on the historic commitment of telephone workers to public service during the regulated period. Internal networking within occupations has helped generate organizational consensus on the need to invest heavily in organizing low-wage non-union competitors that employ workers in similar job categories. Members readily see that huge wage and benefit differences between union and non-union competitors may be unsustainable.

At SEIU, networks of activists and leaders within occupational groups are fostered by meetings within the five divisions. In the health care division, industry meetings are supplemented by national and regional meetings of nurse councils. In conjunction with the "Dignity Campaign," a national nursing home organizing effort, the SEIU regularly brings non-professional health care workers, primarily nurses' aides and licensed practical nurses (LANS) together.

Multi-local meetings on an occupational and industry basis do not take place regularly at AFSCME. For example, even though the federation represents hundreds of thousands of clerical workers who face common pressures as a result of technological change, the expansion of temporary work and privatization, these workers do not regularly come together across employers and local unions. Such contact could promote more effective representation and lay the groundwork for future organizing in the private office worker labour market.

3.8 Shifting resources to organizing

The SEIU, CWA, and AFSCME have all recently shifted resources to organizing. In SEIU, the Committee on the Future outlined a three-year plan under which locals would spend 10, 15 then 20 per cent of resources on organizing, with matching funds available from the national union. SEIU nationally "now spends well over 50 per cent of our resources on growth". CWA allocates 10 per cent of its resources to organizing and a 1997 Constitutional Amendment encourages locals to do the same. This arguably underestimates the importance of organizing in CWA, given the tight link between CWA organizing and bargaining and political activity, and given the union's reliance on cost-effective member organizers. In AFSCME, 20 district councils are now in the process of forming organizing departments.

3.9 Evolving organizing models

With more investment in organizing has come more effort to distill lessons about how to organize cost- effectively. This learning process is more advanced in CWA and SEIU because they refocused on organizing before most other unions.

From countering employers to empowering workers. Over the past quarter-century, organizing by US unions has been shaped by employer opposition to the labour movement. One top official perceived both "models" of organizing – the blitz model and one-on-one organizing – as responses to employers' vigorous campaigns against unionization. They have both:

> ...been invented to try tactically to overcome what the employer does. They presume the employers will beat your brains in. You're either trying to rush quickly before they can get to the workers. Or you're building deeply so that when the employer gets to you there are enough roots that you don't get swept out...They are not models, per se, of trying to persuade workers.

During organizing campaigns, the reality of intense employer opposition tends to reinforce the adversarial orientation of many US unions. Organizing experience, however, is leading unions to question the effectiveness of campaigns that revolve too exclusively around the negative theme of what is wrong with the boss.

At SEIU, for example, the union now perceives its traditional organizing campaigns as aimed at the one-third of the workforce that is pro-union when the campaign begins.

> The first 30 per cent tend to be more aggressive, more class struggle, more angry at the boss. The next 30 per cent, using just broad terms, they're not looking for conflict, they're not looking for hostility, they're looking for a voice. But it's not angry. In health care, our theme among nurses is now 'working together works.'...For many of our class-struggle organizers, it's an enormous challenge because we're so used to being in conflict with the employer. But we don't attack the employer, we inform people about pay practices or whatever. We've polled it, focus grouped it, before and after elections. It's what the swing voters want to hear. It's not what the organizers want to say, it's not what the first people that come to you want, but it's what wins elections.

CWA leaders also see their union as having moved away from the "grievance model" of organizing that dominated its efforts in the public sector in the 1984 to 1992 period.

> You assume the workers have grievances and you appeal to them on the basis of those grievances...With that kind of approach, you tend to appeal to the people in any workplace that actually have some real difficult

grievances. But then there's the other 90 per cent that don't have any personal type of grievance, that just want income security, they want job security, they want a voice on the job...

Organizing "voiced from the inside out". While it may have originated as a tactic to help withstand employer opposition, expanding the workers' role in leading their own organizing campaign has evolved at CWA into a way of ensuring that the campaign responds to those workers' concerns. CWA refers to its organizing as "voiced from the inside out," meaning that workers in the workplace being organized have to lead the campaign. The union describes its philosophy as to "stick with people as long as it takes – it's not about winning an election for us, it's about relationships".

CWA establishes an organizing committee in the workplace and helps take the message out to the rest of the workforce. Internal organizing committees are now encouraged to develop their own mission statement. According to CWA organizing director Larry Cohen:

> The organization, the life of it, emanates from the workplace where people are working together to solve problems... The American Air lines campaign and the US Airways campaign, the inside leaders were very talented, very committed, and had lots of energy. Then our role becomes a secondary role of supporting them to achieve their goal of building a union, versus those workers supporting our goal of enlarging our organization...

CWA, in essence, provides organizational development support for emerging unions in non-union workplaces, helping them plan their own campaign.

> We have come to realize that organizing depends on the systems workers use when building their unions and we share with them what we think are the best systems. One big thing for us is one-on-one personal contact so that workers are not just relying on materials or impersonal media communications, but that they actually have these discussions with folks about what really matters to them...It's got to be built on one-on-one communication with people.

Reliance on member organizers. CWA, particularly, relies heavily on member organizers in its organizing efforts. Contract provisions allow members time off for union business and the union pays them lost wages. The union has only 12 full-time organizers nationally in its nine districts (Nissen and Rosen, 1999, p. 81). The skills of member organizers are developed in regional district organizing networks through formal training, mentoring by district organizers, experience, newsletters that share stories and lessons learned from campaigns, and annual retreats. The organizing network in one district grew from 26 to 62 organizers between 1990 and 1997. The three-day retreat in the district draws about 20-25 people per year, virtually all of them member organizers, for discussions structured around case studies. Industry segments also receive in-depth analysis. On the last day, participants develop an organizing plan for the district for the next year, with targets specified and discussion of how the network can support particular campaigns. The organizing plan is distributed to all locals. The district organizing network thus serves, according to a District 4 Organizing Plan, as a "vehicle for mutual support, exchange of ideas and recognition" (Nissen and Rosen, 1999, p. 77).

At SEIU, "member mobilizers" have played an important part in campaigns for new union contracts with employers that are already organized (Sciacchitano, 1998). At AFSCME, member organizers have been used to augment full-time staff in childcare organizing efforts in Philadelphia.

Over the longer term, the development of hundreds of member organizers may be the only way to turn the tide and start to organize new members by the thousands. CWA sees reliance on member organizers as economical. At Indiana University, for example, the CWA organized 1,800 clerical and technical workers using a staff of three part-time organizers – telephone operators – and eight days a month from a district organizer (Nissen and Rosen, 1999). The campaign cost CWA $250,000 or $138.88 per member organized. This compares with the standard US rule-of-thumb that organizing costs $1,000 for each new union member. Sciacchitano, however, cites an SEIU staff member who found training and developing workers to assume additional responsibilities more time consuming initially than having staff perform those functions (Sciacchitano, 1998). Clearly, the investment necessary to develop member organizers will vary according to the educational background and workplace responsibilities of workers.

Occupational organizing. Several of those interviewed identified "occupational organizing" as a distinct approach. One success that those inside and outside CWA characterized as based on occupational organizing was the unionization of 10,000 call centre workers at US Airways. CWA saw its success with these workers as a direct outgrowth of what the union knew about this kind of work from its representation of operators and customer service representatives in AT&T and regional phone companies. According to CWA organizing director Larry Cohen:

> The reason we won was that we have 150,000 customer service people in the union who do similar work in call centers in a variety of industries...Where people are plowing through screen after screen of very detailed information. Of 150 people on a plane, they've got 100 different fares...That job is much like the calling centre at Bell Atlantic where there's a million ways you can configure your communication set-up ...People interfacing with technology and customers...The job can vary tremendously but it's always about that...Problem-solving and finding the right information for people.

The tone of the US Airways campaign relied heavily on appealing to the professional identity of the agents. It focused on the need to improve customer service, rather than attacking the company per se (Batt, Katz and Keefe, 1999). Twenty-five full-time member organizers staffed the campaign. In the wake of the US Airways effort, the CWA is now aiming for a certification election among 15,000 mostly customer service workers at American Airlines.

For CWA, organizing around the concerns of particular occupational groups is pivotal to its plans to increase density in the telecommunications industry. Mergers and acquisitions have brought large numbers of non-union customer service and technical workers into AT&T and Regional Bell Operating Company subsidiaries. These subsidiaries are often covered by "neutrality clauses" achieved through CWA's bargaining-to-organize efforts. Such clauses limit managers' freedom to use the full scope allowed by US law to convince workers not to vote union in a certification election. Using the access to non-union workers and the protection of these neutrality clauses, organizing outreach can be supported by CWA members in the same occupation.

A former AFL-CIO organizing director offered nursing as an example ripe for more organizing on an occupational basis. In places such as Texas where organizing all occupational groups in hospitals or health care networks would be difficult, nurses show a tremendous interest in having stronger associations. This interest stems from the expansion in the United States of managed health care insurance and for-profit hospitals, as well as a decline in fear of losing jobs at particular facilities.

> The nurses have very strong concerns about their profession, the for-profit nature of their industry, about legislation that is being developed. They are tired of waiting for someone to come and help. They are doing it on their own.

The interviewee believed that a union could organize 127,000 registered nurses in Texas quite inexpensively and that the resulting association would soon be financially self-sufficient. One bottleneck in organizing these nurses is a shortage of trained and experienced organizers and lead organizers.

Organizing workers in non-standard employment relationships. Occupational organizing is seen as a potential approach to representing US workers who are not strongly attached to a particular employer – e.g. those who work for temporary agencies or have short-term contracts. According to the AFL-CIO organizing director:

> The high-tech and contingent workforce area. These folks are not in vertical relationships, with a boss that they are having trouble with, but in more lateral relationships. But they still need an organization to speak for

them...The largest employer in America is a temp agency now. So we have to figure out how to organize this segment, what the glue is and I think that is a different structure in terms of organization and collective bargaining...But it is not either-or and it is not all going to be one kind of organization and representation very soon. Not in my lifetime.

The CWA has led efforts by US unions to represent workers in non-standard employment arrangements. For example, CWA has established pilot "Employment Centers" in Los Angeles, Cleveland and Seattle that perform some of the functions of hiring halls in the construction model of US trade unionism. The Centers provide portable benefits, placement in temporary assignments covered by a collective bargaining agreement (the employer on record may be a telecommunications firm or a temporary agency that acts as an intermediary between the Employment Centre and the telecommunications firm), and training.[10]

In July 1998 CWA chartered the creation of a new local union – the Washington Alliance of Temporary Workers or Wash Tech – by Microsoft temporary workers in Seattle, Washington, the home base of the Microsoft Corporation. About one-third of Microsoft's 6,100 workers are temps and one-third of these have been on the job for more than a year. Wash Tech's goals include: (1) giving workers a voice in any policy decisions, public or corporate, that directly affect high-tech temps; (2) extending sick pay, holiday pay and medical care to all full-time workers in the industry, regardless of their employment status; and (3) educating workers about their legal rights to organize, negotiate contracts, and share employment information. Wash Tech is currently trying to form a workers' cooperative through which workers could contract out their own labour. In June 1999, Wash Tech petitioned four temp agencies for bargaining recognition on behalf of 18 Microsoft contractors. In January 1999, in response to workers' requests, Wash Tech began offering one-month classes on topics such as Java script, web development, database design, digital design and illustration, and career planning.

4. Inventing postindustrial unionism

One AFL-CIO staff member, speaking about unions adapting to new conditions, said "it's not so much the specifics of the change, it's how on earth they ever get to the point of making the change". In fact, however, the specifics of the change – a vision of how unions fit in to the new economy – are part of generating a willingness to change. The difficulties created for unions by the lack of such a vision manifest themselves in various ways.

---

[10] This and the next paragraph are based on duRivage, 2000.

4.1 From industrial to postindustrial organizing

Changes in business and work organization resulting from the shift away from a local craft-based economy, towards a national mass-production economy required a change in the dominant form of trade unionism. The same is true today, with the shift to a global, service-dominated economy. And just as the transition from craft to industrial union organizing was difficult for craft unions – with industrial unions, for the most part, created anew, along with their own federation (the Congress of Industrial Organizations) – the transition to postindustrial organizing has proved wrenching for a labour movement dominated by industrial unions.

Even in the last few years, much of the internal labour movement debate about organizing does not rise above campaign tactics. According to former AFL-CIO organizing director Kirk Adams:

> We do a lot of planning in this town and very often assume the workers want to have a union. I think generally a lot of workers do want to have a union ...But as to why they want to have a union, that's not ordinarily discussed...We talk a lot about the employer but we don't talk that much about the worker...

In the absence of any explicit debate about why workers might associate collectively in today's economy, traditional ideas from the industrial union era continue to have great sway. The most obvious illustration is the idea that hatred of the boss should be the main organizational glue. In some quarters, even to question the universal appeal of organizing "against the boss" is now seen as failing a loyalty test: it is misinterpreted as a retreat from the idea that organizing is about increasing workers' power. However, organizing is still about gaining the collective power to achieve positive transformation in a particular job, industry, or occupation, even if the focus shifts away from the "bad boss".[11] A more subtle but related hangover from the industrial union era is the restricted notion of what unions do. Only a few organizers conceive of what they are doing as part of an effort to transform social relations at work – to increase "worker control". When the language of the high road is adopted it is generally a slogan rather than an expression of a belief that the organization of production could be transformed in ways that benefit customers and society as well as workers.

Especially at CWA, some organizing is now being planned and conducted in ways that expand workers' opportunity to shape their own vision of unionism and then to work with others to find the leverage necessary to realize that vision. In these "best practice" cases, organizer networks include

---

[11] For an illustration of the confused nature of the debate on this issue, see *Labour Notes*, 1999.

internal committees, member-organizers in similar work settings, experienced full-time organizers, and union staff who can bring outside leverage to bear.[12]

The basic challenge for the AFL-CIO is to create an expanding learning network of organizers who have a deep understanding of workers and the nature of work today. This implies a heavier reliance on organizers employed in the occupations and industries being organized. It also suggests a need to re- evaluate the wisdom of having organizers move from industry to industry and occupation to occupation. Such movement may be acceptable if organizers are marketing generic "defence against management" services, but not if the goal is to transcend this and move towards more occupational models. It may also be important to eliminate the hard line that often separates organizers from those who negotiate contracts and oversee the use of union power once it is established. Only if organizers know how unionism will lead to a change in the day-to-day experience of work will they be able to convey the possibilities to new recruits.

There are many ways that AFL-CIO could seek to create the necessary learning network. As with the network of high road practitioners fostered by the Working for America Institute, a priority should be to encourage more contacts among organizers whose perceptions and approaches are not shaped by the past. At present, these individuals appear isolated, which is not a recipe for creativity or success. This interaction might also lead to more dialogue about what workers want, and to a reflection on the lessons of recent organizing successes and failures. AFL-CIO may ultimately need to reinvent its training curricula for organizers and lead organizers, creating, perhaps, a "New Union Organizing Institute" as a successor to the "Organizer Institute" first targeted at college students who would participate in blitz campaigns.

4.2 Inventing the high road

A related challenge for labour today is building the technical capacity in regional economies and labour markets to help pave the high road and block the low road. Implementing the high road requires major changes in public policy and networks of new institutions, many of them operating above the level of the individual firm (e.g. multi-employer unions, labour market

---

[12] Some innovative organizing is more likely to succeed because it is conducted in ways conducive to the development of what Ganz (1999) calls "strategic capacity". Ganz defines "strategic capacity" as the product of three factors: "access to salient information," "heuristic processes" (loosely, processes that help people solve problems creatively – e.g. interaction among individuals with diverse perspectives, brainstorming, telling stories or reviewing case studies of organizing), and "motivation to learn" (i.e. an intense interest in learning how to organize more effectively).

intermediaries that serve multiple employers, institutionalized political alliances between high road employers, unions and consumers). Creating the necessary institutions is outside the experience of most American trade unionists, who were confined to a reactive role within individual companies for most of the time since the Second World War. Especially outside the building and construction trades, most US unionists do not have the habits of thought that would lead them to analyse sectoral development; neither do they have the habits of action that would lead them to organize so as to shift business strategy from the low to the high road.[13]

One place to look for support in building the high road is the public sector. Here, unions confront the extreme free market orientation of even "liberal" US economists and policy makers. The liberal neo-classical paradigm of virtually all economists in the Clinton Administration has no place for the self-conscious construction of institutions designed to push industrial development in more innovative, high- quality directions.[14]

The US labour movement already uses some of its political leverage to free up public resources for technical assistance and institution building that support the high road – the best illustration of this being the Working for America Institute. Additional resources might be released with a strategic focus on that goal, at both state and local level. Some financial support should be sought for institutionally oriented research and graduate training programmes that recognize the role of labour organizations and other institutions in industrial development. The labour movement also needs to fight at all levels of government – including within the next national Democratic Presidential Administration – so that economic decision making is not dominated by neo-classical economists whose insidious influence on policy is impossible to overestimate. (Winning this fight is emphatically not just a matter of influencing the next appointment of Secretary of Labor.)

---

[13] The number of union leaders and activists comfortable with initiatives to promote the high road and rule out the low road will grow if unions expand in services such as childcare, elder care and health care, and if teachers' unions reorient themselves more wholeheartedly to taking the lead in promoting educational quality. In human and educational services, organizing to shift competition in higher quality directions is a natural extension of the professional identity of union members.

[14] Arguably, there was not a single institutional economist in a high level policy position in either of the two Clinton Administrations. In the Carter Administration, Secretary of Labour Ray Marshall, one of the most prominent institutional economists, was isolated within the Cabinet. In the first Clinton Administration, Secretary of Labour Robert Reich espoused some views shared with institutional economists, but saw himself as a one-man source of creativity not the leader of a coherent alternative perspective on economic development. Every Chief Economist at the US Department of Labour since Clinton came to power has been a neo-classical economist.

It must be admitted that it is a lot to ask of the labour movement that it take the lead intellectually, politically and institutionally in pushing for a high road economic strategy. While there are many potential allies for such a strategy once it begins to emerge, there are no other obvious candidates for taking the lead. The statement above is both a recognition of the enormity of the challenge and a rationale for a new economy labour movement.

4.3 Labour's moral purpose

Another obstacle to trade union progress is the decay of a broader sense of social purpose – the idea of a mission larger than the self-interest of a particular union or particular officials. If the upper middle-class income and status of some union leaders and staff may be jeopardized by internal restructuring, the decline of a larger sense of mission can be particularly paralysing. Why sacrifice personal prestige and security if no larger purpose will be served? The lack of a consensus social vision also diminishes labour's ability to attract and retain committed activists and staff who have the alternative of a more financially rewarding career.

Strategic planning and internal reorganization with AFL-CIO and leading affiliates have sought to revive the sense of a larger purpose. One national union leader observed that, within his union, local officials have begun to accept personal sacrifice once they see internal restructuring which is consistent with a principled strategic plan. But a broader regeneration of labour's moral purpose requires a general postindustrial solution to unions' basic dilemma – the need to serve the interests of their members while simultaneously being seen to serve the interests of society as a whole. At the moment, institutional self-interest is too transparently the motivation for many labour actions, large and small. Paradoxically, only transcending the view that labour is just another special interest, and acting to make the world a better place, can restore labour's power.

4.4 Postindustrial unionism

The challenges above are all symptoms of developments in the 1970s and 1980s that rendered obsolete the New Deal solution to the unions' basic dilemma. To end unions' current "identity crisis" within society, and lay the foundation for a substantial increase in membership, unions must, as they did in the 1930s, take a central role in solving persistent economic and social problems. Notwithstanding sustained economic prosperity, the United States at the end of the 1990s does have such problems. They include rising wage inequality, an erosion in big company job ladders that undercuts advancement for low-wage workers and security for mid-career employees, falling rates of health care coverage, and an apparent decline in the value of pension benefits for many workers.

In addition, it is widely perceived that the US invests inadequately in human capital development and that employment instability makes firms less willing to spend money on training (since employees may soon work for someone else). In conjunction with inadequate investment in workforce training, many US employers' competitive advantage is based on paying low wages and benefits rather than raising performance, an approach that retards the growth of living standards.

A potential new economy resolution of US unions' basic dilemma thus lies in their ability to solve these persistent economic and social problems.[15] Adapting the traditions of craft unions, US multi- employer unions rooted in sectoral and geographical labour markets (childcare, elder care, health care, technical occupations, clerical and administrative occupations) could raise wages at the low end of the market, in the process discouraging low-wage strategies. They could negotiate with employers to increase investment in human capital development. They could create multi-employer career advancement, job matching, and health and pension benefit structures. In professional, technical, personal service and customer service jobs – now most of the economy – in which critical knowledge resides within occupational communities, unions could raise performance through apprenticeship and peer learning approaches. In these ways, unions might recapture public support as institutions that raise economic performance and create decent jobs – that "add value as well as values".

A redefinition of unions' place in the economic structure is now the subject of debate at the national AFL-CIO. According to one top staff member:

> There's no more important issue for us in terms of the long-term viability of union organization in this country than workforce skills and preparing people for work, present and future...We organize skill development processes that are critical to your long-term economic security...People will get involved with unions because they build the training structures that allow lots of workers in lots of different situations to get skills and to advance...

In the words of another staff member, the slogan implicit in much union activity in the last two decades is "things could be worse". A new collective identity based on expanding economic opportunity for all and honouring workers' commitment to their customers and their craft would be a more positive and compelling vision.

---

[15] For a longer (but still short) version of the argument in this last section, see Herzenberg, Alic and Wial, 1998b.

Some time ago, the US labour movement developed the marketing slogan "America Works Best When We Say Union Yes", more as an expression of hope and faith than a conviction. The more the union movement discovers, to its immense relief, that this is actually true, and then makes that case to the public as a whole, the sooner we can expect to see a revival of the labour movement.

Bibliography

AFL-CIO. 1985. *The changing situation of workers and their unions.* Report by the AFL-CIO Committee on the Evolution of Work (Washington, D.C., American Federation of Labour and Congress of Industrial Organizations).

AFL-CIO. 1997. *Resolutions and constitutional amendments adopted at the twenty-second AFL-CIO convention* (Washington, D.C., American Federation of Labour and Congress of Industrial Organizations).

AFL-CIO Committee 2000. 1999. *Creating a new alliance with state federations and central labour councils,* Draft proposal, May.

Batt, R.; Katz, H.C.; Keefe, J.H. 1999. *The strategic initiatives of the CWA: Organizing, politics, and collective bargaining* (Cambridge, Mass., MIT Task Force on Reconstructing America's Labour Market Institutions, Working Paper No. 15).

CWA. No date. *Changing information services: Strategies for workers and consumers* (Washington, D.C., Communications Workers of America).

duRivage, V.L. 2000. "CWA's organizing strategies: Transforming contract work into union jobs", in Carre, F.; Ferber, M.; Golden, L.; Herzenberg, S., *Non-standard employment arrangements* (Madison, WI., The Industrial Relations Research Association Annual Research Volume).

Eimer, S. 1999. "From 'business unionism' to 'social movement unionism': The case of the AFL-CIO Milwaukee County central labour council," in *Labour Studies Journal,* Vol. 24, No. 2, pp. 63- 81.

Ganz, M. 1999. *Resources and resourcefulness: Leadership, organization, and strategy in the unionization of California agriculture (1959-1977).* Unpublished paper (Sociology Department, Harvard University), January.

Gapasin, F.; Wial, H. 1997. "The role of central labour councils in union organizing in the 1990s", in Bronfenbrenner, K. et al. (eds.). *Organizing to win: New research on union strategies.*

Herzenberg, S.; Alic, J.; Wial, H. 1998. *New rules for a new economy: Employment and opportunity in postindustrial America* (Ithaca, NY, Cornell University/ILR Press).

—;—;—. 1999a. "A new deal for a new economy," in *Challenge,* Mar./Apr.

—;—;—. 1999b. "New unions for a new economy," in *The New Democrat,* Mar./Apr., pp. 8-12.

Hirsch, B.; MacPherson, D. 1999. *Union membership and earnings data book: Compilations from the current population survey* (Washington, D.C., US Bureau of National Affairs).

Labour Notes. 1999. "The high road: SEIU rethinks hospital organizing tactics," Dec.

Lazarovici, L. 1999. "Launching a new alliance," in *AFL-CIO News*, June, pp. 12-13.

Morris, C. 1998. "A tale of two statutes: Discrimination for union activity under the NLRA and the RLA", in *Employment Rights and Policy Journal*, Vol. 327, p. 330.

NLRB. 1998. *National Labour Relations Act*. Sixty-second annual report of the National Labour Relations Board for the fiscal year ended September 1997 (Washington, D.C., US Government Printing Office).

Ness, I. 1998. "The road to union cities: Labour seeks to transform the culture and structure of central labour councils," in *Working USA*, Nov./Dec.

Nissen, B.; Rosen, S. 1999. "The CWA model of membership-based organizing,"in *Labour Studies Journal*, Vol. 24, pp. 73-88.

Parker, E.; Rogers, J. 1996. *The Wisconsin regional training partnership: Lessons for national policy* (National Centre for the Workplace, Working Paper No. 3, Oct.).

Piore, M.J. 1994. "Unions : A reorientation to survive", in Kerr, C.; Staudohar, P. (eds.). *Labour economics and industrial relations* (Cambridge, Mass., Harvard University Press), pp. 512-541.

Rogers, J. 1994. " A strategy for labour," in *Industrial Relations*, Vol. 34, pp. 367-381.

Sciacchitano, K. 1998. *The union is forever: A comparison of leadership development in SEIU's Dignity Campaign against Beverly Enterprises and SHARE's Campaign at the University of Massachusetts Medical Centre*, Paper presented at the UCLEA/AFL-CIO Annual Conference, San Jose, California, May 1.

Stern, A. 1998. "Jump-starting the labour movement," in *Washington Post*, Sep. 7.

Sweeney, J.J.; Kusnet, D. 1996. *America needs a raise* (Boston, Houghton-Mifflin Company).

Weiler, P. 1983. " Promises to keep: Securing workers' rights to self organization under the NLRA", in *Harvard Law Review*, June.

Part 2

Studies on Chile, Israel,
Republic of Korea and Lithuania

Trade union responses to globalization: Chile

Guillermo Campero

1. Introduction

This chapter presents the policies and strategies pursued by Chilean trade unionism in the 1990s. At this time organized labour was facing challenges caused by the profound economic and political structural changes resulting from the country's entry into a globalized world and an equally globalized political system.

In order to study the case of Chile, it is essential to bear in mind that the process of integration of that country into the framework of economic and political globalization occurred initially, in the early 1970s, under a military government, which had overthrown a democratic government in a coup d'état. The new government, which lasted 17 years, used authoritarian methods to implant an economic model inspired by so-called neo-liberal ideas, introducing a system based essentially on regulation of the market, severely limiting the state's role in the economy, privatizing a major part of the health and social security system, and repealing the old Labour Code, which was replaced by new legislation based on greater flexibility and less labour protection. It drastically opened up trade and finance to the international economy and focused its development policies mainly on the export of commodities. The military government shut down the Parliament, suspended the political parties and severely restricted the activities of social organizations, especially the trade unions. That is why, for Chilean trade unionists, the process of globalization and its structural effects was felt at the same time as the political and social effects generated by the military government. Unlike other countries in the region where the trade union movement faced the challenges of globalization in a framework of political democracy, in Chile those challenges were seen by trade unionists as processes linked to the actions of a non-democratic government. Thus the struggle to restore political democracy in Chile, in which trade unionists were the principal players, was often also linked to combating the new economic model, since they regarded the authoritarian military regime and the new model as two sides of the same coin.

This background needs to borne very much in mind, since it is an important factor in understanding the meaning of trade union policies and strategies in the face of economic and political globalization in the post-1990 period, when political democracy was restored to the country. The effects of the economic, political and institutional changes due to the country's experiences from 1973 onwards had already been consolidated by 1990, so that the structural framework in which trade unionism developed at the beginning of the decade had already been shaped several years earlier. In particular, the economic and social conditions under which the trade unions were working in the 1990s had been established in the previous two decades. Trade unionism and its social and material environment were not those of the early 1970s, although part of its national leadership was the same and its traditional organizational structures were still in place.

This process of major change marked trade unionism in Chile very decisively, because the changes which affected it were not the result, as in other countries, of progressive adjustments due to economic and political modernization strategies in a context of political democracy, but the consequence of a violent, drastic and massive adjustment led by an authoritarian government, which denied social and political freedoms and was overtly anti-trade union.

1.1 Initial restructuring, 1973-1981

After 1973, the trade union growth which had marked the preceding period entered a period of stagnation. Not only did the absolute number of members decline, as a result of high unemployment, but organized labour also became more fragmented as trade unions diminished in size.

In qualitative terms, the impact was significant when it is considered that the manufacturing and construction sectors, the traditional base of trade unionism, seemed to be particularly affected both in total volume and average size. Mining, especially coal (another key sector) also showed deterioration.

In short, as a result of the structural effects of the chosen economic model and the political constraints that stood in the way of trade union development, workers' organization was diminished and its evolution obstructed. The situation was more marked among manual workers than office workers, which demonstrated both the type of unemployment and changes in the composition of the workforce.

The situation can be regarded as critical when it is considered that the weakening was global and that, furthermore, new sectors did not emerge to reinforce and offset the decline in the traditionally most strategic centres.

Consequently, both the political process and the structural changes arising under the new economic model introduced in the early 1970s led to a decline in trade union activity and a drastic change in the composition of the social base on which trade unionism was founded. Nevertheless, it did not mean that the trade union movement vanished completely.

Throughout the period, the action of trade unions, their federations and national bodies consisted of a constant struggle against the military government in an effort to restore the democratic political system. At the same time they waged a battle against the introduction of a neo-liberal economic policy. As we have said, for trade unionism the struggle against the dictatorship and against the economic model were part of the same process. At that stage, to pursue these actions, the trade union movement was forced to organize under its leadership not only trade unions but all social organizations, whatever their composition. Thus, the trade union leadership included urban district associations, many professionals, unemployed people, students and groups linked to religious organizations.

Out of this experience came the idea that under the new structural, institutional and political conditions, trade unionism could redefine its constituent base and move from the traditional purely labour view of its organization to a broader social view. The idea developed to some extent up to 1985, but after that it failed to take hold.

1.2 Economic crisis, recovery and consolidation, 1981 - 1999

Crisis

By 1980 the largest economic, structural and institutional changes had already happened, Chile's integration in the global economy was in full swing, market forces held sway, the culture of the country as a whole was one of incorporation in the globalized world and trends in the main economic variables had proved fairly favourable. However, the chosen model proved to be fragile, both domestically and internationally. The fact was that the economy was centred around significant financial rather than productive development, which made it vulnerable to speculation and limited hard investment in favour of so-called "migrant" capital. Moreover, the country's entry into the globlal economy was not designed to deal with external crises such as occurred internationally in the early eighties. As a result of these and other factors, the Chilean economy fell into a deep recession with a decline in GDP of at least 14 per cent and overt unemployment close on 35 per cent.

The situation unleashed major decisions for change in the management of the economy by the military government, albeit retaining the basic economic model adopted in 1975. Various policies were reformulated, especially those aimed at strengthening productive capacity and controlling the financial system.

On the social level, the trade unions succeeded in leading a vast social protest movement against the military regime and its policies, despite the fact that by 1981-82 trade union membership had fallen to a third of what it was in 1977 (347,470 against 916,569). This led to the "national protests" of 1983-1984. That was the occasion when trade unionism succeeded in promoting most strongly the possibility of leading a social base wider than organized labour. In fact, the protests did bring out much wider groupings of people and organizations under the leadership of the trade unions. These movements were the beginning of the end of the dictatorship, since it was because of them that the military government had to agree to negotiate with the political opposition and allow them room to express their views. However, the trade union leadership was overtaken at that stage of negotiation by party leaders and the new profile that it was acquiring as the cement of a wider social base lost ground and ultimately evaporated.

Recovery

Analysts agree that, once the crisis was over, it was from 1985 onwards that the bases of Chile's current economic process were established. The decade after that was a period of rapid growth. There was permanent job creation and a return to political stability. After the serious crisis of the preceding years, production levels recovered, savings and investment increased, inflation was brought under control, unemployment was reduced and real wages grew in line with productivity.

During the ten years after 1985 a satisfactory macroeconomic equilibrium was achieved. Domestic product grew by an annual 6.6 per cent, inflation was falling steadily, there was a sustained increase in productivity and domestic and external fiscal accounts were sound. There were some significant achievements on the social front. Literacy, school attendance and life expectancy at birth all improved. The number of individuals and families below the poverty line fell significantly.

While these were the general features of the post-crisis period, the distinction between the two stages suggested in the ILO study *Employment trends in Chile 1986-1996* published by the Santiago multidisciplinary team in 1998 should be examined. The study distinguishes a first phase between 1986 and 1989, i.e. up to the end of the military government and the takeover by the democratic government. According to the ILO document, although the process of recovery and improvement in the economic indicators began in 1986, economic growth in that first phase was characterized by excess capacity and the high rates of unemployment caused by the profound crisis that had gone before.

The crisis was overcome by an economic adjustment in 1985 with a high social cost. In order to alleviate some of its effects, policies such as cash subsidies to the poorest sections of the population were adopted as well as the creation of emergency employment programmes, which gave jobs to almost 10 per cent of the workforce between 1986 and 1989.

Although these programmes helped to reduce overt unemployment, it was still above 10 per cent in 1989. Although real wages had risen, they were still 5 per cent below the levels in 1981 and 1982, and the legal minimum wage was 30 per cent less than in those years. The pace of trade union organization and the level of workers' collective bargaining, despite a recovery between 1986 and 1989 compared with the preceding years, was slowing and had reached less than 10 per cent of the workforce.

The second period ran from 1990 to 1996, culminating in a consolidation of the recovery and the formation of Chile's present economic and social environment, the background against which trade unions are tackling the processes of globalization. The period was one of high growth in domestic product, 6.8 per cent on average, a drop in inflation from 21 per cent to 6.6. per cent between 1989 and 1996, strong fiscal accounts and accumulation of international reserves, growth in the level of savings, investment and productivity, more job creation and rising real wages.

The fall in unemployment in the first phase between 1986 and 1989 was mainly the result of mobilizing resources that had been frozen during the preceding crisis. It was only secondarily due to diversifying the production of primary export commodities (wood, fruit, fish) and goods requiring a certain degree of processing (wine, preserves). In any case, this allowed a return to the levels of employment prior to the crisis. However, after 1989, growth was the result of expansion of installed capacity, strongly geared towards exports. Unemployment stabilized at between 6 and 7 per cent.

The social base of unionism in the 1990s

The proportion of women in the workforce increased. After 1989 the rise in employment was mainly due to the entry of more people to the labour force, especially women. Between 1986 and 1994, the proportion of women rose from 29.3 per cent to 35.4 per cent. The expansion of the fruit sector, trade and financial services, among other things, caused the rise in the proportion of women. In the secondary sector, men continued to predominate. Of the total employed in 1996, 80 per cent were men.

Female employment was thus concentrated in the tertiary sector. By 1996, this activity accounted for 80 per cent of working women. Trade had the largest number of women workers, 22 per cent in 1986 and 24 per cent in 1996.

Employment in agriculture and mining grew slightly. In the primary sector, employment in agriculture fell from 20 per cent in 1986 to 15 per cent in 1996. Mining still offered few new jobs.

Manufacturing recovered but did not regain its traditional position. By 1996, the secondary sector had increased its share from 21 per cent in 1986 to 27 per cent. Even so, the recovery in manufacturing employment did not return to pre-crisis levels and began to stagnate after 1994.

The tertiary sector retained a high share of employment. By 1996, the sector was employing some 58 per cent of the total labour force.

Changes within the different occupational categories. The most significant changes in the period occurred in the category of "farmers, livestock breeders, fishermen, hunters and the like" from 21 per cent to 16 per cent, and "manual and casual workers" from 11 per cent to 6 per cent. Other groups increased their share, especially office workers, from 11 per cent to 15 per cent.

Consequently, the main change in the pattern of employment between the mid-1980s and the 1990s was the decline in the number of manual workers and the significant increase in office workers, the latter mainly in the private sector, since those in the public sector had declined by some 30 per cent.

The greater proportion of women was also reflected in a significant growth in the group of "professionals, engineers and the like" and "managers, administrators and directors". This showed that at least some of them were obtaining jobs of a certain quality, although that did not prevent wage discrimination between men and women in these categories of employment.

Changes in workers' educational levels. There was a marked increase in all categories of employees with higher education, from 10 to 18 per cent. Among "managers, administrators and directors", it rose from 39 to 44 per cent, and the profile of "office workers and the like" also changed radically, from 16 per cent to 39 per cent with higher education.

The lowest level of education was in "farmers, livestock breeders, fishermen, and the like", where 80 per cent of those employed were uneducated or had only primary education.

Organization and membership

By 1990, the characteristics and composition of the social base and the socioeconomic conditions in which trade unionism was to develop its activities in the period covered by this study had already been set. What caused a change in the scenarios was the political factor, with the end of the authoritarian government in March 1990 when the country's first democratic elections for 17 years brought President Patricio Aylwin and the centre left coalition, the Concertación de Partidos por la Democracia, to power. This political factor would be significant in creating space for various social and political players to express their views, hitherto rather restricted by the previous regime.

In the case of trade unionism, one of the significant effects was the rapid growth in trade union membership during the first three years of the democratic government, a time when unionization rose by some 25 per cent compared with the end of 1989, reaching a figure of 724,065 members in 1992 against 507,616. Subsequently, the growth in membership levelled off or fell somewhat, with some 600,000 at the end of 1998 (12 per cent of the workforce and 17 per cent of wage earners). Trade unions, for their part, almost doubled in number between the end of 1989 and the end of 1998, from 7,118 to some 13,000. However, although their number increased, the downward trend in average size, which had already begun under the military regime, continued. The average of 84 members in 1980 had fallen to about 67 by 1998.

It should be noted that the recovery in membership and trade unions had already started in 1984, parallel to the recovery from the 1981 economic crisis and the political processes of 1983 onwards, a period when there was a high level of social protest against the military regime. However, the largest quantitative leap occurred, as noted above, during the first phase of the democratic government that succeeded the military government.

Despite all this, the recovery of trade unionism membership to 12 per cent of the workforce was not enough to offset the fall in membership and organizations compared with 1973. In that year the rate of unionization of the workforce was almost 32 per cent, the highest since the late 1920s when trade unions were legally recognized and constituted in the country.

The economic sectors in which trade unionism had traditionally developed recovered their positions in the second half of the 1980s and continued to do so in the 1990s, both in terms of employment and in terms of their relative weight in the economy compared with the period of most acute change (1975-1981). However, the recovery had two features which meant that the process did not necessarily result in the recomposition of the same type of trade union movement as had existed up to the beginning of the 1970s or a reproduction of the social conditions in which it had developed.

The first of these was that although the sectors in which trade unionism had traditionally built its core had recovered, their relative importance in economic and trade union terms had changed compared with the early 1970s. The most significant change was in manufacturing. In 1996 this sector represented 16 per cent of employment compared with 26 per cent in 1973, and by 1997 unionization in the sector was 23.8 per cent of the total, against 31 per cent in 1973. At the same time, the service and trade sectors increased their relative importance in the economy and also in the pattern of unionization, while the importance of mining and construction, two other key sectors in trade union organization, declined.

The sectors that increased their significance in the composition of trade unionism did so, as we have seen, against the general background of a drastic reduction in the pace of unionization. In addition, however, these are sectors that are typically more dispersed and have less tradition of involvement in national trade unionism and trade union federations. Thus, while there was significant growth in those sectors, it was not necessarily a factor in strengthening trade union activities in Chile at national level.

The second characteristic concerns the sectors where trade unionism had traditionally developed; during the years from 1973 to 1990 they generally experienced major changes in technology, forms of organization of labour and management of enterprise and services. Labour markets became considerably segmented and conditions of access to them varied in terms of technical and educational qualifications. Also of crucial importance was the application since 1980 of highly flexible and deregulatory labour legislation on the one hand, accompanied by many aspects that restricted trade union activity, which created a quite different institutional framework, indeed the reverse of the one in which the trade union movement had been developing hitherto. Some of the major aspects of the legislation were reformed after 1990, especially in allowing more scope for trade unions and collective bargaining, but there were still several issues that continued to restrict trade union activities and collective action by workers in general.

These two characteristics, together with entry into the international scene and the market economy, had a powerful influence in bringing about change in the social, technical and cultural conditions under which trade unionism had to operate.

2. Trade union responses to globalization

As argued in the introduction to this paper, trade union responses in Chile to the challenges and structural changes resulting from entry into a globalized economy and a world that had become politically internationalized, were strongly marked by the fact that the process had begun in the early 1970s under an anti-trade union military dictatorship, a feature of which was profound and drastic structural and institutional change, indeed upheaval, on a massive scale imposed in an authoritarian manner in a relatively short period of time.

As a result, the actions and strategies of trade unionism were primarily based on political lines, designed to intervene in national life as part of the restoration of political democracy, and subsequently, from the early 1990s, to consolidate and entrench their position. They thus devoted major efforts to seeking changes in the existing economic model, which, although moderated in concept, continued in many important aspects that made it indistinguishable from the policies pursued by the military government.

In this context, the national organization of Chilean trade unions (Central Unitaria de Trabajadores. CUT) and the leadership generally at federation and confederation level gave priority to policies and strategies aimed at influencing global social policy issues, rather than those aimed at developing ways of restructuring their traditional organization and methods of recruitment in the face of changes in the nature of their social base. That does not mean, however, that such problems did not have a place on the trade union agenda; it simply means that they had lower priority than in other countries.

2.1 Policies and strategies directed towards global issues

Three main focuses of trade union action can be distinguished in this area in the 1990s: policies aimed at social cohesion and social alliances; policies aimed at the institutionalization of labour, labour legislation and social security; and policies aimed at promoting participation and workers' rights in social and economic development.

Social cohesion

The National Agreements. Around April 1990, the most representative workers' organization (the CUT) and the government decided to invite the main employers' organization to seek agreement on a joint document in which they expressed their positions on the issue of labour and its relationship with economic and social development policies, identifying areas of consensus which they were in a position to build. The proposal by the trade unions and the government was to set out the main rules of the game, which could be accepted by the parties as the framework within which the labour issue could be discussed with the advent of the first democratic government for 17 years.

The document, under the title of *National Tripartite Framework Agreement*, signed in May 1990, was the result of that first meeting. Through the CUT, the trade unions played a significant role since, although their positions were generally critical of what they called the "economic model", they were ready to facilitate common ground with employers and the government in order to obtain, from the former especially, an open approach to labour issues and questions of social equity linked to economic growth.

The document to which the framework agreement gave rise was of crucial importance, because it was unprecedented in Chilean experience. Its main value was to signal the readiness of the trade unions, employers and the government to agree at least on the main directions of social and economic development, and the will of the parties to discuss them in a framework in which they were willing to take part. This signal certainly helped to strengthen the transition to democracy.

It should be explained that the agreement was the result of mutual concessions by the employer, union and government sides, so that its content can be seen as a kind of "memorandum of understanding", rather than full agreement on ideas of social and economic development. In fact, trade unions and employers continued to disagree on many subjects, but they agreed to moderate their disagreements as a gesture of readiness to engage in dialogue. The trade unions in particular moderated their positions on many points as an expression of the political will to facilitate the agreement, which they regarded as important in contributing to the success of the democratization process that was beginning in the country.

In particular, they began to look favourably on the role of private enterprise in economic growth and development, as well as the need to consider the demands of an open and competitive economy as a framework for social and labour policies. At the same time, they maintained that a necessary condition of the foregoing was special concern to protect workers during the process of change and adjustment, greater participation in enterprises and their profits, a better balance in labour relations and recognition of the role of the trade unions at grassroots, sectoral and national level, and making workers' access to the fruits and opportunities of growth a priority goal.

The employers, for their part, acknowledged the need to improve labour relations in terms of more cooperation, the need to ensure compliance with labour and pensions legislation. They recognized workers' organizations as valid representatives and expressed their readiness to examine those aspects of institutionalized labour that needed improvement in order to promote labour relations of higher quality and technical calibre. They also recognized the importance of developing policies to help workers obtain better access to the opportunities of growth.

The framework agreement also covered adjustment to the national minimum wage for the period 1990-1991, as well as a range of issues to be discussed in future dialogue. It opened up a readiness to engage in tripartite discussions and helped to ensure that proposed reforms or improvements of labour legislation prepared by the government could then be discussed in consultation with the social partners. Although the government did not achieve full agreement with either the trade unions or the employers on their proposals, the experience of dialogue made it easier to achieve consensus in Parliament when they were submitted to the Congress. In fact, it set a precedent for tackling labour issues in a climate of dialogue and the search for agreement, breaking down the employers' prejudices and opposition to the possibility of change on these issues. This influenced the readiness of Congress to discuss and approve proposals submitted by the Ministry of Labour, under the government's labour reform programme.

Agreements were signed in 1991, 1992 and 1993, which had more practical impact than the first. The main subject was the minimum wage, especially restoration of the link with average wages, and other specific issues. The agreements did not address any other major themes and in many of them it was not possible to finalize everything proposed, other than the criteria for setting the minimum wage, namely estimated future inflation and average productivity in the economy. This was a significant achievement, since it allowed the identification of a precise formula, consistent with the objectives of growth and stability. However, despite their more practical nature, the agreements that followed the first were a focus of constant dialogue and kept alive the idea of social cooperation as a method of high political and social value. That did not, however, prevent conflicts between the parties and the government, some of them quite serious, but the forum for dialogue was preserved as a recourse validated by the partners.

Trade unionism, led by the CUT, kept up this strategy of social cooperation for four years, even though internally it faced constant tensions concerning its validity, since some sectors thought that it was not yielding the results they had hoped for, arguing that the employers were not behaving in accordance with the first framework agreement. In particular, that was because proposed reforms to the labour legislation submitted by government to the National Congress continued to be criticized by various employers' organizations.

Furthermore, although as a result of previous consultations the above-mentioned government initiatives included many objectives put forward by the trade unions, certain union sectors thought that they were still inadequate and that tripartite cooperation and the national agreements were not making an effective contribution to overcoming those shortcomings. Similarly, the attempts at dialogue between the CUT and the employers, prior to and during the four national agreements, were also regarded by their critics as of little value for the same reasons.

These tensions led the CUT leadership to state on several occasions that it was paying a high social and political price to maintain the strategy of tripartite dialogue and that if it were to continue, the strategy would have to allow them to show more positive results, both in law reform and in improving the quality of labour relations at company level, as well as fairer access to the results of economic growth.

According to certain analysts at the time, while the CUT's anxieties were to some extent justified in relation to the matters of concern to them, it also seemed as if the trade union leadership was often inclined not to state its objectives clearly in the process of dialogue, preferring a defensive and even pessimistic tone which obscured its recognized role as national negotiator.

Nevertheless, the CUT leadership kept to the framework of the social cooperation policy throughout the period 1990-1993, which showed that, despite the above, it continued to value it and regard it as a necessary focus for the consolidation of the democracy of which it felt itself to be a constituent part.

Sectoral agreements. The open framework of the national agreements also allowed the conclusion of sectoral agreements. The most important were four in the public sector concerning adjustments in salaries, working conditions and other employment and career issues. The CUT participated in all of them. One of the most outstanding results of the agreements in this sector was the passing of a law allowing civil servants to belong to a trade union. Tripartite agreements were also concluded in the port sector and bipartite agreements in the coal-mining sector.

Other examples of cooperation in the period 1990-1993. The CUT agreed with government on the formation of a National Tripartite Council to advise the Ministry of Labour on vocational education and training. There was also a tripartite agreement to implement a broad programme of publicizing labour laws to encourage compliance. The CUT also agreed with government to establish a National Trade Union Training Fund to finance the training of trade unionists.

Crisis in the policy of cohesion. Following the above-mentioned experiments, from 1994 onwards the policy of national agreements was to end. Both the trade unions and the employers said that the policy had not brought the hoped-for benefits. In particular, the trade unions thought they had not been sufficiently included in important decisions, despite their efforts to achieve agreements. That did not mean that unionists at national and federation level did not remain open to reviving the cohesion policy, but that did not happen except in very specific cases. One such, and a very significant one, was the bipartite agreement between the CUT and the government in 1998 that adjusted the legal minimum wage for three years. Another was the sectoral agreement between trade unions in the forestry sector and the employers to develop and disseminate, with ILO support, a national code of conduct on safety and health at work.

Policies aimed at institutionalizing labour and social security

Since the beginning of 1990 trade unions had focused on drafting proposals to reform existing labour legislation. From their point of view, the legislation in the Labour Code, which had been substantially amended since 1979 during the military government, was the expression of an extreme neo-liberal concept, designed to turn workers into a cheap labour force to help employers enter the global "transnationalized" economy.

In social security, their policy sought to protect their members by better regulation of the private pension scheme, which had also been set up during the military government about 1980. While the system had worked well during the first 16 years, in 1997-98 it began to show signs of lack of profitability, and it was also heavily concentrated in the hands of economic groups. This all reinforced the trade union view of the need for greater government and social control of the scheme.

On both issues, the trade unions did not reach sufficient agreement with the government, which was in favour of substantive reforms, but at a slower pace than demanded by the unions.

Policies aimed at participation and promotion of social rights in economic and social development

In this area, the trade unions, with the government, sought to form a body to allow dialogue between different social sectors on economic and social development policies. This gave rise to the Productive Development Forum, a tripartite body formed around 1994, which developed a major programme of work on a wide range of issues related to the public and private agenda for economic and social development.

To some extent, this body replaced the policy of agreements pursued during 1990-1993, although its purpose was very different, since it was not a decision-making body. The Forum was initially a great catalyst, since it gave rise to debates and meetings at national level with high representation of all constituents. However, by 1998 it had declined in importance for reasons similar to those that had caused the demise of national agreements. The trade unions were not satisfied with the results since they thought that participation at that level was not reflected at intermediate and grassroots levels and, moreover, that the employers were blocking the issues of most interest to the workers. Nevertheless, the CUT and trade union federations continued to express interest in the Forum provided that the above-mentioned limitations could be resolved.

Balance of global policies

The three lines of action making up trade union strategy in Chile relating to global issues were in some ways their most substantial programme of action, designed to tackle, in the existing climate of political democracy, the new conditions created in the country since the beginning of the 1970s under authoritarian policies.

As a corollary to this, it can be said that those policies had allowed trade unionism to be seen by public opinion as a player with clear positions on matters of national interest. It was thus able to overcome the weakness forced on it by the military government since 1973. Its recovery of national presence really began in 1983, when it led the social protests against the authoritarian regime.

However, the representative role achieved by trade unionism in its policies on agreements and the other areas described do not seem to have enabled it to strengthen its capacity to act at grassroots level. In fact, the CUT continued to decline even though it still had over 350,000 members, i.e. almost 60 per cent of total union membership (at the beginning of the democratic government, it had almost 75 per cent). Moreover, much of its membership came from the public sector and it was not growing in the private sector.

According to some analysts, that was because although the CUT and the federations had taken on the major national issues related to macroeconomic and social processes, they had not been so involved in issues and problems arising at the grassroots relating to changes in the composition of the workforce and technological advances which changed the social base in many ways. National trade unionism had taken on a global social and political role, true to its historical tradition, but it had not moved on to identify new areas and forms of action and organization, necessary to interpret and represent a multiplicity of diverse and disparate interests which are now a feature of the labour force.

2.2 Policies at company union level

Strategic agreements in companies in key sectors

Another line of action pursued by trade unionism was the negotiation of long-term agreements in companies with a high economic and social strategic value. The policy was at the initiative of trade unions in those companies rather than a deliberate policy at national level (CUT), but it generally had its support. The purpose of the agreements was to establish a kind of compromise by the company and the workers' organization to ensure the economic performance of the company and a satisfactory level of labour relations. In this way, companies undertook to ensure that improvements in productivity and efficiency would be reflected in workers' pay, that there was adequate information and participation and that there was strict compliance with labour legislation and collective agreements. The workers undertook to maintain industrial peace if the company fulfilled its part of the bargain, to participate actively in all efforts to improve quality, productivity and efficiency and generally to encourage cooperative behaviour.

The policy of participation and cooperation sought to show the employers' side that workers could be partners in the enterprise if employers were prepared to treat them as such. The initiative sought to combat employer attitudes that assumed that any form of worker participation only led to inefficiency and ultimately to higher costs. The trade unions were also trying to show that in a globalized economy, companies could only compete successfully if they faced that competition together and if the workers felt they were being adequately rewarded.

This strategy was most importantly illustrated by two major state companies[1] and two in the private sector. The first three were in the copper mining industry and the fourth was the national and international telephone company.

In the public sector, the companies concerned were CODELCO, the country's largest copper producer and one of the largest in the world with 18,000 workers and ENAMI (National Mining Corporation) responsible for promoting and supporting the development of small and medium-sized mining companies in the country, with a workforce of 2,000. The private sector companies were Disputada de las Condes, with 1800 workers and the Spanish-owned Compañía de Teléfonos de Chile with 8,750 workers.

In the case of CODELCO[2], the company workers' federation entered into a strategic alliance with the management in 1995. Its objective was to identify together the major challenges to the country's largest producer in the future, including expansion policies, technological innovation and human resources. On the basis of those agreements, they reached a consensus on decisions to reduce the workforce in situations of adjustment, on training workers in transferable skills and on labour mobility within the company, which operates five huge copper deposits in the country. Collective bargaining offered appropriate occasions to improve the basis and forms of application of the strategic alliance.

In the case of ENAMI[3], the agreement was called the Strategic Alliance and it began in October 1997. It was a tripartite agreement, since the government participated as signatory, together with company management and its trade unions. The agreement involved commitments on a wide range of issues: the company's aims concerning the mining economy, technical and economic objectives, optimization of management, technological innovation, environmental policy, occupational safety, labour relations with emphasis on participation schemes, communication and information, investment policy and ownership.

From the evidence of interviews and other sources of information, the agreement has had a positive impact and has been widely followed in many trade union sectors throughout the country. That does not mean, however, that there have been no difficulties since it was signed. Indeed, there were problems in collective bargaining, especially concerning productivity incentives, application of the concept of "multi-skilling" and its relationship

---

[1] In Chile, state productive companies are governed by the same economic and labour laws as the private sector.
[2] See statement of the Copper Workers' Federation, 13 Sep. 1995.
[3] See ENAMI document, Strategic Alliance, 6 Oct. 1997.

to job stability, and on procedures to ensure that workers are better informed. However, the issues were satisfactorily resolved and the agreement has gained the trust of workers and management.

In the case of the Disputada de las Condes, management and the trade unions signed a Collective Covenant in 1998, also called the Strategic Alliance, which established targets to be achieved and results for workers for a period of six years. The content is similar to that of ENAMI, although covering a rather more limited range of issues. This experiment has also been widely publicized as a new way of meeting the challenges of an exporting economy, especially in the case of a company with a high degree of modern technology and a major position in the domestic and international minerals market.

Regarding the Compañía de Teléfonos, the Basic Trust Agreement was signed in 1994, with the objective of establishing fully "participatory" arrangements in the area of human resources, technological innovation, working conditions and others, while at the same time modernizing collective bargaining. The agreement has lasted up to the present, although in this case too there have been various disputes over the application of the agreement and in 1998, some trade unions in the company proposed that it should be revised. However, the Basic Trust Agreement has certainly been a useful tool in modernizing labour relations in a company that controls a very large part of Chile's domestic and international telephone business.

The significance of these four cases was that, in a context where it was hard for trade unions to come up with innovative, wide-ranging proposals on issues that were not just macro-level but addressing very specific aspects of working life in companies, the unions in CODELCO, ENAMI, Disputada and CTC succeeded in showing that in large companies of major importance to the country's economic life, this type of initiative can give positive results and open up new opportunities for trade union action.

If so far there have been no other specific experiences of the kind mentioned above, this approach to trade union action has been increasingly publicized. Indeed, through the national tripartite body, the Productive Development Forum, which includes the CUT (United Workers' Centre), the CPC (Confederación de la Producción y del Comercio, Employers' Confederation) and the government, a number of events to publicize these experiences have been held since 1998, and there have been many cases reported of companies considering putting similar agreements into practice. This is a line of trade union activity which will probably be developed in the future.

Policy on productivity agreements at company level

Of more limited scope than the above, company trade unions have also made serious efforts to incorporate new issues in collective agreements. In particular, there have been many initiatives to have company managements negotiate policies to increase productivity with the trade unions and to consider benefits for the workers when they achieve positive results.

Vergara, 1998, reported that at 30 March 1997, of a total of 2,674 collective agreements in force at national level (collective contracts and agreements), 1415 contained productivity-wage clauses: 42.8 per cent of these agreements concerned large companies (over 200 workers), 33.7 per cent medium-sized companies (50-199 workers) and 23.3 per cent, small enterprises (less than 50 workers).

Vergara's study selected a sample of 46 collective instruments from the above population of 1415 and carried out an in-depth analysis into the selected cases. Of these instruments, 46 per cent had been concluded for periods over two years, which is the minimum term permitted under Chilean law; 32 different formulae for calculating productivity were found. The variables most commonly used to measure productivity in those collective contracts and agreements were volume of production, cost of production and company profits. In 62.5 per cent of cases, the agreement set targets for future productivity, linked to a result in terms of pay. In the remaining 37.5 per cent, the criterion was the profits achieved by the company in a given year compared with the previous 12 months.

The majority of collective contracts and agreements preferred to draw up their terms on the basis of collective results, i.e. for all the company's workers and not on an individual basis. Normally, therefore, average productivity was measured and not that of each worker. An intermediate formula consisted of measuring productivity by work teams within the company and awarding differential benefits to each team.

It is clear that the issue of productivity, quality and its relation to pay and career is becoming a matter for trade union action at company level and this will undoubtedly develop in the future. The reason is that at company level, trade unions are becoming aware that considering the variables of productivity, quality and efficiency when negotiating wages, conditions and work patterns allows them to achieve better results and gives them more opportunity to participate in and influence company decisions. Under the conditions of strong domestic and international competition in which most of them operate and in an open market system, company trade unions are coming to understand that knowledge and management of these variables in collective bargaining at company level strengthens their hand vis-à-vis management and allows them to present options in the context of collective bargaining suited to modern realities.

Policy of agreements on vocational education and training

Another novel approach that has recently been emerging in company trade unions concerns the establishment in companies of bipartite committees (management/unions) to draw up company training plans, to be financed by the tax relief granted to companies by the state for that purpose. These committees were set up under a new law passed at the end of 1997, and by May 1999 a total of 435 companies had set up such committees. Trade unions are still slow to push these initiatives and employers have not shown any particular enthusiasm for them. However, it is estimated that this alternative form of participation in an area of such importance will probably spread, especially as the state offers a financial incentive in the form of tax relief to companies that have this type of bipartite committee.

Summary of company level policies

The experiences described in the preceding sections show that a new realism is emerging in trade union actions and strategies in the face of changes and new conditions in the economy and society in the framework of globalization. Indeed, these experiences concentrate on issues that are of interest to both workers and employers. In this way, even when there is a natural degree of confrontation between them, this type of agenda for collective bargaining seems to be a positive help in getting both sides to reach formal agreement on some of the more complex challenges of economic globalization, such as raising productivity, quality, efficiency and upgrading occupational skills. In addition, given that these approaches are part of the collective bargaining process, they also help to moderate the tendency of companies to impose terms on the above-mentioned matters in individual contracts, without any opportunity for the worker to negotiate them and link them to pay and other benefits.

What seems important is how trade unionists succeed in linking their global policies appropriately and in a coordinated way with those at company level. Up to now, there has been no conflict in theory but, in practice, they have not always proved easy to reconcile, giving the impression of a national leadership operating at macro level, based on a grassroots trade unionism which is developing its own action strategies.

2.3 An overview of labour relations

To conclude this chapter, we would like to quote from a National Labour Survey which was carried out by the Department of Labour, the agency responsible for enforcing labour laws in Chile. This study, undertaken in 1998, gives an interesting overview of labour relations on the basis of a representative national survey, allowing us to have a better understanding of the current background to trade union policies and actions.

In the chapter on "Labour relations: The players' view", we quote the conclusion that:

Both players, employers and workers, mostly agree that their relations are cooperative. In a wide range of questions, both employers and workers are very consistent in that view. Data on disputes (legal or de facto strikes or stoppages) confirm the impression that there is a good labour climate in companies and that open disputes do not occur. These assessments contradict both the leading employers' claims (manifestly anti-trade union) and the constant claims by the CUT of persecution, obstruction and hostility to the unions. This perception opens up an important field for analysis of the real scope for development of institutional relations involving "mutual recognition", as we have called them to define a paradigm of modern labour relations....

A simplistic interpretation might question the "veracity of the collected opinion" and thus close the chapter on it. However, situated as they are in a setting of building relationships, it seems more responsible in our view to examine these opinions of actual players who (unlike the more political players) are engaged in the day-to-day reality of production, and are thus more nuanced and complex than those reflected in postures of a political and ideological nature which have their own logic, rationale and even a certain legitimacy in the political arena.

What the labour survey reflects (as well as the other studies on trade unionism carried out by the Department of Labour) is that even against a background of employers' shortcomings, non-compliance with legislation, conflicts of interest, unsatisfied demands and others, there is scope for collaboration (which does not invalidate the conflict of interests) where the players can agree and establish a framework of dialogue. The reason is that there is no escaping the need in a social organization (such as a company) to maintain certain bonds in order to attain the goals or fulfil the functions for which it exists: workers to obtain remuneration for their work, employers to produce goods or services and make a profit. The true mark of success in a modern company is to reconcile profit and fair reward for labour, because both the productive economy and "civilization" demand quality, competitiveness and intelligence. And that means greater involvement of workers in contributing to the attainment of goals.

Trade unionism is a reality that exists mainly in the largest, strongest and most modern companies, and it acts as a valid counterpart to the employer. Thus, the biggest challenge for trade union action seen against that background is for both employers and workers in smaller companies to understand that there are advantages in institutional relations and that achieving them adds to the modernization of their operations.

There is also a challenge for the leading players, both employers and workers. Social cohesion policies are viable if a more pragmatic view is taken of the unresolved issues and employers' traditional posture of unilaterally imposing the conditions of power. There is an enormous range of urgent and vital issues that need to be addressed to improve the working and living conditions of the majority of the country's workers. There is a process of modernization in progress, which needs to be encouraged and completed if Chile is not once again to become a "case of frustrated development" as a brilliant intellectual once prophesied.

3. Conclusions

3.1 The new directions of social and economic development

The conflicts and challenges facing trade unionism, while reflecting in the short and medium term the situations facing unions during the country's transition since 1990, have deeper roots in the need to find a place in the type of society that is arising as a result of structural changes. The new order involves changes to its traditional social constituency and new concepts of the role of trade unionism.

All of this means that the traditional action model is under review and that trade unionism, at international level, is engaged in a complex pursuit of new ideas and strategies. This naturally generates tensions and uncertainties which, in part at least, explain the difficult and uncertain times we are passing though today. We shall examine this process below.

3.2 Tensions arising from changes in the traditional model of trade union action

The process of shifting from one type of trade union action to another creates tensions in adjusting to the new facts of life. In a world of rapid economic, technological and political change, the social organization of workers has faced enormous challenges in keeping up. It has meant not only developing new forms of representation but also tackling the complex task of re-examining social, economic and political ideas deeply rooted in the trade union world, which were the basis of labour culture for over a century.

Unlike intellectuals, specialists and to some extent politicians, who can respond to change more quickly, social movements need longer because identifying, evaluating and adopting new social, political and cultural approaches and finding new forms of organization and collective action involves an arduous process of consultation with the grassroots. It also means carefully collecting the objective and subjective views arising among the grassroots in the face of change and identifying the costs and opportunities involved. Social movements and trade unions especially are representative players and, thus, they have to express the views of those they represent.

Faced with change, therefore, social movements have traditionally suffered periods of acute tension.

Many analysts, perhaps prematurely, then tend to conclude that these movements and trade unionism in particular, have entered a crisis that might even be terminal. Some thus foresee a kind of dissolution of the role of trade unions in our societies. In my opinion, this conclusion is mistaken, because it focuses on the transitional state, but does not consider the long-term view.

While it is true that evidence at the international level, as well as in Chile, suggests that membership and collective bargaining are tending to decline and that there are difficulties in representing the new classes of workers emerging from the changed economic structure and new patterns of employment, and that the influence of the trade union movement appears less decisive, it is important to look at the factors which explain these situations and the way in which they are generating or forcing change in the rationale of trade union action.

Today, just as at the time when the industrialist model of the economy and society arose, changes are taking place in the old forms of organized labour, the way labour markets are structured and operate, the use of technology, the role of workers and institutionalization of labour. The above is due to the introduction of a new development model, which is changing the industrialist model.

The transition to this new situation involves adjustment and restructuring, sometimes drastic, with severe effects on the old way the economy functioned, resulting in reorganization of many sectors depending on their capacity to adapt to the new competitive conditions in changing markets and to absorb rapid technological change. Thus, the entire culture of labour, company management and labour relations that had grown up is being affected.

This process of material and cultural change sets challenges that are completely new to trade unionism, as they are to many other forms of social representation, but it does not eliminate them. To accept that their disappearance is inevitable would be to accept that society has been absorbed by the market or by the state and has completely lost its ability to act collectively. That hypothesis has no historical or sociological basis.

Our hypothesis, on the contrary, is that we are witnessing a progressive replacement of one type of collective trade union action with another type of action and representation that is seeking a place in the new social, economic, technological and institutional conditions. This change is a complex process, involving a major cultural transformation. The feeling of uncertainty is thus persistent. The certainties of the past still often feel safer to many trade unionists. It is an understandable reaction in a world where the basis of an entire social history is being dramatically overturned.

The fact is, however, that despite this fundamental change, there is no evidence that trade union action has been replaced by a preference for individual action, as suggested by some analyses. Nor is there any evidence of the emergence of other forms of representation apart from trade unions in companies or services, where workers are in a position to act collectively.

Trade unions are undoubtedly facing challenges to their traditional model of action, but they have not been overtaken by other forms of representation or the individual option. On the contrary, trade unionism has survived the fierce attacks unleashed by orthodox neo-liberalism, which defined it simply as an obstacle to the free operation of the market and sought to eliminate it wherever the opportunity arose. That first victory demonstrated the historical, sociological and political truth that society cannot exist without players and thus without negotiation of interests. And it is not an inconsequential fact, since it shows the potential of collective action and its cultural permanence in the world of labour. Trade unionism, although weakened in many areas, under tension, seeking new options, is operating as a player in the process.

Although its action is still defensive and its ability to put forward proposals often limited, this also shows that it continues to be an active partner. The recent example of the countries where trade unions have successfully taken part in social and economic debate confirms the above.

For this reason, it is a player that cannot be excluded from the pursuit of a new consensus in the world of labour. Without collective representation of workers' interests it will be difficult to achieve and maintain such consensus.

Chilean trade unionism is not immune to the situation discussed above. Its crises certainly include local components, but their underlying causes cannot be understood unless they are placed in the context of the contemporary changes we have outlined above. Such a view does not mean that we can ignore the issues of leadership and direction nowadays faced by its top leaders, but they entitle us to take a broad view of this social and cultural phenomenon, and not confine our understanding to a limited economic perception.

3.3 Prospects and challenges for the construction of a new model of action

We shall examine here the emerging international trends which can also be found in Chile, albeit in incipient form and with features specific to national circumstances. We will highlight emerging approaches, since they seem to be an appropriate basis for identifying the lines of action which will influence the strategic development and social policy of Chilean trade unionism in the future.

i. First, the trade union debate shows the beginning of a process of reflection aimed at identifying a new form of trade union action, designed to absorb change without abandoning its identity as a movement which represents a social class: the workers. The debate that is beginning concerns the identity and definition of this social class in contemporary terms. It is necessary to decide how to represent its interests without abandoning the traditional nature of social representation, yet accepting that the sociological concept of the workers has lost its specific meaning. This core idea, that trade union action means representation of a social class, is extremely valuable in countering the argument advanced by orthodox neo-liberalism and post-modernist cultures, that modern society is defined by individualism and denial of the existence of class interests. If trade unionism, as a result of this reflection, manages to absorb the new economic, technical and political facts of life, take up the gauntlet of change, but at the same time reassert its traditional involvement in guiding that change and representing workers' interests, it will probably succeed in reconciling its traditions with the challenges of the future. This seems important because in its defence of the social class it represents there is an adversarial dimension to trade unionism which society needs to preserve as a counterweight to economic power and state power. That is why, just as it is necessary for all social forces to be represented in the political system in order to ensure pluralism and act as a safeguard, the same capacity must be ensured in labour relations.

ii. Second, the younger leaders especially value the development of a vision which is more consistent with relations between the economy and social results. This, too, is significant, since the characteristic that in the past marked not only the trade union view but also the political and intellectual views of the so-called progressive sectors, was emphasis on the distribution of the fruits of development and an aspiration to egalitarianism. But that vision, although unquestioned from the point of view of inequalities and the need for social integration, overlooked or paid less attention to the need for growth and the requirement for regulation to achieve the necessary balances in a healthy economy within a legal framework. Thus, for example, the growth in wages and stable employment were often approached as variables which were relatively independent of other factors such as productive investment, labour productivity and the need to adjust the economy, including labour, to market cycles. Increasing wages and ensuring stable jobs for the employed seemed more linked to the political will to achieve it than the capacity to generate sustained growth to achieve those results. This one-dimensional view has its counterpart in that other, neo-liberal, one-dimensional view, that growth alone provides access to opportunities for progress and quality of life. It is thus encouraging to see that trade union thinking is moving towards a multi-dimensional vision which combines the idea of growth with integration and distribution, i.e. with fairness. Development is thus viewed at the same time as a step in the direction of sustained growth and as active policies for generating greater opportunities for a better quality of life for all. This multi-dimensional view is also expressed in the design of a labour policy towards which the new trade union view appears to be moving steadily closer. Under the old approach, labour policy often tends to be seen as the "social" part of economic policy. A kind of counterweight. If the former imposed limits and restrictions, the latter should provide protection against them. Under the new approach, trade unionism is trying to combine growth policy with labour policy, seeking to ensure that both follow the same path in creating sustained growth and distribution of the results, but sharing restrictions and possibilities.

iii. Third, the idea that achieving a greater share of trade union power and participation was in itself sufficient to produce decisions favourable to workers' interests is being questioned. From that point of view (and this is new), restrictions on the functioning of the economy tended to be seen as variables relatively dependent on power and political will, i.e. manageable by these factors. Experience of trade union action seems to have shown that political will is not enough in itself to manage these restrictions and that it is also necessary to accept reasonable criteria for setting objective limits to regulate the economy, which may act as a counterweight to political will. The goals of controlling inflation and linking incomes to productivity, two of today's key themes, demonstrate this. It can also be seen that trade union thinking considers that such regulation cannot be effective unless it is the result of decisions based on fundamental consensus between the players concerned: workers, employers, consumers and various political representatives. The view is thus emerging that political will must be subject to the negotiation of stable support for economic decisions.

iv. Fourth, as shown by the seminars organized by the Productive Development Forum in 1987, a new culture in relationships within the company is emerging. In the seminars, designed to present successful examples of labour relations in real companies, it was noteworthy that the company was identified as the favoured level to deal with technological change, changes in work organization and the new forms of competitiveness and quality affecting working life. In the present circumstances of international competition and rapid technological change, companies have the first direct experience of the changes that later appear as more general phenomena. The role of collective agreements and new management methods is coming to be appreciated as an important area for trade union action in developing new labour relations, as a basis for more general debate, at branch or national level, on critical issues such as flexibility and deregulation. The above does not mean that the sectoral or national level will not continue to be considered as an important strategic level on many matters, but it shows that trade unionism is placing greater value on action at company level.

v. Fifth, the trade union debate concerns the development of forms of representation consistent with the new economic, technical and social conditions. This has been discussed in many meetings with federations and trade unions organized recently by the Ebert Foundation, among others. The meetings highlighted analyses suggesting the value of reviewing the structure of representation peculiar to the industrialist model. The review coincides with the search for a new enterprise culture, which gives a greater role to this level, seeking to link it more closely with the branch and national levels. But other areas of innovation seem to be emerging. These include concern for more democratic methods of choosing leaders. This is because the leadership crisis currently facing trade unionism in Chile has shown that it is becoming more and more urgent to identify the type of representatives suited to the new classes of workers emerging from the technical and organizational change.

The above considerations are leading many national trade union leaders to suggest that greater attention should be paid to leadership within companies, strengthening the trade union career path from the bottom up. It is hoped in this way to strengthen the link between middle and higher management, and also to create a type of representative firmly linked to the new processes of change and capable of meeting their demands.

In addition, in the regions and major federations, the idea is emerging that it is necessary to try greater decentralization, so that the local and regional levels of branch federations acquire greater ability to establish horizontal links between unions within and between branches, and with public and private authorities at that level. If this can mature into a new trend, it may allow a better examination of labour markets and other issues linked to access to services in health, housing, pre-school care, training and other matters. The organization of trade union solidarity, one of the major tasks of trade unionism, may find new areas to work in.

Another subject that emerged in the trade union and specialist seminars was how to strengthen trade unionism in a manner consistent with the new types of contracting. It is necessary to pay more attention to the requirements and specific characteristics of casual, migrant, piece-and subcontract workers, which differ from the traditional permanent company union representation. Given that the trade union base may constantly have to change with this type of worker, the value of strengthening their capacity of representation within the federation and national level is a crucial element. Moreover, it is precisely in these new sectors that anti-trade union behaviour by many employers is most prevalent, which underlines the need to strengthen workers' organization.

In general, decentralizing and diversifying the trade union structure, while maintaining the links between the three traditional levels (grassroots, branch and national) seems to be an important criterion emerging from the new debate.

All the above probably requires the design of appropriate bodies at federation and national level to coordinate and develop the new forms of decentralization and diversification. But at this level, perhaps the biggest challenge is to consolidate a stable institutional framework that combines adjustment to the new forms of representation described above with growing technical expertise to support federation and grassroots activities, especially in collective bargaining, as well as being able to make proposals concerning major national issues. The national level can thus be a key area for the formulation of global strategies, to guide trade union action implemented through a more decentralized and diversified structure. The national trade union leadership must play a role that is more about strategic policy and national coordination, supported by better developed structures at federation and company level. Monitoring of technical and economic change will no longer be just a macro issue, but increasingly the result of individual observation at the face of productive activity and services. Such observation will allow the elaboration of new conceptual approaches, identification of the demands of the emerging classes of workers and the construction of a pattern of representation suited to the challenges of a changing society.

Bibliography

Campero, G. 1982. *El sindicalismo Chileno: Un intento de interpretación y perspectiva.* Discussion Paper, num. ILET. Chile.

—. 1993. *Sindicalismo en los 90: Desafíos y perspectivas.* Revista del Trabajo. PET, num. 3. Santiago, Chile.

—. 1999. *La cuestión laboral en el Mercosur: Procesos, opciones y posibilidades.* Friedrich Ebert Foundation. Santiago.

—.; Cuevas A. (eds.). 1990. «Sindicatos y transición democrática», in *El Sindicalismo Latinoamericano en los 90.* Vol. 1 PLANETA-ISCOS-CLACSO.

—.; Flisfish, A.; Tironi, E.; Tokman, V. 1993. *Los actores sociales en el nuevo orden laboral* (Ediciones Dolmen, Sep.).

Department of Labour. *Trade union statistics*, 1980-1997.

Department of Labour, Department of Research. 1998. *National Labour Survey (ENCLA), Dec.*

Guglielmetti, P. 1999. *Las reformas económicas y su impacto en el empleo y las relaciones de trabajo* (Centre for Public Policy Analysis, University of Chile, Santiago).

ILO. 1998. *Evolución del empleo en Chile 1986 - 1996. (Employment trends in Chile 1986 - 1996)* (Santiago).

Isla, Tarud, Jorquera.1978. *Trade union statistics*. Department of Labour Relations and Organization Studies (DERTO), (University of Chile).

Milet, P.; Gaspar, G.; Rojas, F. 1997. *Chile-Mercosur: Una alianza estratégica.* (Flacso - Chile, Editorial Los Andes), Aug.

National Institute of Statistics. *National employment survey.* 1970-1996. Linked/new series.

Toloza, C.; Lahera, E. (eds.). 1998. «Organización sindical y relaciones laborales», in *Chile en los noventa,* (Office of the President of the Republic, Dolmen Ediciones), Mar.

Vergara, M. 1998. *Incremento de remuneraciones asociados a aumento de productividad (Productivity-linked wage rises),* Aporter al Debate Laboral. (Dept. of Labour, Research Dept.), Sep.

Walker, F.; Arrau, A. 1993. *Las relaciones de trabajo en el Chile de hoy.* Programme of Labour Relations (University of Chile. Labour Relations Series, No. 1), Oct.

Union responses to a changing environment: The *New Histadrut* – The General Federation of Labour in Israel

Roby Nathanson and Associates

1. Introduction

The Histadrut was founded 80 years ago as a surrogate for the state administration which did not exist at that time. Even after the State of Israel was founded in 1948, the Histadrut continued to play a general economic and social role in expanding the industrial sector and providing health care, including medical insurance. Especially during the early years, the Histadrut continued to fulfil many national functions, such as immigrant absorption, rural settlement, and industrialization. Its role in those areas gradually diminished, but its involvement continued to affect the organization, in various ways and degrees, until the end of 1994. Only when the *National Health Insurance Law* of 1995 separated the Histadrut from health care did the organization become predominantly a trade union.

Considering the singular role played by the Histadrut, one that went far beyond any model of trade unionism, it is impossible to detail its history or the evolution of its structure and policies in one short report.[1] Therefore, we must limit ourselves to summarizing the milestones in its recent development. We include a very brief review of the Histadrut prior to 1995, as background to the current special difficulties it confronts in addition to the challenges facing trade unions in general.

---

[1] The Histadrut has been discussed extensively in many works. See for example: Tabb, J.Y. et al: (1961), *Industrial relations in Israel*, Dvir. Tel-Aviv (Hebrew); Shirom, A.: (1983), *An introduction to industrial relations in Israel*, Am Oved, Tel-Aviv (Hebrew); Bartal, G.: (1991) *The General Histadrut, structure and functions*, Histadrut Publications, Tel-Aviv (Hebrew); Galin, A.; Harel, A.: (1978) *Development and change in the industrial relations system in Israel*, Massada (Hebrew); Tabb, J.Y.; Goldfarb, A.: (1971) *Workers' participation in management*, Pergamon Press. Sobel, I.: (1963) "Israel", in Calenson, W. (ed.): *Labor in developing economies*, University of California Press.

1.1 Background: The Histadrut prior to 1995

Before 1995, the Histadrut's main characteristics were its broad membership base and its diverse objectives. Many different units were gathered under its roof. These units often had little in common with traditional trade unionism and some of them could even be considered incompatible with each other or with trade union goals.

Spheres of activity

The Histadrut's main spheres of activity, as expressed in its major subdivisions, were:

Provision of health care: The General Sickness Fund (*Kupat Holim Klalit*), established as an organ of the Histadrut in 1923, remains the largest sickness fund and health care organization in Israel. Until the *National Health Insurance Law* was enacted in 1995 it was the only fund that accepted members regardless of their socioeconomic status or medical condition. It runs hospitals, convalescent homes, neighbourhood clinics and specialized medical facilities throughout the country.

Economic development and employment: This was primarily the function of the economic division (*Hevrat Haovdim*). Established in 1923, it was originally designed as a mechanism for creating employment and providing services to Jewish immigrants in Israel. It included manufacturing, construction, marketing, banking and insurance concerns owned by the Histadrut (known as *The Institutional Economy*). It also included what was termed the "cooperative sector", owned directly by the members. The "cooperative sector" includes the kibbutzim and moshavim (at that time agricultural settlements) as well as their marketing organizations. The dual function of trade union organization and industrial ownership were a feature of the Histadrut for more than 40 years after the establishment of the State of Israel. *Hevrat Haovdim* provided steady employment, and sometimes the only employment in peripheral townships; it was also a leader in establishing fair working conditions. It has been argued that the recession in Israel in the mid-1980s revealed many of the organization's inefficiencies. The consequent reorganization, concluded in the early 1990s, resulted in a gradual privatization of the Histadrut-owned "economy."

Trade unionism: Histadrut members are assigned to individual trade unions according to economic branch, occupation and/or employer. In 1994, there were 44 national trade unions, of which 19 were based on occupation/profession (engineers, social workers, artists, etc.), 19 on industrial branch (textiles and clothing, metals and electronics, construction), and six on employer (government employees, civilian employees of the Israel Defence Forces, etc.). Trade union activity was coordinated by the Trade Union

Division. Contrary to practice in most unions, membership in the Histadrut was general, i.e. individuals joined the cover organization as such, rather than a specific trade union. Afterwards, they were assigned to a union, according to their occupation and/or place of work. Formally, members belonged to a single trade union, but this assignment was a complex procedure because multiple, parallel bases of membership existed (for example, an engineer in industry could be placed according to profession or industrial branch).The trade unions were represented at local level by Histadrut councils, known as local Works Councils (numbering 72 in 1994) and by shop committees in the separate firms. Legally, the Histadrut organs – not the shop committees – represent the workers.

Women's rights: In addition to a special department in the Trade Union Division devoted to women's employment issues, a separate organization, *Na'amat,* was established to promote women's issues and rights in all spheres of life. In addition to proposing legislation and campaigning for gender equality, *Na'amat* operates a chain of subsidized daycare centres and kindergartens as a service for working women.

Social security: The Histadrut established pension funds for workers based on contributions from employers and employees. It owns and operates a chain of relatively inexpensive retirement homes and provides low-interest loans for the needy.

Other services: Additional divisions of the Histadrut structure provided other services, which either supplemented or parallelled state services. The most significant divisions were: culture and education; vocational training; youth movements; athletics; consumer protection; immigrant absorption and development; religious affairs; and many more.

Internal structure

Before 1995, the Histadrut was geographically dispersed, although decision-making power rested with a small number of highly centralized internal institutions.

By 1994, the Histadrut employed a staff of almost 4,000 in its central organizations and local councils, not including the General Sickness Fund, the Economic Division, social security and pension fund administration, the staff of schools and day care centres, or most of the representatives to national and local conventions.

The elected central institutions were the major governing and policy-making organs at national level. These were the National Convention, the Council, the Executive Committee which elected the Central Committee and the Secretary-General. Each national trade union had separate but parallel elected institutions as well, as did *Na'amat, Kupat Holim* and a number of other organizations.

The Histadrut implemented its policy through 72 local councils which attended to most of the functions described, except for health care (handled by *Kupat Holim*)and economic activity (executed through *Hevrat Haovdim* enterprises). Each local council had an elected local (or regional) convention, council, secretariat and secretary. Elected or assigned officials acted as the administrators.

Local shop committees were established in every agency or firm where the Histadrut had organized the workers and where collective agreements were in effect. The shop committees represented the Histadrut, but were not part of its administration.

Elections for the conventions (Histadrut and local council) were run according to political party affiliation. This means that the number of delegates sent by each party to the convention represents the proportion of the total vote won by that party. The parties tend to be identified with the major political parties active in Israel's national political arena. This means that Histadrut elections are related to the political strength and platform of the national parties, and are often lively events. The Histadrut Secretary-General, who used to be the number one candidate of the winning party, was formally elected by the Executive Committee. In all elections until May 1994, the Labour Party won an absolute majority and governed the Histadrut.

Membership

Officially and legally, the Histadrut was a voluntary association with membership decided on an individual basis. Before the *National Health Insurance Law (1995)* was passed, one first had to be a member of the Histadrut and the General Sickness Fund in order to join a trade union. The reverse was also true: in order to belong to the General Sickness Fund, one had to be a member of the Histadrut and thus of a trade union, or at least pay membership dues and hold a Histadrut membership card. For the majority of members, the chief motivation for joining the Histadrut was not the benefit of trade unionism but of medical care.

The General Sickness Fund, reflecting Histadrut ideology, accepted members regardless of their socioeconomic and medical condition, whereas other funds imposed selective criteria stipulating age, medical history, and a minimum income. In consequence, the members of the General Sickness Fund and of the Histadrut came from all strata of Israeli society. They included salaried workers, the self-employed, the unemployed, pensioners, and housewives.

In keeping with the policy of intersecting membership, official Histadrut membership data were based on registered members or, at best, dues-paying members, irrespective of which organization attracted the individual to join. Hence, prior to 1995, there were no reliable data regarding trade union membership. Many Histadrut members did not even know that they belonged to a trade union.

Membership dues: Dues were progressive, according to income, and paid directly to the Histadrut. Payments were transmitted either individually or collectively to the Histadrut "Tax Bureau", which also served as a records bureau. In organized workplaces (i.e., where a Histadrut-negotiated collective agreement was in place) non-members who benefited from the agreement paid an organization fee of 1 per cent.

The Histadrut would allocate a budget to its various activities, including the trade unions, which were, and still are, directly dependent upon the Histadrut budget for funding their daily activities. Prior to 1995, most of the membership dues (73 per cent) were dedicated to health care.

Influence and power relations

As the main labour representative in Israel, supplying services to the majority of the population, the Histadrut has historically played a major role in industrial relations. The fact that the Labour Party was in government until 1977 appears to have contributed to the Histadrut accumulation of power. Among its achievements are an acceptable level of pay and improved working conditions for all employees. These benefits were obtained through general collective agreements and through Histadrut influence on labour policy. For example, the *Minimum Wage Law (1987)* and the *Paid Sick Leave Law (1976)* began as a section in the general collective agreement; later, as a result of Histadrut pressure on the social lobby in the Knesset, the provisions were reformulated and passed as legislation. Yet, even without specific legislation, the conditions negotiated within the framework of collective agreements affected the country's entire labour market. Job security, always an important issue in Israeli labour relations, particularly in the public sector, is another area where Histadrut achievements have influenced policy throughout the economy. The Histadrut has succeeded in negotiating very rigid dismissal requirements for tenured workers. In the organized business sector, dismissals have also become a lengthy process, requiring the agreement of the workers' representatives with respect to individual cases.

We should note here that no specific law concerning freedom of association or trade unionism in general has ever been enacted: in the past, no institutional framework seemed necessary as the strength of the Histadrut appears to have been taken for granted. There seemed to be general agreement that the Histadrut was sufficiently powerful to protect its representatives and prevent any attempt to interfere with free association.

The status of the Histadrut in collective bargaining and in labour disputes is addressed in two laws passed in 1957. According to the provisions of these laws, the Histadrut is practically the only representative organization on these concerns in places of work.

The crisis of 1995: The situation of the Histadrut changed radically with the enactment of the *National Health Insurance Law* in 1994 (it came into force in 1995). This law severed the link between the trade union organization and the provision of health care services. It meant that the Histadrut now had to attract members on its own merits. Separating the General Sickness Fund from the trade union movement removed the basic motivation for mass membership in the Histadrut. Individual membership was automatically cancelled, and with it the flow of funds from these individuals. The status of collective membership became uncertain as the agreements concerning the automatic payment of dues were no longer in force, as of January1995. In effect, the Histadrut had to start recruiting members for a new organization, whose future functions were unclear.

An added element of uncertainty was the fall from power of the Labour Party. For the first time in its history, the Labour Party lost the Histadrut elections in 1994, and a new inexperienced coalition began to rule the organization. Consequently, the new environment has meant a great deal more for the New Histadrut (the name taken by the organization after the 1994 change in leadership) than it does for most trade unions in the industrialized world. Globalization, enhanced competition, technological change, new employment methods and changing characteristics of the labour force are all international trends faced by the New Histadrut but the organization also has to cope with changes in the services it may offer its members. The Histadrut has been compelled, therefore, to "reinvent" itself in a political, structural and economic environment which is less than supportive. The financial costs of transition are becoming increasingly burdensome, especially in view of the deficit accumulated before 1995, by the Histadrut and the General Sickness Fund, part of which still has to be repaid by the New Histadrut.

Thus, we have to take into account the special circumstances of the changing internal environment of the New Histadrut as a central factor in the organization's adaptation strategy. It has become increasingly difficult to differentiate between the Histadrut response to the special circumstances forced upon it as of 1995 and the general challenges facing the trade union movement. It is safe to surmise that a significant part of its response is the effect of the battle for survival. One unfortunate result is the downsizing of its research institution and the cancellation of its longitudinal surveys of labour conditions and the labour market. As a result, information regarding the New Histadrut as an organization and Histadrut functioning as a trade union has become scarce.

1.2 The external environment

Israel's political and economic systems are changing in a way that is having a negative impact on the New Histadrut's status and influence. The traditional partners in the industrial relations system may not necessarily have altered their attitudes towards unionization in general. However, since the late 1980s, fresh impediments have appeared in the organization's external environment that threaten to undermine the *modus vivendi* formerly achieved.

The government

For the past 20 years, all Israeli governments have advocated privatization and increased competition. This policy has been carried out more vigorously of late. Even in corporations still owned by the government, the threat of private ownership and competition dominate planning and policy making. Privatization has already been introduced to some degree in communications and banking. Plans to privatize the nation's electric power company, public transport, seaports and many other activities are being discussed.

Developments of this order always involve the reorganization of employment relations and changes in personnel, particularly under the banner of increased efficiency. According to the common assumption, efficient management involves flexibility in the use of resources, including human resources. Flexibility with respect to human resources has three main aspects: the number of workers, their skills, and labour allocation in terms of time. All three aspects can be considered as obstacles to the stable long-term employment of the same workers in the same occupations. Employer insistence on flexibility raises strong demands for reduced regulation of the labour market, a position opposed to that of the Histadrut's traditional and firm demand for a stable working environment for its members. Moreover, this policy threatens to erode the possibility of long-term employment relationships, the traditional basis of union strength.

Below are some of the main elements of current labour policy.

- For various reasons, the government, as an employer, has introduced an unwritten policy of reducing the proportion of permanent, tenured employees in the public service. The government is hiring more and more of its employees through temporary manpower agencies. Such workers are extremely difficult to organize.
- The official position taken by the government in the course of wage negotiations has been consistent and unyielding during the last few years. The only concession it is willing to grant is to maintain the real wage. Economic recession and high unemployment rates (8.6 per cent in 1998) are used to justify this position.
- Government opposition to strong unions is apparent from steps it has proposed that would restrict a union's right to call a strike in the public

sector. Israel's proposed *Government Budget Act (1999)* includes clauses limiting the right to strike and curbing the unions' decision-making power with respect to strikes. The proposed Act includes an amendment to the *Labour Dispute Act (1957)*, stipulating that the representative trade union has no power to call a strike until such a strike is approved through a vote, by secret ballot, in which at least half the employees of the agency participate.

The employers

Employers in the business sector have been seriously affected by globalization, enhanced competition in their product markets, and technological change. They claim that part of their strategy for survival is flexibility in the allocation of human resources. The present recession and unemployment rates appear to validate these claims.

- Consequently, employers are resolutely demanding reduced regulation of the labour market, which implies less favourable conditions for steady employment and easier dismissal terms. When they fail to modify the regulations concerning present employees, employers attempt to initiate second-generation contracts for new recruits. The second-generation contracts usually include less favourable working conditions and more flexible provisions for dismissal (for instance, shorter periods of notice, reduced involvement of the shop committee and the Histadrut).
- Technological change and the reorganization of production systems make it possible to introduce a variety of employment relationships, such as subcontracting, outsourcing and individual employment contracts.
- The need for flexibility is being used as an argument against the employment of permanent, tenured workers at all levels. Many employers have begun to use temporary employment agencies to provide employees for long-term positions, not just for temporary jobs. This provides maximum flexibility without, as a rule, incurring higher labour costs. Other modes of employment used to avoid collective agreements are subcontracting and individual contracts.
- As a result, Histadrut status and influence in the business sector has declined substantially. Like most trade unions, the traditional stronghold of the Histadrut was large enterprises, with a stable body of employees in the same workplace at the same time. In such enterprises, employees have common interests and are relatively easy to reach and organize. The new employment practices are reducing this body of employees; hence, the source of union support has diminished.

The workers

In consequence of the trends described above, the prevalence of atypical forms of employment is growing steadily in Israel. Employees hired under these conditions pose special difficulties for trade unions because they can be recruited only as individuals. As the terms of collective agreements made by the unions do not directly affect them, their motivation to join is ambiguous.

Individual employment contracts are now more common than ever. The Histadrut, which formerly objected strongly to individual contracts, and which had the power to prevent their expansion, has introduced clauses specifying quotas for such contracts within its collective agreements, primarily with respect to managerial positions. A survey conducted in 1993 found that 36 per cent of the employees questioned were under individual contract. Individual contracts are prevalent in small workplaces in the informal sector, in hi-tech enterprises and in managerial positions in most sectors.

Another popular approach is to recruit through temporary employment agencies. Such workers enjoy neither steady employment nor a permanent place of work. There are no accurate estimates of the number of employees hired through these agencies but from all indications, the phenomenon is expanding rapidly. Temporary employees are a difficult population for trade unions to organize because they are highly mobile between places of work, and they do not work under their direct employer at the same site.

The terms of employment are also affected by the characteristics of young people now joining Israel's labour force. This generation is significantly different from the previous ones, and the entry of the young means an increasingly diversified labour force. They are better educated, more career-oriented, individualistic and less motivated by class interests and solidarity. They reflect changing public and political attitudes towards trade unions, namely a weakened commitment to unionization founded in solidarity. This generation of workers is therefore less motivated to join a trade union and more inclined to look critically at the potential benefits of membership.

The legal system

The involvement of labour courts in industrial relations has increased as the role of collective bargaining has declined.

- The Union of Newspaper Employees requested an injunction against the *Ha'aretz* newspaper's policy of hiring new employees through individual contracts (1996). The National Labour Relations Court did not admit the claim and did not consider the existence of a collective agreement as a factor preventing employment by means of individual contracts in the same workplace. The Court stated that such a practice would be considered illegal only if the collective agreement contained a clause excluding any alternative method of employment. This ruling is intended to protect employers' prerogatives regarding managerial functions.

- On the other hand, the courts have considered the dismissal of permanent employees in favour of individual contract workers as a unilateral substantive change in working conditions that poses a real threat to workers and their representative organization. The courts have acknowledged the trade union right to take collective action, including strikes, against what they consider unlawful dismissal.
- No specific laws concerning the rights and obligations of labour organizations have been enacted in Israel. The Supreme Court, in its role as court of appeal, has recently defined the characteristics of a *bona fide* trade union. One of the fundamental criteria listed in its ruling is that the main objective of a labour organization is to promote the interests of its members, as workers, by negotiating collective agreements. This expresses trade unionism in its traditional sense. It also means that any organization attempting to promote workers' interests solely by rendering individual services and legal counselling cannot qualify as a trade union. However, it is doubtful if an organization devoted exclusively to collective bargaining would be viable in a segmented labour market.

2.   Membership data —Trends in union density

The longitudinal measurement of membership rates in the Histadrut poses serious difficulties due to the redefinition of membership effective as of 1995. The data concerning membership prior to 1995 do not represent union density for they do not represent membership based on trade union interests. With the separation of the General Sickness Fund from the New Histadrut in 1995, one of the major motives for joining the Histadrut was eliminated. Therefore, post-1995 membership is a better indicator of union membership, although it still includes a significant proportion of non-workers, particularly pensioners. Nevertheless, the vast majority of current members are working in firms or organizations where the (New) Histadrut has negotiated collective agreements that include the payment of dues and an organization tax deduction.

In the absence of a better measure, the right to vote in the (New) Histadrut general election is used as the basis of the comparative data presented below. There has been a gradual decrease in the proportion of Histadrut members in the adult population, from 61 per cent in 1981 to 47 per cent in 1994, with no significant change in the absolute number of members. The 1998 data indicate a 60 per cent decline in the number of members, for the reasons stated previously. This decline confirms the conclusion that the gradual weakening of the Histadrut as a central factor in industrial relations has accelerated as of 1995.

It is safe to conclude that membership in the New Histadrut rests between 30-35 per cent of all salaried employees, with a rate of about 25 per cent in the business sector and 50 per cent in the public sector.

2.1 Strategies for organizing new target populations

Many of the employees in Israel's labour market constitute new target populations for the New Histadrut. In 1995, individual membership was automatically cancelled and had to be renewed by all members who wished it to continue. (The situation for members covered by collective agreements was different – their membership was extended, unless specifically revoked by the member.) Among the target populations for unionization efforts are workers considered as difficult to organize, especially newer entrants to the labour force. These groups include women, young people, high-level professionals, workers in the informal sector, and temporary workers. Recruitment on an individual basis is impracticable when the organization cannot offer real benefits. This point is discussed in section 3. Accordingly, the main recruiting effort is aimed at negotiating new collective agreements and extending existing agreements.

A general recruitment campaign was initiated by the New Histadrut on 29 June 1997, before the 1998 general elections. This national "marketing campaign" engaged senior officials and was conducted in the workplaces. The campaign was later extended until 9 September 1997. Workers joining the New Histadrut before the elections, which were held on 9 June 1998, were granted the right to vote in these elections.

Recruitment at individual level is difficult to accomplish. There is little motivation for an individual to join, as the advantages of such membership are not immediately obvious. One appropriate measure is to use local or district council officials who are familiar with potential members. This tactic has not been particularly effective because of the lack of incentives for local staff members to engage in massive recruitment efforts. An important reason for this reluctance is the fact that the dues received go directly to the central Histadrut rather than to the local labour councils. However, in the long term, the capacity to mobilize new members will depend on the New Histadrut's ability to deliver significant results in terms of improved benefits to current members.

As the dominant activity of the New Histadrut has become trade unionism, greater emphasis is being given to collective and individual legal counselling, at local and national level. Many functions previously fulfilled by the Histadrut as an umbrella organization are now relatively neglected. Some of the national unions, especially those in occupational and academic sectors, continue to give high priority to investment in human capital, by organizing and subsidizing vocational training courses. Others are offering consumer benefits through agreements with credit card companies or even individual suppliers. Efforts to unionize newer target populations focus on women, casual or temporary workers and individual contract workers.

Women workers - Special considerations

Women make up about 43 per cent of the civilian labour force in Israel. Until 1995, the proportion of female Histadrut members reflected the proportion of women in the entire population. However, this was not a measure of trade union ability to recruit female workers, as housewives could also be members. In the elections held on 10 May 1994, women comprised 52.6 per cent of those eligible to vote.

The New Histadrut continues to incorporate two organs focusing on women's issues. These are a section of the Trade Union Department which deals with the rights and special working conditions of employed women; and *Na'amat*, the Movement of Working Women and Volunteers, which deals with women's issues in all areas of life.

Women's representation in New Histadrut institutions: The Convention of the New Histadrut includes 3001 members. To ensure more equitable representation, each list of candidates proposed by the internal factions has to include at least 30 per cent women and at least 30 per cent men, i.e. among every ten candidates, there have to be at least three men and three women. It has been recommended that other elected institutions adopt the same system.

The issues concerning working women are high on the agenda of the New Histadrut and *Na'amat*. Their special concerns, such as daycare for children, working hours, training facilities and representation in union leadership are regularly addressed.

The subject of gender equality at work was recognized by the New Histadrut's House of Representatives as the direct responsibility of the New Histadrut. The recommendations prepared by a special subcommittee include an acknowledgement of the contribution of women's labour and a statement of the organization's commitment to equal opportunity and the promotion of women's participation in the labour market. The recommendations are listed below.

- The New Histadrut should exert a direct influence on the educational system. It is proposed to create a lobby pressing for a reformulation of the traditional male-dominant value system in the school curriculum and for the provision of services, such as an extended school day and pre-school education for children aged three to four, free of charge;

- The New Histadrut should emphasize training and education to enhance women's ability to contribute at all levels of the labour market;

- Women should be represented in all union institutions, making up at least 30 per cent of all delegates.
- In order to execute these resolutions in the workplace, local bodies composed of representatives of the trade union, the Department for Employed Women in the Trade Union Division, *Na'amat*, and shop committees, should be established.
- Bilateral (Histadrut– employer) frameworks should be established to supervise implementation of the existing legislation and to draw up new legislation in this area.
- In August 1997, the New Histadrut leadership endorsed the subcommittee's recommendation to include a clause requiring equal pay, promotional opportunity and allocation of responsibility in the workplace within every collective agreement to be negotiated henceforth.

Na'amat, together with other social welfare and women's lobbies, was active in preparing important legislation concerning sexual harassment in the workplace (1998). Beyond the fact that the Act defines harassment in quite broad terms, the activities surrounding its passage focused public attention on this important issue.

Na'amat was also influential in amending the *Women's Employment Act (1954)* to ensure that a woman returning to work after taking maternity leave cannot be dismissed for a period of at least 45 days.

Casual workers

The use of temporary contract labour (or subcontracting) is growing as the need for flexibility in human resources is recognized by Israeli employers. No reliable data are available on the phenomenon in general or on the scope of employment through temporary manpower agencies. However, recourse to casual or temporary labour is known to be very widespread in the private sector. The public service sector and the government are also important users of labour contracted through temporary employment agencies. The government has refused to engage in negotiations with the Histadrut over the employment of temporary labour in the public administration despite the effect of this practice on established labour relations. In Israel, this arrangement does not appear to represent a short-term solution to labour shortages and a "temporary worker" may be employed for indefinite periods of time.

The Histadrut has always strongly opposed any sort of non-collective labour relations, especially in organizations where collective agreements are in force. In the past, it was able to restrict the number of workers not covered by agreements to an insignificant proportion of the workforce. The rationale for this position was twofold, based on orderly labour relations on the one hand, and union interests on the other. First, the employment of direct employees and temporary contract labour in the same organization or firm, especially for long periods of time, undermines the capacity of the union to negotiate for equal working conditions. Second, temporary workers are difficult to organize because of high turnover rates. Even if the manpower agencies, as employers, are party to the collective agreements negotiated with the New Histadrut, the coexistence of two standards for determining working conditions is usually detrimental to both workers and the union. In addition, even if it has a collective agreement with the manpower agency, the New Histadrut does not represent agency workers vis-à-vis management in the actual place of work, a fact that weakens the New Histadrut's position as a labour representative. At present, the threat of transferring staffing responsibilities to manpower agencies is a salient element in the background of negotiations.

Initially, the Histadrut tried to resist the introduction of temporary contract labour by turning to the labour relations courts. But the courts, including the Supreme Court, have affirmed the right of employers to take on temporary workers. A collective agreement may include clauses that prohibit temporary labour in the workplace but, if not specifically included in the terms of the contract, employers may choose any employment relation they wish. Recently, the National Labour Relations Court did recognize the legitimacy of employee resistance to changes "in the fabric of labour relations" initiated by the transfer of responsibility for recruiting part of the workforce to contractors.

Although resort to legal procedures has failed to halt the trend, the New Histadrut has yet to take the serious organizational steps necessary to prevent the expansion of temporary employment. It has often made demands aimed at limiting the phenomenon during negotiations, but employers have rarely agreed to its terms. In effect, although the existing laws do encourage temporary manpower agencies to negotiate collective agreements with their employees, a number of factors are impeding the process. Because casual workers are scattered among numerous places of work, and are easily replaceable, there are practical difficulties in organizing and representing them. (This also applies to public sector temporary workers, although the sector is usually amenable to labour organization). The bargaining power of this segment is relatively low, at least partly because manpower agencies succeed by offering lower labour costs to employers than those entailed by direct employment. Nevertheless, about 40 special collective agreements have been concluded between the New Histadrut and the temporary manpower agencies in their role as subcontractors (1998). One measure encouraging the agencies to sign such agreements is *The Law of Employment by Temporary Employment Agencies (1996)*. According to this law, agency employees who have worked for three consecutive years in the same place of work, must be given working conditions equal to those of the subcontracting firm's regular employees, unless the agency itself has negotiated its own collective agreement.

The New Histadrut, although it does not organize the workers directly, shares the interest of the agency with respect to signing collective agreements. Such agreements include the standard clause concerning union dues. The firm deducts union dues from New Histadrut members and organization taxes from non-members, both of which are transferred to the New Histadrut. The agreements benefit the employees as they guarantee minimum working conditions, such as notice of dismissal, pension rights after a designated period of employment, and paid sick leave. Most of the provisions correspond to the legal minimum, with the exception of pension rights. The agreements do not as yet ensure job security – the worker may still be dismissed at will. Nor do they ensure continuity of actual employment through the agency. Thus, during those periods when a temporary employment agency neither supplies work nor pays the workers, the employees are not entitled to unemployment insurance because they are presumably employed – by the agency.

There is some criticism of these contracts. It has been claimed that by reaching collective agreements with temporary employment agencies, the New Histadrut has, for the first time, recognized the legitimacy of these alternative employment methods. This step is considered detrimental to the workforce in general and damaging to the standing of the organization as a labour representative in particular.

Individual contracts

Worker solidarity and equal working conditions were the cornerstone of the Histadrut's traditional strong opposition to individual employment contracts. This ideology was also the basis of its attempts to include the majority of employees in the framework of general collective agreements. Employees holding individual contracts have always been able to join the New Histadrut, but they rarely do nowadays, apparently because there are few practical advantages to be gained from membership. During the last few years, the New Histadrut's campaign against individual contracts has, to all intents and purposes, failed. Not only are senior managers and high-level professionals increasingly engaged on such contracts, but a significant proportion of the regular labour force also works under those conditions. Some individual contracts are legal documents detailing working conditions and benefits. The majority, however, are verbal agreements regarding general working conditions and remuneration. In all cases where a binding collective agreement is not in force, the terms of employment are established individually. Collective employment agreements are least prevalent in construction, commerce, restaurants and hotels, and personal and other services. The private business sector as a whole includes a large proportion of employment which is not regulated by collective agreements.

At present, the New Histadrut is making a considerable effort to regulate individual contracts in some way. The preferred solution is to include individual contracts within the framework of collective agreements. The attempt to maintain the influence of collective agreements is demonstrated in the revised definition of workers eligible to vote for shop committee members. Previously, all non-managerial permanent employees were entitled to vote, irrespective of the type of contract they held. According to the new definition, workers employed according to individual contracts are denied the right to participate in such elections.

Wage earners from foreign countries

Immigrant workers are a major concern to the New Histadrut. Their presence affects its influence on the welfare of individual workers and the Israeli labour force, and it also affects the New Histadrut's role as an employee representative. The actual number of foreign workers in Israel is unknown; a significant proportion have entered the country illegally and are not registered. Official estimates place the number working in the business sector at 13 per cent of the total employed.

The Histadrut has frequently communicated its position on this issue to the Minister of Labour and Welfare:

- Israeli and Palestinian workers should enjoy preferential treatment. Only special circumstances should justify the temporary employment of a small number of wage earners from foreign countries, not to exceed 2 per cent of the labour force.
- Wage earners from foreign countries permitted to work in Israel should enjoy working conditions and social rights equal to those provided for Israeli or, at least, Palestinian workers, as set out in the respective collective agreements. This policy would prevent unfair competition and unfair labour practices.
- Responsibility for employing only legal workers should be placed directly on the employer. Severe control mechanisms and sanctions should be introduced with respect to employers who do not abide by these conditions.
- The New Histadrut should be the sole representative of wage earners from foreign countries in order to ensure proper working and living conditions. The New Histadrut has drafted a collective agreement designed to protect the rights of these workers. At the time of writing, the New Histadrut has yet to be assigned representation of this segment of the labour force.

Although the government position parallels that of the New Histadrut in many respects, little legislation has been passed and few regulations issued to address the problem.

To summarize: In view of the obstacles to recruiting individual members from new target populations, the New Histadrut is concentrating its efforts on revising the terms of collective agreements and negotiating new agreements on a sectoral basis. This appears to be the only feasible method of reaching new target groups and recruiting them as paying (i.e. membership dues or organization tax) members.

3. The New Histadrut: Financing and structure

3.1 Financing

Before 1995, the Histadrut could boast of a relatively stable membership base, which had been created (almost) independently of its accomplishments as a trade union organization. To repeat briefly, the Histadrut budget was rooted in a general labour tax or dues that included fees for health care insurance (membership in the General Sickness Fund). A fixed percentage of that income was allocated to Histadrut trade union activities. This system did not provide unlimited resources but it did mean that recruiting new members was not crucial for financial survival.

However, as of 1995, the budget of the New Histadrut has depended directly on membership dues and organization tax receipts. The General Framework Agreement, concluded in January 1995, fixes the dues to be deducted in organizations and firms where the New Histadrut is party to a collective agreement. New Histadrut members pay dues of 0.9 per cent of their wages (up to a certain ceiling); co-workers who benefit from the collective agreement but who are not members of the Histadrut pay 0.7 per cent of their wages (up to a certain ceiling) as an organization tax. These payments are deducted from their wages and transferred directly to the New Histadrut.

The separation of the General Sickness Fund from the Histadrut resulted in an immense cut in funding. The number of paying members was drastically reduced and the sum paid by each member to the New Histadrut was significantly smaller because of the decline in the basic payment. In addition, the Histadrut owed significant sums to the General Sickness Fund, debts that accumulated prior to 1995. In order to adapt to its straitened financial circumstances, the first step taken by the New Histadrut was to try to reduce labour costs, which meant dismissing many of its employees (see section 3.2 below).

At the end of 1997, the New Histadrut had accumulated a deficit of NIS 1.35 billion. Although its treasurer claims that the organization will achieve a balanced budget by 1999, the deficit still has to be covered. There is little doubt that in light of the built-in deficit, the New Histadrut's finances require a fundamental adjustment before the organization can expect to cope with the challenges presented by its changing environment. Since 1994, the New Histadrut has reduced the number of employees from 4,000 in 1994 to 2,300 in December 1996, and about 1,500 in July 1999; the long-term objective is 950.

3.2 Structural adaptation

Given the decline in its resources and the consequent reduction in its budget, restructuring became essential; the New Histadrut had no feasible alternative. Stated differently, the drive towards restructuring came primarily from internal sources, and not from a changing external environment. Given that the most significant expenditure item, even before 1995, was wages, especially in the local councils, these became an obvious target for cutbacks. Although considerable efforts were made to reduce the number of regular line employees, there is still an urgent need to reduce the number of administrative posts. Downsizing requires the elimination of many administrative posts and the redefinition of their functions. Contrary to the trends toward union decentralization and restructuring into smaller diversified units, financial stress is driving the New Histadrut in the opposite direction.

In order to reduce redundant bodies, the New Histadrut has considered two types of internal consolidation or merger:
- Merging individual trade unions that serve workers in similar occupations or related economic branches.
- Merging small local labour councils if the number of New Histadrut members in a district and the distance between the councils permits. This option has been examined for some time and was tested in 1989, but without success.

The New Histadrut leadership has preferred the merger of local councils for two reasons. First, the local council budget, especially its personnel costs, accounts for almost half of the regular budget, whereas the Trade Union Department budget accounts for only 23 per cent. An attitude survey conducted in November 1994 showed a high level of agreement or indifference to local council mergers, even in the small localities likely to be affected. This may be another reason for preferring to merge local councils.

Before the 1994 Histadrut elections, 72 local councils were operating; another five were formally established during that year. After 1995, the New

Histadrut launched a drive to form joint local councils. This process was completed by 1998, when elections for the secretaries of the local councils were carried out according to a new district map. The convention and the Chairman of the District Council were elected at district level. No elections were held for the post of secretary in the merged local councils. There are 29 districts at present, some of which represent the union of a number of smaller local councils (the largest number of councils consolidated is seven; generally between two and four councils were merged).

For the time being, the new districts continue to operate through the former local councils, as branches. The branches have retained some of their previous functions, mainly providing trade union services to their members. Most other former services, such as cultural activities and consumer protection, have been concentrated in newly established district offices. Some services, such as legal counselling, are given regularly by district officials at the local council offices.

It is still too early to evaluate the effectiveness of the reorganization. New Histadrut personnel continue to adapt to the new structure, although further dismissals are being met with strong opposition. It appears that the reduction in local functions as well as the constant threat of dismissal may be severely affecting the services offered to members. These conditions pose additional obstacles to recruiting new members. The Histadrut has always prided itself on being in close touch with its members, but this change restricts its ability to offer services in each locality.

Regarding the unions themselves, some national-level trade unions are undergoing unification, whereas others are gaining greater autonomy. The number of national unions has been reduced from 44 to about 30 during the last decade. At the same time, the occupational unions, which had already gained some independence from the Histadrut's central institutions, have achieved even more autonomy. For example, the agreement granting autonomy to the Union of Academics in the Social Sciences and Humanities, revised in 1995, was renewed again in 1997. The agreement provides for financial, organizational and legal assistance to be received by this union from the New Histadrut. The need for such an agreement derives from the basic character of the New Histadrut membership structure (individuals first join the New Histadrut and only afterwards are they assigned to a specific trade union). The renewed agreement grants the union budgetary autonomy, but the number of union personnel and their terms of employment must be agreed in advance. The union may, however, appoint its own officers. In the agreement this particular union undertook to carry out a survey of people holding academic degrees, in order to recruit new members to the union and hence to the New Histadrut.

A *de facto* structural change, not initiated by the New Histadrut, is the growing influence of the large national shop committees, such as those found in the national electric company and *Bezek*, the major telephone and communications company. For the time being, these committees are using their power to influence the New Histadrut from within but it is evident that in a conflict of interest, they will have to be reckoned with. After joining forces during the 1998 elections, the new faction initiated by national shop committees received about 16 per cent of the votes for the New Histadrut Convention.

3.3 New Histadrut leadership and its central institutions

In the Histadrut elections held on 10 May 1994, the Labour Party, which had maintained an absolute majority for more than 60 years, won only 32.6 per cent of the votes; a newly formed party, called *Ram*, took the lead. As so much within the Histadrut was changing at the time, the *Ram* leadership almost immediately decided to rename the organization as *The New Histadrut*. The style of leadership, the centrally elected institutions, and the location of its headquarters were altered, largely because of the new controlling party's agenda. But, as stated previously, the financial constraints were sufficient to induce some of the changes as well.

Elected central institutions

The *General Convention* is the New Histadrut's supreme elected institution. Since the 1998 elections, the number of delegates has doubled, from 1501 to 3001. Each list of candidates (according to political party or faction) has to be made up of at least 50 per cent workplace representatives, who alternate with central candidates. At least 30 per cent of the candidates must be men, and at least 30 per cent must be women.

The name of the *Executive Committee* was changed to *House of Representatives* and the *Central Committee* became *the New Histadrut Leadership*. The number of delegates to the House of Representatives was reduced from 189 to 121. The *General Council*, formerly the Histadrut's central policy-making institution between conventions, was eliminated. Many decisions previously delegated to the General Council are now made by the House of Representatives.

The *Secretary-General* is now called the *Chairman of the New Histadrut*. In 1998, the Chairman of the New Histadrut was directly elected for the first time. Previously, the candidate of the majority was elected Secretary-General by the former Executive Committee. Amir Peretz, who had formed a broad-based coalition prior to the elections, was elected by a large majority (although participation in the elections was less than 45 per cent of those eligible to vote).

The composition of some of the coalitions that participated in the elections is very interesting. The Labour coalition included the *Likud* (Labour and the *Likud* are in opposition in the *Knesset*) and one of the religious parties. The opposing coalition included *Gesher*, a party that has separated from the *Likud*, which has a social rights orientation, and *Meretz*, which is left wing in matters of national security but essentially liberal with respect to economic issues. These alignments, which are rather unusual in Israel's political arena, are viewed as temporary, and expected to change by the next elections, scheduled for 2002.

4. Collective action

4.1 Collective action and institutional benefits

In the past, the Histadrut promoted the negotiation of general collective agreements or framework agreements that set the standard for working conditions and industrial relations throughout the economy. These agreements included the terms of general wage increases and working conditions as well as procedural matters concerning industrial relations. As collective agreements, they are sanctioned by law and appear in the legal code. Traditionally, collective agreements reflected the power of the Histadrut central institutions to obtain comprehensive, acceptable terms and benefits for its members as well as for labour in general. They were also an expression of the Histadrut's perceived responsibility regarding the interests of the economy as a whole. Many clauses (cost of living indexation and coverage of round-trip transport costs) were expanded by government order to include all the workers in the economy or in a sector. Some of these became the basis for later labour legislation.

In contrast to the past, there now seems to be a trend towards the decentralization of collective negotiations. There is a shift from general to occupational and sectoral agreements. The majority of wage increases in recent years (especially between 1993 and 1996) were negotiated at occupational or industrial level. At the same time, local firm-related agreements are becoming more prominent.

A contradiction seems, then, to have developed between the structural changes undergone by the New Histadrut and the shift in bargaining power. A vacuum appears to have been created between the organization's internal structure and the location of bargaining power. Some individual trade unions and powerful shop committees are now filling the vacuum.

An indication of this vacuum is the fact that no framework collective agreement signed since the mid-1990s equals in scope those signed previously. Most of the recent general agreements are extensions of existing agreements, particularly with respect to cost-of-living adjustments. As Israel's annual inflation rate declines, the indexation terms negotiated in the latest agreement are less favourable than those of the earlier agreement. Compensation, at a level of 90 per cent of the increase, is forthcoming only for inflation that exceeds 4.25 per cent per annum; if the inflation rate is 4.25 per cent or less, there is no adjustment.

Two general agreements were concluded in January 1995, one with the government as the chief public sector employer, the other with the Bureau of Economic Organizations, which represents employers in the business sector. The New Histadrut was driven to reach these agreements by the need to renegotiate the arrangements for payment of its dues: the former arrangements were revoked by the separation of the General Sickness Fund. Both agreements include new provisions for collecting and transmitting union membership dues and organization taxes.

Other clauses in the agreement with the business sector concern qualitative and procedural definitions of the industrial relations to be maintained between the parties. The weakness of the New Histadrut is reflected in the concessions made regarding greater flexibility in industrial relations. This is the first general agreement ever signed that recognizes the possibility of applying different terms of employment to new employees in the same place of work. The agreement also establishes joint committees to promote cooperation on issues traditionally opposed by the Histadrut, such as worker mobility, changes in the wage structure, and individual contracts for selected employees. On the positive side, from the employees' perspective, the agreement includes a reduction in working hours — with no cut in wages — from 45 hours per week in 1995, to 44 hours in 1996 and 43 hours in 1997. Another benefit is paid leave during Jewish holidays and after a family bereavement. This section of the agreement was extended, by an order of the Minister of Labour, to cover non-organized employees in the majority of industries. The general agreement signed in May 1996 concerns the notification period prior to dismissal, confirming the conditions which generally apply in Israel. This agreement was extended later to all Israeli employees. The most recent agreement, signed on 21 August 1998 between the New Histadrut and the Bureau of Economic Organizations, guarantees the indexed updating of pensions and social security allowances twice a year.

It is not clear whether the decrease of central New Histadrut influence as revealed in the lack of negotiated framework agreements is a sign of weakness, as it appears on the surface, or an expression of its adaptation to changing circumstances. In any case, the apparent decline is not the outcome of any formal resolution to decentralize activities related to collective action or to yield to the demand for a more flexible industrial relations system.

Rather, it may be attributed to immediate pressures that the New Histadrut is not strong enough to resist.

4.2 Collective action in the case of labour disputes

Before 1995, the Histadrut seldom resorted to "general strikes" in the public sector and when it did, the duration of such strikes was very short — usually only a few hours. The assumption was that the government would cover a budget deficit if it was pressured by labour disputes and the mere threat of a strike.

The New Histadrut, on the other hand, has called three extensive strikes since July 1997. If we consider the range of economic, political and social factors influencing strikes, the data gathered since 1995 are insufficient to determine whether the pattern has changed. Nevertheless, there are indications that the New Histadrut tends to use general strikes in the public sector more often than its predecessor, at least during 1997 and 1998 (July 1997 – government-owned corporations; December 1997 – the entire public sector; September 1998 – the entire public sector). Greater union militancy is considered a sign of weakness because the threat of strike is a sufficient weapon for a powerful union.

Historically, strikes in Israel were always more common in the public sector than in private business, but they were usually restricted to single organizations or agencies. The public sector is relatively easier to organize, and the majority of its direct (as opposed to temporary) employees are Histadrut members. The public administration, and especially some publicly owned corporations, provide essential services, and the workers are extremely powerful in the sense that they can cause great economic and social damage if they strike. During the strike in September 1998, the threatened closure of Ben-Gurion International Airport contributed to reaching an agreement.

The employer in the public sector – usually the government – is highly centralized. The cost of any concession is high for the large number of employees covered or affected by an agreement. In the last instances, the cost of the concessions was a major reason why the government was ready to confront the New Histadrut.

The issues presented as causes for the latest strikes tend to be more general in character than they were in the past, involving basic long-term issues such as terms of employment (temporary employees, outsourcing, individual contracts), pension rights, and protection of workers' rights in firms undergoing privatization. Agreement on these issues, as opposed to wage demands, is usually not clear-cut in terms of cost, and involves further negotiation. On the other hand, direct economic benefits are becoming less dominant as demands.

The following factors may have caused a change in the issues which have led to strikes:

- A period of economic recession and high unemployment (currently 8.9 per cent) in recent years may mean that conditions are unsuitable for substantial wage demands.
- For the union, expansion of non-standard employment practices (e.g. outsourcing), redundancies caused by privatization and global competition, as well as protection of the social rights of workers and pensioners may now be critical from the point of view of representing employees and recruiting new members.
- The rate of inflation in Israel has declined considerably in the last decade. Before this stabilization, most negotiated wage increases were essentially cost-of-living and wage adjustment (up to 78 per cent of the increases). The nominal percentage appeared very significant but, in real terms, it was not always substantial. Still, the nominal size of the increase was obvious and important psychologically. (The annual inflation rate reached a peak of 400 per cent in 1984/5 and then gradually declined to between 10 and 20 per cent by 1994. At such rates, it was practically impossible to assess the real value of wages).With reduced inflation and the government claim that at most the real wage would be maintained, any substantial wage demand may lead to an endless dispute, with uncertain results. From the perspective of the New Histadrut, acceptance of moderate wage adjustments and reduced cost-of-living indexation may be interpreted as another sign of weakness in the public eye.

4.3 Collective action and social alliances

In accordance with the report delivered at the International Labour Conference in June 1996,[2] the three parties to industrial relations in Israel decided to establish a committee, *The Joint Committee of the Government and the Representative Bodies (Histadrut and Employers) for Dialogue and Consultation in the Industrial Relations System in Israel*. The committee, composed of 12 members, is to be convened according to need, but at least every six weeks. The objectives of the committee are mutual consultation, discussion, study and the exchange of ideas on subjects of common interest. It initiates seminars and conferences addressed to decision makers on labour relations and labour legislation. The agenda may include policy questions related to collective agreements and government orders, international treaties, labour legislation, the labour market, pensions, and the normative framework for workers' and employers' organizations.

---

[2] ILO: *Tripartite consultation at the national level on economic and social policy*, Report VI, International Labour Conference, 83rd Session (Geneva, 1996).

The committee gathered for special meetings, seminars and workshops on ten different occasions during 1997. As a rule, the discussions focused, in one way or another, on the future of collective industrial relations and prominent scholars in the field took part. These discussions usually revealed a significant degree of consensus, especially between the Histadrut and private employers. The exchange of ideas tended to be fruitful, with the views of the New Histadrut presented by persuasive speakers. Nevertheless, the operational implications of the tripartite dialogue have yet to be realized.

More recently, in August 1998, the *Socioeconomic Joint Council* was formed by the decision of the Prime Minister. Council members include the Prime Minister, the Ministers of Finance, Labour and Welfare, Industry, Commerce and Transport, the President of the Bank of Israel, the President of the Manufacturers' Association, and the Chairman of the New Histadrut. In announcing its establishment, the Prime Minister stated that the Council would deal with all the important economic issues on the public agenda, but the true impetus was concern over increasing unemployment. The Council's aim is to advise policy makers on issues of unemployment regulation and steps leading to economic growth. Its initial recommendations include:

- transferring unemployment insurance from the individual to employers who recruit unemployed persons and who retain them for a considerable period of time;
- initiating public works and infrastructure projects financed by the government;
- public financing of vocational training programmes organized by employers and the provision of incentives for retraining;
- establishing a special subcommittee that will produce a detailed plan.

In many respects, these recommendations parallel the approach taken by the New Histadrut, which has suggested allocating a percentage of the national budget for investment in infrastructure and research and development projects. Another of its proposals, yet to be acted upon by the tripartite partners, was the guarantee of a safety net to contractors investing in the construction of rented housing. Construction is a leading industry, but contractors do not invest in housing unless there is a reasonable certainty of profit. As there is a shortage of rented housing in Israel, the New Histadrut proposed a government guaranteed safety net for contractors who initiate such projects.

The New Histadrut established an additional joint advisory body on the question of unemployment in September 1997. This forum is comprised of New Histadrut officials, mayors, and officials from local government, especially from towns where unemployment is severe. Joint discussions have been held on the subject but, beyond exchanging views, the forum seems to have no real influence. This impotence results partly from the fact that none of the participants have final control over development budgets.

Examples of other, smaller-scale partnerships aimed at strengthening the capacity for joint action in pursuit of common interests are:

- A pact between the New Histadrut and *L.H.V*, the organization representing the self-employed, which created a joint forum to advance common interests. Some of the issues have been the promotion of social legislation and vocational training for the benefit of the self-employed. The pact includes a proposal to devise a standard collective agreement for employees.
- On the subject of public transport tariffs and government subsidy policy, the New Histadrut has formed an alliance with public transport cooperatives. Both the New Histadrut and the cooperatives oppose the government privatization policy and the exposure of public transport to competition because they believe that this will result in layoffs. The New Histadrut is working with the cooperatives (the employers) and employee representatives on this issue.
- The New Histadrut, in common with the social lobby in the *Knesset*, opposes any step that would lead to a further deterioration in the health care system. The proposed government budget for 1999 contains proposals that threaten the viability of the system.
- The New Histadrut supports the campaign inaugurated by the elderly and their representative organizations against reductions in their social rights. Amendments to the 1999 government budget threaten those rights, particularly in health care.
- The New Histadrut has expressed sympathy with university students who are fighting for a reduction in tuition fees. It called for a solidarity strike lasting one hour in identification with the students.

5. The trade unions and public opinion

Up until 1995, the Institute for Economic and Social Research of the Histadrut carried out periodic surveys of public opinion concerning the organization. A review of these surveys indicates that the public image of the Histadrut remained very stable over the years.

5.1 The general public

Some of the recurring questionnaire items concern the contribution and importance of the Histadrut, its efficiency, and its representatives. The general public usually ranked the Histadrut slighly below average (less than 3.5 on a scale of 1 to 6). Histadrut members ranked the organization somewhat higher. The lowest grades were given to Histadrut representatives, especially as viewed by non-members. Since 1995, no (known) surveys have been conducted.

Compared to survey results obtained in October 1993, the Histadrut's importance to the individual remained the same (44 per cent gave a grade of 4, 5, or 6), although there was a decrease in the assessment of its contribution to the country's welfare (52 per cent in 1993 versus 44 per cent in 1994). The other items were not included in the 1993 questionnaire. To conclude, there were no significant changes between 1986 and 1994 in the attitudes investigated.

An item that appeared regularly in these surveys concerned the credibility of central institutions in Israeli society, such as the legal system, the armed forces, the police, and the government. The surveys consistently reveal that the Histadrut was felt to have little credibility compared to the institutions considered, and was usually ranked 7 out of 8 (as a rule, only the media were ranked lower).

Despite its poor public image, the majority responded that the Histadrut cares for workers more than the government does, mainly with respect to preventing injustice and arbitrary dismissal (55 per cent), as well as ensuring reasonable pensions and fair pay (over 45 per cent). Only 13 per cent stated that the government cares more.

5.2 Women's attitudes towards the Histadrut and the trade unions

The results of the general public opinion surveys indicate no significant differences by gender in attitudes to the Histadrut.

In a 1997 survey on attitudes regarding women in the world of work, conducted solely among women, about two-thirds of the respondents expressed the opinion that greater representation of women in trade unions and on shop committees may enhance the status of women at work. It is noteworthy that only 29 per cent of the sample stated that they were members of the New Histadrut and only 9 per cent indicated that they belonged to a trade union.

5.3 Young workers and the trade unions

Young people aged 15-24 constitute 17.5 per cent of Israel's population (1996). One-third of this group participates in the civilian labour force; about 22 per cent are non-Jewish. In an extensive attitude survey conducted among young people aged 15-18 and 21-24, Jews and Arabs, during March-April 1998, one of the items concerned the degree of credibility of eight central institutions in Israeli society, namely the legal system, the armed forces, the police, the Knesset, religious institutions, political parties, the media and the New Histadrut. The findings revealed that the Jewish portion of the sample had little confidence in the New Histadrut: only 35 per cent of the Jewish respondents had some degree of trust in the organization. As in the general surveys conducted before 1995, only the political parties and the media received lower scores. However, among the Arab respondents, 68 per cent of the sample felt some confidence in the New Histadrut, which is relatively high; among them, the New Histadrut is ranked third (after religious institutions and the legal system) with respect to credibility.

The favourable responses are somewhat lower, in both sample populations, among the 21-24 age group. As the older age group has acquired more working experience, it is feasible that its members have already interacted more intensely with trade unions and that this interaction has undermined their confidence in these institutions.

6. Summary and conclusions

The Histadrut formerly represented one of the most powerful institutions – economically, socially and politically – in Israeli society. Throughout the first 45 years of the country's history, the Histadrut's strength gradually declined, as economic and political conditions changed. But, in 1994, it still covered about half of Israel's population and exerted a substantial influence.

The situation of the Histadrut changed radically with the enactment of the *National Health Insurance Law (1995)*, which severed the link between the trade union organization and the provision of health care. With the basic motive for membership removed, the Histadrut has been compelled to begin anew in many respects, and in a different set of circumstances.

The new situation did not eliminate the organization's need to address the challenges facing the majority of trade unions throughout the world. Like its fellow trade unions, the New Histadrut is operating in a political and economic environment which has a negative impact on its position and influence. Although all Israeli governments for the past 20 years have advocated privatization and increased competition, this policy has been carried out more vigorously of late. At the same time, enhanced international competition and technological change have seriously affected employers in the business sector. In the last two years, recession and high unemployment have caused an unfavourable climate for unionization.

Attempts have been made by government and employers to reorganize labour relations under the banner of increased efficiency. Such policies have raised strong demands for reduced regulation of the labour market, a position antithetical to the Histadrut's firm stance on stability in the work environment. Moreover, these changes threaten to erode the solid, long-term relationships already established between employers and employees, the traditional basis of union strength.

When attempting to analyse New Histadrut functioning in this dynamic environment, we are obliged to consider its internal situation. Although it

is difficult to distinguish between the organization's response to the special
circumstances forced upon it since 1995 and the challenges facing trade unions
in general, we may safely conclude that a significant element in the New
Histadrut's conduct and policy is its battle for survival as an organization.

All the indicators examined in this paper reveal that the combination of
internal and external conditions has eroded the influence of the New
Histadrut. These factors include the following.

- A drastic decline in tax-paying membership. The New Histadrut
  membership rests at between 30 and 35 per cent of all *salaried employees,*
  with an estimated 25 per cent in the business sector and 50 per cent in
  the public sector. Before 1995, more than 50 per cent of the *general adult
  population were* tax-paying members.
- Financial difficulties that limit its capacity to function effectively. This
  situation is caused by the absolute decline in membership as well as
  reduced tax rates.
- The growing legitimacy of non-collective employment relations, such as
  individual employment contracts, temporary employment, and
  subcontracting, despite New Histadrut opposition. Significantly, the
  organization's influence over the employees involved is minimal.
- The increasing proportion of the labour force open only to individual
  recruitment. This situation has evolved from the structural factors listed
  above. Given the New Histadrut's present agenda, staff and budget, an
  appropriate recruitment programme is almost impossible to implement.
- An apparent decline in the power to conduct meaningful centrally
  negotiated collective agreements. Practically no significant agreements
  have been reached at the framework level, and some earlier agreements
  have been abandoned.
- Inadequate union representation at local level.
- Increasing intervention of the courts in deciding industrial relations issues
  and the growing frequency of general strikes since 1995.
- The tripartite bodies serve more as a forum for discussion than as a
  practical policy-making arena.
- Consistently unfavourable public opinion. Although this attitude is not
  new, it has been more detrimental to the status of the New Histadrut
  since 1995.

A number of steps have been taken by the New Histadrut to counteract
its serious predicament. They are summarized below.

Membership

A general campaign to recruit new members was launched before the
1998 internal elections, with the participation of senior New Histadrut

officials. Efforts were focused on recruitment in the workplace. As such recruitment potential is limited, three main groups of workers were targeted:

- Women – by protecting their rights and ensuring better representation.
- Workers on individual contracts – by increasing efforts to achieve some regulation of such contracts and by placing greater emphasis on individual legal counselling.
- Employees hired through temporary employment agencies – by negotiating collective agreements with the agency.

The campaign met with limited success, as the incentives for individuals to join the New Histadrut have yet to crystallize.

Financing and structure

As of 1995, the New Histadrut budget has been directly dependent on its much-reduced membership dues and organization tax receipts. This situation has forced a substantial reduction in expenditure, which was achieved by staff cutbacks and reorganization. Small local councils were merged into regional councils which are responsible for a larger geographical area, and some of the national trade unions representing similar occupations were amalgamated. The reorganization has reduced the availability of services at local level.

The operational costs of the New Histadrut are still much larger than its regular income, and further staff reductions are being considered. The New Histadrut's leadership is attempting to resolve the dilemma of providing effective services and increasing income while operating at lower personnel levels.

Collective negotiation

The pressure to sign collective agreements is partly a result of the organization's financial difficulties. Employees covered by agreements negotiated by the New Histadrut usually become full dues-paying members or at least they pay the organization tax. On the other hand, the capacity of the umbrella organization to negotiate beneficial terms for its members has declined. Consequently, working conditions are being determined more and more at local or individual union level. As the New Histadrut is being judged more on the basis of its achievements, such concessions are undermining its long-term strength and image.

Collective action

The current tendency to demonstrate union power through general strikes has not produced any serious bargaining results although a long period is required before its benefits can be felt. This policy should be considered more as an instrument to unite members around a common cause.

Public opinion

Even among its members, support for the Histadrut has been on the decline for several years despite the public's continued assessment of the organization as a powerful, major institution. It is still too early to assess public attitudes to the revamped New Histadrut, though indications are that no positive change has taken place. Favourable public opinion is significantly more important today for attracting new members than it was before 1995, when membership was necessary for medical insurance.

Future attitudes to the organization will depend to a large extent on its performance. Issues such as promoting the economic and social welfare of members and potential members, improving the scope and effectiveness of trade union and other services, availability, credibility and political integrity, are important factors in creating more favourable attitudes.

Future agenda

The main issues on the New Histadrut agenda reflect its understanding of the needs of the general public. Beyond achieving financial solvency, there are six major issues.

- Retaining the conditions of the present social security system with respect to retirement pensions and social security benefits. Both are threatened by proposed regulations which are detrimental to the eligibility terms and the level of payments.
- Protecting the health care system by combating government plans to increase the health tax or to charge for services previously covered by the medical insurance system.
- Participating in the struggle against growing unemployment and recession.
- Protecting workers' rights in cases of privatization and transfers of ownership, as well as in those cases where efficiency moves jeopardize workers' rights.
- Struggling for the extension of equal rights to women in the workplace, as well as promoting female participation.
- Extending trade union protection to workers in the informal sector who earn less than the minimum wage and have no job security.

Bibliography

Bank of Israel. 1993. *Annual report*, (Jerusalem) (in Hebrew).

Bar-Zuri, R.; Fisher, H. 1997. *Women in the world of work in Israel*, Discussion paper (Tel-Aviv, Israeli Institute for Economic and Social Research) (in Hebrew).

Bartal, G.1991. *The general Histadrut, structure and functions* (Tel-Aviv, Histadrut Publications) (in Hebrew).

Ben-Israel, G.; Fisher, H. 1992 . "Trade unions in the future: Organizational strategies in a changing environment", in *Economy and Labour*, 8 (in Hebrew).

Ben-Porat, A. 1979. "Political parties and democracy in the Histadrut", in *Industrial Relations*, 18(2).

Central Bureau of Statistics. 1997. *Statistical abstract of Israel*.

Dubin, R. 1960. "A theory of power in union-management relations", in *Industrial and Labour Relations Review*, 13.

Fisher, H. 1996. *Structural and functional adjustments of trade unions in the modern era*, Discussion paper (Friedrich Ebert Foundation).

—; Hendeles, Y. 1993. *Evaluation of the merging of local councils*, Internal report (Institute for Economic and Social Research of the Histadrut) (in Hebrew).

Galin, A.; Harel, A..1978. *Development and change in the industrial relations system in Israel* (Massada) (in Hebrew).

Hendeles, Y.; Fisher, H.; Bar-Zuri, R.: "Propensity of labour to organize in Israel", in *Economy and Labour*, 9 (in Hebrew).

ILO. 1996. *Tripartite consultation at the national level on economic and social policy*, Report VI, International Labour Conference, 83rd Session (Geneva).

Institute for Economic and Social Research of the Histadrut. 1985-1995. Public opinion surveys, Internal documents (in Hebrew).

Jiloni, E.1997. *The New Histadrut*, Paper presented at the Conference on Industrial Relations and Collective Agreements in a Changing World (Eilat, Feb.) (in Hebrew).

Manpower Planning Authority, Ministry of Labour and Welfare. 1998 . *Foreign wage earners*, Internal document(in Hebrew).

Nathanson, R.; Livnat Young, R. (eds.). 1998. *Personal, social and national attitudes of Israeli youth* (Tel-Aviv, Israeli Institute for Economic and Social Research) (in Hebrew).

—; Zisser, G. 1997. "The influence of trade unions on wages and labour market – An empirical analysis", in *Economic Quarterly*, 44(3), (in Hebrew).

Ofek, A.; Rosenshtein, E.: "The generality of the Histadrut and separatist tendencies of trade unions", (in Hebrew).

Radai, F. 1998. *The policy of employment through manpower companies*, Discussion paper (Institute for Economic and Social Research and Friedrich Ebert Foundation).

Shirom, A. 1983. *An introduction to industrial relations in Israel* (Tel-Aviv, Am Oved) (in Hebrew).

Sobel, I. 1963. "Israel", in Calenson, W. (ed.): *Labor in developing economies* (University of California Press).

Tabb J.Y.; Goldfarb, A. 1971. *Worker participation in management* (Oxford, Pergamon Press).

—; et al.1961. *Industrial relations in Israel* (Tel-Aviv, Dvir) (in Hebrew).

Labour unions in the Republic of Korea: Challenge and choice

Ho Keun Song

1. Introduction: Unions in transition

For many years unions in the Republic of Korea have struggled for democratic industrial relations despite repressive policies which continued until the end of the 1980s. Unions have also played an important role in the country's remarkable economic growth. Since the industrial revolution really got under way in 1961, state and employers have considered unions as a danger to social stability and economic growth whenever firms and factories are disturbed by labour disputes. Politicians and employers have always maintained that workers involved in industrial disputes are imbued with pro-socialist and Communist ideology. This sort of anti-labour feeling is so deeply rooted in Korean society that organizations such as unions, pursuing social justice and workers' rights, cannot develop normally.

Apart from public hostility towards trade unions, repressive labour laws were the most serious impediment to union development. These laws limited union activity and blocked the intervention of industrial unions in labour disputes and collective bargaining at enterprise level. Labour leaders who dared to call a legal strike were likely to be arrested on charge of violating other regulations. In the first half of the 1980s when authoritarian laws were strengthened, more than 2,000 labour leaders were imprisoned. Many young and innocent workers, male and female, spent years in gaol. This situation received international attention since labour repression generated serious problems concerning human rights and workers' rights. The labour movement remembers the 1970s and 1980s as years of bitter struggle against political repression and unfair labour practices. During this period there were massive and violent strikes at shipyards, automobile factories and steel mills, some of which received worldwide attention, notably the labour disputes of 1987. These continued for four months in most factories and workplaces in support of workers' rights and better working conditions, epitomizing the struggle against state repression and employers' brutal and inhuman treatment. About 1.3 million workers actively joined these disputes which were a watershed in Korean labour history, not only in the number of workers mobilized but also in the impact on industrial relations. The government had to accept workers' demands unconditionally in face of the breakdown of authoritarianism.

As a consequence, repression was relaxed, unfair labour practices largely disappeared, workers' rights improved, and unions gained some power to negotiate with government and employers. The era of bitterness seemed to be over. But unions had to wait a few more years before they had any real influence.

The labour movement had to enter an entirely new epoch after the political opening of 1987 and it went through a period of trial and error in adapting to a new environment. The upheavals of 1987 provided a good chance for workers to organize, so that many unions, big and small, were new. New unions did not have the experience to organize the labour movement effectively and to manage labour demand. Workers began to organize in all industrial sectors, but there was no coherent leadership at the top level to control local unions and rank-and-file workers. Unions, old and new, realized that they had to cope with entirely new issues regarding democratization and globalization. Thus, the years after 1987 are a period of challenge and response, of success and failure, and of satisfaction and frustration to Korean unions. They improved their organizing skills and capacity to manage worker demand, but inter-union alliance and cooperation was seriously weakened by intensified market competition.

The focus of this study is on the successes and failures of Korean unions since 1987. The chapter analyses the strategies and policies that unions have implemented in a time of democratization and globalization. It also sheds some light on the consequences, explaining how the labour movement has been affected, modified and split in the process, and how it has responded to new challenges. The issues and problems that unions have faced are described in the analysis.

2. Labour politics and the structure of unions

2.1 Labour politics

"Labour politics" refers to the policy packages implemented by government and employers to achieve their own goals vis-à-vis organized labour. The term covers the political, legal and institutional instruments regulating interactions between employers and unions in the workplace and the limits imposed on collective action. It defines the legal status of unions, the structure of labour relations, the procedures for organizing workers and the role of unions in politics and the economy. Labour politics are structured through tripartite cooperation between government, employers and workers in democratic countries, while they are enforced by an authoritarian state or monopoly capital in non-democratic settings. The Republic of Korea relied on authoritarian labour politics until 1987.

The approach was authoritarian not only in the workplace but also in the control exercised over workers who rebelled against state policies. The government relied on violent and repressive means to resolve industrial conflict and subdue worker militancy. The police and intelligence agencies frequently intimidated labour leaders who expressed discontent and complained of maltreatment. Industrial disputes were commonly terminated by violent police attacks prior to 1987. The state legitimized repressive labour policies by stressing that workers should accept such practices until economic prosperity was achieved.

Rapid economic growth was supported by authoritarian labour control, which squeezed maximum productivity out of workers. Since authoritarian labour control was a common feature of East Asian NICs (newly industrializing countries), it is often argued that there is a structural affinity between export promotion strategy and labour repression (Deyo, 1987, 1989; Deyo, Haggard, and Koo, 1987; Gereffi and Wyman, 1990; Koo, 1987). The argument is particularly true of the Republic of Korea, which made a radical turn to authoritarian repression with increasing industrialization in 1972. During the Yushin regime (1972-1979) state repression was enforced so strongly that organized labour could not expand its activities and make demands without suffering reprisals.

The labour regime aimed at demobilizing and depoliticizing industrial workers. Demobilization was designed to discourage unionization and destroy established unions which disturbed industrial stability through frequent work stoppages and strikes in protest against state policies. Depoliticization was designed to prohibit organized labour from political participation and deny opportunities for partnership with the government. Organized labour has been regarded as a necessary evil throughout the history of the Republic of Korea since the liberation. The odd combination of rapid growth and anti-labour ideology is an interesting feature of the country's economic miracle. Repressive politics integrated the economy into a coherent policy of export-led industrialization.

During the period of legal and political repression, the labour regime had some distinctive characteristics: enterprise unionism, and administrative and political control. The enterprise union is the basic unit of worker organization and activity. Only regular blue-collar workers within a firm are entitled to join the enterprise union. Enterprise unions can be associated with the industrial union and the Federation of Korean Trade Unions (FKTU), but affiliation is not obligatory. The state vigorously constrains union activity within the workplace, defining the enterprise union as an institution for settling grievances and maintaining cooperation between employer and employees. Apex bodies at both industrial and national level cannot intervene in collective bargaining at plants. They can only send policy recommendations and, sometimes, petitions to employers when collective bargaining has reached a stalemate. According to a survey conducted by FKTU in 1983, only 3 per cent of firms with 500 or more workers engaged in collective bargaining at all: in these firms bargaining concerned only minor issues like paid vacation, work allocation, and some trivial aspects of working conditions.

Second, the Ministry of Labour controls the administrative and legal functions of unions. A new trade union has to get a certificate of registration from the Ministry, known as the Labour Office until 1981. If no certificate is granted the new union has to be disbanded. Before 1987, there were numerous disputes about the certificate of registration especially when the Ministry, in collaboration with employers, refused to issue a certificate to unions that fulfilled all the qualifications. The Labour Code also empowered the Ministry to withdraw the legal status of established unions if they were deeply involved in politically significant industrial disputes, or accused of agitating violent strikes. Besides this, union leaders had to report on their activities and submit their annual budget to the Ministry. If the annual budget was not used for activities permitted by the Labour Code, union leaders could be charged with violating the law. Administrative inspection was an efficient way of controlling unions involved in many troubles and disputes.

Third, the political control of unions relied on institutions such as the police and intelligence agencies. While the Ministry of Labour inspected and supervised the daily activities of unions, including disputes on working conditions, wage negotiation, and unfair labour practice, the intelligence agencies were mainly concerned with security. Their role was to prevent unions from being connected with and affected by militant groups outside factories. It is not long since security police disappeared from big factories and industrial parks. During the authoritarian period, the national intelligence agency frequently intervened in violent strikes which threatened political stability. In these years, numerous workers were arrested on charge of violating the national security laws and imprisoned. This explains why unions have pressed for abolition of the national security laws, as promised by President Kim Dae Jung. Organized labour was thus surrounded with and regulated by multiple types of surveillance. As a consequence, unions could not develop the horizontal and vertical linkages which were essential to the growth of the labour movement. Union activities were confined to the enterprise and those that tried to make alliances across firms were subject to severe and violent repression.

Union leaders in strikes had no legal protection from dismissal and arrest. Once they were gone, it took a considerable time to reproduce leadership and to recover solidarity with the rank and file. Making use of repressive measures, the state aimed at strengthening enterprise consciousness as an essential element of the Korean tradition of paternalism. Employers were basically responsible for the welfare of their employees as sons and daughters, in exchange for discretionary powers of control. In reality, the system generated wealth for the state and employers but failed to include employees in the benefits of high productivity because of its exploitative and repressive character. As social ills such as inequality and political repression became worse, however, workers gradually turned away from the illusion of government promises and began to engage in class conflict in close association with revolutionary student groups. This explains why militant factions of the labour movement were oriented to a radical socialist revolution instead of gradual social reform in the latter half of the 1980s.

2.2 The growth and structure of unions

Union growth

The proportion of organized workers has risen and fallen over the last three decades according to the political and economic climate, but overall it has fluctuated between 15 and 24 per cent. It seems that 25 per cent was the highest organizing rate, during the years of rapid growth. Chun Do Hwan's regime (1980-1987) recorded the lowest figure: unionization was relatively higher during the Yushin regime (1972-1979) than during the period of democratization after 1987. This does not mean that union power to negotiate after the transition to democracy is weaker than in the Yushin regime. The higher rate during the 1970s is mainly attributable to a rapid increase in the number of industrial workers due to growth in heavy industry and chemicals, and also to relaxation of political repression by President Park in the late 1970s. Controls were eased in order to placate growing discontent at workplaces. Unions have grown dramatically in number over three decades although union density has changed very little. Ten industrial federations have recently been established, the number of local unions has tripled, and membership expanded from 200,000 in the early 1960s to approximately two million in the early 1990s. The growth of unionization can be described under several headings.

First, five industrial federations were established during the labour dispute of 1987 by splitting existing federations and unionizing previously unorganized white-collar employees. The Federation of Korean Rubber Workers was created at this time, while newly organized workers included insurance staff, taxi drivers, clerical and financial workers, and city subway workers. The new federations had a progressive and somewhat radical orientation in contrast to the passivity that FKTU maintained over many years. During 1992 five more new federations were created. These brought together the unions representing journalists, hospital workers, university employees, maintenance workers, researchers, professionals, and technicians. These federations sprang up shortly after 1987 and were very active in the period of democratic transition, receiving state recognition in 1992-93. This was a significant time in Korean labour history because it marked the establishment of the first white-collar unions, which were unimaginable in the past. Federations of white-collar unions fought hard for state recognition, in cooperation with progressive groups of blue-collar unions. After 1987 these industrial federations were allowed to decide freely whether to choose FKTU as their national centre or to remain independent. As of November 1995, however, Korea entered an era of multiple unionism at apex level as many unions formed another national centre, the Korean Confederation of Trade Unions (KCTU), competing with FKTU.

Second, local unions grew fast during the 1970s, reaching 5,000 at the end of the decade, but then dropping sharply to just over 2,000. The Chun Do Hwan regime was detrimental to union growth, but the labour dispute of 1987 precipitated an explosion of new activity, and almost 1,500 unions sprang up within six months. Industrial workers had an unprecedented chance to organize in the transition to democracy and almost 8,000 new unions were created in the two years after 1987, the rate of organization rising from 15 to 23 per cent. But this was the high spot of the movement.

Third, the proportion of organized workers culminated at 23.3 per cent in 1989 due to expanded political opportunity, falling back to 13.5 per cent in 1997. The rate was expected to go up again to about 20 per cent when the new labour laws allowing teachers and public sector employees to organize came into force in 1999. It is notable that the trends for male and female workers crossed in the mid-1980s, when more men were joining unions but fewer women. This cross-over was associated with the transformation of Korean industry from labour-intensive to technology- and capital-intensive production. The centre of the labour movement shifted from unskilled women workers in light industry in the 1970s to skilled male workers in the 1980s. The shift altered the goals and orientation of the labour movement, as detailed in a later section.

Union structure

The structure of unions in Korea is relatively simple, since the state did not permit multiple unionism until recently, and enterprise unions were the basic unit of national organization. For many years the Federation of Korean Trade Unions was the only national centre which had official status. However, competing groups of organized labour set up another centre in November 1995, which they called the Korean Confederation of Trade Unions (KCTU). The new centre brought together progressive and active unions which were dissatisfied with FKTU. The new national centre strove for government recognition as a legal organization, and this was finally achieved in 1996. Thus, organized labour in the Republic of Korea has two national centres. Labour laws stipulate that enterprise unions can join a national centre but not individual workers. However, enterprise unions are more closely affiliated with industrial federations than with national centres. Although the national centre is an apex body regulating both industrial unions and enterprise unions, labour leaders at workplaces tend to regard the industrial federation as their supreme organization. The national centre is remote from rank-and-file workers in unionized factories. The tie between industrial federation and enterprise unions tends to be stronger in industries such as textiles and metals, which have had industry-wide collective bargaining for a long time. In general, however, membership in a higher organization meant little because of labour laws that prohibited third party intervention in disputes at the workplace. But now it is likely that the amendments of 1996 and 1998 which abolished the prohibition will make vertical links stronger and more meaningful in the near future.

Another sort of federation grouped the occupational unions which mushroomed in white-collar sectors shortly after 1987. Among the 12 federations of occupational unions that were active at that time, six were successful in getting legal recognition by 1993. They launched another apex body, the Korean Congress of Independent Industrial Trade Union Federations (KCIIF) in 1990. Thus, three kinds of apex body emerged during the transition to democracy.

2.3 Union activities

Collective bargaining

Unions are mainly concerned with collective bargaining and daily routine activities. For a long period, authoritarian governments banned enterprise unions from engaging in collective bargaining. Instead, the Labour/ Management Cooperative Council (LMCC) was set up to deal with working conditions and grievance settlement, while unions were concerned with welfare and safety in the workplace and also outside. The Ministry encouraged monthly meetings of the LMCC, which was composed of managers and worker representatives, and mandated to report on its discussions and decisions to the government. A department of the LMCC was established in the Ministry of Labour to guide and regulate the Council and to send guidelines on state policies to all factories. Collective bargaining was not illegal but was politically banned.

But rules and customs changed dramatically after 1987. Most enterprise unions, old and new, claimed the right of collective action and wage negotiation, sometimes with support from the industrial federation, but mostly on an independent basis. It was a tradition to carry out collective bargaining and wage negotiation separately in the Republic of Korea, even under an authoritarian government. Wage negotiations take place in all industries every spring, as in Japan, while collective bargaining begins early in September and continues until November or December. The system probably originated when the Japanese implanted company welfarism in the colony. Unions deal with job security, worker participation in management and welfare issues through collective bargaining. This dual system actually prolongs the bargaining period over the entire year. However, a consensus between employers and unions emerged in the early 1990s on ways to curtail institutional inefficiency and reduce unproductive costs. The result was a rapid shift from the dual system to a single round of negotiations. Now, most large firms hold wage talks and engage in collective bargaining simultaneously.

Routine activities

Since 1987 enterprise unions have been overwhelmed by large and small demands from rank-and-file workers. Employees in trouble resort to union representatives first instead of seeking help from the head of their production team or a supervisor as in the past. This shows that unions have gained the confidence of the rank and file in most factories. To counteract the increasing influence of union representatives in the workplace some employers have attempted to strengthen the managerial hierarchy by giving more power to section heads and supervisors. This caused serious conflict between employers and unions concerning the direction of managerial innovation in the early 1990s. In addition to dealing with the concerns of individual workers, most large unions have started to publish newsletters which discuss broad labour issues ranging from unfair labour practice to firms' reinvestment schedules.

According to a survey (Yee and Kwon, 1995, p. 180), the priority activities for unions are: wage negotiation, worker welfare and fringe benefits, industrial accidents, organizational consolidation, job security, solidarity with other unions, work sharing, union democracy, job grading, development of policy packages, abolition of discrimination, and reform of work organization.

Industrial disputes

Unions in the Republic of Korea have been known for their militancy. Labour militancy is ascribed mainly to a repressive state that closes the political space through which organized labour expresses and accomplishes its political and economic demands. Factory size and worker homogeneity are other factors enhancing militancy. Chaebol firms (conglomerates) employ over half of all industrial workers and they are not split into different groups by race or religion. Some researchers argue that a high degree of egalitarianism in national society is conducive to labour militancy, which is interpreted as an expression of frustrated upward mobility and income disparity (Kim, 1992).

It is widely accepted that the main causes of labour militancy have been political repression and perceived economic inequality. These two factors were closely interwoven in an authoritarian setting in which the ruling groups always emphasized a "development-first-and-distribution-later" policy when confronted with worker demands. The worker challenge has taken various forms according to perceptions of isolation and discrimination. As economic success reduced absolute poverty in the 1970s, the focus of discontent shifted to the relative deprivation that most workers thought was the result of government reluctance to distribute wealth equally. Worker discontent was amplified by illegal property accumulation through speculation and corruption. Bognanno (1988, p. 435) observed: "at some point during the past five to ten years workers and the public seemed to shift from a concern over absolute poverty to a concern over relative poverty".

Relative poverty and corrupt links between politics and business explain the "strange paradox" that although Korean citizens, including industrial workers, received economic benefits, workers expressed anger at their government, political leaders and business managers (Lindaeur et al., 1997). Research identifies four factors which explain the paradox: the excessive prolongation of authoritarian controls that favoured management over workers; outrage at disrespectful treatment by superiors; an acute sense of relative deprivation; the perception that wealth was acquired by illegitimate means (Lindaeur et al., 1997, pp. 111-113).

A great many industrial disputes occurred after decades of rapid economic growth. Unions were well-prepared to embark on strikes, demonstrations, and sit-ins at a time of frustrated collective bargaining, illegal dismissals, and unfair labour practices. But a careful look at the statistics reveals that, except at the time when the government changed, there were relatively fewer industrial disputes in the Republic of Korea than in some advanced European countries such as France and Italy. The two periods around 1980 and 1987 were extremely unstable. In 1980, most industrial workers took part in strikes and demonstrations, demanding political freedom, equal distribution of wealth, and humane treatment. In that year, a violent revolt occurred in a mining village in protest against a supervisor's appropriation of worker wages and an employer's unfair labour practice. The industrial disputes of 1987 are known as the 'Ulsan Typhoon' since they were ignited by violent turmoil in the Hyundai Heavy Industry Co. located in Ulsan. About 1.3 million workers in 3,300 firms all over the country were involved in these disputes. This was unprecedented in Korean labour history.

Blue-collar workers fiercely attacked employers and managers in a kind of class war. This vociferous and unstable atmosphere continued over two more years of numerous industrial disputes. But the frequency of disputes has declined since the early 1990s and fell below one hundred in 1997.

Labour statistics on type of conflict, number of participants and working days lost indicate that work stoppages and sit-ins are the most common type of dispute in Korea. Whereas industrial disputes were ignited mainly by wage-related issues in the 1970s, workers' concern shifted to diversified issues including collective bargaining, dismissal, and unfair labour practices in the 1980s.

3. Trade unions in the transition to democracy

3.1 Democratization in the Republic of Korea

Undoubtedly, the Republic of Korea has made remarkable progress towards democracy since the political opening of 1987. First of all, the machinery of authoritarian politics was removed and the rules of fair competition were introduced into the political and economic arenas. National politics now satisfy the criteria of procedural democracy suggested by Dahl (1971). In 1998 the door was opened to organized labour when worker representatives were invited to take part in tripartite negotiations, i.e. almost ten years after the political opening. Although the ruling party invited organized labour to the politics of crisis management in January 1998 under IMF regulation, how far this process will go and how it will be institutionalized remain uncertain.

How have unions organized their struggle for better democracy? What did they do during the ten-year transition to democracy? What are the political and economic consequences of the struggle? How have unions themselves been affected? The present chapter addresses these questions. It is helpful to begin with a brief description of the democratization process with regard to the structural obstacles that hindered the political participation of organized labour at national level.

Democratization proceeds through three consecutive phases; political opening, transition and consolidation (O'Donnell and Schmitter, 1986). It is widely accepted that the Republic of Korea successfully passed through the first two phases in a short span of time. *Political opening* began with the general election of February 1985, when the opposition party won a majority in the National Assembly. This phase culminated in the Announcement of 29 June 1987, which set out the political concessions to civil society. The country began its *transition* to democracy with the Rho Tae Woo regime (1987-1992) at the end of 1987. The Rho regime can be defined as a restricted democracy since it reduced political repression but the nucleus of power remained unchanged from the previous Chun regime. Its contribution to democratization was the appointment of Kim Young Sam, an opposition leader, as presidential candidate for the ruling party. This appointment meant the end of authoritarianism strongly backed by the military. The Kim Young Sam government (1993-1997), the first civilian government since the military coup of 1961, started democratic *consolidation* by carrying out a series of reforms during the first half of its term. But the effort was only partly successful due to the lack of political skill and strong reactionary attacks from conservative power groups. Consolidation is protracted. Although it is too early to say whether it will proceed successfully under the Kim Dae Jung government (1998 to present) there are many positive signs.

What role did organized labour play during these three phases? Did unions succeed in expanding organizational and political space as a supreme goal of the labour movement? Have they strengthened their bargaining power vis-à-vis the government and employers? It is notable that organized labour actually gained much less than it contributed to democratization. Organized labour pushed the authoritarian regime to relax political repression by calling mass strikes in the years after 1985, and it expanded the organizational foundation of opposition movements by making alliances with student and religious groups. Finally, it triggered the transition to democracy in 1987 by repudiating labour laws that upheld authoritarian repression. The abolition of authoritarian rules and the achievement of political freedom are by no means negligible. But labour problems were not included in the package of reform policies of the Kim Young Sam government and it was not until April 1996 that the government announced the schedule of labour reform.

Gains are observable in the fact that wage and fringe benefits almost doubled in a short time. Although many warned that the sudden increase in labour costs would eventually ruin national competitiveness it was more urgent to satisfy worker demands than to avoid future economic problems.

Democratization in the Republic of Korea shows distinctive characteristics. First, the process falls into the category of reform democracy rather than rupture democracy. Reform democracy occurs when old authoritarianism does not collapse completely and political power is shared between the old élites and opposition leaders. In this model, authoritarian élites adopt a passive strategy to accommodate the demands of opposition groups. The advantage of reform democracy is that political stability is maintained throughout the process, but fundamental changes are hardly expected. In the Republic of Korea democratization resulted in the removal of authoritarian rules but there was no fundamental change in the party system, electoral system or power structure. In these circumstances it was natural that labour laws remained almost untouched until 1996, and organized labour had no part in reform politics.

Second, Korean politics do not reflect class interests since these were long suppressed by authoritarian governments that gave priority to public rather than private interests, and national rather than individual causes (Stepan, 1978). In this context, labour leaders could not penetrate the power nucleus that was monopolized by politicians.

Third, organized labour did not have access to "the ultra-élitist agreements" which facilitated the transition to democracy. Political agreement commonly emerges in a period of transition to minimize socioeconomic costs and political instability. But in the Republic of Korea, organized labour was alienated not only from these ultra-élitist agreements but also from policy implementation in the absence of "a social pact".

The factors described above determined union experience during ten years of democratization. The consequence is the disparity of union power between national and enterprise levels: union influence is still limited at national level, while it has grown much stronger within the firm. Bridging this gap became the supreme goal of union movements after 1987.

3.2 The rise of democratic unionism

A careful examination reveals that the labour dispute of 1987, called the "Ulsan Typhoon", was not an organized and strategic strike with a clear purpose but an explosion of worker protest against authoritarian repression. Thus, it seemed that meeting worker demands was the best strategy for the state in crisis. The government accepted and announced its intention to reform the Labour Code. The strike gave an impetus to the emergence of informal and progressive groups of workers, who developed a revolutionary and socialist ideology. These groups initiated strikes and street rallies during the labour disputes, supported by student activists, religious groups and political opposition factions. They emphasized the importance of unionism in eradicating authoritarian repression and achieving the "liberation of labour". More radical factions of workers proclaimed a socialist ideology as the most viable ideological weapon against the state and monopoly capital. Consequently, the new unionism grew in pursuit of the liberation of labour and presented a radical and progressive vision of future society. Establishing the Korea Trade Union Congress (KTUC), an apex body independent of FKTU in 1990, unionists rigorously pursued the amendment of labour laws as the platform for mobilizing workers. The new unionism was known as "democratic unionism" because of its goal of abolishing authoritarian repression.

A close look at the components of the new unionism gives us useful information about the origin and nature of democratic unionism. First, the new unionism developed in labour-intensive industries, characterized by low wages and long hours of work. During the 1970s, a period of heavy industrialization, the labour movement was mainly led by workers in textiles and electronics. They adopted desperate means such as suicide and self-immolation to protest against labour repression under the Yushin regime. A militant and revolutionary vision of the new unionism was the legacy of the labour movement in this sector. It also indicates that the new unionism, which had a radical and militant orientation, could not easily penetrate capital-and technology-intensive manufacturing.

Second, owing to its industrial origin, the new unionism had a closer affinity with young female workers at the lowest level of the labour market pyramid. Simply put, workers in lower and less advantageous positions were more likely to support democratic unionism than FKTU compliance with authoritarian rule. The disparity by age and sex is also closely associated with the generational change in the labour movement. The rise of democratic unionism was closely associated with the new generation of workers who were less tolerant of economic inequality and political repression. This was the result of a learning process that was closely linked to student movements and to the presence of student activists in factories.

Third, KTUC workers strongly pursued the "liberation of labour" as a common vision of future society. However, its meaning and the strategy to achieve it showed wide variation. The moderates thought of the liberation of labour in terms of economic affluence but the radicals thought in terms of the political domination of the working class over the state and the bourgeoisie. While the moderates asserted that power should be gained through electoral means, the radicals used revolutionary methods to build a socialist society as an alternative to bourgeois politics. Since the revolutionary ideology was, of course, a menace to the National Security Law, the state imprisoned a number of students and union activists when KTUC was established. This created human rights issues that will be described later.

Comparing the power of FKTU and KTUC, it was reported that KTUC workers numbered 193,000 when the Congress was established compared with 1,739,000 in FKTU. This means that KTUC membership was only one-tenth that of FKTU and only 2.7 per cent of the industrial workforce. Simply put, KTUC represented only a small fraction of industrial workers with a radical and militant ideology. Though the new unionism successfully launched its apex body as the headquarters of worker struggle, it faced formidable pressure. The pressure included state repression, the lack of consistent programmes, and competition with FKTU for members. It is understandable that democratic unionism could not assure autonomy from the beginning.

3.3 Unions in a reform democracy, 1993-1996

The reform politics of the Kim Young Sam government excluded organized labour from policy making and implementation. Although it satisfied the requirements of formal democracy, political power was largely monopolized by individual élites who were loyal to the former leader of the opposition. In contrast to claims made in his election campaign, President Kim did not offer an opportunity to social groups to participate in central politics. Instead, he attempted to bring the leaders of social movements into the ruling party as members of the Assembly, and appointed influential leaders to important government positions. Organized labour was no exception. Some prominent figures in the labour movement became members of the Assembly, while others became independent researchers on labour problems or consultants on labour relations. Political democratization at state and national level weakened political unionism, which emphasized inter-union cooperation and collective action.

Nevertheless, organized labour continued trying to strengthen its influence on politics and the economy. Union leaders adopted various strategies to increase their political influence; these included attempts to establish a labour party, strengthen industrial unions, amend labour laws, and construct a strong national centre by mobilizing the unorganized. Competition between two national centres was a noticeable feature of this period. The centres were FKTU and KCTU (Korean Council of Trade Union Representatives, which was established by combining KTUC and KCIIF in 1993). In 1995, a new KCTU-Korean Confederation of Trade Unions was created. The two national centres sometimes cooperated in pressing the government to start amending the Labour Code, but there were significant differences between the centres in their approach to most labour issues. Government opened channels for negotiation and discussion only to FKTU because KCTU was not officially recognized. KCTU grew faster in size and influence in the first half of the 1990s by incorporating large unions in strategic industries such as automobiles, shipbuilding and metals. FKTU abandoned its passive and submissive attitude to government in order to cure the identity crisis accelerated by its declining membership, but this strategy did not slow the growth of KCTU. KCTU functioned as a centre of the working-class struggle during these years. As a centre of democratic unionism KCTU gained great influence over most large unions in manufacturing industries, as well as over the new white-collar unions. What did the centres do in these years? And what were the main goals they pursued? These can be summarized as follows.

First, amendment of the labour laws was the prime goal that FKTU and KCTU pursued together without discord. The two national centres demanded the repeal of laws which violated ILO labour standards, insisting that the ban on political activity and third party intervention in labour disputes should be abolished first. However, the state did not accept this demand since it would have meant a fundamental change in labour relations, giving more power to unions.

Second, the demand for third party intervention was closely related to the long-term goal of strengthening industrial unions. Industrial unions were a desirable alternative to company unions, as these limited union activity to the enterprise. While the state objected strongly to industrial unionism, the national centres made strenuous efforts to accomplish it. Local union attitudes varied according to labour orientation. A survey reported that labour leaders at plant level who favoured enterprise unionism outnumbered those who preferred industrial unionism (Song, 1992). A survey conducted by Song in 1992 gave further support to this finding. The study of 250 labour leaders in small and large manufacturing firms dealt with union activities, worker attitudes, financing, and other issues. It seemed that labour leaders had less toleration of control by a higher organization. Political liberalization with economic recession pushed labour leaders to be more inward-looking.

Third, KCTU lobbied the government to legalize multiple unionism at both national and firm levels. FKTU strongly opposed this for fear that multiple unionism would wipe out the FKTU advantage and make collective bargaining less effective at workplaces.

Fourth and finally, the two national centres put the emphasis on rapid and broad-based social reform. They pressed for the eradication of links between politics and business, punishment of corrupt politicians and bureaucrats, the introduction of transparency in banking transactions, and finally, tax reform. In April 1993, FKTU accepted wage concessions on condition that the government would immediately implement social reforms. Even though KCTU criticized FKTU's decision at that time, it did not repudiate the social reforms set out in the wage agreement.

In this respect, the contribution of organized labour to democratization is not negligible. It put formidable pressure on government to implement a package of reform policies, regardless of the final outcome. But organized labour continued the struggle to gain its goals until April 1996 when government announced the schedule for labour law amendments.

It is peculiar to the Republic of Korea that white-collar unions collaborated with blue-collar unions in pursuit of social reform in the process of democratization. Most white-collar unions emerged shortly after 1987 as a result of political concessions to worker demands for union freedom. Of the many new unions those representing journalists, hospital workers, clerical and financial workers were influential in terms of size and activities. The journalists' unions achieved solidarity and extended a strong influence on the media through a massive and violent strike at KBS, the public television station, in 1990. They demanded free speech and protested against government control over news broadcasts and other programmes. Workers in all the media joined and supported the KBS strike as a symbol of resistance to state control. The journalists' unions thus earned an image of pioneers at the frontier of democratic labour relations. In 1993, six out of 13 white-collar unions acquired legal status through decisions of the Supreme Court. The struggle of the hospital unions to acquire legal recognition is well-known. Members of these unions were mainly nurses, mechanics and other low-paid workers who had many complaints about working conditions. Their demand for better conditions was naturally connected to the quality of public service. The clerical and financial workers' unions made it their prime goal to implement banking transactions under real names immediately. They claimed that new institutions were needed to eliminate corrupt links between politics and business. It should be pointed out that worker demands for economic well-being and better working conditions included social and political reforms in the three sectors represented by the unions of journalists, hospital staff, and financial and clerical workers.

The white-collar unions established a national centre to organize workers and promote independent occupational unions. In May 1990, the Korea Congress of Independent Industrial Trade Union Federations (KCIIF) was created as an umbrella organization for white-collar unions. It participated actively in general strikes, street rallies, and other public events demanding amendment of the labour laws and union freedom in support of KCTU. (Needless to say, some elements in KCIIF were closer to FKTU.) But, in general, KCIIF contributed to social and political reform by improving the quality of public services and pressing government and employers to change the authoritarian regulation of jobs and workplaces.

The white-collar unions are significant in three respects. First, they are occupational unions mobilizing workers in similar jobs with no distinction between private and public sectors. Occupational unions can easily penetrate the public sector in spite of the legal ban on unionization. Thus, the emergence of white-collar unions was a serious threat to state labour regulation. Second, they have a strong preference for industrial unionism because of occupational similarities across firms. Third, it is highly likely that their economic interests are associated with social and political reform since their jobs are mainly in the public services.

4. Challenges to unions: The impact of globalization

4.1 The impact of globalization

As political liberalization contributed significantly to the introduction of 'new rules of the game' in the political arena, so open competition was encouraged in the national economy. In the state-led capitalism practised in the Republic of Korea, the market had long been distorted by government intervention. Strategic industries and big business enjoyed tremendous benefits in the shape of cheap loans, tax exemptions and tariff rebates. The government invested heavily in strategic industries and protected big business from foreign competition. But the structure of market competition suddenly changed as the state retreated from the forefront of the national economy in response to external pressure to open national markets and follow the international trend towards free trade.

The Kim Young Sam government (1993-1997) turned the focus of economic policy onto globalization in 1994, when the national economy entered a serious recession as a consequence of incomplete industrial restructuring. In the global economy, capital and services move fast and without restriction across national boundaries, due to advanced information technology. In a global economy capital can move anywhere in pursuit of cheap labour and less regulation. Thus, globalization reduces employers' need to negotiate with unions when they demand higher wages and better protection. Just as unions in advanced capitalist countries are all in trouble under a global economy, so the worldwide change may inflict a fatal blow on the Korean unions which have only just settled after the turmoil of 1987.

The introduction of flexible production is a menace to unions. Flexibility has three distinct aspects: employment, wages and skills. Employment flexibility means job instability for workers and a fundamental change in their perception of firms. Workers are no longer paid by contribution and seniority but according to merit and ability once wage flexibility is introduced. Finally, workers are obliged to learn a range of skills in preparation for product diversification and new production technology. The shift in managerial strategy to flexibility was a great shock to Korean workers who were familiar with lifelong employment, high commitment to the firm and a seniority-based wage system. Management attempts to introduce flexibility thus provoked very severe conflict between capital and labour. The situation caused tension during the Kim Young Sam regime from 1993 to 1997, but unions had to accept these changes when the government decided to join OECD in 1996. The changes brought about by flexible production and union response can be summarized as follows.

First, the membership of FKTU and KCTU dropped due to the layoff of numerous workers and the closure of many labour-intensive firms, notably in the clothing industry and textiles. Second, labour unions expressed strong opposition to the massive layoff policy of big firms and conglomerates but could not influence them. Third, when government started to discuss the possibility of selling and privatizing state-owned enterprises in 1994, public sector unions expressed strong and persistent opposition, and called a general strike when it was carried out. As the public utilities had long held a monopoly position, the unions in that sector were well-organized with a high commitment to leadership. Thus, the government inevitably collided with strong unions such as the Korea Electronic Power Corporation and Korea Telecommunications. Public sector unions set up a joint committee to oppose privatization and waged serious and violent struggles in 1994 and 1995. KCTU supported the struggle and public sector unions became the main agent of so-called democratic unionism. The confrontation continued until 1998 when the Kim Dae Jung government announced an official schedule of privatization to overcome the economic crisis. At this time, no opposition was heard because it was channelled through tripartite negotiations that included FKTU and KCTU. Fourth, the conglomerates took huge foreign loans in order to move into new areas such as information and financial services as a means of industrial restructuring. Unfortunately, the new industries in which they invested had little effect on job creation and the reduction of unemployment. Instead, financial deficits accumulated and eventually exploded into the foreign debt crisis of December 1997.

4.2 Union struggle and labour orientation

FKTU and KCTU began to cooperate in the struggle to gain managerial initiative. From 1993 to 1995 there were large-scale strikes against the government's privatization policy and downsizing in the conglomerates. The national centres, FKTU and KCTU, cooperated closely at this time to achieve their common goals of maintaining job security and protecting the rank and file from massive layoffs. They also drew up alternatives to the new wage and promotion system that big firms were trying to introduce. Employers wanted to reduce the seniority element in wage scales and promotion systems and to reward workers according to merit and ability. Unions contended that this would undermine the national employment system which maximized worker commitment to the company. In spite of strong union opposition, the new pay schemes and promotion systems were gradually introduced in most big firms during these years and FKTU and KCTU finally set the amendment of labour laws as a new target.

The conflict surrounding job security and pay schemes significantly affected labour orientation. First of all, political unionism began to lose its attraction for the working class. The "democratic unionism", which was associated with politically active and radical factions of the working class, dwindled and shrank. Attention was focused instead on union democracy. This does not mean that political unionism died out completely or disappeared from the scene. There was a disparity between the national centre and local unions. As Ramos (1981) observed in the case of Japan, while the national apex body attempted to pursue worker interests through political routes, local unions were more concerned with economic well-being and better working conditions.

The rapid economic transition altered the structure of the labour market. Workers who were laid off by large firms tried to find new jobs in the service sector. Small and medium-sized firms in competitive industries went out of business or relocated to less developed countries in search of lower wages. Managerial innovation and industrial restructuring fragmented the labour market and disrupted industrial relations. Increasing heterogeneity in labour markets and intensifying market competition turned yesterday's colleagues into today's rivals.

4.3 The economy, wages and employment

The turn to a market-oriented policy yielded considerable results in the first half of the 1980s owing to the sudden economic recovery in world markets and an improvement in the domestic industrial environment. High economic growth continued until 1988. Surprisingly, the political turmoil and labour disputes of 1987 did not disrupt economic growth. On the contrary, the growth rate was over 10 per cent for three years before and after 1987. A sudden drop occurred in 1989 and the decline continued thereafter. Although there were no signs of crisis in terms of economic indices, the economy has experienced various "crisis phenomena" since 1989. The Rho and Kim governments warned that economic decline would result from political turmoil and labour unrest. Unions accused the government of using the term as a political tactic to suppress the legal demands of workers. For instance, an official alert about economic recession was made every spring when wage negotiations started in all industries. Almost a decade after 1989, and after government warnings of recession, numerous crisis symptoms were actually observed. They included a growing balance of payments deficit, high inflation, wage hikes, excessive expansion of service-related consumption, external pressure to open the domestic market especially from the United States, and finally, the decline of international competitiveness. The GNP growth rate was only 5 per cent in 1992, the lowest since the collapse of the Yushin regime. This rate, still better than the European average, was hardly acceptable to the Korean people who had become accustomed to high growth of about 10 per cent for many years. The economic crisis afflicting the Roh and Kim governments had many causes: exhaustion of the government's export-promotion strategy, the partial failure of structural adjustment in industry, delayed technological upgrading, market opening to foreign manufacturers and foreign capital, and skyrocketing labour costs caused by the wage explosion after 1987. Two points are worth mentioning here.

First, business made huge investments in information and advanced technology during the Kim government as reflected in the high investment rate during this period. This indicates that business chose investment as the best strategy for crisis management. But, unfortunately, most investment was procured from foreign loans and government could not control the conditions of such loans. The annual repayments caused a sudden drain of foreign currency holdings in the second half of 1997 and, eventually, IMF intervention in December 1997.

Second, unions distrusted attempts by government and employers to weaken worker demands for new labour laws by stressing the economic crisis. Although there were signs of a downturn in the economic indices, unions contended that this was by no means a 'crisis'. In addition, the national economy made a sudden recovery in 1994/1995 mainly owing to the short-lived boom in semiconductors. Most conglomerates reported higher profits in these two years. Firms seemed prosperous and money flowed everywhere. In this atmosphere, union distrust of government and business deepened. No one recognized, however, that the national economy would soon be in real trouble.

It is worth studying the effect of the short-term wage explosion in connection with the decline in political activism among labour unions. In spite of the rapid decline in international competitiveness and firms' inability to pay, wages have risen steadily at a pace well above productivity rates since 1987. Moreover, working conditions have gradually improved, with a shorter working day and better fringe benefits including children's education and housing allowances. Improved working conditions, the valuable fruit of the great struggle, promote worker compliance and commitment to firms, bringing employees back from street rallies into the workplace. As usual, the unlimited labour supply in the private sector weakens workers' bargaining power so that unskilled workers are prone to political activism. But better working conditions and a labour shortage in the new sectors of industry caused worker interest to shift from political unionism to economic unionism. Intensified competition in domestic markets as a consequence of economic liberalization and globalization favours compromise between employers and workers in their common fear of bankruptcy and unemployment in the midst of economic recession. This explains the change in labour orientation from the political to the economic and pragmatic.

5. Unions and the politics of crisis management

5.1 IMF regulation

In 1998, the Republic of Korea introduced an IMF austerity policy. The Kim Dae Jung government had no other option but to accept the terms of the IMF intervention, whose main goal was economic stabilization. The direction of the reform policies was imposed before Kim's government was inaugurated. However, implementing the policies and resolving conflicts of interest depended on the political capacity of the new regime. It is not surprising to find more congruencies than divergencies between IMF recommendations and Kim's reform which had been presented to the public during the presidential election. But it remained uncertain how far the IMF package was consistent with and supportive of Kim's political platform, described as a "democratic market economy". The "democratic market economy" has three elements that distinguish Kim's government from previous regimes: a better balance between large and medium-sized firms in the national economy, more equity, and more reliance on the market. President Kim Dae Jung is well aware of the inefficiency and negative effects of state-led capitalism and rapid growth with heavy reliance on conglomerates. The government planned to break up the conglomerates into smaller and more manageable units, but employers argued that restructuring these "chaebols" would ruin national competitiveness. People asked how the government could improve welfare under an austerity policy. Some critics stressed that more reliance on the market could be detrimental to social justice, as was the case in the United States.

As the IMF package emphasized deregulation and structural adjustment, Kim's government put more emphasis on the market economy than on democratic issues such as equity and welfare. In the economic crisis efficiency took priority over social justice. This provoked discontent among wage earners in the lower and middle classes who had voted for him in the presidential election. Employers and shareholders also expressed strong doubts about some aspects of the economic reform, contending that selling out strategic firms would lead to the breakdown of industrial competitiveness in world markets. Crisis management meant implementing unattractive and unpopular policies, but without economic recovery conflicts of interest between different social groups would constrain the capacity of the ruling party.

5.2 The first Social Compact

Even though the ruling party is supported by workers, the middle classes and intellectuals, its power to force the conglomerates to restructure is very limited. The austerity policy is likely to raise popular discontent against the Kim government. With inflation above 10 per cent, a large proportion of Koreans are suffering from wage cuts and drastic increases in interest rates. Mass unemployment has hit consumption and deepened the recession. The longer the austerity policy continues, the more discontented the population becomes.

President Kim decided to construct a consensus-building mechanism, i.e. a tripartite committee of government, employers and workers. In January 1998, shortly after his election victory, he announced the creation of a tripartite committee responsible for negotiating pending issues and setting reform agendas. They include the structural reform of conglomerates, economic stabilization, legalization of layoff, government protection of the unemployed, improvement of social security and the construction of a social safety-net. The committee reached the first Social Compact since the liberation in February 1998. It contains agreements on a number of issues which indicate that government and employers have accepted worker demands for participation in policy making in favour of industrial democracy. In this respect, Kim's government succeeded in including organized workers in the politics of crisis management and persuading them to support the restrictive economic policy imposed by the "Technical Agreement" with IMF.

However, the government could not pacify employers who insisted that massive layoffs were essential in a period of austerity. Unions contended that employers were betraying the spirit of the Social Compact. A tremendous number of firms collapsed during the first half of 1998. Government ordered 15 financing companies to shut down as well as two conglomerates. As unemployment soared with the passage of time, unions began to demand job security in accordance with the Agreement. Workers at Hyundai Motor Company, the largest automobile firm in the country, went on strike in protest against a management decision to lay off a large number of regular workers and reduce production lines and facilities. The struggle was not violent as in the authoritarian past, but continued for almost two months with KCTU support. KCTU leader Kap-Young Lee mobilized 120,000 workers from 16 major cities in the struggle against the layoff policy and job instability. In spite of government efforts to act in the spirit of the Social Compact, the economic crisis and soaring unemployment undermined the tripartite committee. There was a lack of trust between the three parties and increasing discontent among the rank and file.

5.3 The limits of tripartite negotiation

The compromise satisfied the conditions of the "Technical Agreement" signed by the previous government. The Social Compact provided President Kim with a firm foundation on which to base the rigorous reform policies. During the first half of 1998 he frequently reminded the public of the spirit of compromise whenever the media accused the government of delaying the necessary reforms. At first he succeeded in gaining working-class confidence and meeting challenges from business and shareholders. But KCTU threatened to withdraw from the tripartite committee unless the other members accepted the employment security laws. Finally, the Confederation pulled out in February 1999, claiming that the committee had no power to implement any agreement that it reached. FKTU, another labour member of the committee, also threatened to withdraw unless its demands were satisfied. These demands corresponded closely with the points that caused KCTU to withdraw: they included six important questions that had remained unresolved since the labour code was amended. The unions wanted to stop employer-led layoffs and to ensure labour/manager consensus prior to dismissal. They also wanted to introduce an Employment Security Act, to prepare complete unemployment protection, and to improve worker participation in management. They wanted to introduce work-sharing programmes without wage cuts, and finally, to ensure full implementation of the tripartite agreement and recognition of the legal and political status of the tripartite committee. In other words, the second tripartite committee achieved no more than the first committee. In fact the first agreement, containing 90 items of reform, exceeded the political capacity of Kim's regime and, to make matters worse, the relative success of the first Social Compact turned out to be a tremendous political burden. Trade unions began to organize a general strike just after they withdrew from the committee in the spring of 1999.

There are several reasons for the very limited success of tripartite negotiation in the Republic of Korea. First of all, although it takes the form of a tripartite agreement, any compromise is in fact an élitist agreement between leaders at national level. Participation in making policy and monitoring its implementation is required for tripartism to be effective. An organizational and administrative infrastructure is needed to put any tripartite agreement into effect. However, there are no organizational and administrative bodies at regional and local level through which employers and workers can collaborate in implementing policies. It is true that the Social Compact as a national consensus helps to calm unrest and reduce social costs; it also strengthens the political platform on which the ruling party has based its reform policies. However, it is an élitist committee without official networks through which business and labour can work together to produce results at local level; it is therefore extremely fragile. When KCTU threatened to strike just after it withdrew, employers found that the committee was not an effective channel of communication. As the economic crisis was deeper and longer than expected, serious doubts arose about the role of the tripartite committee and its political significance. The broad and vague political slogan "democratic market economy" could not persuade the partners to be faithful to the spirit of compromise. Of the many doubts and questions raised, three are worth mentioning here.

First, to what extent should conglomerates implement downsizing and was the restructuring imposed by IMF and government truly necessary for economic recovery? President Kim seemed to emphasize the role of small- and medium-sized firms in the national economy but that did not have to mean the entire break-up of chaebols into independent firms. It meant that economic concentration should be reduced so that conglomerates would have less influence on politics and society. But how far, in what degree, and in which direction remained uncertain. It is still questionable whether downsizing chaebol firms to fulfill government guidelines ensures competitiveness in world markets.

Second, the legalization of layoff promotes labour market flexibility whereas long-term employment increases labour costs. However, mass layoffs reduce organizational adaptability to new technology and rapidly changing business environments. Since the mid-1980s some Japanese firms have adopted American-style employment systems in response to the rapid decline in international competitiveness. But will American-style flexibility result in productivity improvement in the Republic of Korea, where firm-centred employment is a long tradition, and to be dismissed means "social death", as there is practically no chance of re-entry into larger firms which prefer to recruit young workers without job experience? Firm-centred employment maximizes functional flexibility as employees acquire multiple skills by rotating through many tasks. Does the replacement of functional flexibility with flexibility in the size of the workforce guarantee a rapid recovery from economic recession and high productivity growth, as neo-liberal market theorists claim? No clear answer has emerged as yet.

Finally, will the austerity policy be conducive to economic recovery in spite of the drastic decline in domestic consumption as a result of wage cuts, tax increases and soaring inflation? Wage earners are very doubtful about the government policy of "hardship-sharing" manifest in the sudden reduction of annual income by almost 30 per cent. It is now believed that the debt crisis was caused by an inflow of tremendous foreign loans to conglomerates and undisciplined investment in production facilities. If we admit that large firms and financial institutions are primarily responsible for the foreign debt crisis, does it help the situation to make them bankrupt? What compensates for numerous medium-sized firms, financially solid and prosperous in the product market, if they are in danger of bankruptcy because of the frozen money market? If we accept that there is no other option except to endure economic hardship, what can console frustrated and distressed wage earners? All these questions await a clear answer. The "democratic market economy" is not so clearly thought out as to persuade wage earners to sit and wait until living conditions get better. Moreover, misgivings are growing, since government policy packages have frequently revealed inconsistencies and contradictions.

5.4 Unemployment as a bottleneck

Unemployment is a situation that wage earners cannot tolerate over a long period. Whereas inflation is the most urgent issue for business, wage earners are mostly concerned about unemployment. The National Statistics Office announced that the number of unemployed had almost tripled in the year after the IMF intervention, reaching 1,850,000 at the end of 1998. Statistics for 1961-1998 show that the GDP growth rate fluctuated between 5 and 15 per cent except for a sharp drop to -5 per cent in 1981. Inflation was also unstable during the 1960s and 1970s, culminating at 29 per cent in 1979, the year when the Yushin regime collapsed with the assassination of President Park. Since then, inflation has been relatively stable throughout the 1980s and 1990s. However, the foreign debt crisis terminated the stability and inflation went up to 13 per cent within a few months of the IMF intervention.

Inflation is not new to the Republic of Korea, where rapid growth was inevitably accompanied by moderate rates of inflation. However, high unemployment is entirely new to the Korean people and the government. As reflected in the overall trend, successful economic growth curbed unemployment for four decades, the rate remaining below 5 per cent since the early 1970s. The country has been praised for achieving almost full employment without a rigorous labour market policy. But the record has been broken by an 8 per cent unemployment rate that approximates the average for European countries. Although it may be inevitable, the steep increase in unemployment is problematic.

More serious is the fact that the government is unprepared for mass unemployment. It is often contended that the country is least prepared for unemployment and worker protection since joblessness has been solved by the "growth-first policy". Policy makers in government were convinced for decades that speedy growth would create plentiful jobs for skilled and unskilled workers alike, and that allocating a government budget to unemployment programmes was wasteful. This explains why the government did not respond to unemployment until the mid-1990s and delayed the introduction of employment insurance until 1995.

The Kim government allocated a very large special budget to this policy area. The unemployment budget for 1998 amounted to US$11 billion, one-third of which was reserved for unemployment benefits and living allowances; a small portion was for job creation, job replacement and job training. The allocation was increased to US$16 billion in 1999. As far as the size of the budget is concerned, the government effort was remarkable. Policy makers believed that foreign capital would come back once the right of layoff was guaranteed, and unemployment would then be resolved naturally. President Kim repeatedly emphasized that it would not be long until the crisis ended, possibly within one-and-a-half years. At the beginning stage of policy implementation, however, the unemployment rate was still expected to go up as a result of the massive downsizing of chaebol firms that would be completed in the second half of 1999.

Continuing high unemployment puts tremendous pressure on Kim's regime. It is both a cause and an effect of the politics of reform. If unemployment continues over a considerable period and other reform programmes are delayed, it is likely that the government will face a serious political challenge from its supporters, i.e. wage earners. In addition, the lack of experience in labour market intervention and the loose organization of labour administration make labour politics ineffective. Unemployment is a bottleneck in the politics of reform. It is fair to say that the success of reform depends on maximizing the feedback effect, curbing unemployment effectively, introducing active labour market policies and establishing an administrative infrastructure to carry out the spirit of the Social Compact.

5.5 Improvement of human rights

The Republic of Korea was notorious for human rights abuses - civil rights, political rights and worker rights. For three decades of authoritarian repression, torture, imprisonment and illegal dismissal were inflicted on political dissidents and social and labour activists. Human rights are the most sensitive issue for leaders of the labour movement and rank-and-file workers alike, since political oppression is an obstacle to the improvement of working conditions and workers' standard of living. President Kim Dae Jung promised to improve human rights and eliminate illegal and unfair treatment of political dissidents and labour activists in his inauguration speech. The recognition of human rights has been improved under the present government. In this regard, President Kim deserves praise for taking some positive steps.

In June 1998 when President Kim visited the United States he announced a political schedule for the establishment of a National Human Rights Committee to monitor and indict illegal and violent actions on the part of ruling groups including bureaucrats, the police and employers. His promise was fulfilled in March 1999 when a law was passed creating the National Human Rights Committee. The Committee is a politically neutral and financially independent organ in charge of all official tasks concerning the violation of human rights. It is too early to say how much it will contribute to improving human rights and to eliminating brutality and violence at workplaces. However, the establishment of the Committee is a sign of progress. Before the law was passed the government released most of the labour activists who were in prison, in celebration of March 1st. Over 400 activists were imprisoned in 1998 but many were released in 1999. There are still many laws that hold back the progress of human rights; these are the focus of discussions on legal reform.

In spite of the improvement, there are still many human rights abuses in the labour movement and employment relations. Such cases increased dramatically with the deepening of economic recession and mass dismissals during the foreign debt crisis. Unemployment hit disadvantaged groups disproportionately, so that women, unskilled workers and casual labourers were the first to lose their jobs. Although legislation to prevent discrimination against women at work was introduced by the previous government, young women workers were the first to be dismissed since people did not think of them as the family breadwinner. This was accepted without resistance in the unprecedented economic crisis, but the process hid many cases of abuse. Male workers threatened with dismissal were no exception. Most employees were forced to accept sizeable wage cuts in the face of economic disaster. Otherwise their firm would close down because of bankruptcy and restrictive government policy. Violation of rights falls into four categories.

First is unfair labour practice. Before democratization, unfair labour practice occurred in most workplaces, regardless of firm size. Physical punishment was not uncommon. Employers enforced overtime and if employees refused to work more than their regular hours they could be dismissed without notice.

Second is the imprisonment of unionists who organize protests and strikes. Industrial disputes tended to result in damage to all parties: wounded police officers, arrested workers and broken production facilities. The government used riot police to suppress worker protest, while employers hired guards to protect their production facilities. Even when workers declared a peaceful protest, riot police were deployed in front of the factory. Unionists who organized protests and respected all the procedures stipulated in the Labour Union Laws and the Laws on Arbitration of Industrial Disputes were also subject to arrest on charge of "obstructing business". In1998, when KCTU called a general strike against the restructuring policy that generated and legalized massive layoffs, many strike leaders were imprisoned. The story of Mando machinery indicates how strikes were destroyed by the riot police and the NSL (National Security Law). The Mando strikers were attacked by 10,000 riot police and dozens of workers were arrested and beaten by armed policemen. The strikes occurring in the years just before and after IMF intervention yielded a long list of arrests (Amnesty International, 1999). Most were important union figures, including the Secretary-General of KCTU and the president of the Korean Federation of Public Sector Unions. The number of arrests fluctuated over time, culminating with 611 detentions in 1989. It then declined gradually but began to show a steep increase with the amendment of labour laws in 1996 and the economic crisis of 1998.

Third, illegal dismissal caused concern during the economic crisis of 1998. As mentioned earlier, the number of unemployed increased dramatically from 500,000 in 1997 to 1,850,000 in 1998. It is difficult to calculate how many people were dismissed illegally and how many were allowed to petition their employer. Workers dismissed during this period rarely had an opportunity to appeal because of the economic crisis and firms' desperate battle for survival. Unemployment statistics indicate that the massive layoffs mainly affected disadvantaged groups in the labour market, who lacked skills, experience and education.

Fourth, discrimination on the basis of gender or physical defect is a serious problem. The Republic of Korea is one of the countries that offer lower wages and fewer opportunities of promotion to women and disabled workers. During the last two decades the average wage for women was 60 - 70 per cent that of men, and disabled people could not find jobs in the formal sector. Ironically, however, female workers were over-represented in export manufacturing in those years. Employers with labour-intensive factories liked to hire young female workers to operate assembly lines in order to reduce labour costs and to accelerate labour turnover. Moreover, female workers could not appeal to courts or resist employer decisions on termination of employment. This explains why female workers constituted the main force of the labour protest in the 1970s. But this climate has changed rapidly since the labour dispute of 1987.

The Kim Dae Jung government introduced legislation to outlaw gender discrimination in employment and promotion in 1998. The law stipulates equality of job opportunity and promotion in internal labour markets between men and women, with sanctions against employers who do not respect the law. Government also encourages the recruitment of disabled workers by providing wage support to employers who offer them jobs and training. Despite these efforts, feminist groups and social organizations claim that female workers were the main group to be sacrificed in the massive layoffs of 1998. This claim is supported by statistics that show a sharp decline in the number of young, female, and unskilled workers compared to other demographic groups.

There are many legal and institutional constraints that undermine trade union activities and workers' rights to organize, negotiate and express opinion. Trade unionists began to request international organizations to exert pressure on the government. Such organizations have sent inspectors and observers quite frequently since the labour dispute of 1987. Their reports to the government of the Republic of Korea contain a common recommendation that labour laws and other legislation should be reformed in the light of ILO Conventions. The ILO examined two complaints from Korean trade unions and sent an official letter to the government in November 1998 (Amnesty

International, op. cit.). It reads: "The Committee must express its deep concern over the fact that trade union leaders and members are still detained or on trial, it would appear, for activities linked to collective labour disputes. The Committee is convinced that it will not be possible for a stable industrial relations system to function harmoniously in the country as long as trade unionists are the subject of detentions and judicial proceedings." Although the Republic of Korea became a member of ILO in 1991 and joined OECD in 1996, the government has still not ratified ILO Convention No. 87 on freedom of association or Convention No. 98 on workers' right to organize and to bargain collectively.

6. Politics in unions: Leadership and recent issues

6.1 Recent issues

In the midst of the economic crisis of 1998, workers at the Hyundai Motor Company went on strike to demand the unconditional repeal of the company's layoff policy, claiming that it violated the spirit of the Social Compact which required that efforts be made to avoid layoff prior to the final decision. Since the Hyundai Motor Company, the number one auto manufacturer in the country, was a major contributor to exports, government observed the strike carefully and studied its effect on unions in other sectors. The strike continued for two full months from June to July with no intervention from outside, e.g. shutdown of factories or attack by riot police. Government tried to conciliate angry workers who were protesting against the mass layoffs which were declared unilaterally without negotiation with company unions. Workers claimed that the dismissal of 10,000 workers within a few months was illegal and immoral. After two months the strike was resolved peacefully with government mediation.

This outcome gives the impression that the union won the strike and strengthened its power to negotiate with the state and employers. But the opposite is true. The union lost the game and lost its power to negotiate in the midst of unprecedented economic recession caused by the austerity policy. The union of the Hyundai Motor Company is one of the strongest and most militant in the Republic of Korea. The fact that Hyundai workers finally accepted the government recommendation and the employer's layoff schedule had a tremendous impact on the unions in FKTU and KCTU. Layoff was accepted. After this event workers' main attention turned from aggressive attitudes to defensive and pragmatic issues such as compensation and severance pay. Industrial disputes rarely occurred in the latter half of 1998 and compensation became the most important issue in dismissal.

In 1998, the government undertook four important tasks under IMF surveillance: legalization of layoff for labour market flexibility; privatization;

reform of financial institutions; rationalization of chaebol firms (conglomerates). All these programmes had a negative impact on unions in terms of job insecurity, declining membership, and especially loss of the leading unions in KCTU, i.e. unionized public enterprises. FKTU and KCTU collaborated in the struggle against government policy, KCTU being more active and aggressive than FKTU. KCTU elaborated counter-agendas: job sharing against layoff, opposition to privatizing public enterprises and introduction of Employment Security Laws. FKTU expressed support for this platform. They developed six agendas in opposition to the second tripartite committee, claiming that the committee functioned only to induce workers to agree to government and employer demands. The six agendas are still the most important pending issues for government, employers and workers. Union claims include the following: refusal of employer-led layoff and introduction of labour/management negotiation prior to dismissal; introduction of the Employment Security Act; complete protection for the unemployed; legalization of worker participation in management; introduction of work sharing without wage cuts; reconstruction of the tripartite committee as a legal and political institution.

Government refused to accept these demands, mainly because of their negative impact on economic recovery and national competitiveness. President Kim Dae Jung repeatedly emphasizes the trend towards flexible production systems and unrestrained competition between firms, regardless of nationality. He has pursued neo-liberal policies similar to those of President Reagan and Mrs. Thatcher, stressing that the economy can adapt to world standards by promoting the "market", which was seriously distorted by authoritarian state intervention. In accordance with this firm belief in the market economy, priority has been laid on fairness - fair competition without state intervention, fair transactions between firms, and fair process without violation of 'fair trade laws'. Fairness is acceptable to most actors, but 'which fairness?' raises more debate regarding the neutrality of laws and politics. The government spent US$100 billion on rationalizing banks and financial institutions in 1998. The result was successful. But citizens had to pay higher taxes to make up the financial deficits. Unions ask why wage earners should pay for restructuring. Is massive and unconditional layoff inevitable, as the government insists and are there no other alternatives for maintaining job security and reducing high unemployment? Why are unions excluded from policy making at both enterprise and national level, when these policies are decisive for workers' income and job security? Is the neo-liberal market ideology helpful to workers and unions, or detrimental to worker welfare? Unions are gradually losing confidence in President Kim's policy, which they regard as detrimental to worker welfare and union activities. The Kim government applies labour laws to industrial disputes and especially to illegal strikes. Unions repeatedly contend that the labour laws are not neutral but favour employers. The strike ban in public enterprises is good evidence for the union contention.

6.2 Difficulties of leadership

The reproduction of leadership is the most essential element of the labour movement. If leaders accept government repression and an exploitative labour policy, the labour movement serves the interests of the ruling class and cannot be democratic. Labour leadership is of two kinds, corresponding with the national centres. FKTU tends to cooperate with state labour policy regardless of government characteristics, while KCTU takes an independent position, with the aim of democratizing industrial relations. FKTU and KCTU both supported Kim Dae Jung in the last presidential election since he was more sympathetic towards the labour movement than other candidates. The creation of the tripartite committee is evidence of his sympathy with unions and his political stance.

In spite of significant changes in politics and the union environment, the chief concerns of labour leaders have remained unchanged under the present regime. If unions call a strike, the leaders may be the target of police action, and could face legal penalties. When leaders are arrested and imprisoned on charge of violating labour laws, it takes a long time to build new leadership in the absence of key figures. Usually, it takes two or three years to re-establish authentic leadership after those in the forefront of union action have been removed. Two problems bother labour leaders when they decide to strike against government policy: these are the strong possibility of imprisonment, and the breakdown of allegiance of rank-and-file workers in the face of government intimidation.

Union leaders face a number of difficulties. First, a strike may destroy leadership, especially when the strike is broken by the government. On the other hand, a successful strike is likely to strengthen leadership but success cannot really be expected in circumstances where state and employers are not friendly to organized labour. It takes a long time to reconstruct leadership after the breakdown of union direction. This explains why labour leaders change so frequently in KCTU compared with FKTU.

Second, a frustrated strike undermines the allegiance of rank-and-file workers and reduces solidarity. Many strikers give up when government announces that they will be punished for violating the labour laws. Weak allegiance is detrimental to unions, and it is extremely difficult for leaders to encourage workers in the face of government intimidation. When union leaders are arrested the rank and file have to build up new loyalties. This process generates conflict among workers, and can even split the union into factions.

Third, strikers face hostile public opinion in the Republic of Korea. The only strike which people supported was the labour dispute of 1987 that started democratization. The mass media and leading newspapers strongly criticized the selfishness of the Subway Union in calling a strike, stressing the national economic crisis. The headlines of leading newspapers expressed the fury of Seoul citizens against the strike action which was disrupting their daily transport. Unions need to improve public opinion about the labour movement, but this is extremely difficult in a country where wage earners are hostile to radical and militant action on the part of workers. This explains why union leaders have not won elections even in industrial cities in the past.

Fourth, unions suffer from financial problems, especially at national level. As mentioned earlier, the system is based on enterprise unions. Workers pay 1-2 per cent of their monthly wage to the enterprise union, which pays something less than 10 per cent of these dues to the industrial union and the national centre. As union dues flow upward, financial problems are naturally worse for the apex bodies. The Seoul Subway Union spent most of its funds on the ten-day strike but it is financially stable compared to other unions. The larger the company size becomes, the better the financial situation is. In contrast, the apex body cannot escape financial problems because of its total reliance on member unions. The Federation of Public Enterprise Unions could not provide financial support for the Subway Union because it did not have the means to do so. The lack of funds hampers national centres as well as industrial unions in developing policy packages that require an enormous budget. The bulk of dues from member unions is used to maintain offices and facilities, and pay salaries. Financial conditions vary between the federations, the older ones having a more solid base than those established recently. FKTU is better endowed than KCTU because it receives a government subsidy which amounts to a few million dollars a year. While FKTU has other sources of income from renting out offices and operating small stores, KCTU has to pay rent on its headquarters office every month.

Financial constraints mean that union leaders cannot develop educational programmes and other activities that are important to worker solidarity. FKTU is better off in this respect, but other organizations have to reserve most of their budget for routine activities. A sudden decline in membership precipitated by the bankruptcy of numerous firms during the economic crisis has worsened the poverty of Korean unions. FKTU and KCTU both lost a large proportion of their members when the organizing rate fell from 15 per cent in 1997 to 11 per cent in 1998. Manufacturing and finance are badly hit because most bankruptcies occur in these sectors. Financial problems are analysed more closely below.

Labour leaders face three main negative factors. These are hostile public opinion, apathy of rank-and-file workers and conflict within the union. Public opinion rapidly turns against union activities these days because of economic hardship, and workers on the shopfloor are more interested in wages, job security and company welfare than in social and political issues. The apathy of the rank and file becomes greater when leaders concentrate on social and political issues. Conflict and discord within the union have something to do with the composition of the workforce and ideological orientation. Conflict within unions reflects the structure of Korean society which is based on regionalism and the old school tie. But the ideological orientation of leading groups became more influential in the period of democratization after 1987.

6.3 Union finance and expenditure

It is worth analysing more carefully the extent to which unions suffer from financial constraints and how they try to overcome this problem. As mentioned earlier, the national centres rely solely on dues from enterprise unions, which remit about 10 per cent of their revenue to the federation and the national centre. The federation is considered more important than the national centre with respect to membership dues. Neither the federation nor the national centre can force enterprise unions to pay. Many pay no dues at all, while others pay double dues to both FKTU and KCTU.

According to a survey conducted in 1989, average union dues as a percentage of total wage were 0.68 per cent for all industries and 0.82 per cent for manufacturing. In the metal industry 89 per cent of unions paid a subscription to the federation in 1989 (11 per cent paid nothing). On average, 10 per cent of enterprise unions paid no dues to their federation or national centre in that year. The figures have probably not changed much. It is easy to calculate the revenue of FKTU and KCTU if the number of member unions is known. In 1989, FKTU=s total revenues amounted to 705 million Won (US$ 900,000)and the share of union dues was 66 per cent (Park and Park, 1989).

FKTU expenditure falls into three main categories: maintenance costs and salaries (50 per cent), routine activities (25 per cent) financial costs and others (25 per cent). Since half the revenue has to be reserved for offices and staff, only a quarter can be used for activities. The development of new programmes can hardly be expected in these circumstances. This is why FKTU has relied upon state subsidies in implementing special programmes for members. FKTU has a large building in a financial district of Seoul, and also a training centre donated by the government after 1987 in a satellite city of Seoul. KCTU's yearly revenue is far smaller than that of FKTU because it is newly established, and its membership is just one-third of FKTU's. In addition, KCTU is not entitled to a state subsidy since it is not legally recognized. Financial constraints thus undermine KCTU's capacity to develop and implement policies for worker solidarity and social and political reform.

Most enterprise unions also suffer from financial constraints except large ones with over 10,000 workers. There are approximately 100 unions of this size. These are more affluent than the national centres because of regular income from members. They are able to use funds for outsourcing policy development and special programmes such as constructing horizontal networks with other unions and consolidating worker solidarity across industries and firms. In contrast, small- and medium-sized unions cannot carry out even routine activities because of poverty. During the 1980s these unions sometimes held special fund-raising campaigns selling shirts and calendars for example. But this is no longer efficient as public opinion is against union militancy. Meanwhile, KCTU tries to improve its financial position by encouraging affiliated unions to pay their fees and requesting international NGOs to contribute. But the decline in membership due to the economic recession is undermining its effort. It will take a while for KCTU to become financially stable.

6.4 Exploring new resources for solidarity

As already stated, public opinion is gradually turning against the labour movement, especially in the present context of economic recession. There are two main reasons for this negative trend: one is a deep-rooted conservatism and anti-labour ideology peculiar to Korean society, and the other is the predictable and harmful impact of labour disputes on economic growth. Rapid growth seems natural to the people, and any factor that slows economic growth is considered harmful. The labour movement is considered as a "necessary evil" in the process of economic development. Social support for the labour movement culminated just after the dispute of 1987 and then declined rapidly. It is ironical that the labour movement was unable to strengthen its social and political position in the process of democratization although it was largely responsible for the demise of the authoritarian regime. There is a strong tendency in Korean society to oppose the rise of organized labour in politics and the economy. Conservative groups viewed the tripartite committee of 1998 with suspicion and discontent. Thus, it is a matter of urgency for labour leaders to develop new resources for worker solidarity and cooperation with other social movements. Labour leaders think that the new social movements (NSMs) which are emerging are good resources for solidarity.

Two factors accelerate the new solidarity between unions and NSMs. One is the expansion of common interests in the process of democratization. As unions become more active in social and political reform, NSMs invite union leaders to workshops and conferences on regional issues more frequently than before. Unions and NSMs are developing networks for information exchange and cooperative action. Second, a survey reports that many NSM activists are recruited from the labour movement as public concern has moved to postindustrial values since the early 1990s (Song, 1998). For instance, activists who were union leaders in female-dominated factories in the past are now playing a leading role in the feminist movement. Such activists are also found in the welfare movement, consumers' rights groups and the human rights campaign. They have deep sympathy with workers and develop close ties with union leaders. Labour leaders make use of formal and informal networks in expanding links with NSMs (Kim and Song, 1997).

How far this effort will be successful and what sort of solidarity will be achieved are still uncertain. It is desirable for unions to develop solidarity with social organizations, but common agendas such as peace, environmental protection and human rights may undermine the cause and purpose of a labour movement based on class. Nevertheless, solidarity with NSMs is pursued as a desirable way for unions to escape from the conservative social atmosphere that is hostile to the labour movement.

7. Conclusion: Future tasks

The union movement in the Republic of Korea is considered to predict the future of organized labour in Asia. It is not inappropriate to state that the Korean movement is the most influential in the continent B influential in volume, impact of strike action and power to mobilize workers in the struggle against authoritarian labour practice. It is influential not in the exercise of legal and institutional power but in the struggle to gain such power. The movement is extremely fluid in pursuit of its goal. This strength and fluidity attracts much attention from organized labour in countries such as Thailand and Malaysia. Several points are worth mentioning in this regard.

First, the Korean union movement is fairly healthy and not corrupt in comparison with some Latin American countries where official unions were under state control for a long period. It is not so imbued with "give-and-take politics" even in the case of the Federation of Korean Trade Unions (FKTU), the only apex body which had official recognition before the 1988 amendment of labour laws. Thanks to its clean image the movement grew fast and gained more support from the middle and lower classes in the 1990s.

Second, the labour movement played the most influential and decisive role in the struggle against authoritarianism in the past two decades and in triggering the transition to democracy in 1987. Organized labour put formidable pressure on authoritarian leadership in all three major regimes when NSMs were underdeveloped. It also made ordinary people aware of the importance of social justice and political freedom. Although progressive groups of organized labour were accused of extremism in the 1980s, democratization would not have been promoted without the unions' contribution.

Third, unions have achieved an outstanding record of development, despite repressive practices and legal restrictions, formal and informal barriers to organizing workers: most large firms are unionized except the Samsung conglomerate. The organizing rate still remains low but the fact that large firms are mostly unionized and that major factories carry out cooperative labour/management actions explains the union impact on politics and the economy. Large unions in big firms enjoy a financial surplus due to labour legislation that permits company unions to collect dues from member workers. In large unions, financial affluence hides a danger of corruption as reflected in frequent quarrels within unions.

Fourth and most important, attempts to overcome the limits of enterprise unionism cannot go unmentioned. Before the labour law amendment of 1996, industrial unions were marginalized by the legal ban on third party intervention in enterprise labour disputes and collective bargaining. Thus, the legal recognition of industrial unions was an important aim of the labour movement. It was finally achieved in the labour law amendment of 1998.

The Republic of Korea is a contested terrain between the European model and the Japanese model, i.e. industrial unionism and enterprise unionism. While the European model is more common in textiles, finance and services, the Japanese model dominates big manufacturing firms. This situation is a source of optimism for other Asian labour movements which, they feel, are limited by enterprise unionism combined with foreign capital.

Future tasks can be divided into three types: organizational, political, and economic. First is the question of organizing the trade union movement. It took almost ten years to construct an umbrella organization competing with FKTU and to obtain legal recognition. The attempt was frustrated several times but succeeded eventually. For the first time in Korean labour history worker representation was split between FKTU, KCTU, and KCIIF (independent unions). There were unbridgeable differences in policy orientation, political attitudes and goals between the three apex bodies: there are more differences than similarities between them. The country has thus entered an era of multiple unionism.

Building up strong industrial unionism was another task vigorously pursued by some unions and this was finally achieved in the new labour laws of February 1998. But big unions with 10,000 or more members are reluctant to be controlled by a national federation. The umbrella organizations are not yet able to support newly organizing unions and expand organizational boundaries by careful policies. Due to the weakness of national centres and industrial federations, the horizontal and vertical alliances that are the key to the growth of unionism are not yet fully developed. Therefore, the organizational task is to build strong alliances between unions.

Second is the political task. Organized labour played a crucial role in the transition to democracy in the Republic of Korea. But it failed to expand its organizational scope and political space. Unionization rates increased sharply for a few years after 1987 but began to drop from the mid-1990s, finally reaching the lowest level in the past three decades. In addition, organized labour was entirely excluded from the reform politics of Kim Young Sam's government. President Kim did not change the principle of labour politics but stressed a closer adherence to labour laws. Unions had no place in the political arena and no opportunity to exert pressure on policy makers. The party-labour link does not exist in Korean politics. In such an environment, union efforts to establish a political party cannot be fruitful. The development of party-labour links is necessary if unions are to gain some political influence. But the precise nature of these links is still open to debate.

The final task is economic. In advanced capitalist countries, unions are regarded as an important partner in improving productivity and competitiveness in world markets. Workers expect their union to ensure that they have good wages and working conditions. These two functions are usually contradictory and hard to satisfy simultaneously since high wages undermine firm competitiveness, especially in a country that has relied largely on cheap labour for comparative advantage in world markets. The Korean economy had long enjoyed benefits from a protectionist policy and was not prepared for globalization, free trade and world markets. But industrial restructuring for the global economy was not so urgent for unions, most of which were newly established and more concerned with raising wages and improving working conditions. Employers had to forego profits and sell their assets to pay increased wages and benefits in the early 1990s. Employers believed that a 'cost-pushing strategy' could placate angry workers and gain their commitment to the company. Employers made strenuous efforts to meet the new pressures from inside and outside by a managerial revolution that included downsizing, new pay schemes and employment systems. In this sense, the decade after 1987 was a period of industrial restructuring and re-engineering in terms of technological upgrading and managerial innovation. However, these efforts were not supported by unions because of distrust and animosity against employers. Distrust became stronger in the course of dispute settlements in the early 1990s. The amendment of labour laws in 1996 provoked another conflict between business and labour, instead of resolving tensions. Employers and unions both failed to improve flexibility in employment and production despite the fact that flexibility was essential to cope with the global economy.

The IMF intervention of December 1997 altered the entire atmosphere of conflict between employers and unions, as the government was obliged to implement new policies including labour reforms. The employment system has been significantly changed so as to reduce job security as well as lifelong employment. As layoffs became legal in February 1998, numerous workers lost their jobs. Unions realized that they were no longer on the offensive; they became passive and defensive in the midst of economic crisis and increasing unemployment. Unions are alert to the high rate of unemployment which, they know, encroaches on their organizational base and weakens their power to negotiate. Now it is desirable for unions to be more policy-oriented than strike-oriented in the deepening economic crisis.

The 1970s and 1980s were the era of struggle for political freedom and worker rights; the decade after the political opening of 1987 was the era of attempts to cultivate a mature partnership between politics and the economy. During the last ten years, unions have weathered democratization and globalization simultaneously. They have realized that to maintain worker unity across enterprise unions is not easy in a democratizing and globalizing economy due to the diverse interests of workers and intense market competition among firms. Although it will take time for unions to overcome these challenges, past experience indicates that they will grow into strong and healthy organizations in the Republic of Korea.

References

Amnesty International. 1999. *Workers' rights at a time of economic crisis in Republic of Korea* (AI Report ASA 25/02/99, Feb.).

Bognanno, M.F. 1988. *Korea's industrial relations at the turning point* (Seoul, KDI).

Collier, R.; Collier, D. 1980. *Inducements versus constraints: Desegregating corporation,* Working Paper No. 432 (Institute of Industrial Relations).

Dahl, R. 1971. *Polyarchy: Participation and opposition* (New Haven, Connecticut, Yale University Press).

Deyo, F. 1987. *The political economy of the new Asian development* (Ithaca, New York, Cornell University Press).

—. 1989. *Beneath the miracle* (Berkeley, California, University of California Press).

—. 1987. Haggard, S.; Koo, H.: "Labour in the political economy of East Asian industrialization," in *Bulletin of Concerned Asian Scholars*, Vol. 19, No. 2.

Freeman, R.; Medoff, J. 1984. *What do unions do?* (New York, Basic Books).

Gereffi, G.; Wyman, D. 1990. *Manufacturing miracle* (Princeton, Princeton University Press).

Kim, K.-D. 1992. *The sociology of industrial relations* (Seoul, Kyungmunsa).

Kim, Y.-H.; Song, H.K. 1997. *Network of trade unions in Korea* (Seoul, FKTU).

Koo, H. 1987. "The interplay of state, social class, and world system in East Asian development: The case of South Korea and Taiwan," in Deyo, F. (ed.): *The political economy of the New Asian development.*

Korean Confederation of Trade Unions. 1996. *KCTU White Paper* (Seoul, KCTU).

Lindauer, D.; et al. (eds.). 1997. *The strains of economic growth: Labour unrest and social dissatisfaction in Korea* (Cambridge, Massachusetts, Harvard Institute for International Development).

Martins, L. 1986. "The 'liberalization' of authoritarian rule in Brazil," in O'Donnell, G.; Schmitter, P.; Whitehead, L. (eds.): *Transition from authoritarian rule: Latin America* (Baltimore, Maryland, Johns Hopkins University Press).

O'Donnell, G.; Schmitter, P. 1986. *Transition from authoritarian rule: Tentative conclusion about uncertain democracies* (Baltimore, Maryland, Johns Hopkins University Press).

Park, K.-S.; Park, D.-J. 1989. *Korea's union* (Seoul, Korea Labour Institute) (Korean).

Przeworski, A. 1985. *Capitalism and social democracy* (Cambridge, UK, Cambridge University Press).

—. 1991. *Democracy and the market: Political and economic reforms in Eastern Europe and Latin America* (Cambridge, UK, Cambridge University Press).

Ramos, E.T. 1981. "Industrial relations strategies of trade unions in South East Asia: A comparative analysis", in *Agenda for Industrial Relations in Asian Development* (Tokyo, Japan Institute of Labour).

Song, H.K. 1992. *The state and organized labour in the transition to democracy,* Paper presented at the European Consortium for Political Research and later published as Working Paper (Hallym University).

—. 1993. "Working-class politics in reform democracy in South Korea," in *Korean Journal of Population and Development* (Seoul National University), Vol 23, No. 2.

—. 1998. "The analysis of participants in the new social movements in Korea: Mobilization and networks," in *Korean Social Sciences*, Vol. 20, No. 3 (Korean).

Stepan, A. 1978. *State and society: Peru in comparative perspective* (Princeton, New Jersey, Princeton University Press).

Valenzuela, S. 1989. "Labour movement in transition to democracy: A framework for analysis", in *Comparative Politics*, No. 2.

Yee, J.; Kwon, H. 1995. *Korea's labour union of the 1990s* (Seoul, Federation of Korean Trade Unions, Research Center) (Korean).

Trade union responses to globalization in Lithuania

Roma Dovydeniene

Introduction

In 1990 Lithuania rejoined the international community as a sovereign state. The transition from a centrally directed political and economic structure to one based on market principles and democracy has been longer and more complex than many people anticipated ten years ago. Economic transition is being accomplished under the influence of globalization and European integration. The first imposes ready-made models and rules for adapting the national economy to world markets, while the second involves an institutional and political model which must be implemented as a condition for accession to the European Union. Transformation is a challenge. This chapter analyses the response of trade unions to economic and social changes in Lithuania. It illustrates how far unions have maintained their position with respect to the traditional demands of constituents, which focus on wages, working conditions, employment and social security, and such demands as human resource development, gender equality and legal assistance.

The chapter gives an overview of the situation since the establishment of a liberal economic regime and it describes trade union responses to the changing environment. It shows the development of unions, their membership and structure; interrelations and international cooperation; the role of unions in establishing a legal basis for labour rights; their tasks in the labour market; union activities in training and education; promotion of equal opportunities; development of industrial relations, collective bargaining and tripartism. Finally, the chapter presents public and political attitude towards trade unions in Lithuania.

1. Overview of the situation since the establishment of a liberal economic regime

1.1 Social and economic conditions

Lithuania is the largest of the three Baltic countries with a population of 3.7 million and an area of 65,300 sq. km. Lithuania has borders with Latvia, Belarus, Poland and the Russian territory around Kaliningrad. The capital Vilnius has a population of 600,000. The country regained its independence on 11 March 1990 and since then the government has been committed to a market economy.

Lithuania re-emerged as an independent state with a fragile economic structure; it was formerly entirely dependent on the Soviet economic system. The country was particularly reliant on the USSR for primary energy resources: oil and other energy constituted 60 per cent of its imports from the USSR at the beginning of the decade. On the export side, Lithuanian industry and agriculture were mostly oriented to USSR markets. This meant that industries were not internationally competitive and they have faced major obstacles in finding alternative markets.

Lithuania had to deal with considerable difficulties during the short period when it was moving away from outdated traditions, lifestyle and modes of thought. The costs of transformation are reflected in the basic changes in Lithuania's GDP and the rate of inflation which reached 1162.6 per cent in 1992, falling to 2.4 per cent in 1998. Change in GDP was estimated at -34 per cent in 1992 and at +4.4 per cent in 1998.

New economic foundations were laid in 1991-1993: the share of agriculture in the national economy declined, services expanded and private business became a prominent sector. Industrial production fell because of adjustment problems linked with Lithuania's reorientation towards Western markets; foreign trade had similar difficulties and its share of GDP wavered. Economic problems are reflected in the unstable structure of domestic savings and investment and their reduced share of GDP.

New open markets and their respective social and economic structures were created in Lithuania in 1993-1994. The country's economy stabilized and private property emerged as the leading form of ownership. Lithuania became economically and politically open to Europe.

The first stage of privatization was carried out between 1991 and mid-1995. During this stage, state assets were sold off into private ownership in accordance with the *Law on the Initial Privatization of State Property* and other laws of the Republic of Lithuania. Investment vouchers were distributed to citizens in 1991 and these were used to buy divested property. The sold-off capital amounted to 3.4 billion Lt, which accounted for 30 per cent of total state assets.

During the second stage, privatization is being carried out for cash. The list of objects to be privatized is drawn up annually and approved by the government. The privatization process accelerated in 1997-1998. Sales of state property in 1998 were 17 times higher than in 1996/1997, amounting to 2.3 billion Lt (US$ 5.75 million).

The growth of consumer- and cost prices started to decline in 1993. The previous upsurge in prices was brought about by the elimination of price controls in 1991 as well as by more expensive production inputs from Russia.

In addition, Lithuania suffered from rouble-linked inflation, since Russian currency was used until October 1992. After the new currency, called the Litas, was introduced in 1993 Lithuania started to implement measures to stabilize the economy.

Economic stability is reflected in the structure of GDP, which shows that the basic macroeconomic proportions – private consumption, investment, separate industrial branches, etc. – are relatively fixed. During the seven years of reform a stable macroeconomic environment has been created with growth rates of more than 5 per cent. This is consistent with the Lithuanian goal of rapid integration into the EU.

Significant labour market problems have emerged during the process of economic restructuring. The official level of employment (ratio of employed to people of working age) fell from 66.7 per cent in 1991 to 58.1 per cent in 1996, and unemployment increased from 0.2 per cent to 8.3 per cent over the same period. Since 1996 there has been some improvement in the labour market and unemployment has declined to 7 per cent. In that year 49 per cent of workers were employed in services, 24 per cent in agriculture, 20 per cent in manufacturing industry and 7 per cent in construction.

The official unemployment rate is not high compared with other countries, but regional and structural differences are pronounced. The level of unemployment is two to three times higher in the worst affected areas than in those which are least affected. A particularly high level is noted in areas where economic activity is concentrated in a single industry or a small range of firms.

Due to the decline of traditional activities and the privatization of state enterprises certain groups of workers are facing severe difficulties in adjusting. This includes older workers, women and the unskilled. The traditional high employment of women is decreasing, and they now account for 50 per cent of the workforce, down from 56 per cent.

During the Soviet period, under a planned economy, wages were the most important source of income and the main factor determining consumption. Wages were determined through a system applied to all companies; low salaries and insignificant wage differentials were characteristic of that system. In 1991 the *Law on Wages* was adopted granting companies and organizations the right to regulate wages themselves depending on labour demand and supply, work load, quality and business success. However, the *Law on Wages* authorizes government to establish the minimum hourly wage and a minimum monthly salary. Wages cannot be lower than the minimum established by the government. From 1991 to January 1998 the minimum monthly salary changed 34 times. Despite this the real value of the minimum salary fell dramatically. The ratio of the minimum monthly salary to the average salary was also inconsistent. For the first three years this ratio dropped and in 1994 the minimum monthly salary (MMS) made up only 15.5 per cent of the average labour salary (ALS). Later on, the growth rate of MMS increased, reaching 45.8 per cent in 1997 and 41.75 per cent in 1998.

In 1990 the *Law on Citizens' Income Guarantees* was passed. The law was designed to guarantee a minimum standard of living to every citizen during the process of political and economic reform. In 1991 a minimum income was established for receipt of social benefits and this was expected to be linked to inflation. However, during a period when prices increased 13 times, the minimum income was increased only three times.

Although the average monthly wage increased by 5 per cent between 1997 and 1998, income disparity expanded significantly. There are great wage differentials between occupations. For example, the salaries of bank staff are 4-5 times higher than those of health workers or teachers. People working in the electricity supply system make 6-7 times more than those in large agricultural companies. In addition, the salaries of government officials are 2-3 times higher than the average salary for the total economy. The income of the wealthiest group is ten times higher than the income of the poorest.

According to a poverty line of 50 per cent of average expenditure per household member (an indicator used in poverty studies by European Union countries) in 1997 Lithuania's poor made up 16.6 per cent of the total population. As many as 37.2 per cent of households with three or more children are living below the poverty line. There is a very clear problem of impoverished families with children.

1.2 Social security

Social security guarantees the necessary financial support and services to persons who, due to old age, disability, sickness, maternity/paternity, guardianship of close relatives or unemployment cannot provide for themselves or their family from wages or other income. The social security system is composed of two main parts: social insurance and social assistance. There are also special social benefits.

Social insurance is the largest and most important part of social security. Current laws provide for compulsory insurance for the majority of workers, including those who also receive special benefits (military officials, scientists, etc.). The aim is to apply the principle of universal social insurance so that nobody is deprived of the rights and responsibilities inherent in this system.

Everybody also has the right to social assistance but, unlike social insurance, this is provided irrespective of contributions to those considered to be in need of such assistance. Social assistance takes the form of cash benefits and social services. Special benefits are usually paid as a supplementary pension.

2. The role of trade unions in a democratic society

2.1 The development of trade unions

During the years of Soviet occupation trade unions were the largest non-governmental organizations, representing 97 per cent of all employees. Union membership was more mandatory than freely chosen, due to the link between social insurance benefits and union membership. The unions also provided facilities for culture, sports and leisure activities, distributed goods and provided apartments that were difficult to obtain otherwise. Union leaders were elected by the managers and directors of the companies, therefore there were no serious labour conflicts or disputes. The conclusion of a collective agreement was formal and it was usually prepared by the company's administration. All trade unions were joined into 21 branch organizations and belonged to the Lithuanian Trade Union Council (LTUC). LTUC was affiliated to the Trade Union Council of the USSR, which was a member of WFTU.

The emergence of democratic and independent trade unions started with the independence movement "Sàjûdis", which spread to all spheres of public life: political, economic and social. A Sàjûdis group was established for trade union reconstruction, and three alternative approaches to trade union development were discussed:

- all unions that existed during the Soviet era should be closed down and new ones should be established;
- nothing should be changed within trade unions, as economic development will cause them to change by themselves;
- everything that is positive should remain (e.g. structure, members); democratic elections should be organized and unions should be reformed so as to operate in a market economy.

The Sàjûdis group raised the idea of a Trade Union Congress. Before the general Congress, unions had to convene congresses at branch level, adopt a new statute strengthening the principle of free choice and organize democratic elections of representatives and chairpersons.

The Committee for Congress Preparation was formed by representatives of the Lithuanian Trade Union Council, the Sàjûdis group and the Lithuanian Workers Union, at that time registered as a political organization. The general Trade Union Congress took place on 11 April 1990.

During the Congress the unions split, as only seven branch organizations had fulfilled the requirements. After the Congress these branch organizations remained independent and chose not to join the national centre, which was renamed the Lithuanian Free Trade Union Confederation.

In 1991 the Trade Union Community was established; this was an amalgamation of unions representing workers, farmers, teachers, researchers and the blind and deaf.

On 11 February, 1991 the Coordination Centre of the Lithuanian Trade Unions was established. It was founded by unions representing workers in local industry and services, those in the food industry, and radio and television employees. The Lithuanian Coordination Centre introduced a new concept for the establishment of a trade union structure. Based on Western unions' experience the authors of that concept suggested that all national trade union organizations should create structures reflecting the specific interests of blue-collar workers, white-collar workers and managers.

However, this idea was not very popular and specific unions represented people of the same profession. For example, the journalists' union, accountants' union, engineers' and architects' unions registered as public organizations and did not carry out the functions characteristic of trade unions.

On 20 February 1992 the Trade Union Federation was established, replacing the Union Coordination Centre and uniting seven branches: the communication workers' union, metal workers' union, union of health care employees, trade union federation of public services, union of food industry employees, union of commercial and cooperative workers, and the union of creative workers of radio and television.

The Federation brought together occupational unions which were willing to implement new work methods and exert a stronger influence on legislation; it aimed for social partnership and negotiation with government, the Supreme Council (Parliament at that time) and emerging employers' organizations. At its inaugural conference the Trade Union Federation adopted a resolution on collaboration with political parties, public organizations and movements, aiming for the development of a democratic Lithuanian state and supporting legal trade union demands.

At the end of 1990 the workers' union demanded a change in its statute, from a political organization to a registered trade union. As an alternative and newly established union it was financially and morally supported by AFL-CIO in the United States. The Lithuanian government also gave one-off financial support to the workers' union. This was opposed by other unions and caused doubts about the independence of the workers' union among the other national centres and branch organizations.

At the end of 1991 a Christian union - the Lithuanian Labour Federation - was established.

2.2 Trade union membership and structure

Despite the fact that trade unions are seeking an active and constructive role in society the government has ignored them almost completely in the development process. In 1990-1991 the Seimas (Parliament) legally and almost completely nationalized union assets, leaving only about one-third of the property for indirect union management. This issue has not yet been solved and it seems unlikely that the property will be transferred to unions before the year 2006. In 1991 the Seimas adopted a resolution prohibiting the centralized deduction of union membership dues. Previously, employers used to deduct the dues and transfer the money to the union account. The membership dues had to be paid in cash, with a signature on a special financial document. This strongly influenced the membership.

Another reason for the decrease in membership is the restructuring and privatization of companies. With the rapid change in enterprise structure the unions fell behind in adapting to the new situation and were slow to appoint representatives who could organize workers and keep up the membership. The establishment of trade unions within new private enterprises became practically impossible. Employers strictly forbade their employees to join unions and threatened to dismiss anyone who showed initiative or took part in any union activity. Workers, threatened by unemployment, had little choice in the face of such exploitation. The government implicitly approved the employers' attitude and actions. Publicly it did not say that unions were unnecessary, but described them as a relict of the past which would not be able to represent workers' interests in market conditions. In 1990-1991 there was a common belief that affiliation to the unions contradicted the idea of Lithuanian independence and that some union activities such as strikes, pickets and demonstrations might damage the vulnerable economy and ruin the developing capitalist industrial relations. The vast majority of Lithuanians believed that only the Seimas and government knew the rate and scale of change to be implemented. They just waited for the state to start taking care of citizens' welfare.

As a consequence of this objective and subjective environment, union membership fell to 20-25 per cent of all employees. During the first years of independence membership declined dramatically in certain sectors of the economy. Branches where privatization started earlier suffered the most.

According to data from the Ministry of Justice on 1 January 1999, there were 100 registered unions which had members from more than one district. Most of them are affiliates of the four national trade union centres: the Lithuanian Trade Union Centre (LPSC); the Lithuanian Trade Union Federation (LPSS); the Lithuanian Workers Union (LDS); the Lithuanian Labour Federation (LDF). Representatives of all these national centres are members of the Tripartite Council and other tripartite institutions.

The Lithuanian Trade Union Centre (LPSC) joins together 13 branch unions and one regional union. The declared membership is 142,000. This number is questionable as the number on the list presented to the Special Fund Commission on Supporting Trade Unions (for the resolution of union property issues) was 80,000. In the 13 branch organizations, ten shop stewards have continued from Soviet times, hardly changing their work methods and style. That is one of the obstacles to collaboration and mutual understanding between the national centres. The LPSC is seeking to join ICFTU. Six LPSC branch unions are members of international trade union secretariats.

The Lithuanian Trade Union Federation (LPSS) joins together ten branch unions. Eight of them are members of international trade union secretariats (ITSs). The Federation joins together 50,000 members. In 1994 the LPSS became an ICFTU member. The newly established unions most frequently choose this national centre or its branch organizations. During 1997-1998 the union of state workers and the union of theatre employees joined the LPSS. Union organizations are now being established by the police, customs, border protection service and cultural institutions.

LPSS branches have managed to unionize workers in multinational companies in Lithuania. At Craft Jacobs Suchard (USA), 381 employees out of 750 are union members and at Philip Morris 143 workers out of 311 belong to the union. Members from these companies belong to the trade union of food industry employees.

Seventy-nine employees out of 210 at McDonalds (USA) joined the union but, due to the company's negative attitude to unions and labour turnover there are now only 16 members. In Statoil (Norway) 120 employees out of 300 are unionized; they belong to the union of commercial and cooperative employees.

At the beginning the Lithuanian Workers Union (LDS) organized members on a geographical basis, but later on industrial federations emerged. The LDS declares that it brings together 78,000 members. That is doubtful, but it is not possible to check the figures as the LDS does not submit its membership list to the Special Fund Commission on Supporting Trade Unions. In 1994 the LDS became a member of ICFTU.

The Lithuanian Labour Federation (LDF) was a workers' organization in the 1920s and 1930s; it was resurrected by the Christian Democrat Party which has close ties with it. The LDF has 13,000 members. At the beginning the LDF established geographical structures, but its members have now started to organize on an occupational basis. Since 1996 the LDF has been a member of WCL.

In addition to branch organizations within these four national centres there are many independent trade unions active at the level of the company. These small unions operate more as welfare organizations: they do not influence employment policy or tripartite collaboration.

2.3 Relations between trade unions

All Lithuanian trade unions understand that only a united movement can properly represent employees and protect their rights and interests. However, at a practical level they were not able to reach an understanding or find a common language for a long time. The reason was conflict over trade union assets which had not been shared between the unions. Different national centres have different interests in these assets. The law suggested that property should be distributed in proportion to the size of union membership, but LDS and LDP refused to divulge this information.

The LPSS recommended that trade union property should not be distributed to the branch unions but should be used to establish insurance and other funds for members. Branch unions or associations should only be given work premises. This was rejected by the workers' union and trade union centre. The workers' union suggested selling union property and using the money to build flats and create new workplaces. Other unions did not support this idea.

Finally in April 1999, with the support of ICFTU, all four national centres signed a joint agreement concerning trade union property. It was agreed that ILO should be consulted on the control of union membership. It was also agreed that the remaining property should be sold and a Trade Union Fund established. This Fund would support all unions in the following activities: education, research, occupational safety and health, consultancies, employment benefits and other social issues.

Despite some disagreements trade unions have been searching for a consensus on different issues through tripartite institutions, presenting amendments to the law, participating in joint training and joint union institutions such as the Commission on Trade Union Rights' Violations; the Committee on Integration into EU; the Commission on Cooperation with EU; the Commission on Cooperation of Trade Unions; Special Fund Commission on Supporting Trade Unions.

Relations between trade unions are being improved by joint youth summer camps, joint conferences and regional events. Unions in other countries are also promoting the labour movement in Lithuania. In 1998 the Swedish LO/TCO and NFS suggested that Lithuanian trade union centres organize a joint round-table on the power of a united labour movement. During these discussions the reasons for establishing different national federations, relations with employers and government, and the influence of globalization were analysed.

2.4. Trade union demands

During the first years of independence the main issue facing trade unions was to help members keep their jobs and preserve at least a minimal standard of living. They tried to ensure that economic reforms were carried out in a consistent way, paying due regard to the social consequences and human needs.

The parliamentary elections of 1992 confirmed that neo-liberal reforms were not acceptable to the majority of the population. The right-wing Sàjûdis movement was replaced in government by the leftist Democratic Labour Party which gained an absolute majority with 73 parliamentary seats out of 141. This result had little to do with ideological issues: rather it was a clear message that voters would not tolerate a continuation of the economic "shock therapy" with its immense social costs, but wanted a slower and more controlled reform process.

The unions understood that market forces and economic structures were effective and dynamic, but that market forces themselves do not provide full employment or socially acceptable outcomes. They believed that health and social insurance, education, police, justice and security should remain under state control.

On 2 April 1993 European Trade Union Day was celebrated in Lithuania. The President of the Republic, Algirdas Brazauskas, was invited to a joint trade union meeting. The unions protested against the consequences of economic reform: unemployment, inflation, declining production levels and a catastrophic fall in living standards. They adopted a resolution which called upon the Seimas:

- to implement privatization on an economic and not an ideological basis;
- to adopt the law on pensions as a matter of urgency;
- to decentralize and demonopolize social insurance;
- to ratify Conventions of the International Labour Organization.

The resolution made the following demands on government:
- to consult unions on economic affairs;
- to present its economic action plan to the public;
- to approve increases in the minimum wage and adjust living standards;
- to prepare an employment programme and ensure its implementation;
- to regulate local and international accounts so that employees are paid on time;
- to set priorities for economic development.

Unions requested employers to:
- fix salaries at a level which ensured an adequate standard of living;
- pay salaries on time;
- maintain workplaces, prepare business plans and increase production;
- avoid artificial bankruptcy and save company property;
- create conditions for the establishment of unions at enterprises;
- convert collective contracts into the company's constitution;
- create decent working conditions and ensure occupational safety.

Most of the union requirements were ignored unless sufficient pressure could be exerted to alter the existing legislation.

Trade unions argued that the principles of social partnership should be strengthened in the new labour relations system. But the Lithuanian government has selected a complex method for the regulation of labour relations. The government considers that workers' and employers' organizations are weak and insignificant; therefore it controls implementation of the most important workers' rights and guarantees, delegating very little authority to unions and employers' organizations. This complex model, which gives the state a preponderant role, is reflected in the new labour laws.

3. The role of unions in establishing a legal basis for labour rights

3.1 Labour legislation

The basic reform of labour relations started in 1990, and the *Law on Support to the Unemployed* was passed that year. The *Law on Trade Unions* was passed in 1991. This law provided the basis for union activities and rights in relation to employers, government and ruling bodies. In the same year the *Law on Collective Agreements* was passed, regulating dialogue between employers and trade unions.

The *Law on Employment Contracts* was also passed in 1991 and lays down the general procedure for concluding, amending or terminating an employment contract.

The constitutional provision that every person has the right to rest and leisure, as well as to annual paid holidays is specified in the *Law on Holidays* passed in 1991.

The *Law on Wages* (1991) regulates the wages of people who work under employment contracts in enterprises, institutions and organizations, regardless of their form of ownership.

The *Law on Regulation of Collective Disputes* was passed in 1992. Disputes between unions and employers have to be settled in accordance with the procedure established by this law.

Another very important Act is the *Law on Labour Protection* passed in 1993. This takes into consideration the constitutional provision of the right of every person to acceptable, safe and healthy working conditions.

The *Law on the Social Integration of the Disabled* was passed in 1991. It aims to implement the rights of disabled people as stipulated in international laws which concern their integration into the mainstream of national life.

The Lithuanian labour laws are comprehensive and leave little room for collective bargaining to develop. Despite their comprehensive nature the laws are often changed, their contents and intentions are not precise and sometimes they even contradict each other. The *Law on Employment Contracts* has been changed 11 times during the last 7 years. The laws are frequently amended in response to political pressure or the interests of specific groups.

3.2 The role of unions

Being unable to influence the reform of labour relations through bilateral or tripartite consultations (the first bilateral agreement with government was signed in 1993, and the first tripartite agreement in 1995) trade unions had to try and establish a workable relationship with the most favourable political parties, so that the social and economic interests of employees could be heard and incorporated in law.

In 1991 the Trade Union Coordination Centre signed an agreement with the "centre fraction" of Parliament concerning bilateral collaboration. In 1992, after the Trade Union Federation was established, an agreement was signed with the Lithuanian Social Democrat Party.

The experience of seeking political support for normal union objectives resulted in other trade union centres starting to look for political partners. The Lithuanian Workers' Union found some support from the Lithuanian Conservative Party, and the Trade Union Centre looked for sympathizers in the Lithuanian Democratic Labour Party (previously the Communist Party).

Trade unions actively participate in discussions concerning the preparation of draft laws or amendments. They present their suggestions, participate in discussions at the Seimas' Committee meetings, and organize public debates with union members in order to explain the benefits and disadvantages of amendments.

The unions have had some success in this effort. In 1991, for example, during a debate on the *Law on Labour Contracts*, trade unions successfully argued for the inclusion of a clause requiring employers to apply to the elected body of the union for agreement to dismiss an employee-union member in case of redundancy. In 1994 this norm was expanded and union agreement was required even when employees were dismissed due to their own fault.

In March 1994, through the initiative of trade unions, a new section was added to the *Law on Collective Agreements*. Trade union branches and national centres were granted the right to negotiate collective agreements with the government, ministries and employers' organizations. However this did not bring a new quality to collective bargaining because the new section did not adequately specify bargaining procedures or the validity of agreements. After these amendments, collective agreements were concluded at certain companies but not in the whole branch of industry.

Another success came in 1994 when it was made clear that only a recognized trade union had the right to sign collective agreements on behalf of workers. Until that time employee delegates were able to represent workers in collective negotiations. At the same time the *Law on the Regulation of Collective Disputes* was amended, granting unions the exclusive right to initiate a collective dispute and participate in its solution.

In 1994 the *Law on Trade Unions* was amended to provide more guarantees for the representatives of elected union bodies. Employers have to apply for union approval not only in the event of dismissal but also when they desire to transfer union officials to another job or take disciplinary action against them. This law recognized the union right to represent not only members but all employees in situations such as bargaining on collective contracts or settling collective disputes. Under the Resolution of 14 January 1999 the Constitutional Court admitted that unions can represent not only members but all employees.

At the initiative of the metal workers' union, supported by other unions, important amendments were introduced in 1996 to the *Law on Labour Contracts* and the *Law on Labour Payment*. Employees' and employers' obligations in the event of involuntary unemployment were amended in the law. During times of economic crisis "involuntary unemployment" was very popular. Employers forced their workers to stay at companies, giving no work for weeks and sometimes even for months. Based on old legal norms, management was allowed to pay the minimum wage for idle time. Trade unions successfully argued that during "involuntary unemployment" an employer does not have the right to require an employee to stay at work for longer than one hour per day. If other work is not given, the employer must pay two-thirds of the average salary.

The *Law on Labour Contract* was amended in light of these arguments. Presently the law allows an employee to stop working if involuntary unemployment lasts for 30 consecutive days, or if it adds up to 60 days in a year, or if the salary is not paid for several months. In this event an employer must dismiss the employee and pay the compensation that would normally be available on dismissal.

Trade unions fought to make the procedure concerning unpaid leave more strict. Due to economic difficulties employers regularly used to put a worker on unpaid leave for several months, regardless of the fact that the person might have no income. The law now requires the written agreement of the employee before the employer can give unpaid leave.

At the insistence of trade unions, the *Law on Arrears Definition for Delayed Payments Related to Labour Relations* was adopted in 1996. Until that time there was no law in Lithuania regulating compensation for delayed payments that related to labour relations. The *Laws on Labour Contract and Labour Payment* were frequently violated, when salaries were not paid on time. In addition, compensation for dismissal was often not paid on time. The period from the employees' application to court, to the court decision and actual compensation used to be more than four months. Due to rapid inflation the income of the employee fell significantly as a result of these delays.

Union representatives take an active part in task forces drafting new legislation. At present union members are participating in the task force preparing a draft *Law on Labour Disputes* and a group revising the *Law on General Agreements and Collective Agreements*. Labour disputes concerning workers' rights are regulated by the Labour Code of 1972. The norms of this Code are out of date and do not correspond to the present social and economic situation in Lithuania. The draft law provides for the establishment of a reconciliation procedure, as well as for the establishment of tribunals. Such courts would radically change the way in which labour laws are applied and would facilitate dispute settlement; at present labour disputes are decided in the general courts, where the process takes several months. According to the new law a tribunal would comprise one professional judge, one union representative and one employer representative. The draft *Law on Labour Disputes* has been agreed by the social partners and discussed with the government, which will submit it to Parliament.

The draft *Law on General Agreements and Collective Agreements* was initiated by trade unions and employers' organizations. The task force has prepared amendments to the law, and these will be discussed at the Tripartite Council. The draft sets conditions for the legal recognition of branch-level and national collective agreements, and stipulates procedures for their conclusion and application.

A new Labour Code is under preparation in Lithuania. A draft is being drawn up by a group of legal experts, and representatives of unions and employers are included in the observer group, which analyses the draft and provides comments. Trade unions have unanimously resisted a suggestion in the draft that elected Works Councils have the right to represent employees and sign collective agreements. In the opinion of the unions this amendment would prevent the further development of the labour movement, as well as depriving unions of the possibility of representing employees in collective bargaining.

However, the main guarantee for the protection of workers' rights is the inclusion of international labour standards in national laws.

4. Policy on international social standards

If they are ratified and implemented, ILO Conventions together with European Council and European Union legislation can raise the quality of labour standards. On 12 June 1995 Lithuania signed a European Association Agreement with the European Union and submitted an official application to become a member of the EU. Based on this agreement the government is obliged to: grant equal protection to all employees; analyse ways of strengthening the labour movement; create a social security system and bring Lithuanian laws into line with EU requirements concerning the protection of workers, including occupational health and safety.

The White Paper concerning *Preparation of the Associated Countries for Integration into the International Market of the Union* provides a basis for the integration process. The White Paper describes how applicant countries should develop their legislation in order to achieve the necessary harmonization with EU law. For trade unions it is extremely important to influence the setting of priorities, to ensure that the social dimension is not at the bottom of the list.

The European Trade Union Confederation (ETUC) has strongly supported Lithuania and in 1995 the Committee on Trade Union Integration into the European Union was established. This Committee strives for the implementation of EU social policy and attempts to ensure that all components of government policy have a social dimension: investment, privatization, finance, industry restructuring, agriculture, education and vocational training policy should all be directed to promoting employment. Under EU policy, social partnership between trade unions and employers should be increased, bilateral negotiation should be improved and collective agreements should be concluded; equal opportunities for men and women not only in the labour market but in all spheres of public life should be implemented.

Social policy and labour issues have been included in the national programme for the adoption of acquired rights, as medium-term priorities. Since 1997 the laws on occupational health and safety, as well as those on legal norms and equal opportunities have been refined. The draft Labour Code should guarantee implementation of EU directives concerning collective dismissal, enterprise relocation and other important matters. The social security systems for migrant workers are being coordinated.

Lithuania has ratified 34 international labour Conventions. Three to five Conventions are ratified every year. Trade unions have been very much concerned to ensure that the provisions of these Conventions are reflected in national laws. For example, in connection with the new *Law on Bankruptcy*, trade unions held meetings, organized demonstrations and used the mass media to fight for the inclusion of Convention No. 173 in the national legislation, particularly the clauses dealing with labour relations.

In June 1997 the new *Law on Bankruptcy* was adopted; it failed to include a provision that would give priority to employee claims over other debts incurred by the enterprise in the event of insolvency. In the new law creditors were granted priority and money owed to employees had to be paid afterwards.

In September 1997 trade unions achieved the creation of a Fund to meet the obligations of bankrupt companies to their employees. The goal of this Fund is to provide financial support for insolvent companies which are unable to pay salaries or provide benefits to employees for sickness or disability. However the Fund is not a guarantee institution, and provides loans only when there are financial resources and the enterprise has property to mortgage. During the last meeting of the Fund in 1998, seven companies asked for a loan of 9 million Litas, and there were only 2 million Litas at the Fund's disposal at the time. Therefore unions are seeking to change the Fund into a Guarantee Fund, to provide financial support for all companies and to pay employees at least part of their wages.

In 1995, the ILO studied the new labour laws and concluded that basically they comply with the Conventions ratified by Lithuania. However, dispute settlement, liability, work guarantees and compensation, employers' organizations and tripartite mechanisms are not sufficiently developed in the present laws. There is also no adequate consultation system for workers' rights. The principal consultations are provided through the Ministry of Social Security and Labour and the State Labour Inspectorate.

People must become more involved in defending their own interests and rights; workers have to develop more solidarity among themselves, including an awareness of their rights and how to defend them. This can be achieved only by constant and consistent education and training. Unions have a vital role in educating workers and offering legal advice.

5. Education and training

Trade union activities in the sphere of education fall into two groups: vocational training and workers' education.

5.1 Vocational training

Vocational training is offered in vocational schools, high schools and adult training centres. A legal basis is provided in the *Law on Vocational Training* (1997) and the *Law on Informal Adult Education* (1998). Both laws provide a close link between vocational training institutions and the social partners.

According to the *Law on Vocational Training* the structure and management of this training system is based on cooperation with the social partners. The Vocational Training Council is an advisory institution which analyses strategic vocational training issues. The Council has an equal number of members representing the state, employers' and workers' organizations. Employers as well as trade unions can submit to the Council their requirements for vocational training programmes and qualifications: they can participate in testing and certification.

Organizations representing trade unions and employers, as well as other public bodies, political parties and religious groups, have the right to participate in informal adult education programmes and targeted projects. Informal adult education as a form of ongoing training is quite new, but it is spreading rapidly. Trade unions have always supported adult education and informal training related to the needs of the labour market. For a long time unions have been lobbying for paid study leave and for financial support from employers for training and education. The *Law on Informal Education* allows additional paid vacation only in the event that this is included in a collective agreement.

Since 1998 employers and trade unions have taken a more active role in formulating vocational training standards. Following the German example 14 expert groups corresponding to different economic sectors were established at the Ministry of Education for a tripartite discussion on vocational training standards. Trade unions are not very experienced in vocational training but their representatives take part in seminars and conferences, and are gaining expertise.

5.2 Workers' education

Workers' education has been receiving more attention since the very first days of independence. During the transition to a market economy it has been important to understand the changing goals of trade unions. They realize that to influence government policy and gain credibility in collective bargaining they need many members and also a high degree of awareness among members.

In the absence of a single centre for workers' education, separate union branches organize courses for shop stewards, union leaders and members in accordance with their individual resources. The priorities for training are based on information derived from the actual situation, sociological surveys and data collected from local organizations and members.

Workers' education has made significant progress as a result of close cooperation with unions in Scandinavia and Western Europe. Union members were trained by their foreign counterparts at courses and seminars where they were taught active new training methods. As they had no professional trainers, unions trained their economists, financial specialists, lawyers and leaders for educational work. The major part of trade union training covered an analysis of legal relations in the labour market and explanations of newly adopted laws and social care.

At national level the first education centre was established in 1992 at the workers' union. The establishment of this centre was financed by AFL-CIO and FTUI (Free Trade Union Institute). The Free Trade Union Institute organized seminars on trade unions, democracy in a market economy, occupational safety, implementation of labour laws, privatization and social insurance.

In 1994 some printing equipment was purchased for the Lithuanian Worker's Union, which then established the Trade Union Training Centre and

Research Institute, organizing regular seminars and producing training materials. Since 1992 the workers' union has been publishing a newspaper called *The Lithuanian Worker*.

Until 1996 the Lithuanian Trade Union Federation implemented training activities at branch level, and held several joint seminars with ILO and the Danish LO. Information bulletins were published at branch level, together with educational material on the role and training of shop stewards, how to establish a trade union, and a trade union manual. The Trade Union Youth Centre, established in 1995, took an active part in the educational activities of the Federation.

In 1996 joint training projects involving the Trade Union Federation, the workers' union and the Swedish LO/TCO started. At seminars and courses training is given in traditional subjects such as collective bargaining, social partnership, and training-of-trainers, and also in new issues such as integration to the EU, project management techniques, lobbying, and labour rights' protection in courts. Courses are also arranged for journalists.

In 1996-1997 the Federation and the workers' union, together with colleagues from Latvia, Estonia and Saint Petersburg, participated in a project known as SODICOBA "Concerning the role of trade unions in politics and society".

Seminars and discussions on legal issues attracted major public interest. The Federation organized these in seven Lithuanian cities. The seminars were targeted to the unemployed and to workers, but management representatives and employers attended them as well.

In 1998 the Trade Union Federation devoted all its efforts to involving employees in a union campaign called "The union belongs to you". With financing from the Swedish LO/TCO, the leaders of the Federation organized radio programmes on the most important labour and union issues during the campaign. Open days were arranged and advice was given on establishing a trade union and registering statutes. Discussions were held on the possibility of introducing national structures.

At the beginning of 1999 the Education Fund was established. This is to be used for basic training for union leaders; for vocational and informal education; for public information and education on integration into the European Union; for the production of training materials; for information campaigns concerning the trade union position on social policy; for tripartite partnership; and for national and international projects.

At the Lithuanian Trade Union Centre education was mostly organized at branch level. At national level it has become more active during the last year with the establishment of the Education Centre. The Education Centre organizes workers' education at regional and national level, and deals with legal and social issues. Speakers from the State Labour Inspectorate, social insurance and other institutions are invited to these seminars. Since 1994 the Trade Union Centre has been publishing a newspaper called "The Lithuanian Trade Unions".

In 1998 the Youth Federation Centre was established, working for international cooperation and participation in national and international projects.

Public education in legal rights and human rights promotes democratic change and encourages the participation of all citizens in the process.

Before the changes in Lithuania, as well as in Central and Eastern Europe, women had achieved a formal equality with men in many areas of economic and social life. In reality, however, women encountered many of the same problems in society and at work as they do in other parts of the world. During the transition to a market economy the gap between employment opportunities for men and women has grown wider. Most trade unions in Lithuania have large numbers of women workers in their industries. Therefore strengthening women's opportunities in the labour market is an important part of their activities. Trade unions started the active promotion of equal opportunity in employment in the late 1990s.

6. Promotion of equal opportunity

The Lithuanian Constitution declares equal rights for every person regardless of gender, race, nationality, language, origin, social condition, religion, beliefs or attitudes. All laws regulating labour relations, wages, professional and vocational training, and social security prohibit gender discrimination. In two cases specific rights for women are defined by legal act. The first deals with conditions for the state retirement pension for women (based on the *Law on State Social Insurance Retirement Pensions* - 1994); the retirement age is gradually increasing to 60 for women and to 62½ for men. The second makes special provisions for pregnant women or women with small children. Although the principle of equality is enshrined in the law, the provisions are not properly implemented. Traditional culture and stereotyped beliefs still mean that women have to take care of the children and the household, and that men have to earn the family income. In addition, there is no specific institution responsible for ensuring that equal rights are respected.

The most frequent cases of discrimination concern different pay for the same work. Income disparities are mostly horizontal rather than vertical (more men are employed in well-paid jobs and in senior positions, while women are engaged in social work, education and medicine), but average pay for women is 20-30 per cent lower than for men.

In all sectors of the economy and nearly all occupations women earn less than men. In 1997, women earned an average 74 per cent of men's salaries.

Female legislators, top executives and managers earn 80 per cent of their male counterparts' salaries. Even in sectors where women make up the majority of employees, their salaries are lower then men's.

In 1998 the number of unemployed women was 2-3 per cent higher than unemployed men. Women are frequently forced to work part time or on short-term contracts. Women, being traditionally responsible for the family, accept unfavourable labour conditions and low salaries in order to keep their jobs. There is no doubt that their conditions of employment are less favourable than conditions for male workers.

Women make up 70 per cent of all union members in Lithuania. The majority of women are members of the following unions: education union – 75 per cent; manufacturing workers' federation – 80 per cent; cultural employees' union – 90 per cent; communication workers' union – 75 per cent, health and social care employees – 80 per cent; public service – 73 per cent; food industry union – 70 per cent; commercial employees' union – 89 per cent; workers' union – 75 per cent.

Women also make up a higher percentage of elected shop stewards. For example, 97 per cent of shop stewards in the commercial employees' unions are women.

Only one of the four national centres (the workers' union) is chaired by a woman. The Trade Union Centre is the most male-dominated. Of 13 branch unions only two are chaired by women. Female participation is highest in the Trade Union Federation; of the ten industrial unions making up the Federation, six are chaired by women.

Trade unions have always supported the active participation of women in public, economic and political life. This attitude is reflected in the fact that the number of women leaders elected to representative bodies is significantly higher at branch level and at local organization level.

Trade unions support women's employment, equal rights in the labour market, in training and in pay. They also support equality in the labour movement.

For some time unions did not see the need for separate structures to deal with women's questions. The Lithuanian Worker's Union was the first to establish a Women's Federation. Two years ago a Women's Centre was established at the Lithuanian Trade Union Federation. The "Phare" micro-project funded by the EU on *The role of employed women in democratic society* stimulated the creation of this Centre. During the first year of project implementation special attention was paid to women's psychology. For the majority of participants this helped them to know themselves, to conquer their fear and submissiveness. After an active women's movement was started, even more women were attracted to trade union activities. In 1998 women's committees were established in all branches of the Federation.

Conferences and seminars were convened during the project period in all branch trade unions. Women were widely informed about union activities in favour of women all over the world and about labour laws. Every women's committee issued an information bulletin describing the work of its organization and the situation of women. Early in 1999 a Women's Federation was established at the Lithuanian Trade Union Centre. Women's Councils are now being established at branch organizations.

Lithuania has ratified ILO Conventions No. 111 on Discrimination in Employment and Occupation and No. 100 on Equal Pay for Work of Equal Value. In 1993 Lithuania ratified the UN Convention on the Elimination of All Forms of Discrimination against Women.

In 1998 a special state programme to accelerate the progress of women (Action Plan 1998-2000 on Women's Progress in Lithuania) was adopted by the government. The programme foresees active and practical legal measures to promote gender equality.

Trade unions are also aiming to promote equality between men and women at work by means of collective agreements. Relevant issues include:

- equal pay for work of equal value;
- the same criteria for men and women in quality assessment;
- equal opportunities for promotion, training and retraining.

The Law on Equal Opportunities for Men and Women, which came into force on 1 March 1999, should promote these goals. The first draft Law On Equal Opportunities for Men and Women was prepared in 1995. The second draft was prepared in the lead-up to the Beijing Conference on the initiative of the Lithuanian national committee. However, Lithuanian politicians paid little attention to these drafts, although they were discussed at seminars and conferences. At that time women made up only 7 per cent of all Seimas members.

After the 1996 elections the situation changed drastically. Twenty-five women (18 per cent) were elected to the Seimas. Through their initiative the Parliamentary Women's Group was established, which actively promoted adoption of the draft law. Seimas members, as well as representatives of women's organizations, referred to the conclusions of an EU Commission, which stated that the principle of non-discrimination was not always respected in Lithuanian law and that the country had to work hard to ensure the harmonization of its laws with EU requirements, specifically with regard to labour law and equal opportunities. These arguments were sufficiently important to ensure that equality was included in the legislative process.

On 1 December 1998 the Law on Equal Opportunities for Men and Women was passed in Lithuania, which was the first post-Soviet country to adopt such an Act. The 1998 law aims to ensure the implementation of equal opportunities in the Lithuanian Constitution. It obliges state and managerial institutions, education and science institutions and employers to implement equal rights. It defines discriminatory advertisements, sexual harassment and conduct which violates equal treatment.

An Equal Opportunities Inspection Service is being established and application of the law will be supervised by the Equal Opportunities Inspector. The law defines procedures for registering complaints, conducting investigations and implementing the Inspector's decisions. Employers who fail to implement equal rights are liable to a fine.

7. Tripartism

With changes in the political, economic and social situation the nature of labour relations has also changed. Employers and workers and their organizations have been granted greater possibilities of collective bargaining. Tripartite cooperation is being strengthened in Lithuania and the principle of tripartism was accepted in 1994 when the Seimas ratified the relevant Conventions of the ILO.

In democratic societies social dialogue is executed at bilateral and trilateral levels. As already mentioned, bilateral partnerships in Lithuania used to be implemented through collective bargaining, and collective agreements were concluded at company level. The main obstacle to social partnership at a higher level was the fact that for a long time there were no employers' organizations, or they were very small. In addition Lithuania lacked a stable centralized negotiation mechanism, as well as a sound legal basis for collective bargaining. In addition, the social partners lacked knowledge and experience.

As a result it was not until 1995 that the first tripartite agreement was concluded between the government, trade unions and employers. The agreement was signed by representatives of four national trade union centres: the Lithuanian Trade Union Centre (LPSC), the Lithuanian Trade Union Federation (LPSS), the Lithuanian Labour Union (LDS) and the Lithuanian Labour Federation (LDF). It was also signed by representatives of the most influential employers' organizations: the Lithuanian Industry Confederation (LPK) and the Lithuanian Business Confederation (LVK). On behalf of the government, the agreement was signed by the Prime Minister of the Republic of Lithuania.

This agreement is a short document more like a declaration, stating that it has been agreed to solve social, economic and labour problems on a tripartite basis, to cooperate in implementing social, economic and labour policy, to establish a Tripartite Council and to sign an agreement every year.

Many observers are sceptical about the impact of the new Tripartite Council. Decisions taken by the constituents are rarely reflected in legislation adopted by the Seimas or administrative decisions implemented by government. There is an impression that the government seeks political credit for playing the game of consultation but is not prepared to allow other parties any real influence over the decision-making process.

Between 1995 and 1998 the Tripartite Council met 24 times and discussed 170 issues. On many occasions employers at the Tripartite Council tried to influence government decisions on the minimum wage. However, until 1999 suggestions from the social partners did not have a significant influence on government policy.

Trade unions and employers have submitted proposals for a new *Law on General Agreements and Collective Agreements*, aiming to establish salary levels and terms, especially the minimum wage.

The European Commission has positively influenced the work of the Tripartite Council, indicating shortcomings in the level of social dialogue and the influence of tripartite institutions in the labour market in its conclusions concerning Lithuania's readiness for joining the EU. This forced the government to pay serious attention to union and employer suggestions and to allow the Tripartite Council a decisive vote on certain issues.

On 11 February 1999 a new general tripartite collaboration agreement was concluded. This agreement was signed by the Prime Minister, chairpersons of the trade union national centres, and the presidents of three employers' organizations. The group was supplemented by one more business confederation.

The parties agreed on:

- exchanging information on labour, social and economic issues, holding consultations, preparing and coordinating draft legislation, and discussing the most serious problems at the Tripartite Council;
- respecting the terms of tripartite agreements in their activities and accepting the decisions of the Tripartite Council.

The parties' obligations were laid down in the agreement. The government undertook responsibility to:

- inform the social partners about draft legislation on social and economic issues and submit draft laws for discussion at the Tripartite Council;
- inform the Seimas of the conclusions of the Tripartite Council;
- ensure that decisions on serious labour, social and economic issues are adopted after the Tripartite Council discussions.

Having signed this agreement trade unions and employers' organizations undertook not to initiate disputes or other actions on the understanding that government will respect its obligations.

This agreement also provided that:

- an annual tripartite agreement on the minimum hourly wage (monthly salary), on income tax and on other serious social and economic issues should be signed;
- the structure of tripartite cooperation should be developed; a committee should be established at the Tripartite Council and tripartite bodies in the provinces and municipalities should be expanded to increase the effectiveness of their activities;
- the social partners should collaborate in preparation for EU membership, hold consultations and exchange information concerning their representation in international organizations;
- trade unions and employers' organizations should work together in concluding collective agreements and contracts;
- consultation should be strengthened and joint training activities should be promoted.

The government has undertaken to publish tripartite agreements in the official journal called "The State News".

During the last two years, cooperation between trade unions and employers has become more active. Some amendments to draft laws, such as the *Law on Labour Disputes*, the *Law on Collective Agreements*, and the *Law on Extra Payment for Hazardous Conditions* were put forward by the joint employer/union task force.

The unions are constantly looking for ways to obtain information at company and national level. One possibility might be to establish cooperation committees which would collect information about the company's economic situation and short-term plans, orders implemented and the market situation, future changes, reorganization and reductions in the workforce. The role of cooperation committees would be to discuss, to influence labour relations and to inform employees of planned changes. Although employers' organizations did not support the above suggestion, positive changes have been achieved in the sphere of information.

At present the government is amending the *Law on Support of the Unemployed*, granting unions the right to be informed of layoffs beforehand and to consult with employers on protecting workers. Employers will have to inform trade unions or employees (in the absence of unions) of planned collective dismissals two months in advance. Labour exchanges and local government offices will also have to be informed in advance.

7.1 Tripartite bodies

The National Tripartite Council is composed of 15 members, five representatives of each partner. Government is represented by the Ministers of Social Security and Labour, Finance, Industry, Agriculture, and Justice. The Council analyses and makes suggestions on social, economic and labour issues. The chair is appointed for a four-month period and rotates among members of the Council. In addition to the National Council there are a number of other tripartite bodies functioning at national level.

In 1991 the State Social Insurance Fund Council was established. It consists of 15 members (five representatives each of trade unions, employers and the state). All social insurance matters are within the competence of the Council, which is the longest serving tripartite institution and has decision-making power.

A Tripartite Committee of the Labour Exchange of the Republic was established in 1991, as well as Tripartite Committees for local labour exchanges in the cities and regions.

The social partners were not active on the Tripartite Committees for local labour exchanges during the early years because employers and trade union representatives were not ready for the role, as they lacked competence and knowledge. Activity was low and there was submissive approval of projects prepared by local labour exchanges. However, these Committees have made good progress in the last few years due to special training courses for representatives. The government is making promising efforts to develop these activities, based on the experience of EU countries in solving employment and social problems on a tripartite basis.

In 1996 the Citizens Employment Council was formed at the Ministry of Social Security and Labour. The Council is the Employment Fund's management board, operating on a tripartite basis.

In 1995 an Expert Council was established at the Lithuanian Labour Market Training Service. This is a tripartite advisory and supervisory institution. Its task is to support the development of a labour market vocational training and consulting system, to improve its functioning and relations with labour market partners.

The Lithuanian Occupational Safety Committee was established in 1994. It consists of 15 members (five representatives each of employers, workers and government).

In 1997 the Compulsory Health Insurance Fund Council was established. Two-thirds of the members represent the health system and there are also two trade union representatives.

In 1995 a permanent commission was established for tripartite consultation on labour standards implementation.

In 1997 the Council of the Fund to Fulfil Employees' Claims Related to Labour Relations of Bankrupt Enterprises and Enterprises under Bankruptcy was established.

8. The development of industrial relations and local trade unions

At present there are more than 100 laws regulating labour relations. As most issues are regulated by law the social partners at enterprise level have little freedom of action. The rights of the unions and employers in the formation of industrial relations are defined by the *Law on Trade Unions, Law on Collective Agreements* and *Law on Collective Disputes*. The Constitution provides that trade unions in Lithuania may be created freely and act independently. Their purpose is to protect employees' rights and interests in labour, economic and social matters.

The right to trade union membership is promoted for all workers who are not younger than 14 years of age and who are employed under a labour contract or on any other basis. The employer and the employer's attorney are not allowed to join trade union organizations at enterprise level.

Trade unions may be established on an occupational, enterprise, industry or regional level, or any other level defined by the trade union itself. Most unions are organized on an industry basis, and include all workers in an industry regardless of qualifications or position. A trade union may be established in any enterprise, institution or organization by not less than 30 employees or one-fifth of the workforce, whichever is less. (However, there is a minimum requirement of three employees to form a union). A trade union is considered to be established when employees hold a constituent meeting, adopt statutes and elect representatives and a chairperson.

Unions must act in accordance with their statutes. They have a general duty to monitor management compliance with labour laws, health and safety issues, and agreed terms of payment. Employers must grant unions the necessary facilities and provide them with the information they need to carry out their functions.

Unions have the right to demand that the employer reverse decisions which are in breach of the economic and social rights of union members. If an employer fails to reverse a decision within ten days of the union demand, the union may take the issue to court.

8.1 Collective bargaining

Collective bargaining is still not very widespread in Lithuania.

A collective agreement is an agreement entered into by employers and employees on labour, working hours, salaries, occupational safety, job security and other social and economic matters. Collective agreements may improve upon the rights set out by law, but may not reduce them.

The legal right to collective bargaining, established in 1994, extends only to trade unions. If more than one union is operating within an enterprise, a joint mission of the unions is established. This body has the right to sign collective agreements. If the unions do not agree on the establishment of a joint mission, the dispute will be settled at a General Meeting (conference) of employees by means of a secret vote. The union with most votes has the right to conclude a collective agreement.

Collective agreements may be established in companies regardless of the form of ownership, number of employees or legal status. Agreements may not be made with state or local government officers.

The unions are not able to engage in meaningful collective bargaining if they do not have access to relevant information about the enterprise or industry. The *Law on Trade Unions* provides the right to monitor whether employers have met their obligations concerning workers' rights as specified by economic and social laws and collective contracts. The unions can set up inspections, legal support services and other institutions. Persons authorized by unions have the right to visit companies, enterprises and organizations where union members are employed and can analyse the documents concerning labour, economic and social conditions. However, because there are no sanctions for violating the regulation, this legal norm is ineffective. As the financial and economic documents of the company are frequently considered a commercial secret, this information is usually not accessible to unions.

The procedure for bargaining is laid down in the law. Negotiations must begin within ten days of a request from one of the parties, or such other period as is agreed. Where an existing agreement is coming to an end, negotiations on a new one begin two months before the termination date.

Before negotiations start, the parties are supposed to provide each other with proposals from employees and the necessary information concerning the economic, social and working conditions of the enterprise.

The parties prepare a draft agreement which is discussed at small group meetings of the employees (structural divisions) and then presented for the discussion at a General Meeting (conference). If the draft agreement is not approved, the parties amend and supplement it and are required to submit it again for discussion at a General Meeting within 15 days. If the draft is accepted, representatives of the social partners sign the collective agreement within three days.

Local collective agreements enter into force from the day they are signed. There is no requirement for such agreements to be registered in order to become valid. Collective agreements at national and branch level have to be registered at the Ministry of Justice within ten days of signing.

Collective agreements are valid until a new agreement is signed, but may not exceed a two-year span. Parties to the collective agreement report to employees on progress in implementation at least once in a half-year period.

Disagreements and disputes among the parties during negotiations, or at the conclusion and implementation of collective agreements are settled according to the procedure for collective disputes. Disputes between employees and employers concerning violations and improper implementation of the collective agreement are settled in the courts.

8.2 Individual disputes

Individual disputes are still resolved according to rules established in 1974, i.e., they are studied by the Labour Dispute Commissions established by companies. These Commissions usually consist of an equal number of employer and union representatives. If an agreement is not reached the dispute is discussed by the local trade union committee, whose decision is binding on the employer. In the event that the employer disagrees with a decision, the dispute can be brought to court.

Disputes concerning dismissal, removal from work or transfer to other positions are discussed in court. The Supreme Court has indicated that cases concerning payment (salaries, compensation, paid leave, etc.) can be brought to court. If there is no union in the company, individual disputes are settled in court.

At present a new draft law providing for the establishment of labour courts is in preparation. Labour Courts (tribunals) will include professional lawyers and representatives of workers' and employers' organizations.

8.3 Collective disputes

Collective disputes concern disagreements between union and employer resulting from demands which have been duly submitted and registered, but have remained unsatisfied. Workers' demands must be considered by the employer within seven calendar days of their submission in writing. If the employer's decision does not meet the requirements, the matter has to be discussed according to a reconciliation procedure.

The Reconciliation Committee consists of representatives of the parties, but no more than five for each party. If the Committee fails to agree on all or some of the demands the matter may be submitted to arbitration. A strike is permitted by law if a dispute has not been settled in accordance with the procedure set out above.

The decision to go on strike (or to issue a strike warning) rests exclusively with the trade union. A strike is called if the decision is approved by a secret ballot. Two-thirds of the employees have to approve the strike at enterprise level. At unit or branch level two-thirds of the employees of that unit and more than half the total number of employees have to approve. The employer must be given written notice of the strike seven days in advance. A so-called warning strike lasting no more than two hours may be held 24 hours after written notice is given. Lockouts are not recognized by law.

Workers in vital services, utilities, medical emergencies, national defence and national security are forbidden to strike. The demands of workers in these services are negotiated directly with government.

During a strike employees maintain continuity of employment, length of service, maintenance of state social insurance and assurance of safety at work. Employees taking part in a strike do not work and do not receive pay. Trade unions are liable for any losses incurred by the company should a strike be declared unlawful.

Strikes are not very popular in Lithuania, primarily because there is no tradition of strikes since they were prohibited in Soviet times. In addition, the *Law on Regulation of Collective Disputes* creates barriers to the urgent and effective resolution of disputes.

Employers often refuse to establish a Reconciliation Committee (the first stage of dispute settlement). The only sanction for ignoring the collective dispute decision is strike action, but because of complicated procedures (employee vote, long warning period), strikes are ineffective. Therefore dispute settlement is not based on legal requirements. Since the law came into effect only a few legal strikes have been organized. Most strikes are spontaneous and occur when employees are not paid because of involuntary unemployment or a long period of unpaid leave.

Collective disputes as well as collective bargaining mainly take place at enterprise level. Collective agreements have been adopted at approximately 8-10 per cent of enterprises.

9. Trade union strategy on employment

Recent labour market developments have been significantly influenced by the transition to a market economy. Since 1990 Lithuania has experienced a period of high inflation, declining production and falling living standards.

Until 1990 the official economy was directed to meet the needs of the Soviet Union and was totally dependent on Soviet raw materials and production markets. After the political reforms most markets and sources of raw materials diminished or disappeared. Due to a relatively small internal market and limited possibilities for participation in world markets, the operation of large enterprises producing for the former USSR became very problematic. Production levels declined and they were not operating to capacity. In 1995 the average capacity utilization level in industry was 44 per cent. Twenty per cent of companies were operating at less than 30 per cent capacity.

In 1989 the highest ever employment rate was registered in Lithuania; 1,903,000 people were employed at that time. With the start of economic reform the employment rate decreased year by year.

Very significant changes took place in rural labour markets. With the implementation of land reform the structure of agricultural holdings and farming conditions changed drastically. Due to the low mobility of rural residents a very specific closed labour market was formed. The proportion of rural residents among the unemployed is 35 per cent.

The decline in production has inevitably led to a fall in employment in industry, construction and other sectors. However, the level of production declined more rapidly than the total number of workers, because many employees were transferred to part-time work, or were put on unpaid leave.

Mistakes in economic restructuring and privatization have not been avoided. Attempts to maintain some non-competitive enterprises only enhanced the atmosphere of delay and uncertainty, thus hindering the search for more efficient economic management.

In 1991-1995 the number of employees decreased by 250,000 in all economic branches. Only in 1996, when positive economic growth was restored, did the employment rate begin to rise again.

Some basic shifts in the labour market can be observed:

- from public- to private-sector employment;
- from production to the service sector;
- from the formal labour market to unemployment and the informal or "black" economy.

The loss of employment was concentrated in the public sector, and was only partly offset by an increase in the private sector. Uncertainty about taxation and state support for investment encouraged investment in the "shadow" economy, first of all. This set the conditions for unofficial employment and a "black" labour market to expand.

It has been calculated that approximately 300,000 people or almost one-fifth of the economically active population are employed illegally for a certain period. Informal employment is widespread in agriculture, construction, trade and car repairs.

The creation of a policy environment that will preserve existing jobs and generate new employment opportunities is one of the most important tasks of trade unions. In 1991-1992, with the start of the privatization process, trade unions argued for beneficial conditions and priority for employees when enterprises were privatized and vouchers were distributed. Trade unions at first resisted privatization of commercial enterprises because they were afraid that private persons, having illegally accumulated capital, would accumulate the power to privatize other state property. It was expected that privatization through employee share ownership would help to save jobs. However due to rapid and large-scale privatization (through vouchers) a large number of stock companies were established in a very short time (1991-1993). These stock companies were actually managed by the old (state) enterprise administration, although formally they were owned by small-scale shareholders, frequently employees of the company. Such privatization was not very effective, as the new owners did not have the financial resources to purchase modern equipment. Also the turnover of resources was insufficient and the actual restructuring of industry was implemented through declining living standards - salary increases were very small in comparison to the rapid rise in consumer prices.

Several stages can be traced in the development of the Lithuanian labour market. The first stage was a comparatively short period from the end of 1990 to the beginning of 1991. The labour market of that period had the following political goals:

- creating a legal basis for labour market regulation;
- ensuring that employment guarantees are provided for all citizens;
- changing negative attitudes towards the labour market and unemployment.

The second stage lasted for two years from the second half of 1991 to the first half of 1993. The main goals of this stage were:

- expanding the range of active labour market policy;
- completing the establishment of state institutions for labour market regulation;
- strengthening the activities of the state labour market.

The model for regulating the national labour market was established on the basis of the Lithuanian Labour Exchange and Training Service, which has a wide network of local divisions.

The Lithuanian Labour Exchange is a public organization, with 47 regional offices and about 100 offices in the bigger towns. The regional offices analyse labour demand and supply, study changes in the labour market, collect data on job vacancies and register job seekers. They place people in employment, grant and pay out unemployment benefits. In case of mismatch between labour demand and supply, local employment programmes are drawn up with the municipalities, and active labour market policies are implemented to assist vulnerable groups of workers.

The Lithuanian Labour Exchange has a modern information system. Its work is facilitated by independent job centres which offer information and counselling. The activities of the state labour exchange are supplemented by those of non-governmental employment agencies, which often concentrate on unusual occupations and highly qualified workers. .

The vocational training system is quite well developed, and ensures that workers' skills correspond to employer demand. Since 1992 vocational training has been organized by the *Labour Market Training Department*, which has six regional offices. Fourteen training centres are in operation, including three for enterprises financed by foreign capital. These centres offer training and retraining for 120 occupations that are in demand on the labour market. A survey has revealed that about 75 per cent of the unemployed succeed in finding a steady job after retraining.

During the second stage of labour exchange development in Lithuania unions took an active role in the preparation of laws regulating labour relations.

Due to inefficient restructuring of large state enterprises in 1992 a significant increase in unemployment was expected. The trade unions requested government to adopt measures such as restricting layoffs as well as expansionary economic measures.

Having evaluated the financial resources of the Labour Exchange and the possibility of increased unemployment the government issued the following resolutions:

- during the first year after privatization new owners cannot cut the number of jobs at the enterprise by more than 30 per cent;
- managers of state and state-stock companies cannot cut the number of non-administrative staff without the agreement of the founder, with the exception of employees violating labour laws. After some time this position was changed and a cut in the number of employees was allowed as long as it did not exceed 10 per cent of the average number on the payroll per quarter.

These measures resulted in an official unemployment rate of 1.5 per cent. At the same time the decrease in production was faster than the decline in employment: hidden unemployment and unofficial employment increased. Compulsory part-time employment or hidden unemployment and unofficial employment concern 15-20 per cent of the economically active population.

Trade unions are strictly against illegal work, as informal workers do not pay taxes or social insurance. Moreover, employers in the informal "black" economy do not guarantee safe working conditions and do not provide social guarantees in the event of job loss.

During the last few years strict measures to control clandestine employment have been introduced, but unions believe this is not the only way to stop informal work. Due to the inefficiency of the current taxation system most private companies are forced to engage illegal workers and use a double accounting system in order to survive. An improved taxation system rather than heavier fines would help to eliminate illegal labour.

9.1 Labour market priorities

The main labour market priorities for the government are: unemployment prevention, employment promotion and protection. Special attention is paid to active labour market policies designed to help people who have lost their jobs to find work and use their skills. Active labour market policies are implemented through employment exchanges, vocational training, job creation and small enterprise promotion schemes.

A passive labour market policy is implemented through unemployment benefits which provide temporary and partial compensation to the unemployed. Eligibility for unemployment benefit, as well as the amount and duration, are defined by the *Law on Support for the Unemployed* (1996) which, together with its amendments, created new provisions for the unemployed. The right to unemployment benefit and the amount received are based on state social insurance records and the reason for unemployment. The minimum unemployment benefit is the same as state income support (135 Lt per month in 1998) and the maximum is twice the minimum subsistence level (250 Lt per month in 1998). On average, unemployment benefit is paid for six months. The number of recipients is steadily decreasing; in 1996 they accounted for 28.1 per cent of the total number of unemployed, in 1997 for 21 per cent and in 1998 for 19 per cent.

9.2 Financing labour market policies

Active labour market policies, as well as unemployment benefits and labour market institutions (labour exchanges and the Labour Market Training Department), are financed by the Employment Fund, which is managed by the Ministry of Social Security and Labour. The main source for this fund is the compulsory unemployment insurance contribution paid by employers.

However, due to the unstable economic situation and illegal employment, not all expected payments are collected. This results in a deficit in the State Social Insurance Fund budget and at the same time a shortfall in the Employment Fund resources. As the priority of the Social Insurance Fund is retirement pensions, the necessary financial resources do not reach the Employment Fund. Very little is left for vocational training, retraining, supported employment, business promotion and job creation. The inadequacies of the Employment Fund increase unemployment and hinder economic restructuring.

9.3 The role of unions in the labour market

With the change of government, priorities in the labour market have changed. However, trade unions have consistently criticized the state for failing to develop and implement a programme for industry restructuring and employment.

The further development of the internal labour market has to become a priority goal in preparation for entry into the EU. The trade unions aim at full employment whereas the government priority is freely chosen employment. Trade union demands include implementation of a national restructuring and economic development strategy aimed at employment promotion. Unions believe that:

- workplace protection has to be strengthened in industry;
- economic policy measures have to be coordinated so that any negative impact on employment is avoided;
- it is necessary to introduce a tax system which encourages job creation;
- there has to be a balance between attracting foreign companies and encouraging local companies to create new jobs;
- state investment programmes are needed to set up new companies in regions with high unemployment or in problematic sectors of the economy, where it is hard to attract private capital;
- government should promote small and medium-size business, and provide legal and financial assistance to help small enterprises to expand;
- a rural employment programme should be prepared promoting rural tourism and non-traditional agriculture;
- workers should be protected from mass dismissals due to economic restructuring, bankruptcy or downsizing;
- education and vocational training have to be improved;
- measures are needed to integrate the long-term unemployed into the labour market;
- regional and local initiatives should be supported;
- the public should be informed about the social consequences of economic reform and its impact on employment.

Trade unions also stress the need for a *Law on Unemployment Insurance* and the establishment of an independent insurance fund for the unemployed. This should be managed by the social partners. Trade unions have also suggested that government should support active labour market measures through the state budget and not from the residue of the Employment Fund.

10. International cooperation

Since the very start of independence Lithuanian trade unions have sought membership in international trade union structures. The experience of free trade unions will help Lithuanian unions bridge the gap which the world labour movement has overcome during the last hundred years.

The Danish and Norwegian LO and the Nordic Trade Union Council NFS were the first foreign unions to extend help. However, the most active work was done at branch level in the international trade union secretariats.

The Lithuanian unions joined nine international secretariats and were thus included in international projects and bilateral cooperation with similar unions in the Nordic countries and Western Europe.

In 1994 the Lithuanian Trade Union Federation (LPSS) and the Lithuanian Workers Union (LDS) were accepted by the International Confederation of Free Trade Unions (ICFTU). That was a very important event, making it possible for the national centres to participate in an international union movement; it also helped increase the authority of unions within the country.

In 1995 all four national centres started collaboration with the European Trade Union Confederation (ETUC), and in 1996 the Lithuanian Labour Federation (LDF) was accepted by the World Confederation of Labour (WCL).

Due to the ETUC the Committee for Lithuanian trade union integration into the European Union was established. The Committee aims to support national trade unions' integration with Europe, to form workers' opinion on integration consequences, to represent workers' interests and influence the process of Lithuanian integration with the EU. In 1998 the LPSS and LDS became associate members of the ETUC.

Lithuanian trade unions cooperate with unions in the Nordic countries and with the Nordic Trade Union Council (NFS). During recent years the Swedish LO/TCO has given more attention to the Trade Union Federation and to the Lithuanian Workers' Union. Education projects financed by LO/TCO have been conducted for three years.

The Lithuanian Trade Union Centre (LPSC) works closely with the Danish SID.

The Workers' Union has cooperated with AFL-CIO since 1992 and the Polish "Solidarnosc" has a good relationship with the LDS and LPSS. The Lithuanian Labour Federation collaborates with Belgian Christian Unions. Lithuanian unions also cooperate with the Danish LO, Finnish SAK and STKT, and the German DGB. Lithuanian trade unions participate in the work of the International Labour Organization (ILO). An especially close relationship has been established with the Budapest office.

In 1993 the Lithuanian, Latvian and Estonian unions established the Baltic Trade Union Council. The Council was also promoted by the Baltic Assembly, created for political reasons by the Parliaments of Lithuania, Latvia and Estonia. The Baltic Trade Union Council meets several times a year, rotating between member countries. Discussions are held on the most important economic, social and labour issues. All four Lithuanian national centres are active in the work of the Council.

All the unions in the Baltic countries work closely together. In 1998 they agreed that in 1999 an official Confederation of the Baltic States should be established to represent workers at the annual meetings of ministers from these countries. The Lithuanian trade unions approved the proposal and expressed a wish to participate in the Confederation.

International trade unions support the integration of the Lithuanian trade unions into the European Union, emphasizing the social dimension.

International unions provide strong and active support for projects designed to build strong, free and democratic trade unions in Lithuania. Through meetings, projects and other forms of cooperation they promote the development of unions, with particular attention to ensuring a trade union presence in multinational companies and other private enterprises.

They assist Lithuanian trade unions in their contacts with institutions such as the European Union, the World Bank, the International Monetary Fund and the European Bank for Reconstruction and Development. They try to ensure that unions are included in development programmes and cooperation projects. International trade unions also initiate cooperation and solidarity between Lithuanian unions and other unions in Europe and the world.

11. Public opinion

After the restoration of independence the economic, social and political situation changed dramatically in Lithuania. Life became safer politically, but it did not become secure from an economic, personal or health standpoint.

Until the country regained its independence Lithuanian citizens were "locked" in an economically safe society, where salaries were fixed and the state social system was firmly established. When the centralized state fell apart and the long-awaited freedom was gained, new problems emerged. Such problems are characteristic of a market economy, but most citizens knew about them only from Soviet propaganda. They included inequality, poverty and homelessness. Social problems reflected the psychological dependence of people unable to give up a lifestyle characterized by state guarantees of their personal welfare. Still others were used to the order imposed by government. They did not see the difference between democracy and anarchy and did not respect laws and institutions. Criminal activity increased and antisocial behaviour spread.

As the economic and social situation developed and the nature of labour relations became more apparent, the influence and prestige of unions started growing. Workers and employers were given more opportunities to participate in shaping labour relations. Trade unions made proposals for the revision of labour legislation and they took the initiative in activating labour/

management partnerships. Special attention was paid to labour contracts, collective contracts and dispute settlement.

Public opinion surveys indicated that unions gained wide support when their activities were seen as attempting to promote the general public interest. Demonstrations and pickets were not popular, but they were considered to be acceptable.

The Trade Union Federation organized a survey of its members in 1998 to determine whether members approved of union activities when the government did not meet their demands. The main purposes of the survey were:

- to identify ways to increase union members' activity;
- to get a better understanding of the priorities for union demands;
- to collect ideas for cooperation with local organizations.

Research results showed that most respondents approved of meetings, demonstrations and picketing. Eighty-two per cent of respondents fully approved, 15 per cent were undecided. Several respondents stated that there was not enough consultation with local bodies when organizing such action. However, the vast majority of union members were not ready for decisive action and thought that tripartism and negotiation were the most appropriate ways of promoting union objectives.

The general public also seemed to share the opinion that social, economic and labour problems as a whole should be solved by tripartite consultation and action. Moreover, most people thought that tripartite councils and committees should have more mandatory power.

The authority of trade unions has increased through educational activities. Realizing that only those members who are aware of their rights are in a position to defend their legal interests, the unions pay careful attention to workers' education. A vast amount of union training is devoted to the analysis of legislation, and to explaining newly adopted labour laws. At training seminars and in the mass media unions explain the impact of political and economic changes and clarify the role of unions in a market economy.

The legal services provided by unions are very popular. Although the number of full-time employees in union branch organizations and in the centres has declined, the unions still manage to find lawyers to advise employees on labour law and to represent union members in court. The authority of trade unions has also been increased by their active participation in international organizations.

All the points above indicate that the role of unions in the development of civil society and the implementation of human rights is growing stronger.

Conclusions

A top priority for the labour movement in Lithuania is to influence the environment. Therefore unions have been active in suggesting changes in macroeconomic policy, employment policy, labour legislation, industry and tax policies, social security and European integration. The degree of success in influencing policy has been limited. Perhaps the greatest achievements have been to establish: legislation that promotes collective bargaining and a framework for dispute settlement; an institutional mechanism for social dialogue and annual framework agreements; legislation governing health and safety, social security, redundancy, gender equality and employment. In practice, however, there are serious problems with implementing legislation in all these fields due to the attitudes of employers, the absence of adequate labour inspection and the slow procedures of the Labour Court.

During the last decade of the twentieth century the labour movement went through profound internal reform and it emerged as truly democratic and accountable. However, until recently divisions and disputes between and within the unions have exacerbated image problems that were inherited from the Soviet period. Privatization and changes in the labour market caused union membership to decline drastically between 1990 and 1997. In 1998 and 1999 this decline was arrested and some very marginal increases in union membership were achieved. Collaboration and coordination between the different centres also improved in these two years. One of the great success stories is the extent of workers' education on a wide range of topics.

In conclusion, therefore this has been a period of internal change and major adjustment to external forces. On any objective basis the political strength and influence of unions has declined. However the internal reforms should place the labour movement in a position to re-establish itself as a powerful force for social justice in the twenty-first century.

Bibliography

All data for this report have been provided by the Department of Statistics, unless otherwise stated in the text.

Interest groups, power and politics. 1997. Text of Annual Conference (Vilnius) 21-22 Nov.

Lazutka, R. 1999. *Assessing poverty and preconditions for reducing it* (Vilnius University).

Maculevicius, J.; Tiazkijus, V. 1977. *Legal regulation of labour relations. World experience and Lithuanian practice* (Vilnius).

Paukõtë, A.D. 1997. *Report on the situation of trade unions,* Inaugural conference in Lubeck, 25-26 Nov.

Perkumas, L. 1996. *Development and perspectives of the Lithuanian labour market*, Paper for the International Conference, 27-28 Mar.

Petrauskas, A. 1997. "Unofficial employment", in *Labour Exchange News*, Vilnius.

Report of the Lithuanian Trade Union Centre Council for the VIIth Congress. 1997. Vilnius, Oct. unpublished document.

Reports of the Lithuanian Trade Union Federation Annual Conferences. 1995-1998. Vilnius, unpublished documents.

Social report of the Ministry of Social Security and Labour. 1997. Vilnius.

Sysas, A. 1996. *The role of the state in industrial relations*, Country Report (Pestiany, Slovakia), 2-3 Mar.

UNDP. 1997. *The Lithuanian human development report 1997* (Vilnius).

Part 3

Studies on Ghana, India, Niger and South Africa

Trade union responses to globalization: Case study on Ghana

Kwasi Anyemedu

Introduction

There have been two principal driving forces of the process of globalization. The first is vastly improved transport and communications which have greatly reduced the importance of geographical distance. The World Bank (1995) estimates that by 1960 maritime transport costs were less than a third of the 1920 level, and they have continued to fall. The jet aircraft has made most parts of the world accessible in a relatively short time The fall in the cost of communications has been even more dramatic. According to the World Bank, the cost of an international telephone call fell six-fold between 1945 and 1970, and ten-fold between 1970 and 1990, and has continued to fall. The fusion of traditional communications technology and computer technology which has created the e-mail, Internet etc. has revolutionized worldwide communications and virtually eliminated geographical barriers since there is now instantaneous transmission of information throughout the world.

The second principal driving force has been the dominance of free enterprise, market-oriented, liberalized trade policies and development strategy since the early 1980s. The collapse of the Soviet Union and the socialist regimes of Eastern Europe at the end of the 1980s has intensified this dominance since it removed the major contending economic strategies. Through the medium of "policy-based lending", the World Bank, the International Monetary Fund (IMF) and Western donor countries have ensured that an economic orthodoxy which favours liberalized trade and the free flow of capital, though not of labour, has been embraced by virtually all the developing countries.

What has been called the " triumph of economic liberalism" is one of the driving forces of globalization. This triumph of neo-liberal ideas on economic management, as well as the free movement of goods and capital and the relative immobility of labour, has led to a situation in which the influence of organized labour has been considerably weakened. The need to be "internationally competitive" has often meant reducing labour costs and increasing profits so as to enhance "shareholders' value". The desire to attract foreign investment has prompted even centre-left governments to turn a deaf ear to union preferences. Almost all governments now have to institute neo-liberal reforms

> that have only spelled trouble for labour. Tighter fiscal controls prompted
> governments to downsize public-sector payrolls and pensions. Stabilization
> policies aimed at reducing inflation and controlling prices in some cases
> included wage freezes. Liberal trade policies have led to increased
> competition, which often meant that inefficient industries must shed labour
> and, in some cases, may be forced out of business entirely. In this climate,
> unions in many countries have had increasing difficulty delivering tangible
> results to their members (Newland, 1999).

In large parts of the developing world, the economic liberalist reform objectives of privatization, deregulation, and open trade and investment have been introduced mainly through structural adjustment programmes (SAPs), supported by the World Bank and the IMF. Since 1983 the government of Ghana has been implementing such a programme of economic reforms aimed at reducing the role of the state in the economy, increasing the role of the private sector and the market, liberalizing the economy and integrating it more fully into the global market. The policies pursued have included fiscal and monetary restraint; exchange rate adjustment/devaluation; trade liberalization; divestiture of state-owned enterprises; and private sector promotion.

The present chapter examines the impact of these reforms on Ghanaian workers and looks at the response of organized labour to the new environment created by the reforms. We begin with some background information on the country and its labour market, the Trades Union Congress (TUC) of Ghana and its relationship to successive governments. The next section presents the current structure of organized labour institutions, and the central role played by the Trades Union Congress. The third section reviews some aspects of the economic reforms introduced since 1983, with special attention to measures aimed at integrating Ghana more fully into the global economy. This section also reviews the impact of the reforms on employment and earnings. The fourth section analyses the response of the Trades Union Congress to the challenges posed by the reforms. First we review the attempts made by the TUC to influence economic policy through a critique of some of the reform measures and also by participating in the implementation of specific policies. The objective of these activities has been to mitigate what the TUC perceives to be the adverse effects of the reform measures on its members. The second part of the fourth section is devoted to attempts by the TUC to shore up its declining membership and improve its capacity to represent and protect the interests of its members.

1. Background information

Ghana, formerly a British colony called the Gold Coast, attained independence in 1957. It is a small low-income country in West Africa with a population of about 18 million (1997) and a land area of 228,000 sq. km. It had a Gross National Product (GNP) of $6.6 billion in 1997 and a per capita GNP of $370 the same year.

The political history of the country since independence has been dominated by frequent military interventions in government, with successful military coups in 1966, 1972, 1979 and 1981, a palace coup in 1978, and numerous unsuccessful attempts to overthrow the government, whether it was in civilian or military hands. Political instability has been the principal cause of the deteriorating economic fortunes of the country, which was considered a middle-income country at the time of independence, and had a standard of living which was high for an African country. The past two decades have seen a reasonable measure of political stability. The military regime, which took power at the end of 1981, managed to continue in government despite some challenges. After elections in 1992, it transformed itself into a constitutional regime.

Information on the labour market in Ghana has traditionally been characterized by its paucity and unreliability. The Statistics and Research Division of the Ministry of Employment and Social Welfare has recently attempted to remedy this situation, and the discussion in this chapter is based mainly on its *Key Indicators of the Ghanaian Labour Market*.

Agriculture, forestry and fishing provide about 60 per cent of total employment; retail trade is the second most important source, accounting for 21 per cent of total employment. Manufacturing provides about 5 per cent of total employment; the service industries 10.2 per cent; and construction 2 per cent of total employment. Transport/communications/utilities provide 1.7 per cent of total employment; mining 0.3 per cent; finance /insurance/ real estate 0.3 per cent; and wholesale trade accounts for 0.5 per cent of total employment.

The Trades Union Congress (TUC) of Ghana was formally inaugurated in 1945 when the existing 14 unions registered under the Trades Union Ordinance of 1941 came together under a central coordinating body. Associations of workers for mutual protection had existed in the Gold Coast from about the 1920s, but organized trade union activity is usually dated from 1941 when the Trades Union Ordinance provided for the registration of unions, which could be formed by any five workers. The 1941 Ordinance, however, did not confer bargaining rights on the unions. Employers could agree or refuse to negotiate with their employees.

Four years after the formation of the Trades Union Congress, a militant nationalist party, the Conventions Peoples Party (CPP) was formed. The CPP was devoted to seeking immediate self-government, and the ending of colonial rule in the Gold Coast. The party courted organized labour, many union leaders were active in the party, and there appeared to be some coordination of activities between the party and the unions. Thus although a general strike called by the Congress in 1950 was ostensibly to protest against dismissals in the Meteorological Department, the demands made by the workers included a call for the immediate grant of Dominion Status to the Gold Coast; and a day after the outbreak of the strike, the CPP decided to embark on a "positive action" campaign for immediate self-government.

The collaboration between the Congress and the CPP appeared to pay off when the party led the country to independence in 1957. A year after independence, the CPP-led government introduced the Industrial Relations Act of 1958 (Act 56) designed to strengthen trade unions in Ghana. The 1958 Industrial Relations Act gave legal backing to trade unions for the first time. It gave legal recognition to the Trades Union Congress as a corporate body. It made collective bargaining compulsory, and the provisions of collective bargaining agreements legally binding on employers and workers. It gave legal backing to the check-off system under which trade unions dues were deducted at source. An amendment in 1959 made it impossible for any union to stay outside the TUC's new structure. The CPP government also passed the Civil Service Act and the Civil Service Interim Regulations of 1960 which had the effect of making trade union membership compulsory for all civil servants. This was intended, among other things, to strengthen the financial standing of the TUC. In 1958 the government provided the TUC with the building which houses its headquarters as a "tribute to the contribution that Ghana labour has made in our struggle for liberation".

The Industrial Relations Act of 1958 was replaced by the Industrial Relations Act of 1965 which remains the principal instrument governing industrial relations in Ghana. [A new Labour Code has been prepared but is yet to be enacted.] The 1965 Act echoed the 1958 Act, including the provision making the TUC the sole representative of the trade union movement in Ghana. This monopoly status has been criticized as contravening ILO Convention No. 87, and the country's constitution. The proposed new Code seeks to make changes in this area.

Collaboration between the TUC and the CPP government did not only produce benefits for the labour movement; it also entailed costs in terms of a loss of independence. From about 1959 onwards, the CPP regarded the TUC as a wing of the party and felt free to interfere in union matters in several ways, including making appointments to leadership positions in the TUC. This generated resentment among some unionists, and the difficult economic situation in the mid-1960s turned many rank-and-file workers against the government. When the CPP government was overthrown by the military in 1966, many workers welcomed the change. The arrival of Ghana's first military regime, however, represented a setback to the TUC in some respects. Some of its leaders were arrested and held in custody for a while, and the new government, the National Liberation Council (NLC), repealed section 24 of the Civil Service Act of 1960, which made trade union membership compulsory for civil servants. This naturally led to a loss of membership. Membership in the Public Services Workers Union fell from 40,000 in January 1967 to 26,000 by June 1968 (Arthiabah and Mbiah, 1995). The NLC also implemented an IMF-supported stabilization programme which involved the retrenchment of an estimated 60,000 workers in state-owned enterprises over the period 1966-67. These developments adversely affected the financial position of the TUC.

The TUC was to suffer an even more serious setback with the return to civilian rule in 1969. The party which won the 1969 elections had been in opposition to the CPP before and after independence. It was not known to be a natural ally of workers and their unions. Indeed the claim was made that many of the party's leaders had "a class-based disdain for union leaders". There was soon to be cause for confrontation between the government and the TUC. At the third biennial congress of the TUC held in August 1970, a resolution was passed calling for a 100 per cent increase in the minimum wage (from C 0.75 to C 1.50). The request was turned down by the government as unreasonable and potentially inflationary. Given the initial mutual suspicions, and fearing that a national strike might be called to support the demand for an increase in the minimum wage, the government decided to strike first at the TUC. On 13 September 1971, under a certificate of urgency, Parliament passed the Industrial Relations (Amendment) Act 1971 (Act 383) to replace the Industrial Relations Act 1965 (Act 229). The new Act dissolved the TUC with immediate effect and empowered the government to appoint a board of receivers to dispose of all the properties of the TUC.

The government argued that the TUC as set up by the Industrial Relations Act of 1965 was undemocratic and an infringement on the rights of workers to associate freely. The new Act, therefore, in addition to dissolving the TUC provided that: "Any group of trade unions shall have the right to constitute themselves into any association, federation, confederation or congress of trade unions for the attainment of their common aims". There can be no doubt that the primary motivation for introducing the Industrial Relations Act of 1971 was to disorganize and weaken the labour movement. However, the government was able to claim that the Act of 1971 was for the "purposes of protecting the rights or freedoms of other persons in terms of the spirit of the constitution". This claim was justified by the legitimate criticism of the monopoly status conferred on the TUC by the 1965 Act.

The military took power again only four months after Act 383 was passed. The new rulers who came into power in January 1972 promulgated the Industrial Relations (Amendment) Decree of 1972, which repealed the 1971 Act and restored the Industrial Relations Act of 1965 and the TUC.

2. Current structure of the trade union movement

The Industrial Relations Act 1965 (Act 229) recognizes the TUC as the sole representative of the trade union movement in Ghana. Section 3 of Act 229 requires that any union wishing to apply for a collective bargaining certificate from the Registrar of Trade Unions has to apply through the TUC. The TUC has 17 national unions organized along industrial lines. These and their declared membership are:

Table 1. Trade union membership

	1985	1998
1. Communication Workers Union (CWU)	7000	6026
2. Construction, Building & Material Workers Union (CBMWU)	39553	36750
3. Ghana Mine Workers Union (GMWU)	27, 018	24834
4. Ghana Private Road Transport Union (GPRTU)	56138	37400
5. General Agricultural Workers Union (GAWU)	100000	86690
6. General Transport, Petroleum & Chemical Workers Union (GTPCWU)	29185	15683
7. Health Services Workers Union (HSWU)	30000	32745
8. Industrial and Commercial Workers Union (ICU)	120000	106483
9. Local Government Workers Union (LGWU)	35000	33126
10. Maritime and Dockworkers Union (MDU)	31085	29012
11. National Union of Seamen (NUS)	5011	1871
12. Public Services Workers Union (PSWU)	63000	89324
13. Public Utility Workers Union (PUWU)	20000	10081
14. Railway Enginemen's Union (REU)	898	884
15. Railway Workers Union (RWU)	8955	5907
16. Teachers and Educational Workers Union (TEWU)	40000	31448
17. Timber and Woodworkers Union (TWU)	18000	24334
TOTAL	630843	572598

Source: 1985 figures are from Arthiabah and Mbiah, 1995, and 1998 figures are from the Secretary-General's Report on Activities of the TUC (Ghana) for the Third and Fourth Quarters of 1998, presented to the Executive Board, Dec. 1998.

In September 1993, a new union, the Textile, Garment and Leather Employees' Union (TGLEU), whose members were formerly with the Industrial and Commercial Workers Union (ICU) of the TUC, was registered by the Registrar of Trade Unions under the Trade Unions Ordinance of 1941. As required by the Industrial Relations Act of 1965, the new union, though not affiliated to the TUC, applied through the TUC for a collective bargaining certificate, which was duly granted by the Registrar in October 1993. Thus since 1993, there has been an eighteenth trade union operating under the Industrial Relations Act of 1965, but not affiliated to the TUC. (The new Labour Code is expected to regularize the situation.) In addition, there are a number of workers' associations representing public sector employees, which are not certified to operate under the Industrial Relations Act of 1965. These are the Civil Servants Association of Ghana, the Ghana National Association of Teachers, the Ghana Registered Nurses Association, and the Judicial Service Staff Association of Ghana.

Since December 1992 these associations have had a form of negotiating power with their employer (the government) under the Public Services (Negotiating Committee) Law. Strictly, however, only unions which hold a collective bargaining certificate can call a legal strike, as only they fulfil the conditions laid down by Act 229 to make a strike legal.

These associations and the TUC came together in August 1985 to establish a National Consultative Forum of Ghana Labour (NCFGL). The Forum does not negotiate on behalf of its constituent members, but creates a cordial atmosphere for negotiations. The public sector workers' associations have constituted a Joint Consultative Forum. These associations are represented on the National Advisory Committee on Labour, which advises the Ministry of Labour. At the Tripartite Committee on Salaries and Wage Guidelines, they participate under the umbrella of the TUC.

In 1998, a new labour centre, the Ghana Federation of Labour, was established by the Ghana National Association of Teachers, the Ghana Registered Nurses Association, the Textiles, Garment and Leather Employees Union, the Lotto Receivers Union, the Cooperative Transport Association, and the Tailors and Dressmakers Association. The latter three associations/unions are made up of self-employed operators in the informal sector. Subsequently, the Civil Servants Association and the Ghana National Association of Teachers withdrew from the new labour centre.

3. Economic reforms and their impact on Ghanaian workers

Since April 1983, Ghana has been carrying out a number of macroeconomic and structural reforms aimed at reviving the economy. The reforms have covered a broad front, including exchange reforms; fiscal reforms; removal of price controls; privatization; restructuring of the public sector; and reforms in agriculture, manufacturing, health and education.

The fuller integration of Ghana into the global economy has been a fundamental objective of the reforms, and a number of policy measures have aimed at achieving this. Of particular mention are the exchange reforms and import liberalization. The previously fixed and highly over-valued exchange rate has been replaced by a flexible, market-determined one. In the process the local currency, the cedi, has undergone massive depreciation, from C2.75=$1.00 when the reforms started, to the April 2000 rate of C4,000=$1.00. The measures taken to liberalize imports have included the abolition in January 1989 of the import licensing system established in 1961, a reduction in tariffs, and the lifting of restrictions on access to foreign exchange.

Considerable success has been achieved in increasing Ghana's integration into the world economy. Exports grew from about $450 million in 1983 to about $2,090 million in 1998, while imports increased from about $500 million in 1983 to about $2,900 in 1998. The trade intensity index (the sum of exports and imports as a share of GDP) increased from 20 per cent in 1984 to 59 per cent in 1997. In line with most of sub-Saharan Africa, Ghana has not been able to attract large volumes of foreign investment despite vigorous efforts to promote the country as an attractive location for such investment. Some progress has, however, been achieved in recent years.

What has been the impact of these reforms and increased integration into the world economy? Real GDP has grown at an average annual rate of about 5 per cent since 1984. This contrasts with an average annual rate of –2.4 per cent over the pre-reform years of 1978-1983. An evaluation of the impact on employment is more difficult because figures on "recorded employment' from the Ghana Statistical Service terminate in 1991. The recorded figures, based on a survey of establishments, show that employment rose steadily from 280,000 in 1982 to 464,000 in 1985, and then began to fall, dropping to 186,000 in 1991. The decline occurred in both the private and public sectors.

The initial increase in recorded employment was largely due to the greater availability of imported raw materials brought about by the easing of foreign exchange constraints, and the lifting of restrictions on imports. The subsequent decline in employment was due to two main factors. The first was increased competition from imported goods, and the inability of some manufacturers to face this competition. Electrical equipment, textiles, clothing and leather goods were particularly hard hit by the very strong competition from imports. The second factor was the retrenchment of labour in the public sector. An estimated 73,000 workers were retrenched from 1987 onwards under the Civil Service Reform Programme. Another 100,000 workers are estimated to have been retrenched from the Ghana Cocoa Board from the mid-1980s to the early 1990s. The layoffs caused insecurity among workers about their future employment prospects. With respect to incomes, it is a fact that wage restraint has been a constant feature of the reform programme. In the early part of the programme, wage restraint was deemed necessary as an anti-inflation measure. It was also necessary to ensure that the incentive effects of the exchange rate depreciation for the export sector were not eroded by wage increases. Later, the emphasis was on the effects of public sector wage increases on the budget deficit. Currently, it is also emphasized that "prudent wage policies" are necessary to "enhance Ghana's competitiveness and attract foreign investment". Hard data on incomes are as difficult to obtain as employment figures. The Ghana Statistical Service's survey of establishments, which produced the "recorded employment" figures also produced data on "average monthly earnings per employee". These figures, of course, also terminate in 1991. Analysis of the figures shows that "real monthly incomes in 1989 were about double their level in 1980 but declined by more than ten percentage points between 1989 and 1991" (Boateng, 1998).

There are indications that real wages have declined since 1991. A survey of manufacturing firms over the period 1992-94 under the Regional Programme on Enterprise Development (RPED) showed that, for the enterprises surveyed, real wages had declined by 9 per cent over the period of the survey. The survey also revealed a widening gap between low-paid and higher- paid jobs. Thus, for instance, while the real wages of management personnel had increased by 30 per cent and the real wages of sales personnel had increased by 46 per cent, the real wages of production workers and apprentices had declined by 13 per cent and 56 per cent respectively. This widening in the wage differential is a result of policy, as well as demand and supply factors. For the public sector, for instance, the government's medium-term programme calls for measures "to reorganize the functions of the Civil Service and subvented organisations, reduce staffing levels, rationalise hiring practices, and raise relative pay in favour of managerial staff".

It can be said that the changes brought about by the reforms have not been particularly friendly to the workers represented by the TUC. In a speech delivered at the launching of the TUC/ICFTU "New Approach to Structural Adjustment in Africa" in Accra on 9 July 1998, the Secretary General of the TUC declared: "(The) standard of living of the average worker and for that matter the average Ghanaian has fallen during the last fifteen years of adjustment. Unemployment has been high, real incomes have reduced drastically....". The perception of the leaders of organized labour as to the impact of the reforms on their members is important because, irrespective of the evaluation of outside (non-union) analysts, informed or otherwise, the response of the labour movement to the changing economic environment will be determined by what the trade unions perceive it is doing to their members.

4. Trade union responses

The reaction of the TUC to what it perceives as an unfavourable environment has taken many forms, but can be classified into two main sets of responses. First, the TUC has attempted to influence the (policy) environment and make it less unfriendly; secondly, it has attempted to adjust to the changed environment as far as possible. This has also involved shifts in organizational focus and action. The TUC is trying to adjust to a new environment which itself is still evolving. Therefore some of the responses are only in the form of proposals at this stage.

4.1 Attempting to influence policy

The TUC has been aware from the start of the reform process that the changes taking place have serious implications for its members. It has therefore sought in various ways to influence the direction of policy through memoranda, conference resolutions, seminars and workshops, and through representation on bodies dealing with the implementation of specific policies and measures. In 1993, in the tenth year of the economic reforms, the TUC and the ICFTU organized a *Conference on the Social Dimensions of the Structural Adjustment Programme*.

This meeting deliberated extensively on the performance of the Economic Recovery Programme/Structural Adjustment Programme in Ghana, and made observations and recommendations on privatization, trade liberalization, external debt, agriculture, small businesses and the informal sector, consultation and participation.

The TUC has made its views known on government policies, highlighting what it perceives as the negative effects on workers and society generally, and proposing remedial measures. In May 1986, the TUC issued a statement setting out its views on economic, social and political affairs. Reference was made to a comprehensive position paper on the national situation presented to the government in February 1985, as well as other memoranda on economic and social issues submitted in the previous two years. Expressing regret that these representations to the government and its agencies "have hardly even received acknowledgement", the statement expressed in forthright terms the dissatisfaction of the TUC with the prevailing economic conditions:

> The situation that we face today is one in which harsh sacrifices are exacted from the mass of the working people in the name of economic recovery at the same time that their interests are overlooked. In the name of the efficient utilisation of resources, the basic health, education, and housing needs of the people, as well as access to utility services like water and electricity are

all continually undermined through increasing fees and prices. In the meantime, self-reliance and genuine mobilisation of the resources of the nation in which the people play a central role has been abandoned for reliance on foreign aid and loans (TUC Ghana, 1986).

The TUC thus took the position quite early that the opening of the economy to foreign capital, and reliance on development strategies imposed from outside were related to the situation in which the interests of the working people were overlooked. This theme was taken up again at the quadrennial congress of the TUC held in March 1988, which addressed among other issues the national economy. The congress came to the conclusion that "the current worsening economic situation in the country, the brunt of which is being borne by the working people, is attributable in the main to the conditionalities imposed on the economy by the multilateral lending agencies, namely the IMF and the World Bank". The congress called for condemnation of the strict adherence by the government to the IMF/World Bank conditions.

The quadrennial congress thus launched a fundamental and frontal attack on the whole reform programme. It requested the government to "discontinue forthwith" the major elements of the liberal reform agenda: currency devaluation, import liberalization, privatization, expansion of exports, decontrol of prices, etc. All these were denounced as not favourable to the working people of the country. The congress, of course, also noted the increasing burden of external debt servicing payments.

The 1988 Christmas and New Year message of the Secretary-General of the TUC continued this trenchant criticism of the reforms and the prevailing economic situation, detailing the negative effects of the reforms on organized labour:

> The year 1988 has been a difficult year for the working people in the country. Workers have had to put in a lot to survive the intolerable hardship. It is five years now since the inception of the nation's Economic Recovery Programme (ERP), but although the policies of the ERP affect the various social classes one can say without equivocation that as workers we have felt the brunt of the policies despite the great sacrifices made by us under the programme. The year 1988 has not been different from the four previous years of the ERP. As workers we have had to work under severe constraints with the hope that things would get better for us to enjoy the fruits of our sweat and toil, but after five years we are yet to see the light of hope at the end of the tunnel. Rather, things are getting worse from all indications.

> Employment in the public sector has ceased to grow. In fact, it has declined due to the retrenchment exercise going on. Workers are becoming redundant because several local industries, which have been subjected to unfair

competition from outside under the trade liberalization programme, have folded up. The army of the unemployed is now being urge to seek refuge in the so-called informal sector and this has brought about a massive increase in casual work. Men, women, young people and even children are driven to seek insecure, inadequate, and even dangerous jobs on the fringes of society just to survive.

Those of the working population in gainful employment have also been hard hit by the effects of ERP/SAP and they are having to fight to protect their jobs because they are the first victims of the retrenchment exercises.

During the 1990s the TUC continued to comment on government policies and the national economic situation, but the criticisms were muted. With the SAP firmly entrenched, and the prospects for reversal virtually non-existent, recommendations to the government to discontinue the entrenched policies "forthwith" would probably be futile. In addition, the collapse of the worldwide socialist alternative has meant that people everywhere have had to accommodate themselves to what appears to be the only viable development path. The TUC has concentrated its attention in more recent years on ensuring that the process of policy formulation and implementation is as inclusive as possible in the hope that this will raise the quality of policies and improve the prospects of their being implemented efficiently and with fairness.

In this connection, the TUC was one of the institutions that pressed for the National Economic Forum which took place in September 1997 with the theme *Achieving a National Consensus on Policy Measures for Accelerated Growth within the Framework of Ghana- Vision 2020*. The TUC took an active part in planning the forum as well as in its deliberations. The Secretary-General of the TUC chaired the syndicate group, which discussed the theme *Increasing Employment Opportunities and Promoting Human Development*.

The TUC has also accepted, and indeed sought, representation on bodies charged with policy implementation because it believes it can better protect the interests of workers in this way. Thus, although the TUC was critical of the divestiture programme, it nevertheless agreed to serve on the Divestiture Implementation Committee (DIC). This made it possible for the TUC to fight for compensation for workers laid off in the process of divestiture. The TUC is also represented on other implementation bodies such as the Export Processing Zone Board and the Public Utilities Regulatory Commission, which is responsible for approving the tariffs charged by public utilities.

There has been some debate about the wisdom of the TUC participating in such bodies. Some hold that the small number of TUC representatives are unlikely to influence the decisions taken, while TUC participation will reduce its moral right to criticize the decisions if they are unfavourable to workers.

The dominant view in the TUC, however, is that it is better to ensure that the concerns and interests of labour are taken into account when the decisions are being taken, because very little can be done later. The TUC reserves the right to criticize decisions taken by bodies on which it has representation.

The return to constitutional rule in early 1993 meant that the attempt to influence policy requires not only memoranda and comments on executive actions or participating in policy implementation. It also requires lobbying Parliament to ensure that legislation takes account of the interests of workers. In 1994, the TUC appointed a parliamentary liaison officer as a means of establishing a formal and continuous relationship between the labour movement and Parliament. The officer has been formally introduced to Parliament and recognized by the House. The officer, who has exhibited dedication to the job, briefs TUC leaders on developments in the House and impending legislation. When a bill is published it is examined for provisions concerning workers, the TUC is alerted, and if it decides to make representations to Parliament, the necessary contacts and arrangements are made.

A labour caucus has been established, comprising members of both the majority and minority parties, and meetings are organized with the TUC to discuss issues and impending legislation of particular interest to workers. Among the major achievements of the TUC's lobbying efforts are the changes effected in legislation on the export processing zones (EPZs). The TUC was able to ensure that the rights of workers to organize within the zones were not compromised, and it also secured representation for the TUC on the EPZ Board.

4.2 Adjusting to a changed environment

4.2.1 Attracting new members

Union membership has traditionally been derived principally from junior employees in the formal economy, mainly from relatively large establishments in both the private and public sectors. To counter the erosion in membership, there has been an intensification of the effort to organize self-employed workers and others in the informal sector. Increased efforts are also being made to unionize senior staff and professional workers.

TUC initiatives to establish links with operators in the informal sector are not new. Indeed, one of the 17 affiliated unions, the Ghana Private Road Transport Union (GPRTU) ranked fifth in terms of membership, consists very substantially of self-employed transport operators. However, there has been a definite intensification of efforts to "organize the unorganized" as a means of shoring up declining membership. The organization department of the TUC and almost all the national unions are devoting time and energy to meetings with micro and small-scale operators with a view to affiliating them to one of the national unions.

The task of organizing the unorganized appears to be easiest with respect to operators who already belong to some form of association. Thus the Ghana Hairdressers and Beauticians Association has been affiliated to the ICU, and constitutes the most organized informal sector group within the unions. Other groups of self-employed operators such as butchers (LGWU), carpenters and charcoal burners (TWU), and small-scale miners have been organized. The General Agricultural Workers Union (GAWU) has also organized groups of self-employed rural workers. In the capital city, efforts are being made to organize the large numbers of street hawkers, roadside traders and newspaper vendors.

Unions provide various services to their informal sector members or affiliates. In some cases, as with GAWU's farmer organizations, there is provision of limited credit and help with access to other forms of institutional credit. Many unions provide educational and skill development services. They also provide channels for collective bargaining with public authorities on matters of interest to the operators. In some cases, legal support is provided for members.

Based on experience so far, K. Adu-Amankwah (1990) has summarized the main obstacles which have faced union organization in the informal sector. These are the low financial returns from the sector in relation to the cost of organization, the absence of a ready package of benefits to attract informal sector operators, and lack of previous experience in union organization. The financial constraint is likely to be the most serious, for if increased membership only worsens the financial plight of the unions, the sustainability of the membership drive will be jeopardized and the capacity to offer benefits to attract informal sector operators will be weakened.

In view of the number of redundant workers, some attention has been given to retaining links with retrenched former members of unions. It has been proposed, for instance, that life membership of unions may be granted in some cases. Another approach is to encourage the formation of associations of pensioners and retrenched workers. These may be assisted with training to function as self-employed operators. One such association of mainly retrenched workers is the Self-Employed Women's Union (SEWU), affiliated to the Industrial and Commercial Workers Union (ICU). This is an association of about 300 women engaged in micro and small-scale manufacturing and craft industries. The TUC has helped with their organization and has arranged a number of workshops on entrepreneurship and small business development for them.

The unionization of senior staff and professional personnel is going to be crucial for the continued vitality of the TUC and its unions. Globalization and technological developments are reducing the demand for unskilled labour while increasing the demand for highly skilled and professional personnel. Unions which continue to recruit only blue-collar workers are likely to suffer a diminution in numbers. In addition, senior staff generally earn higher salaries and their financial contribution through union dues can be particularly valuable.

Many unions have mounted aggressive membership drives with respect to senior staff and professional employees. Other factors are also working in favour of the unionization of senior staff. Retrenchment in the public sector, downsizing in the private sector, and the notion that wages and other labour costs have to be restrained to make Ghana attractive for foreign investment have made many senior and professional personnel feel as vulnerable as junior staff to possible redundancy and erosion of income. Many senior staff have also realized that being covered by a legally binding collective bargaining agreement puts them on a firmer basis for negotiating for improved service conditions than the informal arrangements that their staff associations have had with employers.

The intensified drive by unions to attract senior staff has provoked a counter-offensive from the employers. The Ghana Employers Association (GEA) has issued public statements, organized conferences and published articles opposing the unionization of senior staff. The GEA's stated reasons for its opposition are many and varied. There is first the genuine problem of deciding which employees are representatives of employers or shareholders, and therefore to be excluded from union membership. On this, the ILO Committee on Freedom of Association (1963 and 1966) has advised as follows:

> It is important that the scope for managerial staff and the like should not
> be defined so widely as to weaken (worker) organizations by depriving them
> of a substantial proportion of their present or potential membership.

The GEA has tended to define "shareholder's representative" rather widely. In the view of the Executive Director of the GEA, a shareholder's representative is "anybody selected by the shareholder as his representative or any staff whose functions entail taking important decisions which have serious repercussions on the shareholder's business, assets or liabilities".

The employers cite among their reasons for opposing the unionization of senior staff, possible divided loyalty and misuse of confidential information by unionized senior staff/management personnel. The employers also argue that it would be distasteful for managers to belong to the same trade union as their subordinates, or even worse, for union leaders who may be junior staff to direct the affairs of a union in which their superiors are members. The employers believe this would tend to undermine or erode the authority of the senior officers concerned.

It seems that the employers are particularly concerned about what they believe would be the negative effect of senior staff unionization on foreign investment. On this issue, the Executive Director of the GEA has written as follows:

> The government is invited to take a position on the issue with a view to discouraging the unionisation of management staff. The GEA is of the view that government's efforts at attracting foreign investment may be seriously undermined if senior and management staff of companies are allowed to unionise, knowing the history of trade unions in the country. Foreign investors in particular may feel insecure in the sense that they cannot have loyal senior and management staff they can rely on to ensure increased profitability and reasonable profit, which is the driving force behind any investment (K. Amoasi- Andoh, 1998).

The country's Constitution and laws guarantee freedom of association and the government has declined an invitation from the employers to intervene. In a statement issued in October 1997, the Ministry of Employment and Social Welfare declared as follows:

> The Ministry recognises the fact that every Ghanaian is guaranteed freedom of association including the freedom to form or join a trade union of his choice. Senior staff members in any enterprise are therefore at liberty to form or join trade unions. However, since the levels of management responsibility vary from one organization to the other the Ministry's position is that Employees and Management should look at their organizational structures and determine which categories of employees should be unionized.

Both sides in the debate accept the prescription in principle, the problem is where to draw the line.

The unions have been reasonably successful in unionizing senior staff. The two largest, the Industrial and Commercial Workers Union and the Public Service Workers Union, have strong senior staff representation in their unions. The ICU has about 4,000 senior and management staff from 29 companies among its members, and the companies include most of the major private sector establishments in the country. According to the PSWU senior officers have numbered among their ranks from the inception of the union. The unions have not had things all their own way. The three biggest unions have all had instances in which management resisted the unionization of senior officers, and cases of unionized senior officers renouncing their union membership.

4.2.2 Training union officers and activists

Within the limits imposed by the prevailing environment, the task of mobilizing members and obtaining improved conditions for them depends to a considerable extent on the skills of trade union officers and activists in the areas of organization and negotiation. The Ghana TUC has recognized this and made the education of its members one of its priority concerns. The preamble to the TUC's educational policy affirms that:

> Trade union education has clearly established itself as one of the most important services that trade unions can provide for their members. Properly designed and implemented, trade union education plays an indispensable role in raising awareness among union members and providing them with skills to meet the challenges that confront the unions.

The institutional arrangements for giving effect to the educational policy centre mainly on the Education Committee and the Labour College. The Education Committee, consisting of seven members of the Executive Board, is responsible for implementing all aspects of the TUC's educational policy, and is required to promote the full participation of national unions in seeking to achieve the objectives of the policy.

The Labour College, which is regarded as the focal point for developing and managing the educational programmes, has the following specific functions:

i)   to develop study material and provide the technical and administrative support for executing education and training programmes;

ii)   to train trainers and develop a pool of educators to handle trade union education and compile a list of trainers for the national unions and regions;

iii) to implement a comprehensive education and training programme for the trade union movement;

iv)   to liaise with institutions of higher learning for support in programmes;

v)   to promote learning and studying in the labour movement by organizing seminars, outreach programmes, academic and non-academic courses and discussions.

The Labour College will certainly need additional resources, material and human, to discharge the above functions, but there is already vigorous activity. Training programmes are being organized for various categories of members and officers such as shop stewards, local/branch officers, union staff/field officers, national officers/ members of the Executive Board, and women/ youth activists. Training at the Labour College covers three broad areas; trade union education (collective bargaining, grievance handling, organizational skills, health and safety, conduct of meetings and labour laws); trade union history (in Ghana and generally, but with special reference to European trade union history); and special programmes, covering topical issues of interest both at home and worldwide. Basic accounting is offered for some levels of officers, and there is said to be a general request for more emphasis on management training.

There are some acknowledged problems in the field of education. The first is that there is not enough of it. Financial limitations mean that not as many people as desired are currently being catered for. Another problem is that there is no clear division of labour between the unions and the Labour College as to the courses offered, leading in some cases to avoidable duplication of effort, which is particularly regrettable in view of the resource constraints. Another problem mentioned is insufficient attention to participant selection, leading to persons of widely different backgrounds being enrolled in the same course. This tends to reduce the utility of the course, the level being too low for some participants and too high for others.

The educational programmes of the TUC depend quite substantially on external funding. The courses at the Labour College receive funding from the Netherlands Trade Union Federation, the Commonwealth Trade Union Council and the ICFTU Afro among others.

4.2.3 Negotiating for improved wages and working conditions

Wage restraint has been a constant element of public policy throughout the reforms, and the current emphasis is on wage restraint as a means of attracting foreign investment. This preoccupation with making Ghana attractive for foreign investors has produced an alliance between government and private business in opposition to demands for wage increases by organized labour. At the Tripartite Committee, the TUC has had to face the combined strength of the employers and government, who have coordinated their position on the minimum wage, for instance. This government/private employer collaboration is motivated by more than the fact that the government is also an employer. It appears that the government considers it part of its economic management responsibilities to ensure that the division of the national value-added between wages and profits is biased in favour of profits as an incentive to private investment.

The government and employers have succeeded in installing the capacity to pay of employers as virtually the only factor to be taken into account in wage determination. At the same time, deregulation and privatization of the utilities and other vital services have produced steep increases in the prices of these services. This is justified by what is said to be the economic cost of providing the services.

There are clear indications that the real value of wages declined in the 1990s. To a large extent, trends in the minimum wage can be used to approximate what is happening to wages generally since the minimum wage serves as a benchmark for incomes, especially in the low and middle ranks. The real value of the daily minimum wage (April 2000) is about half its value in 1991. This is roughly in line with the change in the dollar equivalent of the minimum wage over the same period. In July 1991, when allowances were first consolidated into wages, the daily minimum wage was equivalent to $1.25, while it is now equivalent to about $0.60.

The serious erosion in the income of large numbers of workers is generating considerable soul-searching on the part of organized labour and pressure on wage negotiations.

4.2.4 Participating in job creation

In the face of dwindling formal sector employment opportunities, the TUC has been mobilizing resources from its members to invest in productive enterprises as a means of creating employment as well as strengthening the financial base of the unions. In pursuit of this objective the TUC has established a Labour Enterprise Trust (LET) which holds members' contributions and invests the money either by itself or in collaboration with others.

The decision to institute what has been called an enterprise ownership policy was taken at the quadrennial congress in 1996, and was presented as an "important initiative to meet the challenge of job creation and employment security and the need for organized labour to establish itself as an obviously equal and constructive partner in the national development of Ghana".

The broad objectives of the enterprise ownership policy were stated as:

i)   to create and secure employment;
ii) to promote the national development of Ghana through appropriate investments;
iii) to secure a fair return for workers as shareholders;
iv) to strengthen the economic base of trade unions in Ghana; and
v)   to create the conditions for promoting workers' participation as an integral aspect of labour relations in Ghana.

At the inception of the trust, it was expected that all the estimated 500,000 unionized workers would purchase a minimum of 100 shares at 50, 000 cedis each. The collection of subscriptions was to be spread over 20 months, and by the end of 1998, a total initial capital of 25 billion cedis (equivalent to about $10 million at that time) was expected to be realized. Actual contributions fell far short of the projected sum, however, and at the end of the subscription period only a little over 90,000 had been contributed, yielding about 20 per cent of the expected initial capital.

So far the LET has made three major investments. It has purchased a 20 per cent share in a $5 million car park project located in the commercial centre of the capital city of Accra. It is also the majority shareholder in an insurance company and it has invested in four tankers to provide water at competitive rates to residents in Accra.

The LET Board has had to ensure a balance between safe investments and number of jobs created. Only the insurance company, designed to employ 27 full-time staff and 200 full-time agents, can be said to provide a reasonably large number of jobs but the LET has made an initial modest contribution to job creation. Upcoming projects include the establishment of a commercial bank, a security service, service stations, and radio taxi services. These will make further modest contributions to job creation.

4.2.5 Women and unions

Women are under-represented in the unions with an estimated share of 9-10 per cent in total membership. This is substantially below women's share of formal sector employment, which is about 25 per cent. The Ghana TUC has a long-standing commitment to mobilize women for the national unions, to encourage them to take leadership positions so that the concerns of female members can be effectively articulated, and also to ensure that the policies of the TUC take account of women's concerns. In accordance with this commitment, a women's section was established in the TUC in 1969, and in the same year women organizers were appointed for the regional offices at Kumasi and Cape Coast.

The Ghana TUC has formally adopted a gender policy based on the conviction that "the integration of women and achievement of gender equality are matters of human rights and a condition for social justice which should not be seen in isolation as a women's issue". The TUC believes that a gender policy is needed because, owing to the marginalization that women have generally suffered, they need to be treated differently by means of affirmative action in order to achieve greater social justice for all members. The broad objectives of the TUC's gender policy are stated as:

i)   to create gender awareness within the movement;
ii) to secure proportionate representation within the union structures;
iii) to promote the integration of gender considerations in collective bargaining agreements;
iv) to strengthen the legal rights of women in society and at the workplace;
v)   to formulate strategies for the protection of workers in the EPZs and in the informal sector.

Considerable emphasis has been placed on increasing the involvement of women in decision making in all the structures of the labour movement. In addition to the women's desk at the TUC, seven national unions have set up women's wings and committees at national as well as regional levels.

Some unions have also appointed women organizers and coordinators, and there is an increasing trend towards assigning negotiating responsibilities to women. Four unions have women on their joint negotiating committees.

The idea is growing that the inclusion of women in the negotiating committees will ensure that the peculiar problems of female employees are taken into account in negotiations. It is expected that the practice of including women in negotiating teams will be embraced by all the national unions. Various training programmes have been arranged for women organizers as well as rank-and-file members.

The TUC is convinced that grooming female members to assume leadership positions will help raise its image and will strengthen the TUC and the national unions. It is also true, however, that there has been some pressure from the international trade secretariats (ITS), to which some of the unions are affiliated, for unions to include women in decision-making positions. Some ITS are said to have made this a condition for their unions to benefit from programmes which they sponsor. The activities of the women's desk of the TUC have also benefited from considerable financial contributions from international organizations and NGOs. This pressure or encouragement from outside has been useful for there are still substantial problems militating against women's active involvement in union work. Some of the problems identified include; lack of knowledge about unions on the part of women; difficulty in combining union work with family responsibilities; lack of confidence and unwillingness to compete against men in elections; and preference for men during elections to union offices. On the last issue, there has recently been a welcome development from an unlikely source. The local union of the Ashanti Goldfields Corporation, which makes up about 40 per cent of the total membership of the Ghana Mine Workers Union, has elected as its secretary a female union member. In the elections, this lady unionist polled about 90 per cent of the votes.

The TUC and its women's section, in collaboration with other women's organizations, have been making efforts to improve the economic and social status of women. A large part of this drive has centred on encouraging the education of women at all levels and countering the social attitudes that tend to give priority to the education of boys. The TUC emphasizes the importance of educating girls. The TUC has also participated in campaigns to promote the welfare of women in the workplace and in society generally. The women's desk has played a leading role in raising awareness about the problem of sexual harassment at the workplace, and in emphasizing the need for adequate paid maternity leave. The TUC has also been very vocal in condemning violence against women and in calling for stiffer punishment for such crimes as rape.

4.2.6 Collective action and social alliances

It has been pointed out (Newland, 1999) that trade unions tend to benefit when they take an expansive view of their role, seeking to represent not only the concerns of their members but those of broad-based political parties. In Southern Africa, trade unions such as COSATU have participated actively in popular political and social struggle, and such activities, it is claimed, can enhance the labour movement's popular esteem and boost membership.

An extraordinary congress of the TUC in 1969, when a national election was due, decided that the TUC would not align itself with any political party, and that national union leaders should be debarred from party politics. This non-political party stance was reversed by the second quadrennial congress of the TUC held in September 1978, which endorsed:

> "the Executive Board's decision to enter into alliance with other progressive organizations and collaborate with such other persons or groups of persons that might share the aspirations of the working people for the purpose of fulfilling the *labour movement's initiative to create a political force for the defence and protection of the interest of the broad masses of the Ghanaian people*" (author's emphasis).

The TUC accordingly sponsored a political party, the Social Democratic Front, to contest the general elections held in 1979. This party was spectacularly unsuccessful in the elections, winning only 3 out of 140 parliamentary seats, and performing badly also in the presidential elections. Suitably chastened by this experience, the TUC subsequently effected an amendment in its constitution, which reaffirmed its neutrality in party politics.

The TUC has forged alliances with other workers' organizations and other elements of civil society in pursuit of common objectives. Within the labour movement, the TUC has established an alliance with bodies such as the Civil Servants Association, the Ghana National Association of Teachers, the Ghana Registered Nurses Association, and the Judicial Service Staff Association. These other workers' organizations and the TUC are united in a Workers' Forum, which deliberates on issues related to the salaries and conditions of service of workers and puts up a common front when appropriate. The TUC as the most representative workers' body often takes a leadership role. In consultations on the minimum wage and other issues determined at the National Tripartite Committee, it is the TUC which represents workers, but the TUC consults extensively with these other organizations and includes their representatives in its delegation.

Outside the labour movement, the TUC has often made common cause with civil society organizations such as the Ghana Bar Association, the National Union of Ghana Students and the Ghana Journalists Association in support of national objectives such as ensuring free and fair elections; promoting freedom of expression; encouraging the independence of the judiciary; and promoting economic development and stability. Freedom of expression has received particular attention in the TUC's endeavours, no doubt because it is so central to the achievement of the other political and economic goals. The TUC has persistently called for the media, especially the state-owned media, to be freed from government control. The TUC is currently represented on the National Media Commission, the body charged by the national constitution with responsibility for ensuring the independence of the media and for insulating the state-owned media from governmental control.

In Ghana, as in many African countries, distinctions of ethnicity, gender, income and wealth, and sometimes religion constitute potent divisive forces making for civil strife and social disintegration. There is often a need for conscious attempts at social integration based on a policy of inclusion under which all sections of the population have a say in national decision making. The rich and the powerful always have their say, the TUC provides an avenue through which the underprivileged can ensure that the interests of ordinary people are taken into account. Poverty is often a source of social alienation, and the TUC's struggles for an improvement in the living standards of working people, and the achievement of social justice generally, make important contributions to social cohesion.

4.2.7 Regional and global coordination

The work of the TUC is greatly aided, especially in the area of capacity building, by the collaborative interactions it undertakes with international and external trade union bodies in Africa and in the rest of the world. The Ghana TUC is affiliated to the Organization of African Trade Union Unity (OATUU) and to the International Confederation of Free Trade Unions (ICFTU). Some of the national unions are also affiliated to their corresponding international trade secretariats. The Ghana TUC also has fruitful bilateral collaboration with many national trade union centres, particularly in Europe. The Netherlands Trade Union Confederation and its Swedish counterpart appear to be the most active bilateral collaborators of the Ghana TUC. As the most representative labour organization in the country, the TUC participates in ILO meetings and programmes on behalf of the labour movement in Ghana.

These international connections have proved very beneficial to the TUC in many respects. Through reports, commentaries and other publications of the leading international trade union organizations and the ILO, the Ghana TUC is brought up to date on developments in the international economy and their impact on the labour movement globally as well as locally. But perhaps the greatest contribution of these international bodies is the organization both locally and overseas of a large number of conferences, workshops, seminars, and training programmes on issues of importance to the work of trade unions.

The establishment of an African Office for the ICFTU has been particularly important in terms of generating programmes of support targeted at African trade unions. The main programmes that ICFTU-Afro has brought to the Ghana TUC include the 1993 *Conference on the Social Dimensions of Structural Adjustment Programmes*, a workshop on export processing zones, and the recently launched *New Project Approach to Structural Adjustment*.

The Organization of African Trade Union Unity has also been active in marshalling trade unions to confront the challenges posed by the structural adjustment programmes in African countries. Its activities are, however, hampered by inadequate funds. Financial difficulties also led to the demise of the Organization of Trade Unions of West Africa (OTUWA), although efforts are being made to resurrect it.

It is now acknowledged by trade unions in the developed as well developing countries that the challenge of global capital can only be met by unions which have international connections, and that the forging of strategic links between organized labour groups in different countries is an imperative in an era of globalization. Developing country trade unions, in particular, stand to benefit from the alliances being forged at international level between trade unions, environmental associations and human rights groups to ensure that the rights of workers everywhere are respected, and that globalization produces not only profits for capital but also improved conditions for workers and their families.

5. Summary

Globalization has altered the balance of power between capital and labour decisively to the disadvantage of labour. The free movement of capital across national boundaries and the intense competition between countries for foreign investment have meant that investors'/shareholders' interests are given priority over workers' interests. Supporters of free capital mobility argue that increased inflow of capital produces productivity gains that generate competitive jobs and higher wages. In sub-Saharan Africa, efforts to attract foreign investment have not achieved much success due, in part, to non-economic factors such as civil strife in some countries. This lack of success compels some countries to try even harder at such policies as wage restraint, further trade liberalization, labour retrenchment, privatization etc., policies which, for the time being at least, appear to disadvantage workers.

We have reviewed the policies and actions that the TUC of Ghana has taken to meet the challenges posed by this unfavourable environment. These have included criticizing policies deemed not to be in the interest of workers, advocating and lobbying for more labour-friendly policies, extending the coverage of unions to previously unorganized workers, building alliances, and intensifying the education of officers and activists. Some of these initiatives have been modestly successful. But the labour movement still faces formidable obstacles in its endeavour to achieve improved wages and conditions for workers in the country.

Substantial support is emerging within the labour movement for more radical and robust approaches to defend the interests of workers. This is in accord with developments in other parts of the world where a radical mass "movement for social justice" has emerged to counter what are perceived to be the growing inequalities generated by globalization

References

Adu-Amakwah, K. 1990. "Trade unions in the informal sector: Finding their bearings", Ghana Country Paper, in Labour Education, Vol. 3, No. 16 (Geneva, ILO).

Amoasi-Andoh, K. 1998. "Unionisation of senior and management staff: A study of some problems", in Business Chronicle (Ghana), Mar 24 - Apr. 26.

Arthiaba, P.; Mbiah, H. 1995. *Half a century of toil and progress: The history of the Trades Union Congress of Ghana* (Accra, Friedrich Ebert Foundation).

Boateng, K. 1998. "Impact of structural adjustment on public and private sector employment and incomes in Ghana", in TUC Ghana/ICFTU-Afro: *New project approach to structural adjustment in Africa*, Oct.

Centre for the Study of African Economics. 1995. *The Ghanaian manufacturing sector 1991-1993: Findings of waves 1-3*, Report from the Regional Programme on Enterprise Development (University of Oxford and Dept. of Economics, University of Ghana), Sep.

Fosu, P.O. 1999. *Industrial relations in Ghana: The law and practice* (2nd ed.) (Ghana Universities Press).

Mazur, J. 2000. "Labour's new internationalism", in *Foreign Affairs*, Jan.-Feb.

Nayyar, D. 1997. "Globalization: The past is our present", in *Third World Economics*, No. 168, 1-15 Sep.

Newland, K. 1999. "Workers of the world, Now what?", in *Foreign Policy*, Spring.

Preeg, E. 1988. *From here to free trade* (University of Chicago Press).

TUC Ghana. 1986. *Views on economic, social and political affairs: Our perspectives*, 15 May.

— . 1988a. *Resolutions adopted by the Third Quadrennial Delegates Congress*, Mar.

— . 1988b. *Christmas and New Year Message to the Workers of Ghana*, Dec.

World Bank. 1995. *Workers in an integrating world*, World Development Report (Washington, DC).

Organized labour and economic liberalization in India: Past, present and future

Debashish Bhattacherjee

1. Introduction

This paper examines the role of organized labour in India in a structural and historical context, tracing the economic, political, and social effects of the trade union movement over time. We look at union strategies at the level of the enterprise and/or firm, the industry, the region and the nation. The effects of changing economic conditions on the evolution of trade unions and bargaining institutions are described in largely urban labour markets in the post-independence period (1947 onwards). Then we consider some contemporary issues affecting the organized labour movement in India today.

The paper has two main objectives: a) to present a history of Indian industrial relations, broadly understood as the changing relationships between workers, trade unions, employers, the economy and the state; and b) to posit a political economy of trade unionism in India. The contrasting views of Freeman and Medoff (1984) of trade unions as "monopoly" institutions, or as the "collective voice" of workers, serve as a theoretical framework here. From a policy perspective in democratic and pluralistic societies, the objective must be to minimize the "monopoly" effects and to strengthen the "collective voice" effects.

The position taken here is "that the evolution of labour institutions is determined by the objective interests of social groups inherent in the logic of a modern industrial society" (Zeitlin, 1987, p. 163), and that these "interests" are inevitably "ambiguous and context dependent". Consequently, it is difficult to establish mechanisms to ensure that labour institutions, such as trade unions, collective bargaining and the state, continue to play the parts assigned to them. The second proposition of this essay is that "no single approach to the study of labour organization is at present adequate – which is to say that the study of these matters is usually informed from several points of view" (Williamson, 1985, p. 241).

2. Contrasting views on trade unions as institutions

Freeman and Medoff (1984) examined the impact of unionism on the employment relationship in the US economy, contrasting the "two faces of

unionism": the "monopoly" versus the "collective voice" view. These lead
to a completely divergent analysis of the union as an economic and political
institution; the policy implications of the two views are therefore
fundamentally incompatible.

The first view analyses unions as large monopolies in the labour market
whose basic objective is to increase their members' wages above the market
level by restricting labour supply. This "wage mark-up" leads to a
misallocation of human and capital resources, and is therefore not only
economically suboptimal, but may also be socially undesirable in that it leads
to greater inequalities within the workforce. In addition, strikes of all kinds
impose an easily measurable loss on the economy. Finally, "union work rules",
embedded in contract provisions often lower the productivity of both labour
and capital by creating inflexibilities at the workplace. While these arguments
typically emanate from free-market economists, social theorists who subscribe
to this view often characterize unions as undemocratic and crime-riddled
institutions.

In sharp contrast, the collective voice view asserts that unions have
positive economic, political and social effects in pluralist democracies. The
union's collective voice, determined by a "median voter", provides
management with information on workplace and shopfloor issues, acting as
a communication channel. This leads to the development and retention of
specific skills, improves worker morale, provides conditions that eliminate
quitting, and enables the union to pressure management to act fairly and
efficiently in its daily operations. It is believed that unionized work
environments are more productive than comparable non-unionized
environments. Finally, unions are socially beneficial as they represent the
interests of lower income groups and vulnerable sections of society.

2.1 A comparative framework

It is now a truism that economic performance is related to the nature of
labour market institutions (see Horton et al., 1991; Nelson, 1991; Freeman,
1992; Buchele and Christiansen, 1992). Economic performance here means
controlling inflation and generating employment, which implies productivity
growth. In the world of unions and collective negotiations, the key variables
frequently cited as determining economic performance are: the level at which
bargaining takes place (plant, firm, industry/region, nation), and the nature
of trade union structures.

Until at least the mid-1980s, the literature suggested that economies with
a decentralized bargaining structure (enterprise-based unions negotiating at
the plant and firm level, as in East Asian countries, Japan and Switzerland)
and economies with a centralized bargaining structure (national agreements

with centralized trade union federations, as in Austria, Norway and Sweden) "performed" better than economies having industry-wide agreements with industry-wide unions, as in the United States and United Kingdom. Put another way, "collective voice" effects seem to be maximized in centralized bargaining structures, whereas "monopoly" effects seem to be greatest at medium levels of centralization.

While most commentators would agree that labour market flexibility is required for facilitating economic restructuring, heated controversy surrounds the question of how this flexibility is to be achieved. As transition will involve considerable social costs, what is to be the role of the state and the trade union movement in managing this transition? The debate acquired particular significance with the release of the World Bank *World Development Report*: *Workers in an integrating world* (1995) and an ILO report: *World Employment 1996-97 – National policies in a global context*. The World Bank report hypothesizes increasing employment and labour incomes with greater integration of nations into the global market, positing a reduced role of the state in the labour market and expecting trade unions to be responsible and non-political. On the other hand, the central message of the ILO report is that state intervention with centralized bargaining institutions can return economies to full employment policies, which it sees as the only way to create jobs and better earnings opportunities (D' Souza, 1998).

Where does India fit in this comparative framework? The Indian economy represents a mix of all three bargaining levels and a variety of union structures. In the private corporate sector, plant-level bargaining takes place with enterprise-based unions that may or may not be affiliated to parliamentary political parties. In public sector enterprises, centralized trade union federations affiliated to political parties bargain with the state (as employer) at the industry-and/or national-level. Central and state government employees in the service sector (transport, postal services, banking and insurance, police and firefighters, etc.) are usually represented by politically affiliated unions bargaining at the national and/or regional level. Most of these centralized bargaining and union structures were stable during the period of planned industrialization while India pursued a policy of import substitution. However, since the mid-1980s the economy has opened up to greater domestic and international competition and these structures have come under increasing pressure to decentralize. These pressures have become stronger since the economic liberalization programme was introduced in 1991, especially in the public sector. As in other countries, the state has gradually retreated from its earlier role of creating permanent employment and regulating union/management bargaining.

India has had mixed experience with creating labour institutions that are compatible with a pluralist industrial relations model. In the early years, the government officially promoted industrial pluralism and bilateral collective bargaining, but the institutions responsible for this were largely controlled by the state. This "state-dominated" pluralism, coupled with ambiguous labour laws regarding trade union recognition and "industrial disputes", eventually led to a multiplicity of party-based trade unions. This considerably weakened the political power of the organized labour movement as a whole, although in some strategic sites in the public sector centralized unions had considerable bargaining strength. Although unions could impose severe costs on key sectors of the economy, the organized labour movement as a whole was not strong enough to impose a cooperative solution at the national level. This is still true today.

With economic liberalization, competitive forces began to affect the structure of the union movement. In several private enterprises, "independent" rank-and-file led unions came into existence and engaged in informed and militant bargaining, often with multinational employers, securing substantial wage and non-wage gains in the process. As these unions "traded off" increased wages against employment growth, and as employers shifted to "outsourcing" from non-union sites, the traditional party-based unions found their potential recruitment terrain both challenged and curtailed. More recently, since the liberalization process officially began in 1992, many of these centralized party-based unions have united under a common front to resist government attempts at privatization and decentralization in the public sector. However, the organized labour movement as a comprehensive organization continues to face a fractured and segmented constituency, divided by skill, region, industry and ethnicity. In addition, major labour law reform continues as an unfinished (and forever postponed) agenda.

In terms of the "monopoly" versus the "collective voice" framework, the early years after independence witnessed the state acting as the "collective voice" of workers for the purpose of rapid industrialization with minimum industrial strife. In so doing, the state minimized the potential "monopoly" effects; wages and working conditions were administered rather than decided through collective negotiations in the public sector. An implicit "incomes policy" kept the "union wage mark-up" in check. Over time, however, as both inter- and intra- industry differentiation developed, especially within the private sector, other, more radical and militant union "voices" emerged that quite effectively began to challenge the state hold on the organized labour movement. In the private sector, efficient productivity bargaining with informed unions kept "monopoly" effects within the firm in check while "collective voice" effects increased. However, in public sector enterprises and services, the union "voice" led to rigid and inflexible contract provisions. With pay increases unrelated to improvements in productivity, union "monopoly" effects intensified. There seems to be some agreement now among labour commentators and researchers that (since at least the early 1980s) some segments of the organized workforce made substantial wage and non-wage gains in the more profitable sectors of production. The large majority of workers, however, continue to face increasing employment insecurity, if not lower wage growth, both in declining industries in the formal sector and in the growing informal sectors. With the onset of economic liberalization, these "negative union spillover" effects may accentuate inequalities within the workforce. Clearly there is need for a concerted attempt by the state and the organized labour movement to actively reverse these trends by levelling up the labour market institutions which affect the wages and working conditions of the unorganized.

3. The changing economic environment and its effects on organized labour in India

3.1 The four phases of unionism: An evolutionary approach

3.1.1 The first phase of unionism (1950 to mid-1960s)

The first phase of the (post-independence) Indian trade union movement generally corresponds to the first three Five-Year Plans (1951-56, 1956-61, 1961-66), a period of "national capitalism". A state-led industrialization policy with an import substitution strategy resulted in the formation of large, employment-intensive public sector enterprises, mostly in the capital and intermediate goods sectors. This massive development of the public sector aided the private corporate sector in terms of supplying the necessary intermediate and capital goods (Desai, 1975). Between 1951 and 1965, industrial production increased at an average annual rate of 7.7 per cent, and manufacturing output increased at the rate of 7.6 per cent (Nayyar, 1981). High growth rates were sustained by public investment in capital and intermediate goods, while growth in consumer durables slowed down. Rigid import-substitution policies guaranteed the domestic market and stimulated private sector investment (Patnaik and Rao, 1977).

The expansion of large public enterprises led to employment growth in the formal economy, mainly in such enterprises, but also in the private sector, notably in services, transport and education. Average employment growth increased rapidly from around 0.4 per cent per annum from 1951 to 1956 to around 2 per cent per annum from 1961 to 1966 (Papola, 1994). Public sector employment quite naturally led to public sector unionism. The number of registered trade unions increased from 4,623 in 1951/52 to 11,614 in 1961/

62; membership in the registered unions that submitted returns more than tripled during this period (Venkataratnam, 1996).[1]

The Communist-led All India Trade Union Congress (AITUC) had dominated the organized labour movement since before independence (for example, in the textile and engineering industries of Mumbai, Calcutta, Kanpur). The growing public sector now provided a new terrain for large-scale unionization. It is here that the Congress Party-controlled Indian National Trade Union Congress (INTUC) made early inroads. Unlike the AITUC, which rose from the rank and file, the INTUC was imposed on the labour movement from the outside. There were no ambiguities in the chain of command from party to union.

When confronted with a choice between the patronage of the ruling party and genuine worker support, the INTUC usually opted for the former (Chatterjee, 1980). Since chief ministers, labour commissioners, registrars of trade unions, inspectors, conciliators, tribunal officials, magistrates, police officers and all other officials who dealt with unions (during this first phase) were appointed by the Congress government, management officials were often requested or pressured to assist INTUC unions to establish themselves or defeat rival unions (Kennedy, 1966).

This relationship between the state (i.e. ruling government) and its affiliated trade union federation during the first phase of unionism seems to have tied in neatly with the provisions of the Industrial Disputes Act (IDA) of 1947 which, according to Datta Chaudhuri (1996, p. 12), is "the single most important piece of legislation between the worker and his employer". The Act makes no provision for procedures to determine the representative union in what would normally be a single bargaining unit, and as employers were under no legal obligation to bargain with unions, there were no built-in incentives for either party to engage in collective bargaining. Early writings on Indian industrial relations consistently pointed to this aspect of the Industrial Disputes Act and the way in which it impeded collective bargaining during this period (Kennedy, 1966; Punekar, 1966). Coupled with this was the Indian Trade Union Act of 1926; the Act allowed any seven workers to register their trade union, but made no provision for union recognition (e.g. through a "secret ballot" procedure). While the opposition unions were for a "secret ballot" to determine union strength, the INTUC was against it, favouring instead the "check-off" system of membership receipts, a system that could easily be manipulated.

---

[1] Statistically, there are three types of trade union in India: those that do not register and are statistically invisible, those that register but do not submit returns to the Registrar of Trade Unions on membership size, and those that register and submit returns on membership figures.

The Industrial Disputes Act also made it very difficult for the unions to call a "legal" strike. Most disputes were first referred to conciliation, then to the labour commissioner. If this solution failed, the dispute was usually settled in an industrial or labour court, or occasionally through binding arbitration (Kennedy, 1966).

During the late 1950s, however, some attempts were made to introduce labour legislation promoting genuine collective bargaining through voluntary arrangements such as the Code of Discipline and the inter-union Code of Conduct (Venkataratnam, 1996). If these arrangements were made legally binding on the parties, the question of determining the representative union in a single bargaining unit might have been solved for good. Effective dispute resolution through voluntary arbitration was also suggested. Various bills were drafted and debated at several tripartite forums, but none were enacted (Kennedy, 1966). Further, the executive branch of the government ultimately vetoed the proposed Trade Unions and Labour Relations Bills. These are known as the "Giri Approach", after the Labour Minister who resigned in protest, and many commentators see this as a major setback to the development of a mature industrial relations system (Ramaswamy, 1984).

State intervention in the determination of wages and working conditions was the norm during the first phase; wages were determined by political and institutional considerations (Myers, 1958; Fonseca, 1964; Jackson, 1972). The structure of bargaining was very centralized, usually at the national level, but at industry level in some regions (e.g. Mumbai textiles). In a few cases private sector bargaining was at the enterprise level. Wage determination during this first phase was known at the time as "tripartism" and "political bargaining".

In terms of the movement of real wages of industrial workers during this first phase, India was held out as an example of the Lewis model of growth at work, with both product and consumption wage growing more slowly than labour productivity (Jackson, 1972). Low unionization, inter-union rivalries sharpened by political affiliation, excess supply of labour and state intervention of a complex and peculiar type contributed to a wage lag (Deshpande, 1992). The labour relations regime promoted "responsible unionism" subject to maintaining industrial peace (Johri, 1967). Both the number of strikes and the number of workers involved in strikes during the first phase were significantly lower than during the second phase and beyond (Johri, 1967; Sengupta, 1992). By the end of the first phase of unionism, further splits had occurred in the labour movement: the Socialists broke away from the Congress and formed their own trade union federation, the Hind Mazdoor Sabha (HMS), and during the Indo-Chinese conflict, the radicals broke away from the Communist Party of India and formed the Communist Party of India (Marxist) which generated its own trade union, the Centre of Indian Trade Unions (CITU).

3.1.2 The second phase of unionism (mid-1960s to 1979)

The second phase of unionism more or less corresponds with the Annual Plans for 1967-69, the Fourth (1969-74) and Fifth (1974-79) Five-Year Plans. "The rate of inflation rose above the politically sensitive danger-mark of 10 per cent in 1966/67 and 1967/68, and food price inflation was even higher (around 20 per cent)" (Joshi and Little, 1994, p. 48). Inflation worsened in 1973/74 and there were food riots in various states. The period is associated with industrial stagnation (Nayyar, 1981). Thus, between 1965 and 1975, the average annual rate of growth in total industrial production and in manufacturing output increased at only 3.6 per cent and 3.1 per cent respectively (Nayyar, 1981). In addition, the economy suffered oil price shocks in 1973 and in 1978. During this phase, especially during the Fourth and Fifth Five-Year Plans, actual growth rates for industrial production were far below plan targets (Ahluwalia, 1991, p. 11). It is quite clear that the deceleration adversely affected the level of employment in the economy as a whole.

The second phase of unionism saw significant changes in collective bargaining practices. The Industrial Disputes Act of 1947 did not provide for the compulsory recognition of a representative union as the sole bargaining agent, nor did it encourage or compel parties to bargain in good faith; more importantly, it gave no legal status to collective bargaining agreements. However, the 1965 amendment to the IDA gave a "higher legal footing" to agreements reached through conciliation and adjudication. Patil (1982) describes how employers and unions have used the 1965 amendment to transform agreements into legal documents. First, there is a form of coalition bargaining between multiple unions and the employer in an enterprise so as to arrive at a satisfactory settlement. Then conciliation is sought (not after the failure of direct negotiations as in the first phase) in order to convert the agreement into a legally binding document. The terms of the agreement are signed in the presence of the conciliation officer, making the contract legally binding on all parties.

The states can add their own labour legislation to the central labour statutes, and in the early 1970s, Maharashtra, Gujarat, Rajasthan and Madhya Pradesh enacted laws on trade union recognition. The Maharashtra Recognition of Trade Unions and Prevention of Unfair Labour Practices Act became effective from 1975. Failure to bargain with the (now-defined) representative union became an unfair labour practice under this Act. Its actual capacity to penalize is, however, questionable (Deshpande, 1992).

In terms of wage dynamics in the urban labour markets, the second phase of unionism was marked by significant changes as well. While the evidence suggested declining, or at best stationary, real wages during the first phase of unionism, Madan (1977) pointed out that the data used in earlier studies suffered from a serious downward bias as they referred to a restricted category of low-paid workers. Using wage data generated by the Annual Survey of Industries (all workers) he found that the real wages of manufacturing workers had in fact increased since the early 1970s; he also showed that the proportion of low-paid workers to all workers had declined during the second phase.

It could be hypothesized that since the mid-1970s, segments within the union movement shifted their goals from those of right to those of interest. This distinction roughly corresponds with the value placed by unions on centralized lobbying (rights) vis-à-vis decentralized collective bargaining (interests). Various factors conditioned such a shift and these became apparent during the third phase of unionism; see below. Some of the key factors were as follows: (a) uneven development of firms within an industry, as well as increasing inter-industry differentiation, meant that some sites were considerably more profitable than others. Unions in these sectors exploited the increased "capacity to pay" during collective bargaining, while unions in the declining sectors had no such opportunity; (b) workers and unions in the profitable sites were more aware of their firm's financial performance through their informed bargaining practices and/or through management willingness to share this information with unions; and (c) workers in these units realized that the leaders of many traditional party-based unions were averse to intense decentralized bargaining, because of their party commitments and their more national concerns.

These shifts and fractures within the organized labour movement had serious implications for union strategies, especially in maintaining solidarity across the entire organized labour movement. Specifically, it becomes increasingly difficult for the trade union movement in India to act as an "all-encompassing" organization, especially during the third phase of unionism. A rather pessimistic variant of neo-institutional analysis of labour unions and collective action (Olson, 1971) can partly explain the above difficulties. According to this "logic of collective action", the assumption of rationality and self-interested behaviour on the part of individuals does not always lead to groups acting in the (collective) interest. This is because of the "public goods" nature of this collective interest: "though all of the members of the group therefore have a common interest in obtaining this collective benefit, they have no common interest in paying the cost of providing that collective good" (Olson, 1971, p. 21). In our context, the "cost" of obtaining collective benefits is different for the various segments of the organized labour movement. To the extent that these "costs" become similar across certain sectors with the onset of liberalization (especially in sectors facing closure, privatization and restructuring), there will be fewer barriers to the trade union movement acting as an all-encompassing organization.

3.1.3 The third phase of unionism (1980-1991)

This phase corresponds to the Sixth (1980-85) and the Seventh (1985-90) Five-Year Plans, as well as the two Annual Plans (1990-92). Average annual growth rates during this decade were about 5.7 per cent but employment grew at only around 1.8 per cent (Papola, 1994). Employment elasticities in major sectors, especially in services, fell drastically during this time (Papola, 1994). In terms of Joshi and Little's (1994) analysis, the third phase of unionism corresponds to two distinct sub-periods: 1979/80 to 1984/85 and 1985/86 to 1990/91.[2] During the first part, the economy suffered from severe internal and external shocks: one of the worst droughts since independence occurred in 1979, there was trouble in the northeast, an industrial recession in 1980/81, rising inflation and increasing oil bills. All this led to a balance of payments crisis and then to a massive IMF loan. In May 1984, India terminated the programme after drawing SDR 3.9 billion (Joshi and Little, 1994, p. 60). This period was also turbulent on the political front with Mrs. Gandhi's return to power in 1980, the assault on the Golden Temple in Amritsar, Mrs. Gandhi's assassination in October 1984 and the landslide victory of the Congress Party with her son Rajiv as Prime Minister.

The second part of this phase is associated with Rajiv Gandhi's economic liberalization measures. The economy moved away from import substitution towards strategies that encouraged export promotion and domestic competition. Partial deregulation, financial liberalization, exchange rate policy, taxation, and export incentives brought this about. After 1988 the country experienced severe unrest. Economic recession and political turmoil followed the 1990 Gulf war.

India was now facing a full-scale macroeconomic crisis. "Agreement was reached with the IMF in January 1991 on a loan of $1.8 billion, partly out of the Compensatory Financing Facility (to offset increased oil imports) and partly as a first credit tranche standby" (Joshi and Little, 1994, p.66).

The macroeconomic changes during this phase had a profound effect on the political economy of trade unionism and labour markets, as well as on the structure of industrial relations. On the union front, this phase started with a massive public sector strike in Bangalore during 1980/81 which involved giant public enterprises such as Hindustan Machine Tools, Hindustan Aeronautics Limited, Electronics Corporation of India, and Indian Telephone Industries.

The event that characterized the first part of this third phase was the famous, and much studied, Mumbai textile strike of 1982 (see Patankar, 1981;

---

[2] This discussion on macroeconomic trends relies heavily on Joshi and Little (1994).

Pendse, 1981; Bhattacherjee, 1988; 1989; Van Wersch, 1992). This started as a wage and bonus issue in a few mills in late-1981, and soon developed into an industry-wide stoppage that ultimately became the longest strike in post-independence labour history. The basic cause was disquiet among the rank and file about the 1947 Bombay Industrial Relations Act, which had imposed an industry-wide bargaining structure with an unrepresentative union (affiliated to the Indian National Trade Union Congress) as the sole bargaining agent of workers. As a result of the internal differentiation within the mills that took place during the 1970s, workers wanted more control over their labour market- and industrial relations outcomes at the level of the individual mill. They approached Dr. Datta Samant to lead their struggle: his main project was to form and lead an "independent" trade union movement in western India.

The textile strike ended in a whimper late in 1983: many workers returned to their villages, their lives ruined; employers restructured their mills in the advanced textile sector, and the credibility of the government-installed union in the industry declined to levels from which it could never recover (Bhattacherjee, 1988). Evidence from the immediate post-strike period seems to suggest that workers and unions, at least in the profitable mills, negotiated their own decentralized bargaining agreements (Bhattacherjee, 1989; Van Wersch, 1992). After Datta Samant formed the *Kamgar Aghadi Party* and won a few seats in Parliament in 1984, many commentators felt that this was a new and encouraging beginning for the organized labour movement in India.

Another important feature of this third phase was the proliferation of "independent" unions operating in the major industrial centres and competing with the traditional party-affiliated trade unions (both of the Congress and of the Left). In Mumbai, for example, the decline of the Left unions is partly attributable to their general opposition to intense decentralized bargaining (Pendse, 1981). Segmented and uneven developments in the industrial sector tied workers' earnings to the fortunes of the plant in which they were employed. An analysis of plant-level contracts from the Greater Mumbai-Thane industrial corridor revealed that, *ceteris paribus*, the "independent" unions delivered a higher wage and fringe package than did the affiliated unions at the beginning of this third phase (Bhattacherjee, 1987b). In a number of multinationals, it was found that workers with their "independent" unions exerted considerable control over the labour relations process, often more than their counterparts in the host country.

In the late 1970s there was a phenomenal rise in the number of disputes led by unaffiliated unions and the importance of politically affiliated unions declined (Bhattacherjee, 1987a, p. 57). The ratio of registered unions that submit returns about their membership size to the total number of registered unions fell sharply from 60 per cent in 1962 to 21 per cent in 1974 to 13 per cent in 1982 (Bhattacherjee and Datta Chaudhuri, 1994a, p. 70). This would support the hypothesis of the rise of "independent" unionism, if the total number of registered unions that submit returns proxies the traditional party-affiliated trade unions.

Finally, increasing inter-regional, inter-state, and inter-city variations in the nature of labour/management relations marked this phase. In a study of Bombay, Calcutta, Madras and Bangalore, Ramaswamy (1988) points to significant inter-city differences in the texture of labour/management relationships. He writes (1988, p.17): "The driving force of the Bombay labour movement are union leaders who disclaim allegiance to political parties and their trade union federations. What we find here is the most evolved Indian version of business trade unionism", and "the city has witnessed the steady decline, if not eclipse into oblivion, of ideological trade unionism". This clearly has something to do with the fact that private and multinational firms dominate Mumbai's urban economy.

In sharp contrast is the case of Calcutta, where a highly politicized industrial relations regime prevails with the dominant trade union federation (the CITU) under the close watch of the dominant political party (the CPI-M). This has created considerable inflexibilities for management, and has partly prohibited the growth of independent trade unionism. Bangalore, a city where both private and public sector enterprises thrive, especially those in the information technology industry, has witnessed the rise of plant and firm-based unions (as in Mumbai). Inter-city differences, attributable no doubt to different political, social, and urban histories, emphatically suggest the inherent difficulties in trying to generalize about an "Indian" labour relations system. With the passing of time, especially with the onset of the fourth phase (see below), attempts at this kind of generalization will become more and more difficult.

Changes in union structure, together with macroeconomic developments, considerably affected both employment and the wage structure. Between 1980/81 and 1988/89, while employment growth declined, the capital/labour ratio and labour productivity increased by 8 per cent and 7.5 per cent per year respectively (Ahluwalia, 1992). According to Ghose (1992, p. 95): "The most striking fact is that the 80s have been the best decade in terms of economic growth but the worst decade in terms of employment generation." Moreover, employment growth decelerated in all sectors of the economy and open unemployment increased in the 1980s (Ghose, 1992). The search for labour market flexibility in Indian manufacturing led labour-intensive firms and those engaged in the production of consumer non-durables to subcontract and outsource their production to the unorganized sectors (Ramaswamy, 1999).

Unions in the organized and more profitable sectors (often "independent" unions), managed to secure part of these productivity increases through militant bargaining and/or through productivity bargains that contained effective incentive structures. This resulted in slower employment growth. In the relatively unorganized and less profitable sites, workers and unions lost out. While formal sector employment as a percentage of total employment in manufacturing fell from 24.5 per cent in 1972/73 to 17.4 per cent in 1987/88, real wages of workers and "other employees" in organized manufacturing increased at a rate of 5.8 per cent and 4.1 per cent between 1983 and 1986 respectively, whereas low-paid workers suffered declining real wages (Ghose, 1992, p. 97). As the union wage effect increased significantly in the profitable sites (especially in consumer non-durables) during this phase, employers cut back on hiring and started retrenchment, increasing the capital/labour ratio which in turn increased labour productivity. Thus, according to this scenario, the faster growth of real wages in the 1980s played a role in slowing employment creation (Ahluwalia, 1992).

Bhattacherjee and Datta Chaudhuri (1994b) found that: (a) in the high-paid sector, real wages increased after the late 1970s and there were wage returns from striking; (b) in the low-paid sector, real wages declined after the early 1980s, and employers could lower wages by imposing lockouts; and (c) in terms of union structure, low-paid workers gain as unions submitting returns (proxy for traditional unions) increase their dominance within the union movement, whereas high-paid workers gain as registered unions not submitting returns (proxy for plant-specific unions) increase their dominance. The traditional unions predominant in the older industries provided overall protection to their members as long as these industries grew. As they declined, and as plant-specific unions reaped returns in the high-paid sector, workers in the low-paid sector "became more vulnerable to competitive forces and could no longer count on the traditional 'wage-welfare' functions provided by the party-based unions. Workers in this segment will find it difficult to form strong plant-specific unions due to increasing instability in their product markets" (Bhattacherjee and Datta Chaudhuri, 1994b, p. 459).

Jose (1992) examined earnings, employment, and productivity trends for 19 industry groups for the period 1970/71 to 1987/88. His findings were: (a) whereas the 1970s are associated with employment growth in both high and low wage sectors and with stagnant and even declining productivity levels, the 1980s are associated with slower employment growth with rising productivity levels, especially in the high-wage sectors; (b) higher productivity brought about the (modest 2-3 per cent per year) increase in real earnings in the high-wage sectors. These findings seem to fit with the characterization of different types of union dominating these two labour markets since the early 1980s. Jose (1992) maintains that technological change led to the rise in wages and productivity, whereas subsequent analysts inverted the hypothesis to argue that union militancy and higher wages resulted in technological change that subsequently led to a decline in employment.

Labour researchers towards the end of this third phase focused on employment inflexibilities embedded in the Industrial Disputes Act (see Mathur, 1992). The 1982 amendment of the Industrial Disputes Act provided that a firm employing more than 100 workers (reduced from more than 300) needed permission from the state government to lay off or retrench workers. Fallon and Lucas (1991) showed how employment would have been higher in several sectors without the 1976 and 1982 amendments. Mathur (1992) recommended that the sections pertaining to permission for layoff, retrenchment or closure be deleted from the Act.

To remedy the limitations of the Industrial Disputes Act and the Trade Union Act, from both the union and the employer point of view, a number of changes were proposed in the Trade Unions and Industrial Disputes (Amendment) Bill, 1988 (Mathur, 1992). The proposed changes would reduce the fragmentation and multiplicity of unions, clearly define the bargaining agent by providing for a secret ballot, promote internal leadership, create state-level industrial tribunals, force employers to set up comprehensive bargaining councils to facilitate internal grievance settlement, and so on. After considerable debate, however, the bill was rejected because of controversy over the definition of "industry" (Mathur, 1992, p. 50).

3.1.4 The fourth phase of unionism (1992-2000)

In June 1991, the ruling minority government decided to adopt the World Bank-IMF stabilization and structural adjustment programme. "In July 1991 the rupee was devalued twice, quotas on the import of intermediate and capital goods were reduced, tariffs were brought down, the state monopoly on exports and imports was ended and a statement on industrial policy was presented along with the Union Budget, which was aimed at reducing the fiscal deficit by two and a half percentage points" (Mathur, 1993, p. 333). The fourth phase of unionism more or less corresponds to the Eighth (1992-97) and the Ninth (1997-2002) Five-Year Plans.

According to Nagaraj (1997, p. 2870) "On average, the Indian economy grew at 5.3 per cent during the first five years of the reforms (1992-96), compared to 5.9 per cent during 1986-91." The tertiary sector grew fastest in the 1990s, at about 6.8 per cent per year. The economy has become considerably more "open" than ever before. There was some apprehension that government expenditure in the social sector would decline significantly, but Nagaraj (1997) found that social spending, averaged over four years since the reforms, did not suffer; most of the cuts were made in defense and economic services. Again, contrary to expectations, investment performance in India actually improved after the reforms, with private corporate business emerging as the economy's "leading sector". However, in terms of industrial growth performance, "the manufacturing growth rate since the reforms is lower and its composition is uneven" (1997, p. 2875). Even though public investment had witnessed deep cuts since the reform, "public sector output growth and profitability improved" suggesting better resource utilization. Nagaraj concludes: "In sum, the good news (so far) is that there is no major, unqualified, bad news."

Transnational corporations, as expected, have reacted very favourably to the new economic policy. Chaudhuri (1995) examines the mechanisms through which transnational corporations have achieved entry and growth: through the ousting of Indian partners, through extensive mergers and acquisitions, and through expansion and fresh entry. The gross inflow of foreign direct investment rose from Rs.5.3 billion in 1991 to Rs.141.9 billion in 1994 (US$1 is approximately Rs. 0.47), and although Chaudhuri is sceptical about the prospects of this investment leading to export-oriented growth in India, it is expected to generate some employment.

If the 1995-96 period was a slowdown, and 1996-97 was a year of "industrial recession and political uncertainty", the year 1997-98 can be described as an "elusive economic recovery" with a "hesitant government".[3] A whole range of issues on the economic reform agenda remain incomplete: infrastructure development, greater transparency in investment procedures, restoration of business confidence, review of import duties, further banking sector reforms, and most important, public sector and labour market reforms.

The available data seem to suggest that economic reform has led to an increase in rural poverty and a decline in urban poverty; in fact, urban poverty was lower in 1993-94 than in any pre-reform year (Sen, 1996). Deshpande and Deshpande (1996) found that although the initial stabilization years "took some toll of organized manufacturing employment", subsequent structural adjustment led to employment growth at around 2.3 per cent between 1992/ 93 and 1994/95. If this rate continues for the next few years, "employment in the factory sector would be about 12 per cent higher at the turn of the century than in 1990/91" (1996, p. 18). In terms of the structure of employment, these authors found that in some sectors the employment share increased after the reforms (textiles, transport equipment, chemicals, beverages, metal products) while in others the employment share decreased (machinery).

Mundle (1992) presented employment and unemployment projections under "high" and "low" growth scenarios taking into account employment

---

[3] I am grateful to my colleagues, Professors A. Ray and A. Sinha, for permitting me to use expressions from their unpublished annual economy reports.

elasticities and labour force participation rates. Even under the most optimistic scenario in the private sector, given declining employment elasticities in organized manufacturing and the unlikely expansion of employment in the public sector, it is quite evident that a "large majority of the nearly 80 million persons who will join the labour force during 1999-2000 will have to find work as self-employed or casual workers" (Visaria and Minhas, 1991, p. 978). In terms of the impact of economic reforms on women workers, Deshpande and Deshpande (1992) believe that female unemployment may go down but the openings available will be low-wage jobs in secondary labour markets. In light of the above, it seems imperative to expand the existing public employment schemes. However, the most appropriate strategy for a predominantly agrarian economy such as India must be to raise labour force participation rates and shift the workforce away from agriculture into more productive sectors so as to generate large economy-wide productivity gains (Bhaduri, 1993).

One of the main objectives of the economic reform package is the restructuring of unprofitable public sector enterprises. These enterprises are free to reduce their workforce through voluntary retirement schemes (VRS) assisted by the national renewal fund (NRF) instituted by the government, and by amendments to the Sick Industrial Companies Act 1985. The strengthening of the Board for Industrial and Financial Reconstruction considerably facilitated this process (Mathur, 1993). The objectives of the NRF were to provide assistance to cover the costs of retraining and redeployment made necessary by modernization, technological upgrading, industrial restructuring, and possible closure. In 1993-94, Rs.7 billion (US$1 = approx. Rs. 0.47) were allocated to the VRS in the central public sector enterprises; nearly Rs. 4.9 billion was allocated to the textile sector alone (Muralidhar, 1993).

While recruitment was all but frozen (especially at lower levels), the government also froze the centralized wage bargaining process for a few years after 1992. It later opened the negotiation process and attempted to decentralize bargaining by announcing that any wage increases would have to be absorbed by the specific enterprise as these could no longer be passed on to the final price. In other words, the new policy clearly stated that any additional wage burden would not receive budgetary support (Venkataratnam, 1996).

The need for tripartite consultation was clearly felt during the early years and many meetings took place. Mathur (1993) documents the experience of consultation during the early phase of structural adjustment in India (1990-92), and suggests that although the government partly diffused possible tension through its consultative approach, unions had "serious misgivings about the adequacy of consultation at (the) industrial or enterprise level" (p. 344).

Labour commentators have found that the centralized and traditional union structures often fall short of worker expectations, and in many instances, they are giving way to independent and decentralized union structures (Davala, 1992; Muralidhar, 1994). However, this (current) fourth phase has witnessed the growth of the Bharatiya Mazdoor Sangh, affiliated to the Bharatiya Janata Party. In the state of Maharashtra, the trade union movement has become quite volatile since the locally based Shiv Sena party and its affiliated union, the *Bharatiya Mazdoor Sena*, made deep inroads. During this phase the public has become acutely aware (largely through the print and visual media) that trade unions represent a declining "sectional interest group".

On 10 January 1999 the government announced the second National Labour Commission (the first NLC was set up 30 years ago). The terms of reference laid down that the commission should suggest rationalization of existing labour laws in the organized sector and recommend umbrella legislation to ensure minimum protection for unorganized workers. The commission has a two-year term and is made up of representatives from government, trade unions and industry. Trade unions feel that workers have little protection from the whims of errant management, and that any alteration in the law would only add to managerial power. For example, the proposal to relax the law on contract labour in order to generate more jobs on contract for the unorganized sector is interpreted by the unions as a move to undercut permanent unionized jobs. More recently, proposed changes in the Industrial Disputes Act will make it difficult for trade unions to call wildcat strikes and the amendments will dilute the need for employers to have government approval for a lockout. On the other hand, they give the tribunals more power to penalize errant employers.

The present government dissolved the National Renewal Fund and entrusted the corpus to the Ministry of Industry. The money in the fund will now be given to public sector enterprises directly by the Ministry. The government hopes to monitor the use of funds more effectively by not involving the administrative departments that control these enterprises. More recently, the government has announced that it will develop a comprehensive strategy to deal with unprofitable public enterprises and "hammer out a mechanism which makes it easier to close chronically sick units". Officials in the Ministry of Finance announced that more funds have to be pumped into the voluntary retirement schemes so that workers can be retrained and redeployed in viable public sector units.[4]

---

[4] *The Business Telegraph* (Calcutta), 28 May 1999.

3.2 The issues

The above discussion on the four phases of Indian trade unionism sketched out the interaction between changes in the overall economy and their effects on the labour market and on industrial relations. In this section we examine several issues that arise from the discussion and speculate on trends in the near future. These issues are: unionization and employment; union structure and union density; wages and working conditions; collective bargaining; industrial conflict; labour/management relations; inter-state variations; unionization and women workers; and the changing public perception of trade unions.

3.2.1 Unionization and employment

Declining employment elasticities imply that more output is attained with less employment. This could be due to the fact that employers are investing in more capital-intensive technologies, and that there has been a considerable amount of labour shedding in private-and public-sector enterprises since the mid-1980s. Unions can affect these employment elasticities by resisting technological change that increases the possibility of substituting between capital and labour and by limiting the availability of goods and services that compete with the output of unionized firms. In addition, union bargaining power varies indirectly with labour's share in total costs: unions are more powerful in relatively more capital-intensive firms and industries, as the demand for labour is relatively inelastic compared to labour-intensive sectors. Employers in capital-intensive firms find it much easier to meet union wage demands compared to employers in labour-intensive firms. Finally, it is in the interest of unions to raise the price of other inputs, particularly non-union labour, as this increases the cost of switching from union to non-union labour (see Borjas, 1996, pp. 126-127).

Over time, average annual growth rates in GDP have outstripped average annual growth rates in employment and employment elasticities in major sectors have fallen. During the first phase of unionism, public sector employment increased sharply and private sector employment increased marginally; during the second phase, public sector employment increased rapidly, whereas private sector employment remained sluggish; during the third phase, employment growth in both sectors sharply tapered off; and during the first few years of the fourth phase, growth in both sectors remained nearly static.

With regard to the sectoral distribution of employment in the formal economy we note two trends: since the third phase, growth in employment in manufacturing, both in the public and private sectors, has remained virtually stagnant; however, during the third phase, employment increased in public services. We also observe the phenomenal growth in employment in services (especially in the public sector) relative to manufacturing. Finally, except in manufacturing, the public sector continued to be the dominant employer in the organized economy. A sector-wise ranking of the number and membership of trade unions that register and submit returns over the four phases of unionism shows that: (a) manufacturing leads in the number of unions and membership size; (b) construction lags behind most other sectors.

Given that the macro data on employment and unionization in India are riddled with problems and contain errors of omission, detailed case studies of specific industries and regions have revealed significantly different trends. The *Friedrich Ebert Stiftung* study (Davala, 1992) is an example. It covers tea plantations and the jute industry in West Bengal, the coal sector, ports and docks, the engineering industries of Andhra Pradesh and West Bengal, the power sector in Andhra Pradesh, and the chemical and pharmaceutical industry in Maharashtra. Although the study shows a fair number of inter-industry and regional variations, there were some striking similarities. The trend everywhere was a downsizing of permanent employment and the proliferation of contract, temporary, and casual jobs. There were very low rates of unionization of contract and casual labour, with the unions being more sensitive to the plight of such workers in the newer industries. In the state of Maharashtra, permanent workers and their unions in the chemical and pharmaceutical industries have realized that their well-being is ultimately tied to their fellow workers in the "reserve army of labour". The study found that unions organize on an industry- and/or region-wide basis in the older industrial sectors, but the enterprise becomes the unit of organization in the newer industries. This pattern corresponds with the prevalent bargaining structure (i.e. industry- and region-wide in the older industries, and plant-level in the newer industries).

The "market friendly" views of the relationship between unionization and employment in India, especially during the third and fourth phase, was elaborated earlier, but needs to be emphasized in this section as well. The "monopoly effects" of trade unions, together with inflexible labour laws, have enabled employers to move up their demand curves and have practically frozen employment growth in permanent unionized jobs. Due to union wage mark-ups, employers have increased the capital intensity of production, thereby raising productivity. But this route can only lead to jobless growth, clearly a suboptimal outcome in a labour surplus economy. Those who oppose this view point out that wage increases took place not because of union power but largely because of an intensification of the labour process resulting from a decline in union power. A disaggregated analysis probably comes closest to reality: in the more prosperous sectors, with low elasticities of labour demand, "selfish" plant-specific unions managed to extract generous wage increases; in the less prosperous sectors, largely in the public sector, "altruistic" unions affiliated to political parties have had little success with centralized bargaining procedures in unstable product markets.

In the buoyant sectors of production, even before 1991, employers have managed to execute viable exit policies through generous voluntary retirement schemes, with the cooperation of enterprise-based unions. In these largely private sector sites, "bringing the union in" has clearly paid dividends in terms of generating "strongly efficient contracts" (that is, when the labour contract leads a unionized firm to hire the competitive level of employment). In the public sector, however, exit schemes (available through the National Renewal Fund) have few individual takers or else they face union resistance at national level. The practice of "featherbedding" (employing more people than required) in a whole range of public enterprises is no longer financially viable. The union movement as a whole, especially the large centralized and industry-wide public sector unions, may benefit more from unionizing the unorganized than from attempting to preserve unproductive jobs.

3.2.2 Union structure and union density

The number of registered unions increased from 3,766 in 1950/51 to 55,784 in 1993, whereas the average size of those that submitted returns decreased from 577 to 460 during the same period. As stated earlier, not all registered trade unions submit returns on their membership. If we assume that the registered unions which submit returns are the large, established, politically-affiliated unions with the organizational resources to engage in this process, whereas the registered unions that do not submit returns are the plant-based independent unions, then movements in the percentage of unions submitting returns to total registered unions make for an interesting interpretation. It appears that the centralized unions dominated during the first phase, lost ground during the second phase, and then sharply declined during the third phase, dropping to an all-time low of only 12 per cent in 1993. Although this is only one possible reading of the data, several detailed case studies have also pointed to these movements in union structure (Ramaswamy, 1988; Davala, 1992). The fourth phase is also associated with the sudden rise of the *Bharatiya Mazdoor Sabham*, especially in those states governed by the Bharatiya Janata Party.

The decentralized independent unions have in some instances attempted to generate firm-wide agreements but they have been unsuccessful because of considerable employer resistance at firm level. Some recent commentators have suggested that these unions have been on the defensive ever since the reforms. This is partly because they lost staff through voluntary retirement schemes; it was also due to the strategies of multinationals which severely cut back on permanent unionized employment. Other factors were the setting up of non-union facilities at new sites and the practice of subcontracting work to the informal sector (Banaji and Hensman, 1995; Noronha, 1996).

3.2.3 Wages and working conditions

Standard neoclassical economic theory would argue that increased global trade raises the earnings of unskilled workers relative to those of skilled workers in a country such as India, which has unlimited supplies of the former. This implies that India's exports are largely unskilled labour-intensive products. Nambiar et al. (1999) found that wage disparity for the period 1980/81 to 1992/93 increased but only marginally. In addition, they found that the disparity rises from less skill-intensive to more skill-intensive sectors. To the extent that the union voice reduces earnings inequality within the unionized workforce, employers, especially in the private sector, have "manufactured consent" with the unions in setting up ingenious pay incentive systems.

Wage determination in the organized economy varies significantly between the private and the public sector (Datta Chaudhuri, 1996; Anant and Sundaram, 1998). In the private corporate sector, where collective bargaining largely takes place at enterprise level, unions that are willing to accept some risk have benefited from a form of gainsharing by agreeing to tie a significant part of the monthly pay to incentives. The incentive structures are designed to generate cooperative behaviour at the departmental, plant and firm level. Risk-averse unions, usually more concerned with employment growth than with members' wages, have resisted management attempts to impose such systems.

In many of the older sectors, such as tea plantations and jute in eastern India and textiles in western India, industry-wide bargaining is the institutional norm. With the advent of economic liberalization, this bargaining structure will be under pressure to decentralize some of the outcomes as inter-plant and inter-firm differences become wider (see 3.2.4 below). Similar decentralizing pressures will be felt increasingly in public sector industries, even though the Bureau of Public Enterprises "sends guidelines for wage settlement to all administrative ministries, setting down norms to be followed in determining basic salaries and the various categories of benefits for different classes of employees" (Datta Chaudhuri, 1996, p. 18). In Coal India, for example, employees in the better-off units feel that their earnings could increase substantially if they were linked more closely to productivity at the unit level. Centralized public sector unions will have to come to terms with these decentralized union "voices".

Salaries and benefits for central government employees in public administration, academic institutions, posts and telegraph, etc., are determined in detail by the Pay Commissions which are periodically set up by the government. As Datta Chaudhuri (1996, p. 18) puts it: "The award of the Pay Commission for the Central Government employees becomes the reference point for wage determination in the rest of the public sector." The Pay Commission is the object of considerable lobbying by various unions and employees' associations prior to and during the deliberations.

The recommendations of the Fifth Central Pay Commission have been implemented and employees in the central and state governments have seen their incomes rise substantially. If it is true that the disparity between the average salary of government employees and per capita income is far higher in India than in most other countries, the public clearly need to see vast improvements in productivity in this sector given the fairly high additional cost involved in delivering the pay recommendations (Joseph, 1997).

Industrial accident rates in India, both fatal and non-fatal, are extremely high compared to most countries. While it is true that the occupational health and safety monitoring agencies are weak, it is also the case that unions can intervene significantly more in this area than they are presently doing. Often, workers demand higher wages for increased safety measures during contract deliberations. But there are other examples where unions have been closely involved in occupational health and safety matters. One such case is the Occupational Health and Safety Centre that operates out of two union offices in Central Mumbai and was set up largely due to the inefficiencies of the Employees' State Insurance (ESI) Scheme. Among its many achievements, the Centre was able to get the ESI medical board to recognize and compensate mill workers suffering from occupational bysinosis in 1994.

The linking of minimum labour standards and trade agreements, i.e. the "social clause", has generated considerable debate and discussion among trade unions and labour commentators (FES-IIRA, 1996; Hensman, 1996; Bhattacherjee, 1997). There are various economic arguments in favour of the imposition of international labour standards (ILS). To the extent that labour markets in developing countries are beset with imperfect and asymmetric information (for example relating to industrial safety), ILS may level up labour market institutions to correct for market failures of this type. ILS can be used as a redistributive mechanism if the government feels that the market-determined income distribution profile is skewed towards the more skilled workers in relatively protected environments. Trade unions in India interpret this imposed link as a disguised form of protectionism (for the various trade union views, see FES-IIRA, 1996, and Hensman, 1996). This argument leads to the same outcome as those put forward by the 'comparative advantage' trade theorists that the imposition of ILS will lead to a reduction in the net gains from trade, and therefore individual countries should decide on their own labour standards. But surely one has to question this simple view. Why is it that countries with relatively abundant and cheap labour find it difficult to compete in international markets, except in those sectors that have (relatively) lower labour standards? Clearly, this kind of participation in global trade, where inferior labour standards are the comparative advantage is unlikely to lead to social progress. Since it is not enough to wait for sustained economic growth to upgrade domestic labour standards, the unions need to forcefully generate demands, both from above and below, for improvements in working conditions. Hensman (1996) spells out an agenda for trade unionists and NGOs that strongly believe that labour standards in India have to be substantially improved, perhaps even through trade links and other forms of international pressure.

3.2.4 Collective bargaining

Two critical aspects of the collective bargaining system are an expansion of the coverage and scope of long-term agreements and the increasing pressure for decentralized bargaining. These tendencies originated during the third phase of unionism and became acute during the post-reform fourth phase. The restructuring agreements cover (among other things): ban on recruitment, job transfers to non-bargainable category, introduction of parallel production, automation and flexibility, transfer of production to subcontracted units, introduction of voluntary retirement schemes, transfer of permanent jobs to contract/temporary workers, merger of units, and a host of other shopfloor restructuring provisions (Venkataratnam, 1996). Concession bargaining in several units has led to job and wage cuts, a freeze on cost-of-living allowances, and suspension of industrial action for a period of five years. While the above suggests that management has had the upper hand in recent years, Venkataratnam (1996) also lists some "unusual" clauses that suggest a positive union "collective voice" effect: linking allowances such as house rent and children's education to attendance, permitting pregnant women to refuse to work on computer terminals, voluntary retirement schemes for contract labour, and so on.

We have already mentioned government attempts during the post-reform period to decentralize bargaining in public sector units by tying unit-level wage increases to productivity increases (rather than passing them on as price increases), and by consistently announcing its refusal to provide budgetary support to these wage increases. The central trade unions are uniting to pre-empt a government attempt to switch to a 10-year wage settlement in public sector units instead of the present 5-year duration. Union leaders say the move will affect the pay revision prospects of about 2 million workers in the public sector. Private employers have been lobbying for some time to increase the duration of contracts in public sector units so as to prevent disruptions arising from frequent industrial disputes, the costs of which they often have to bear.

Unions, especially the All India Trade Union Congress and the Indian National Trade Union Congress, are strongly against such a move.

Even outside the public sector, pressures for decentralized bargaining are emanating from both workers and employers. What happened in the textile industry is now being repeated in the jute industry in and around Calcutta. Due to the uneven development of textile firms in Mumbai in the early 1980s, and due to the undemocratic nature of union representation in the industry, both employers and unions in the more profitable mills wanted to break away from the industry-wide agreement in force and set up their own mill-level agreements (Bhattacherjee, 1988; 1989). Recently, employers in two jute mills defied the industry-wide agreement between the Indian Jute Mills Association and the many unions by offering a higher cost-of-living allowance to avert mill-level strikes. The central trade unions are in a dilemma for the first time in the jute industry: on the face of it, they oppose any kind of bipartite settlement by insisting on an industry-wide agreement at tripartite level. But by encouraging strikes at individual mills, they are indirectly opening up routes for direct negotiation between management and mill-level unions. The trend towards decentralization is reflected in the rising number of unions which have signed the industry-wide agreement: in 1972, there were only four signatories, in 1979 there were 11, and in 1992 there were 16 (Sen, 1997, p. 104).

By decentralizing bargaining structures and expanding the scope and duration of labour contracts, employers and the government are trying to minimize the "monopoly effects" of union work rules embedded in contract provisions that lead to considerable labour market inflexibilities, especially at micro-level. The determinant of public sector negotiations has been pay parity, and as a result there are few incentive structures in this system. Centralized public sector unions will have to come to terms with the microeconomic requirements of productivity growth and increased competition. They can learn from union responses to restructuring programmes in Europe.[5]

3.2.5 Industrial conflict

Even though union density is very low by international standards, India loses more days every year as a result of strikes and lockouts than almost any other country (ILO, 1997/98, pp. 253-254). However, the number of workers involved in strikes and lockouts is considerably lower in India than in Brazil, Italy or Spain (pp. 251-252). This raises the classic question of whether conflict reflects union power or union weakness? It certainly indicates

---

[5] ILO, 1997/98, Ch. 5 and 6.

that the basic premise of industrial pluralism, the regulation of conflict, has not been achieved.

The answer to this question in India depends on whether workers resist strikes or whether employers are on the offensive during lockouts. During the third and fourth phase, the number of lockouts rose whereas the number of strikes decreased. The same applies to the number of workdays lost and the number of workers involved. Until 1989 industrial conflict occurred mainly in the private sector in terms of number of disputes, workdays and wages lost, and lost production, although the actual number of workers involved in disputes was higher in the public sector in the early 1980s. Since 1990, however, industrial disputes in both sectors have increased significantly (Venkataratnam, 1996).

Since the economic reforms of 1991, successive national governments have had to deal with considerable industrial conflict in the public sector, especially in banking, insurance, and transport. At regional level, some state governments have had to contend with continuing inter-union and inter-party rivalries, leading to the disruption of public life. Of late, the government has followed a tough line on striking public sector unions, as demonstrated in the dismissals and criminal proceedings against air traffic controllers. There is an imperative need for industrial relations reform in dispute settlement as the average consumer and voter has increasingly come to be a key actor and end-user of the industrial relations system. There are significant differences between the main trade union federations on the issues of secret strike ballot, prior notice to striking and the period of notification, layoff provisions, the role of voluntary arbitration, multiple union situations, etc. The country as a whole would gain if the union movement could arrive at a consensus and if the recommendations of the Ramanujam Committee (statutory recognition of "representative" trade unions and the creation of an independent authority to arbitrate, mediate and enforce) were implemented. The institution of arbitration, if effective, fair and credible, will significantly improve the quality of industrial pluralism.

3.2.6 Labour/management relations

Since the mid-1980s the practice of human resources management (HRM) has significantly altered traditional union/management relations in the advanced sectors of production, notably in multinationals and other private firms. Since the economic reforms of 1991, some public sector firms have also incorporated modern HRM practices into their otherwise traditional labour/management relationship. Some of the essential characteristics of these HRM practices are: attempts at direct communication between managers and employees; individualized and/or contingency pay systems; modular organization of production through work teams with team leaders who often form part of the management structure; carefully designed and fairly implemented performance appraisal systems. While many would argue that modern HRM practices undercut union effectiveness at the enterprise level, there is no clear evidence of this in India. Unions have a strong presence in the firms where modern HRM practices are implemented successfully, and it is only with cooperative union/management behaviour that this has been possible. But this applies mainly to the manufacturing sector.

In the skill-intensive service sectors such as information technology, HRM practices continue to pose a challenge and possibly create permanent barriers to union entry and organization. To the extent that information technology redefines the nature of work in banking and insurance, unions will have little success if they resist modernization, given the entry of new, mainly foreign, players in these sites. It is no coincidence that the most publicized post-reform industrial conflict at the national level has been in banking and insurance.

If labour law reforms facilitate competitive pluralism and lead to efficient collective bargaining in the private sector, and to tripartism with responsibility and accountability in the public sector, we can postulate that the effectiveness of unions would not necessarily diminish if modern HRM practices were introduced in enterprises.

3.2.7 Inter-state variations

One critical reason why labour law reform has been continually debated but ultimately shelved, is the lack of a consensus within the labour movement and across different state governments. Since economic liberalization, every state government has attempted to attract national and international capital. This has involved significant media costs, and many states have even hired international consultants to draw up economic renewal agendas. A vital consideration in this post-liberalization discourse has been the question of work ethic and comparative union militancy.

One of the most important concerns of social scientists in India today is the effect that economic liberalization will have on inter-state variations in human development, social productivity and civil society at large. States with a less organized labour movement, if controlled by pro-capital state governments, may attempt to attract capital with implicit promises of a union-free environment. This has clearly happened to some extent and has often taken violent forms. Ruling governments in other states with a long history of proletarian politics are desperately attempting to change their signals. These attempts are causing confusion within the union movement, both among the leaders and the rank and file, and they are also leading to chasms between political parties and their affiliated unions. In several instances, temporary or issue-based alliances have been formed between unions affiliated to opposition parties, especially with regard to privatization of public sector services and utilities.

One example of a state government changing its signals after being in power for over 20 years is the case of the CPI(M) in West Bengal. For the last 20 years, the CPI(M) and its trade union wing, the CITU, have been at the forefront of proletarian resistance to capitalist production processes and management hierarchies that control the labour process. Many commentators attribute the large-scale flight of industrial and commercial capital from West Bengal, which has been occurring since at least the mid-1960s, to heightened industrial conflict supported by a sympathetic state government. In the meantime, the state's reputation declined, fuelled by a hostile local press. But the fact that the industrial health of the state withered during this time was there for everyone to see and experience.

Since the mid-1990s, the CPI (M) has attempted to attract national and international capital at several well-publicized gatherings in Calcutta, through government funded ministerial visits abroad, and through promotional advertising. The state government has been sending strong signals to the trade unions in the state to accept the requirements of industrial regeneration. After nurturing (some would say pampering) the trade unions in the state for so long, it is now very difficult to change attitudes, behaviour, customs and institutionalized practices to facilitate capitalist expansion, a process that was anathema to the CPI(M) for so many years. With hindsight, one could argue that if the party had thought out a strategy only a decade ago, the state could have reaped considerable returns from an effective model of social democracy. In the meantime, trade unions are now realizing that there is nothing voluntary about the 'voluntary retirement schemes' being imposed on workers in some well-known large firms.[6]

Calcutta exemplifies the failure of state-controlled unionism where "class consciousness" is dominant. In contrast, the market-driven industrial relations system of Mumbai exemplifies a centralized regime where the important role played by individual trade union leaders in the city's labour history has added to the "job cononscious" nature of industrial relations. Although considerable growth has taken place in Mumbai, this regime has led to almost uncontrollable and corrupt links between politics, the real estate market and the organized labour movement. It is no wonder that post-reform capital has invested in newer industrial locations, and this logic is slowly but surely changing the industrial geography of India (Shaw, 1999). It will thus become increasingly difficult, if not impossible, to generalize about an Indian labour relations system.

---

[6] *The Business Telegraph* (Calcutta), 16 March 1999.

3.2.8 Women workers and unionization

The percentage of women members in trade unions that submit returns rose from 7.3 per cent in 1951-52 to 10.3 per cent in 1985; in 1992 it was 11.6 per cent. Detailed information on the extent of unionization among women workers is not available, although there are rich case studies of specific sectors/industries where women workers form a substantial section of the workforce (see the chapter on tea plantations by Bhowmik in Davala, 1992).

There is considerable controversy on whether there has been an increasing "feminization" of the workforce over the last decade, especially since the liberalization process began. Deshpande and Deshpande (1992, p. 1998) assessed the short-run impact of liberalization on female employment and participation. They found that: (a) in urban areas, both male and female participation rates increased after liberalization; (b) gender-based wage differentials widened among regular wage/salaried rural and urban workers; (c) women workers were increasingly taking to self-employment and to the informal sectors as their proportion in manufacturing declined even though women's share in the urban workforce rose slightly.

Although in several countries globalization has led to feminization of the manufacturing workforce, Banerjee (1997) argues that in India the reverse has taken place: women's opportunities in the secondary sectors have fallen drastically in all states. However, there has been a slight increase in work opportunities for rural women in agriculture and some gains were made in the tertiary sector. According to Banerjee (1997, p. 433), it would be unrealistic to expect a "mechanical reproduction of international trends in a country the size of India". Women workers account for only 17 per cent of the manufacturing workforce that in turn is only 13 per cent of the total workforce. She goes on to suggest that even if the entire export sector (commodities) were staffed by women, "it is doubtful that this would result in a feminization of the Indian manufacturing workforce as a whole".

Given that a substantial section of women workers in India today are engaged as "homeworkers" in several industries (such as bangle makers, cobblers, dye makers, flower workers, kite makers, lace makers, leather workers, etc.), it is encouraging that the Indian trade union movement, under the leadership of the Self-Employed Women's Association (SEWA) has taken a lead in drafting an ILO convention on homeworkers (Mukul, 1998). A bill was introduced in the upper house in 1988 that attempted to equalize treatment of homeworkers with other wage earners in terms of remuneration, health and safety, minimum wage and maternity protection, with tripartite boards as the enforcement mechanism. Although the bill was dropped, it did contribute to initiating a national debate, according to Ela Bhatt, general secretary of the SEWA (Mukul, 1998, p. 758).

The SEWA model, where poor working women in the informal sector are organized so as to improve their wages and working conditions, and also assisted with credit from banks and cooperatives, needs to be replicated elsewhere in India with considerable urgency. This is already happening in the *Working Women's Forum* in Chennai and *Annapurna* in Mumbai. Established trade union federations have to take a lead in fostering these organizational models and cooperating with local NGOs where the situation warrants, especially in states where gender equality is a serious problem (Seeta Prabhu et al., 1996). The CITU has made considerable progress in organizing women workers in the informal sector.

Trade unions should lobby central and state governments to improve education for women and increase state intervention in favour of women's employment. There is also considerable scope for increasing the number of women in leadership roles within the established trade union federations.

3.2.9 Changing public perception of trade unions

The memories of nationalism and independence struggles sustained the image of trade unions as the collective voice of the oppressed, dispossessed and the exploited during the first two phases of unionism. In the third phase, segmented and uneven economic growth fractured union voices, and the public was able to distinguish between them. The Mumbai textile strike of 1982-83 generated considerable solidarity, not just within the organized labour movement, but among the urban citizenry at large. At the same time, however, impatience with the declining work ethic and a growing lack of accountability in the public sector, especially in services and education, often reached critical levels.

Since the liberalization process in 1991-92, the print and visual media have clearly supported globalization. By and large, organized labour, especially in the public sector, has not received a sympathetic press; in fact, coverage of trade union matters has declined considerably. At the same time though, considerable media attention is given to the conditions of unorganized workers, child and women workers, and to the attempts by non-governmental organizations to improve the status of disadvantaged groups. Trade unions in India today face the challenge of convincing the public that they can act on behalf of all employees, unionized or not. This requires the formation of strategic alliances with community bodies, social movements, and other non-governmental organizations. Trade unions will have to accept that the credibility of political parties is at a very low level. There is considerable scope for the trade union movement to capitalize on potential alliances, and a concrete beginning can be made by first forging alliances among themselves. However, this could entail a weakening of links with their political parties.

4. Future role of trade unions in India: Organizing the unorganized

The future role of the trade union movement is linked with a broader concern for ensuring the social cohesion of working people in a large and diverse country. In this final section, we examine union strategies in the private corporate sector, in public sector enterprises, and in the informal sector. It is imperative for the trade union movement to concentrate on organizing the unorganized, so as to create secure incomes and safe working conditions for those with irregular and precarious jobs.

4.1 The private corporate sector

On average, private enterprises employ around 30 per cent of all formal sector workers in India; in manufacturing and trade, this proportion is around 70 per cent, whereas in transport, electricity and construction the figure is less than 5 per cent (Datta Chaudhuri, 1996).

In successful private companies enterprise-based trade unions (that may or may not be politically affiliated) will have to accept that pay is partly (if not largely) determined by productivity. Rather than blind resistance to this kind of pay structure, a cooperative strategy may yield greater dividends in terms of gainsharing at enterprise level. Unions will have to use their "collective voice" effectively in collective bargaining when incentive structures are proposed and negotiated. While the independent unions will find this strategy quite natural, those which are affiliated to the centralized federations may find it difficult. In either case, the extent to which a union is willing to take a risk will partly determine the composition of pay (performance-based "risk" pay and "steady" pay).

While the majority of contracts in this sector are (and probably always will be) negotiated at enterprise- or plant-level, unions in some organizations, possibly in the multinationals, could concentrate on attaining firm-wide agreements in the face of considerable management opposition. Firm-wide agreements will strengthen union power at the corporate level, and to achieve this, unions may have to trade off some plant-level gains. An example of this situation is being played out at Bata India. Management recognizes the ennterprise unions in its various plants across the country, but the loosely united All India Bata Employees Federation is not recognized. It appears that management is willing to talk to the federation if it agrees to restructuring plans at the plant in Faridabad. If the federation agrees to these plans in exchange for management recognition, this would clearly reduce union influence at the plant.

In the older industries in the private sector, where industry-wide bargaining is the dominant structure and where inter-firm differentiation has grown considerably since liberalization, unions and employers are finding it difficult to reach industry-level agreements. Unions will continue to face obstacles to industry-wide solidarity in this sector.

What have been the effects of economic liberalization on the connections between unions and political parties, and what has this meant for the private corporate sector? To the extent that most of the centralized trade unions continue to oppose the basic implications of economic liberalization, there has been a surprising reconciliation of unions affiliated to opposing political parties on a range of issues at both regional and national level. There has been a gap between the preoccupations of political parties and the macro-objectives of trade unions since the reforms. This has created a dilemma for most of the unions in this sector: while the loosening of ties with the parent body inevitably leads to greater autonomy in decentralized decision making, it also means a lessening of centralized lobbying power. Market forces will increasingly dominate union strategies in this sector.

4.2 Public sector enterprises

On average, the public sector employs around 70 per cent of all formal sector workers in India; in transport, mining, construction, electricity and services this proportion is high (more than 80 per cent), but it is considerably lower in agriculture (40 per cent), manufacturing (less than 40 per cent), and trade (less than 35 per cent) (Datta Chaudhuri, 1996).

In non-viable public sector enterprises that are ready for closure, most of which are in the east, the situation continues to be very grim. Workers have not been paid for several months and the endless talk of revival now sounds hollow. The closure of these firms seems to be the only solution and unions can do no more than see that layoffs are implemented fairly and as generously as possible. In several state-owned enterprises and organizations unions have accepted that privatization is the only way of saving the unit, and that informed negotiation is required.

As a result of increased competition from both domestic and international producers, the output of public enterprises and services has improved substantially. Nowhere is this more true than in the state-run airlines. But unions in the public sector, especially those in services such as medicine, education, the police and municipal workers, can substantially increase their credibility by agreeing to enforceable accountability procedures. This would mean internal monitoring, which the unions are reluctant to accept.

Although the government has indicated a preference for decentralization, the centralized bargaining structures have not yet been dismantled. Unions could campaign for a restructured central system that allows for greater local autonomy and minimizes bureaucratic inflexibilities. For the public sector to deliver long-run productivity improvements in the post-liberalization period, unions will have to partly align their objectives with those of the end-user – the average voter/consumer – who has become an important voice in the labour relations system.

4.3 The informal sector

In terms of union density, India fares rather badly compared to other large developing countries. According to the ILO *World Labour Report* 1997-98, union membership as a percentage of non-agricultural labour dropped from 6.6 per cent in 1985 to 5.5 per cent in 1995 (the corresponding figures in 1995 for Argentina were 23.4 per cent, Brazil 32.1 per cent and Mexico 31 per cent). Union membership as a percentage of formal sector workers in India declined from 26.5 per cent to 22.8 per cent between 1985 and 1995 (the corresponding figures in 1995 were Argentina 65.6 per cent, Brazil 66 per cent, Mexico 72.9 per cent). If the figures are derived only from registered unions that submit returns, it is possible that they may somewhat underestimate union density in India. According to the above source, less than 2 per cent of workers in the formal and informal sectors in India are covered by collective bargaining agreements. Clearly, a large proportion of workers (certainly those in the formal sector) fall within the ambit of labour legislation, even though they are not covered by a collective agreement. Nevertheless, it is apparent that considerable organization of workers remains to be undertaken in the Indian economy.

If one were to assume that the formal sector corresponds with the unionized sector (in reality, the unionized sector is a subset of the formal sector), then the following figures give an idea of the extent to which unions in future can organize workers in the various sectors. In total, less than 10 per cent of all workers are in the formal sector. The proportion of workers in this sector by industry groups is: mining and quarrying (56.9 per cent), manufacturing (19 per cent), construction (17.5 per cent), trade (2.1 per cent), transport (38.7 per cent), and services (38.7 per cent). Clearly, there is enormous potential for organizing workers in construction, manufacturing and trade. In addition, detailed surveys in several industries have found that the existing unions do not sufficiently represent the interests of casual and temporary workers (see the studies in Davala, 1992). Finally, according to National Sample Survey Organization data, there is a "high incidence of women's involvement in unorganized sector activities, ranging anywhere between 20 to 25 per cent of total employment in urban areas and anywhere between 30 to 40 per cent of total employment in rural areas – figures which far outweigh women's recorded involvement in productive activities from Census sources" (Mukhopadhyay, 1997, p. 485).

In sharp contrast to the formal sector, "the unorganized sector has little by way of protective legislation or union representation" (Anant and Sundaram, 1998, p. 833). In this site, the "not so invisible" forces of demand and supply determine wages and working conditions. There are no automatic cost-of-living adjustments and substantial improvements are required in designing need-based minimum wages for unorganized workers (Jhabvala, 1998) and providing them with assured employment for a minimum number of days (Unni, 1998). In this regard, the government's recent signal about labour law reform consisting of "umbrella legislation for welfare of unorganized sector workers" as part of the agenda should be critically examined. The government proposes to relax contract labour laws so as to generate more jobs, arguing that this would ensure better overall security and welfare provisions for unorganized workers. Unions, however, feel that any such move will only undermine permanent jobs. In any case, there are strong economic reasons why the wages and working conditions of informal sector workers should be improved through welfare legislation. Such measures improve the capabilities of the disadvantaged and vulnerable sections of working people. In the absence of enhanced capabilities the economy suffers a net loss.

It is clear that unions have a whole range of workers to organize in the coming years, since the majority of labour market entrants will probably work as self-employed or casual/temporary/contract workers. Visaria and Minhas (1991) estimate that nearly 80 million people will join the labour force between 1990 and 2000. A whole range of non-governmental organizations have successfully organized (not necessarily unionized) several informal sector occupations and sites in India during the last decade, but it seems that these interventions are resented by the established trade union federations as an intrusion into their terrain (often, it is claimed, with financial backing from abroad). These fears are probably unwarranted, and cooperation between trade unions and NGOs is required to level up working conditions in these relatively neglected labour markets.

One way of organizing workers could be through union mergers and a joint trade union front. However, the latter presupposes a certain number of shared objectives among the large centralized trade union federations, and this unity is not yet on the agenda. The All India Trade Union Congress, the Hind Mazdoor Sabha, and the Indian National Trade Union Congress have talked of mergers and unity, but the Centre of Indian Trade Unions has taken a different approach; they have proposed a confederation of central trade unions which will preserve the individual identities (Muralidhar, 1994). The large unions have considerable differences on the efficacy of a secret ballot system to generate the legitimate bargaining agent. However, one good sign is the increasing willingness of trade union federations to work together in spite of the differences between their political parties on reform. In many states acute differences are surfacing between political parties and their affiliated unions and these issues are now being openly debated.

It is well-known that the informal sector in India contributes significantly to employment generation and to value added in industry. It is also true that there are considerable links between the formal and informal sectors and that there is a crucial regional dimension to informal sector manufacturing (Shaw, 1990; 1994). The attempt to unionize the unorganized in India has been difficult, although some progress has been made in certain regions with sympathetic state governments. But in other states, the situation of informal sector workers remains grim, and will probably get worse unless there is a concerted effort by trade unions and NGOs, hopefully with the assistance of local and state governments, to level up the labour market institutions of the informal sector. In these endeavours, the organized labour movement should not view NGOs as competitors.

To what extent will alliances between trade unions break the links with their respective political parties? Or, will such alliances lead to the emergence of national unions without explicit political affiliation? It is too early to answer these questions but the tensions between some political parties and their trade union affiliates have come onto the regional and national stage since economic liberalization began in the early 1990s. In the private sector, these tensions emerged during the third phase of unionism and resulted in the proliferation of independent unions. It may be premature to suggest that independent unions, if they can be organized at industry/regional level, will lead to far greater "collective voice" effects and less "monopoly" effects than the existing industrial relations system. With economic liberalization and its effects on regional variations in economic activity, it seems that battles over working conditions will increasingly be fought at local and regional levels. Trade unions will have to forge deep links with neighbourhoods and communities, urban movements, environmental groups and regional NGOs to enhance their effective power. Ultimately, it all depends on "public action", participation in the process of social change. Public action refers not to what the state does for the public, but to action taken by the public (Dreze and Sen, 1989). The trade union movement could trigger this much needed "public action" through broad-based alliances.

In sum, the organized labour movement will have to come to terms with global competition, technology, new industrial organization and structural/ demographic changes in the workforce. The earlier, relatively insulated, systems for regulating employment will have to give way to more market-sensitive and flexible systems, ultimately even in the public sphere. Unions, especially in the service sector, will have to become sensitive to consumer needs. In the private sector, trade unions have adapted their structures in response to the decentralization of industrial relations, but these adjustments are painful and difficult in the public sector. There is no other way but to increase membership, which means organizing vulnerable workers in the informal sector. This is the most obvious way for unions to win broader community support. Finally, trade unions can only gain by cooperating and working together. Perhaps the new millennium will witness a series of mergers leading to a united and independent labour movement.

References

Ahluwalia, I.J.1991. *Productivity and growth in Indian manufacturing* (New Delhi, Centre for Policy Research) (mimeo).

. 1992. *Redefining the role of the state: India at the crossroads* (New Delhi, Centre for Policy Research) (mimeo).

Anant, T.C.A.; Sundaram, K. 1998. " Wage policy in India: A review", in *The Indian Journal of Labour Economics*, Vol. 41, Oct.-Dec., pp. 815-834.

Banaji, J.; Hensman, R. 1995. "India: Multinationals and the resistance to unionised labour", in *International Union Rights*, Vol. 2, No.2, pp. 5-6.

Banerjee, N. 1997. "How real is the bogey of feminization?", in *The Indian Journal of Labour Economics*, Vol. 40, July-Sep., pp. 427-438.

Bhaduri, A. 1993. "Orthodox development theories and their application to less developed countries", in Vaggi, G. (ed.): *From debt crisis to sustainable development: Changing perspectives on north-south relationship* (London, St.Martin's Press).

Bhattacherjee, D. 1987a. *Union-type, labour market structure, and bargaining outcomes in Indian manufacturing*. Unpublished Ph.D. thesis. (Urbana-Champaign, University of Illinois).

—. 1987b. "Union-type effects on bargaining outcomes in Indian manufacturing", in *British Journal of Industrial Relations*, Vol. 27 (July), pp. 247-266.

—.1988. "Unions, state and capital in Western India: Structural determinants of the 1982 Bombay textile strike", in Southall, R. (ed.): *Labour and unions in Africa and Asia: Contemporary issues* (London, Macmillan), pp.211-237.

—. 1989. "Evolution of unionism and labour market structure: Case of Bombay textile mills, 1947-85", in *Economic and Political Weekly*, Vol. 24 (May), M67-M76.

—. 1997. "Labour truths", in *The Telegraph* (Calcutta), 19 Sep .

—; Datta Chaudhuri, T. 1994a. "Modelling trade union growth in India", in *Indian Journal of Labour Economics*, Vol. 37 (Jan.-Mar.), pp. 67-72.

— ; —. 1994b. "Unions, wages and labour markets in Indian industry, 1960-86", in *Journal of Development Studies*, Vol. 30 (Jan.), pp. 443-465.

Borjas, G. 1996. *Labor economics* (Singapore, McGraw-Hill).

Buchele, R.; Christiansen, J. 1992. "Industrial relations and productivity growth: A comparative perspective", in *International Contributions to Labour Studies*, Vol. 2, pp. 77-97.

Chatterjee, R. 1980. *Unions, politics, and the state: A study of Indian labour politics* (New Delhi, South Asian Publishers).

Chaudhuri, S. 1995. "Government and transnationals: New economic policies since 1991", in *Economic and Political Weekly*, Vol. 30 (6-13 May), pp. 999-1012.

D'Souza, E. 1998. "World employment: ILO perspective", in *Economic and Political Weekly*, Vol. 33 (26 Sep.-2 Oct.), pp. 2537-2545.

Datta Chaudhuri, M. 1996. *Labor markets as social institutions in India*. IRIS India Working Paper No.10 (College Park, MD).

Datta Chaudhuri, T.; Bhattacherjee, D. 1994. "A structural model of strikes and wages in Indian industry, 1960-86", in *Indian Journal of Industrial Relations*, Vol. 30 (Oct.), pp. 144-155.

Davala, S. (ed.). 1992. *Employment and unionization in Indian industry* (New Delhi, FES).

—. 1992. "Chemical and pharmaceutical industry in Maharashtra", in Davala, S. (ed.): *op.cit.*, pp. 191-222.

Desai, M. 1975. "India: Emerging contradictions of slow capitalist development", in Blackburn, R. (ed.): *Explosion in a subcontinent* (London, Penguin), pp. 11-51.

Deshpande, L.K. 1992. "Institutional interventions in the labour market in Bombay's manufacturing sector", in Papola, T.S.; Rodgers, G. (eds.): *Labour institutions and economic development in India*. Research Series No. 97 (Geneva, International Institute for Labour Studies).

Deshpande, S.; Deshpande, L.K. 1992. "New economic policy and female employment", in *Economic and Political Weekly*, Vol. 27 (Oct.), pp. 2248-2252.

—; . 1996. "New economic policy and response of the labour market in India", Paper presented to a seminar on *"Labour markets and industrial relations in South Asia: Emerging issues and policy options"* (India International Centre, New Delhi, 18-20 Sep.)

—; . 1998. "Impact of liberalisation on labour market in India: What do facts from NSSO's 50th round show?", in *Economic and Political Weekly*, Vol. 33 (30 May), L31-L39.

Dreze, J.; Sen, A.K. 1989. *Hunger and public action* (Oxford, Clarendon Press).

Fallon. P.R.; Lucas, R.E.B. 1991. "The impact of changes in job security regulations in India and Zimbabwe", in *The World Bank Economic Review*, Vol. 5 (Sep.), pp. 395-413.

FES-IIRA. 1996. *Social clause in trade: Trade unions' perspective* (New Delhi, FES).

Fonseca, A.J. 1964. *Wage determination and organized labour in India* (Bombay, Oxford University Press).

Freeman, R. 1992. "Labor market institutions and policies: Help or hindrance to economic development?", *Proceedings of the World Bank Conference on Development Economics*, pp.117-144.

—; Medoff, J. 1984. *What do unions do?* (New York, Basic Books).

Ghose, A.K. 1992. "Economic restructuring, employment and safety nets: A note", in *Social dimensions of structural adjustment in India* (New Delhi, ILO-ARTEP), pp. 94-102.

Hensman, R. 1996. "Minimum labour standards and trade agreements: An overview of the debate", in *Economic and Political Weekly*, Vol. 31 (20-27 Apr.), pp. 1030-1034.

Holmstrom, M. 1984. *Industry and inequality: The social anthropology of Indian labour* (Cambridge, Cambridge University Press).

Horton, S.; Kanbur, R.; Mazumdar, D. 1991. *Labor markets in an era of adjustment.* Policy, Research, and External Affairs Working Paper No. 694 (Washington, D.C., World Bank).

ILO. 1996/97. *World employment – National policies in a global context* (Geneva, ILO).

—. 1997/98. *World Labour Report, Industrial relations, democracy and social stability* (Geneva, ILO).

Jackson, D.A.S. 1972. "Wage policy and industrial relations in India", in *Economic Journal*, Vol. 82 (Mar.), pp. 183-194.

Jhabvala, R. 1998. "Minimum wages based on workers' needs", in *Economic and Political Weekly*, Vol. 33 (7-13 Mar.), pp. 500-502.

Johri, C.K. 1967. *Unionism in a developing economy: A study of the interaction between trade unionism and government policy in India, 1950-65* (Bombay, Asia Publishing House).

Jose, A.V. 1992. "Earnings, employment and productivity trends in organised industries in India", in *Indian Journal of Labour Economics*, Vol. 35 (Jul.-Sep.).

Joseph, K.P. 1997. "Piped music and telephone attendants: Report of Fifth Pay Commission", in *Economic and Political Weekly*, Vol. 32 (22 Mar.), pp. 563-565.

Joshi, V.; Little, I.M.D. 1994. *India: Macroeconomics and political economy, 1964-1991* (Washington, D.C., The World Bank).

Kennedy, V.D. 1966. *Unions, employers and government* (Bombay, Manaktalas).

Madan, B.K. 1977. *The real wages of industrial labour in India* (New Delhi, Management Development Institute).

Mathur, A.N. 1992. *Employment security and industrial restructuring in India: Separating facts from folklore – The exit policy controversy* (Calcutta, Indian Institute of Management).

—. 1993. "The experience of consultation during structural adjustment in India (1990-92)", in *International Labour Review* (Geneva, ILO), Vol. 132, No. 3, pp. 331-345.

Mukhopadhyay, S. 1997. "Locating women within informal sector hierarchies", in *Indian Journal of Labour Economics*, Vol. 40 (July-Sep.), pp. 483-492.

Mukul, 1998. "Homeworkers: High hopes and hard realities", in *Economic and Political Weekly*, Vol. 33 (4-10 Apr.), pp. 758-762.

Mundle, S. 1992. "The employment effects of stabilisation and related policy changes, 1992-1994", in *Social dimensions of structural adjustment in India* (New Delhi, ILO-ARTEP), pp. 25-40.

Muralidhar, S. 1993. "Slipping through the holes in the safety net", in *Economic Times* (Calcutta), 26 Dec., p. 7.

—. 1994. " In tune with changing reality", in *Economic Times* (Calcutta), 13 Feb., p. 9.

Myers, C.M. 1958. *Labor problems in the industrialization of India* (Cambridge, MA, Harvard University Press).

Nagaraj, R. 1997. "What has happened since 1991? Assessment of India's economic reform", in *Economic and Political Weekly*, Vol. 32 (8-14 Nov.), pp. 2869-2879.

Nambiar, R.G.; Mungekar, B.L.; Tadas, G.A. 1999. "Is import liberalization hurting domestic industry and employment?", in *Economic and Political Weekly*, Vol. 34 (13-19 Feb.), pp. 417-424.

Nayyar, D. 1981. "Industrial development in India: Growth or stagnation?", in Bagchi, A.K.; Banerjee, N. (eds.): *Change and choice in Indian industry* (Calcutta, K.P. Bagchi), pp. 91-118.

Nelson, J.M. 1991. " Organized labor, politics and labor market flexibility in developing countries", in *World Bank Research Observer* (Washington, D.C.), Vol. 6, pp. 37-56.

Noronha, E. 1996. "Liberalisation and industrial relations", in *Economic and Political Weekly*, Vol. 31 (24 Feb.), L14-L20.

Olson, M. 1971. *The logic of collective action* (Cambridge, Harvard University Press).

Papola, T.S. 1994. "Employment growth and social protection of labour in India", in *Indian Journal of Industrial Relations*, Vol. 30 (Oct.), pp. 117-143.

Patankar, B. 1981. "Textile workers and Datta Samant", in *Economic and Political Weekly*, Vol. 16 (Dec.), pp. 1981-1982.

Patil, B.R. 1982. "Coalition and convertive bargaining", in *Indian Journal of Industrial Relations*, Vol. 18 (Oct.), pp. 241-262.

Patnaik, P.; Rao, S.K. 1977. "1975-76: Beginning of the end of stagnation?" in *Social Scientist*, Vol. 5 (Jan.), pp. 120-138.

Pendse, S. 1981. "The Datta Samant phenomenon", in *Economic and Political Weekly*, Vol. 16 (Apr.), pp. 695-797 and 745-749.

Punekar, S.A. 1966. "Aspects of state intervention in industrial relations in India", in Ross, A.M. (ed.): *Industrial relations and economic development* (London, Macmillan).

Ramaswamy, E.A. 1984. *Power and justice* (New Delhi, Oxford University Press).

—. 1988. *Worker consciousness and trade union response* (New Delhi, Oxford University Press).

Ramaswamy, K.V. 1999. "The search for flexibility in Indian manufacturing: New evidence on outsourcing activities", in *Economic and Political Weekly*, Vol. 34 (6-12 Feb.), pp. 363-368.

Rudolph, L.I.; Rudolph, S.H. 1987. *In pursuit of Lakshmi* (Bombay, Orient Longmans).

Seeta Prabhu, K.; Sarkar, P.C.; Radha, A. 1996. "Gender-related development index for Indian states: Methodological issues", in *Economic and Political Weekly*, Vol. 31 (26 Oct.), WS72-WS79.

Sen, A. 1996. "Economic reforms, employment and poverty: Trends and options", in *Economic and Political Weekly*, Vol. 31 (Sep.), pp. 2459-2478.

Sen, R. 1997. "Changing employment and industrial relations in the jute industry", in Venkataratnam, C.S.; Verma, A. (eds.): *Challenge of choice: Industrial relations in Indian industry* (New Delhi, Allied), pp. 65-104.

Sengupta, A.K. 1992. *Trends in industrial conflict in India (1961-87) and government policy.* Working Paper Series No. 174/92 (Calcutta, Indian Institute of Management).

Shaw, A. 1990. "Linkages of large scale, small scale and informal sector industries: A study of Thana-Belapur", in *Economic and Political Weekly*, Vol. 25 (17 Feb.), M17-M22.

—. 1994. "The informal sector in Indian manufacturing activities: A regional study", in *Indian Journal of Labour Economics*, Vol. 37 (July-Sep.), pp. 335-350.

—. 1999. "Emerging patterns of urban growth in India", in *Economic and Political Weekly*, Vol. 34 (17-24 Apr.), pp. 969-978.

Unni, J. 1998. "Wages and employment in the unorganised sector: Issues in wage policy", in *Indian Journal of Labour Economics*, Vol. 41 (Oct.-Dec.), pp. 875-892.

Van Wersch, H. 1992. *Bombay textile strike 1982-83* (New Delhi, Oxford University Press).

Venkataratnam, C.S. 1996. "Industrial relations in India", Paper presented to a seminar on *"Labour Market and Industrial Relations in South Asia: Emerging Issues and Policy Options"* (New Delhi, India International Centre, 18-20 Sep.).

Visaria, P.; Minhas, B.S. 1991. "Evolving an employment policy for the 1990s: What do the data tell us?", in *Economic and Political Weekly*, Vol. 26 (Apr.), pp. 969-979.

Williamson, O. 1985. *The economic institutions of capitalism: Firms, markets, and policy control* (New York, New York University Press).

World Bank. 1995. *World Development Report, Workers in an integrating world* (Washington, D.C., World Bank).

Zeitlin, J. 1987. "From labour history to the history of industrial relations", in *Economic History Review*, Vol. 40, No. 2, pp. 159-184.

Globalization and union strategies in Niger

Souley Adji

1. The context of the social struggle

Since the installation of a democratic government in 1991, and particularly since the inauguration of the Fourth Republic in 1996, many of the recognized rights of workers and unions have been challenged, if not severely restricted, by the state authorities and employers. This is because successive governments have been trying to meet the conditions of the structural adjustment programme (SAP) advocated by the international financial institutions. The successful implementation of such an economic policy is bound to have a significant impact on the purchasing power of workers, and on the living and working conditions of all social groups, particularly since the devaluation of the CFA in 1994. The unions were not slow to react and, since independence in 1960, the country has never known such intense social conflict as during the present decade. However, the results of union action are rather limited.

1.1 The first adjustment programmes and their consequences

Niger began its catastrophic decline in the early 1980s, when the government first appealed to the International Monetary Fund (IMF). One of the 30 poorest nations in the world, Niger was still the richest country of the Sahel, thanks to its mineral resources. It was the fourth world producer of uranium at that time. Twenty years later, with an education rate of 29 per cent, an illiteracy rate of 83 per cent, access to health services for 32 per cent of the population and clean water for 41 per cent (10 million people) Niger is still one of the poorest countries.

In 1980, uranium represented 40 per cent of state revenue, bringing in 28,000 million FCFA. The government invested in ambitious prestige projects at that time, but the collapse of the uranium market put an end to the euphoria. During 1981 the repercussions of the world economic crisis and the cancellation or reduction of nuclear energy programmes began to hit Niger. The sale of minerals brought in a mere 6,700 million FCFA in 1982, only 7 per cent of government revenue, while the debt rose to 16,600 million FCFA the same year. There were food shortages and price rises: this trend continued in the years that followed, as the economic crisis deepened.

Faced with this catastrophic situation the government signed an agreement with the IMF in October 1983, whereby the Fund provided significant financial assistance on certain conditions. Some years later the IMF effectively imposed an SAP which was expected to improve the country's economic position. The drastic measures consisted mainly of a significant cut in the number of government employees, a reduction in the volume of state subsidies and price controls, as well as the liberalization of banking and commerce. It also advocated government withdrawal from the education and health sectors, and the privatization of many enterprises. In a poor country, where the state is the main employer and where the modern private sector is very small, such measures are likely to drive down still further the living conditions of the majority of workers.

It was in this context, and after 30 years of political monolithism (including 15 years under a military regime) that Niger entered its Second Republic with the election of a National Assembly. But the elections were not democratic as the President of the State Party was the only candidate. At the same time the international financial institutions took charge of economic policy, notably in the implementation of structural adjustment.

The austerity measures which were introduced resulted in a popular discontent which was without precedent. Moreover, the foreign debt, and particularly debt servicing, became a real problem at this time, even though the sums involved were smaller than those owed by several other countries. Since the beginning of structural adjustment in 1983 the country has seen an exponential growth of its foreign debt.

In these circumstances the government was unable to honour its commitments to its workers or to its foreign partners. The state was in a crisis that the very young Second Republic could not survive. From that time on, economic liberalization and democratization have gone together.

1.2 The union awakening

Since its 1978 Congress the USTN (Union des Syndicats des Travailleurs du Niger), the only federation of unions, had advocated 'responsible participation', and collaborated with the military regime. However, the weakness of the government at the end of the 1980s gave the union movement an opportunity to separate itself from the State Party. The real turning point came on 1 May 1990 with the demand for a multiparty democracy and a National Conference. Since then, together with the student movement, the USTN has been at the forefront of the struggle for democracy.

This awakening promised to be fruitful but the rank-and-file workers quickly became disillusioned. Having based their hopes on solving the economic and social problems which were at the root of the social conflict, workers became the victims of economic stabilization. During the transition, as under the Third Republic and even more under the Fourth Republic, their purchasing power collapsed. The drawing up of a new Constitution and the creation of democratic institutions did not compensate for this economic failure. Furthermore, the unions had to face the growing economic hostility of the democratically elected authorities.

It was in this context of economic and political liberalization that the cohesion and unity of the labour movement, so remarkable during the struggle for democracy, began to break down. There were conflicts between unions affiliated to the federation and divergences among union leaders suspected, rightly or wrongly, of playing the political game.

1.3 Planned reforms under the new programmes

The struggle against the economic measures recommended by the IMF and the World Bank, particularly in the field of education, led to the fall of the Second Republic and the introduction of political democracy. The National Conference rejected the SAP and adopted a series of measures designed to stimulate the national economy. The transitional government was faced with a great challenge. The fall in the uranium market meant a reduction of 34.48 per cent in the value of mineral exports between 1986 and 1990, according to the IMF. Disruptions in distribution, the destruction of equipment and the closure of more than half the country's small and medium-sized enterprises left the economy in a desperate position. According to the World Bank, Niger's foreign debt amounted to 1340 thousand million FCFA at the end of 1989, including 331 thousand million FCFA of long-term debt. There were shortfalls in tax revenues, overdue salaries in the public sector, and unemployment in the private sector. One-fifth of the population of the capital city was without an income as a result of the closure of numerous small businesses. Employment fell by 22.68 per cent between 1978 and 1990.

Incapable of mobilizing internal resources and faced with the timidity of development partners, each successive government has appealed to the international financial institutions. Formerly decried and contested by unions and political parties the SAP thus came back through the front door.

Niger's financial situation had deteriorated to the point where it was necessary to give priority to budgetary adjustment. The imperative reduction in salary costs required a restructuring of the public service and a revision of government objectives in education. Significant measures were introduced to cut production costs in order to make the economy competitive. These were the principal IMF recommendations which were made in 1992, and successive governments have attempted to implement them despite the reluctance of many social groups. Owing to political instability, however, no government has been able to carry out the reforms in full and the programmes and facilities have been continually renegotiated.

Nevertheless, massive layoffs have occurred in both the public and the private sectors, and workers' interests have been sacrificed. The sacrifice is all the more painful as unions have not been involved in economic reform, despite the fact that Niger has ratified international Conventions which prohibit this type of action without prior consultation. It must be said that the political context of the Fourth Republic is not favourable to negotiation.

1.4 Union attitudes

There are many obstacles to the implementation of economic reform. But despite union opposition unpopular measures have generally been applied and workers have suffered. The lack of real direction on the part of leaders has meant that unions have not been very effective in their efforts to defend workers' interests. The USTN document *Analysis of structural adjustment in Niger* gives the impression that the federation considers structural adjustment as a neutral technique for solving economic and financial problems, and that the SAP is inevitable.

The federation seems to accept layoffs as workers' contribution to national recovery, despite the fact that the burden is not spread evenly over all social classes. Nevertheless the unions are trying to initiate strategies to combat the social cost of globalization. Their demands relate to four vital areas: preserving democratic structures, safeguarding union rights, protecting employment and defending wages. The following sections describe union strategies in the face of globalization.

2. Recent reforms and their effect on production

2.1 Reasons for privatizing enterprises

Privatization/restructuring is one of the principal elements of the SAP. The entire public sector is affected by economy measures and retrenchment. Salaries were cut by 30 per cent across the board in 1997, and early retirement became mandatory for everyone aged 50 and over, or having 30 years service. Eight enterprises are concerned by the reforms foreseen in the structural adjustment programme.

2.2 The institutional framework and collective agreements

Employment in public sector enterprises is governed by the Labour Code and by collective agreements. In other words, public sector workers are treated like those in the private sector. They are automatically promoted every two years, moving from one grade to the next.

Strictly speaking there is no collective agreement between the state and the public sector unions. The negotiating body is the Consultative Committee of the Public Service, which has six members representing government ministries and six representing employees. The Committee gives an opinion on human resource policies and practices in the public sector: it also studies draft texts dealing with changes in the status of government employees.

There is a collective agreement between employers and unions in the private sector, which dates from 15 December 1992. This agreement incorporates the principal union rights enshrined in international texts; it also outlines the practical modalities of applying the provisions of the Labour Code, particularly those relating to acquired rights. It stipulates that an employer cannot discriminate against an employee who belongs to a union. Discrimination is also forbidden on grounds of the political, philosophical or religious beliefs of employees. With regard to union rights the agreement authorizes absence from work to take part in union activities, the provision of premises and facilities for union meetings and the collection of union dues inside the enterprise. Like the Labour Code, the collective agreement protects unionists from discrimination. The dismissal of a union delegate is not valid unless approved by the Inspector of Labour.

2.3 Effects on employment

Between 1988 and 1992 about 5000 people who were employed in public enterprises lost their jobs. Many of these people will join the ranks of the unemployed as there are few openings for job seekers in the context of privatization and restructuring. 'Voluntary retirement' is really a disguised form of layoff. Workers are offered an attractive payment if they resign rather than wait to be dismissed. They are encouraged to start their own business and create new jobs, but many of these enterprises fail. The reason generally given is the lack of institutional support and the unfavourable economic situation.

2.4 Effects on acquired rights

- The 30 per cent reduction in public sector wages was a heavy blow to government employees. Salaries have also been cut in private enterprises, ostensibly to save the enterprise and thus preserve the jobs. In other words, workers are given the choice of accepting a lower wage or losing their job. Unfortunately many workers have suffered both.
- Public sector wages have been withheld because of strike action, without regard to actual responsibility for the stoppage. These strikes have been justified by the non-payment of wages, so that the state (the employer) is responsible because it fails to honour its commitments to employees. Withholding salaries is thus a step backwards. Civil servants have also lost the right to a salary increase on promotion. This allows the state to save on salaries, at the expense of workers.

- The check-off system which assured the payment of union dues has been challenged by the Ministry of Finance, in order to weaken the unions.
- The president of USTN, the main union federation, automatically chaired the Administrative Council of the CNSS (Caisse Nationale de Sécurité Sociale), which made it possible for the unions to promote the social rights of workers. This privilege has now been withdrawn.
- The right to strike has been seriously undermined by individual and collective reprisals. Picketing is forbidden and unionists have been arrested and imprisoned. Government forces have been deployed at workplaces to obstruct the action of union delegates by violence or intimidation.
- Union leaders have been imprisoned and dismissed, in contravention of the Labour Code. Strikers have been wounded during protest demonstrations.
- Temporary workers have been hired in order to break strikes. These workers are not familiar with the equipment they have to use, and they often damage it, which makes the conditions of work more difficult after the strike. Some employers dismiss strikers.
- Two police unions were dissolved by the government, in defiance of international Conventions, the police having made many demands for improved pay and conditions. The pretext for dissolving the unions was that police strikes were against the public interest. The union representing customs officials was also dissolved, as a strike in this sector would sabotage the government's economic programme.
- The freedom of the labour movement has been seriously threatened by state intervention in union affairs. Government has made appointments to union offices and created new unions favourable to the ruling party.
- Unions have lost the right to organize demonstrations as marches are forbidden on the pretext that municipal services cannot cope with them. Only meetings are allowed.
- Unions have lost their access to the public mass media.
- Unions are not involved in the privatization process.

Since a democratic government was installed at the beginning of the 1990s unions have managed to preserve some of their rights by resorting to judicial procedures. They have prosecuted employers, including the state, who do not respect their obligations to workers. Some positive results have been achieved, notably:

- the reinstatement of workers who were illegally dismissed;
- the restitution of their salaries and other rights and benefits;
- the release of imprisoned unionists;
- the preservation of threatened jobs;

- the cancellation of arbitrary assignments of unionists;
- the recruitment of young graduates to the public sector, notably in health and education.

Under the authoritarian government of the Fourth Republic economic liberalization seriously affected workers, enterprises and business. The immediate effects were felt in:

- purchasing power – workers were impoverished;
- civil liberties – demonstrations and marches were forbidden, and unions were denied access to the media;
- enterprise productivity – workers were demotivated by salary cuts;
- foreign investment – industrial unrest deterred foreign investors;
- union activities – some unions lost the right to organize meetings at the workplace;
- union militancy – loss of workers' rights undermined union action, particularly among women and young people. Some workers were obliged to take a second job in order to make up the income lost as a result of salary cuts. They were discouraged and had no time for union activities.
- degree of mobilization – the massive demonstrations organized in protest against public sector wage cuts failed to achieve any result. This caused workers to lose heart and leaders to become apathetic. Some union leaders were suspected of colluding with the government.

2.5 Union strategies

In the period before privatization began unions preferred action which required a minimum of human and material resources. This stage was generally peaceful as unions were trying to ensure a 'soft' process of privatization which would not be prejudicial to workers. Six types of action were undertaken during this period.

Before the reforms were implemented

Preventive action

Unions carried out research and collected data on the enterprises which were to be privatized and on the public sector generally. The information allowed them to combat the options preferred by employers, which threatened workers' interests. Unions made counter-proposals which they publicized in the media and among their members. They only accepted measures which they considered were justified and only on condition that unions took part in the entire process.

Internal promotion

Unions denounced certain enterprise directors who deliberately mismanaged the company in order to profit from privatization. They fought for internal promotion so that people inside the enterprise would be appointed to management positions. They believed that directors appointed from outside were not able to defend the enterprise and the people working there.

Negotiation and mediation

In order to obtain the reinstatement of workers illegally dismissed the unions denounced the layoffs and demanded talks with the employer. If employers refused to negotiate a strike warning was issued. The strike was highly publicized to gain public sympathy and alert other unions. The strike was also brought to the attention of unions in other countries.

Judicial proceedings

For private sector employees hearings were held at works tribunals. The first recourse in the public sector was to the bipartite authorities, before going to the Supreme Court. In the case of imprisoned unionists publicity campaigns were organized to exert pressure on the government and the matter was brought to trial if there was no response from the authorities.

Lobbying

Unions lobbied the government for the reinstatement of workers. If negotiations broke down they also lobbied influential politicians.

Administrative measures

The union defended workers who were illegally dismissed and helped them prepare the documents necessary to challenge the employer through the official channels.

After the reforms were implemented

If the types of action described above were not effective, the unions moved on to different strategies. This has caused considerable disturbance because the unions are trying to achieve by force what they failed to achieve by peaceful means. This stage continues as the privatization programme is still being pursued. Three principal strategies are deployed:

The indefinite strike

The traditional union strategies of strikes and negotiations are still preferred but their nature has changed since the introduction of the SAP and economic reform. Thus, when the government refuses to negotiate, or if negotiations fail, the unions individually or collectively decide to:
- call an indefinite strike, sometimes with no guaranteed minimum service;
- suspend activities because of the 'impossibility of working'.

These methods were used during the political struggles of 1991 when, for the first time in its history, the USTN called an indefinite strike to demand a multiparty government and the withdrawal of structural adjustment measures. This strike, which was massively supported by workers, students and the general population, led to the fall of the Second Republic and the introduction of multipartism.

Under the democratic regime the USTN used this strategy in 1994 to combat government measures affecting salaries and unionists. The federation organized an indefinite strike which lasted for 55 days but achieved no more than a promise of arbitration. This did not meet the expectations of workers, particularly as the authorities had drafted in temporary workers to maintain skeleton services in the public sector. The strike thus had very limited success, particularly as workers were not paid during the action. Indefinite strikes seem to have given way to intermittent strike action now, although the suspension of activities is still used.

The strike relay

Under this strategy all the unions affiliated to the USTN declare a strike in turn. As soon as a strike is called off in one sector employees stop work in another sector, so that the authorities are constantly importuned. Sometimes no skeleton service is maintained, which is a real declaration of war on the government. Unions in the health sector, education and electricity are able to use these strikes to the best advantage as they cause the most serious problems for the government and employers. This strategy has made it possible to start a dialogue and even to satisfy some union demands.

The general strike

Unions paralyse all the vital sectors of the economy for one or two days, thus disrupting national life and embarrassing the government. This strategy is used when the political situation is extremely critical, when negotiations have failed or the government offer falls far short of workers' demands, and also when democracy and national unity are under threat. It was effective in 1991 in the struggle for democracy, and also in 1992 and 1994 against an army mutiny during which the established authorities were illegally confined by rebellious troops.

3. Union structures and finances

3.1 Reconfiguration of the union landscape

Niger now has five unions affiliated to the Confederation Nigérienne du Travail (CNT) and 21 which are not affiliated. A total of 26 unions are not affiliated to the USTN, which is the principal federation. These fall into three main groups:

- The disaffiliated unions which created a new federation, the CNT, with five members. The CNT represents workers in the parapublic and private sectors, and is discussing whether to extend its membership to unions in the public sector as well.
- Many new unions which have been created because of a split in existing unions. Most new unions would like to be affiliated to one or other of

the federations but the USTN has to submit applications for the approval of existing members in the same sector. Approval is unlikely to be given when the new union arose out of a clash of interests between leaders.
- Autonomous unions which prefer to remain outside the existing federations. These mostly represent white-collar workers.

It is possible that new federations may be created, particularly if the USTN refuses requests for affiliation from new unions. Economic liberalization and privatization have influenced the union movement in Niger. In the context of globalization the authorities, always inclined to divide and rule, have encouraged the quarrels between union leaders. This situation has affected both the structures and the finances of the labour movement.

3.2 Effects on USTN functioning

- The withdrawal of four unions from the USTN has not affected the structure of the federation, as they represent only a few urban sectors which are also represented by other unions.
- Since its last Congress in 1996 the USTN has stopped producing the membership cards which were sold by its local offices to subsidize their activities. These offices are no longer effectively supported financially and consequently they are unable to address local needs adequately.
- The CNT has recently created a network of structures below the national level, and these seem to be functioning well.
- The federations and the non-affiliated unions advocate centralized democracy as an organizing principle. The impulse for action comes from the centre and the communal, local and regional offices implement decisions and orders from the national executive office.
- Training is the prerogative of the national level and depends on financing from (northern) partner unions, international bodies to which the national unions are affiliated, or state subsidies. The lack of training at grassroots level means that the labour movement is not very democratic as rank-and-file workers are not sufficiently informed to play a meaningful role in union affairs. The movement tends to be unbalanced, with the mass of workers unaware of their rights and the leaders holding too much power, for which they are not held accountable.

Unions can be grouped into five types according to their internal structures:
- those which have local structures with regular activities, an accounting system and a procedure for renewing mandates as they expire;
- those which have found ways to finance themselves, through local subscriptions or the direct payment of dues;

- those which are subsidized so that they can organize conferences in their locality and benefit from the proceeds;
- those which have effectively suspended operations and which rely on the USTN to support unionists in their area;
- those in difficulties because of unfair competition which is undermining the sector (e.g. taxi-motos which are destroying the urban transport business in some towns).

3.3 New types of relationship between the different structures

Relations between the different unions generally reflect the solidarity which is the cardinal principle of union action. Nevertheless, there is some degree of polarization between unions representing workers in the parapublic and private sectors on the one hand, and those in the public sector on the other hand. The disparity of interests often makes it difficult to organize a common struggle in support of specific demands. This situation requires the USTN to make its own structure flexible enough to take account of the interests of its various affiliates. Respect for the federation's basic documents on the part of its affiliates and its own leaders is a necessary condition for good relations between them and for viable democratic unionism. Unfortunately, however, it should be noted that:

- only 10 per cent of affiliated unions paid their subscription to the USTN in 1998;
- the mandate of 80 per cent of union offices expired long ago, but they continue to operate;
- some labour leaders openly declare their political allegiance, despite the fact that the statutes insist that unions remain apolitical;
- weak USTN leadership has led to a crisis of confidence, with affiliates tending to act independently.

Relations between the CNT and its affiliates are based on the principles of equality and equity. They all have the same rights and duties and they act together to solve individual problems.

There are no formal or official relations between the two federations. When the CNT was first created there was open hostility between them and no attempt was made to come together. They now seem to be moving towards an understanding, however. They need to agree to differ on certain points in order to work together and develop a common platform.

3.4 Relations between the union federations, the employers and the state

Relations between unions on the one hand and employers and the government on the other hand may be considered at two main levels, i.e.

respect for union rights and liberties, and the viability of the social dialogue. Union rights and liberties are enshrined in the Constitution and the law, as well as in the national and international Conventions ratified by Niger. However, only limited progress has been made in the exercise of these rights, which often means a battle. The resolute action of unions has sometimes succeeded in dissuading employers and the state from disputing workers' rights and forced employers to go back on measures which would threaten them. Examples include:

- non-access or restricted access to the mass media;
- interference in union business;
- violation of agreements concluded between the state and workers' organizations;
- suppression of workers' demonstrations permitted by the Constitution and international Conventions;
- reprisals against union leaders;
- threatened or actual layoffs of workers involved in union activities;
- suspension or dissolution of unions.

The social dialogue is ineffective. There is no systematic discussion and dialogue serves as part of the employers' strategy, notably the government's strategy in its role of employer. The state ignores its obligations towards the social partners, giving priority to its commitments under the SAP. Workers remain fairly passive; they do not insist on being consulted on decisions which concern them very closely. Nevertheless, bipartite discussions between unions and the sectoral authorities are an effective forum for dealing with many problems. In addition, non-affiliated unions are included in many USTN meetings and they contribute to clarifying the union position.

A change of attitude could improve the tripartite mechanism. For many years the unions projected an image of 'political opposition', which aroused the hostility of the government in power and undermined the establishment of a constructive partnership.

3.5 Effect of the reforms on union finances

As shown in the table below the USTN has lost about 87 per cent of its income since 1993.

Changes in USTN revenue, 1993 - 1998

	1993	1994	1995	1996	1997	1998
Cards bought & union contributions	3.380.000	2.338.000	2.099.000	1.209.000	400	433
Overall receipts	128.173.861	55.963.362	67.110.585	43.644.591	69.688.857	42.985.818

It is difficult to estimate CNT losses, but some of its affiliates are suffering financial constraints, which have repercussions on the federation.

3.6 Services for union members

Health

The USTN is developing a health insurance project in collaboration with the Confédération Française de Travail (CFDT). The union representing employees working for the national social security scheme (CNSS) is preparing a social fund designed to provide a supplementary pension and to pay the 20 per cent of medical expenses which are not covered by the national scheme.

Training

The USTN is running a project to provide low-cost training to workers and one of the unions is organizing and training workers in the sectors which it represents. In January 1999 an international cooperation project was launched (ILO/DANIDA) with the aim of supporting the efforts of USTN and CNT to provide workers' education in the informal sector. The three-year project has the following objectives:

• to organize informal sector workers into representative structures;
• to draw up a list of trade union indicators and seek to improve them;
• to combat child labour;
• to fight against illiteracy;
• to promote union solidarity.

The USTN is also running a training school and an agricultural project.

Financial services

Loans and financial support may be available through the federations or some of the unions. But they depend on the financial situation of the union itself, and very often members have to make a special effort to help colleagues who are in difficulty.

3.7 Effects of budgetary constraints on union functioning

The USTN and its affiliates have been seriously affected by budgetary constraints. The USTN has great difficulty in covering its running costs and paying salaries. The telephone and fax have been cut off for three years, so that it is difficult to communicate with local offices. Activities have therefore slowed almost to a standstill. Even worse, the USTN cannot keep up its subscription to international federations, which means that the training programmes supported by international cooperation are under threat. The union councils and the Congress cannot be held as often as the statutes require. The mandates of about 80 per cent of the offices of USTN affiliates have expired, which casts doubt on their representativity and legitimacy. The government's economic measures are demoralizing unionists as unions seem unable to defend their members and safeguard their interests.

The CNT is in a similar position to the USTN, although the problems are less acute. The services offered to members have shrunk and those that remain depend heavily on international union cooperation.

3.8 Strategies for financial viability

The double strategy consists of cutting the budget for some activities in order to maintain others, at the same time as attempting to increase revenues. The measures include:

- imposing special subscriptions on affiliates which can afford to pay them;
- making the payment of membership fees obligatory by introducing proportional representation;
- organizing informal sector workers in order to enlarge the union base;
- holding campaigns to make unionists aware of the importance of finance for union activities;
- undertaking income-generating activities such as buying crops at harvest time to sell when there is a shortage;
- requesting special contributions from members to cover the most urgent needs;
- maintaining good relations with the social partners to favour the collection of union dues at the work site, particularly in the public sector;
- striving to get the check-off system accepted as the normal way to finance unions;
- managing the income generated by conferences as economically as possible.

4. Building alliances

Unions often undertake collective action with other groups, notably political parties, humanitarian associations and student bodies. Collaboration with women's groups is discussed in section 6. These alliances have become much more important since 1990-1991, when the state entered an unprecedented period of crisis.

4.1 Characteristics and objectives of the partner organizations

At the beginning of the 1990s the groups fighting for a democratic government had certain characteristics in common:

- They were hostile to the one-party state. At that time the multiparty system and freedom of association had just been authorized after a 30-year ban. The new associations and political parties were thus practically unknown to the public, and they had no experience of mass organization.
- They had no real roots among the people, and they were identified only by the charisma of their leader. They were thus built up on the model of union structures and they echoed union demands.

The most important occasions in the building of alliances were:

- 1990-1991: Unions were involved in the Preparatory Commission for the National Conference and took an active part in the Conference itself. Most members of the Preparatory Commission represented groups fighting for democracy (the 'democratic forces'), while the Conference brought together all sectors of society.
- 28 February 1992: Five months after the transition government was formed there was an army mutiny and political leaders were seized. The democratic forces, notably the unions and political parties, acted together to oppose this challenge to the democratic process.
- 1994-1995: The democratic forces struggled to maintain national unity in the face of an armed rebellion in the north of the country.
- 1996-1997: The USTN formed an alliance with the non-affiliated unions. The objectives of the alliance are the preservation of constitutional liberties and the defence of employment and workers' rights. The alliance itself is open only to unions but a subgroup fighting for freedom of association is open to community organizations.

Since the political parties became more firmly established in Niger there has been little collective action between them and the unions. They no longer share the same interests and objectives.

4.2 Union involvement: Problems and interests

In 1990, in the absence of any political opposition, workers and students led the struggle against the SAP and they dominated the fight for democracy. Union structures compensated for the lack of direction and leadership in the battle against one-party government. They acted as a kind of political opposition.

In principle the labour movement is 'apolitical', being neither for nor against any party: unions are autonomous and independent. But the USTN reserves the right to express an opinion on questions concerning national life, and until 1990 it maintained relations with successive governments. It even sat on some of the one-party political authorities. This practice was known as 'responsible participation'. It is only since the early 1990s that the USTN has really been politically independent. During the early 1990s it became closely involved in the national political debate. The stakes were high, with five crucial questions to be addressed at that time:

- The future of the country's schools, which were threatened by project 'Education II' designed by the international financial institutions. The proposals included two sittings in primary and secondary schools (morning classes and afternoon classes, i.e. half-day schooling), restrictions on the number of students admitted to higher education, and massive reductions in teaching staff.
- The end of the one-party state.
- The holding of a National Conference to evaluate 30 years of authoritarian government.
- The installation of a transition government paving the way for the creation of democratic institutions.
- During the army mutiny of 1992 the newly created democratic framework was at stake, as well as the transition government. These had to be restored and strengthened. It is important to note that no alliances were formed during the military coup of 1996, the unions being hostile to the coalition which was overthrown. A few months later, however, they rallied to combat the junta in power.

4.3 The formation and management of alliances

During the early 1990s the USTN was the only union federation, and it had branches throughout the country. The opposition parties had only recently been created, so that the USTN effectively controlled the new socio-political scene.

- The Secretary-General of the USTN acted as spokesman for the opposition.
- The Assistant Secretary-General of the USTN chaired the Preparatory Commission for the National Conference.
- The USTN was a kind of headquarters for the opposition and many meetings were held there.
- Unions affiliated to the USTN had 100 seats at the National Conference, the non-affiliated unions and the students also had 100 seats, and the 24 political parties had 14 each.
- The preliminary address to the National Conference was made by the president of the Preparatory Commission. The conference was opened by the Head of State.

All the collective action led to positive achievements in the fight for national unity. The government ceded to demands for the withdrawal of Education II, the introduction of multiparty politics, the holding of a National Conference and the ending of the army mutiny.

On the other hand, the alliance between USTN members and non-affiliates has not produced the expected results. Nevertheless, it has raised awareness among workers of the interests at stake.

5. The trade unions as development partners

5.1 Workers' organizations and economic development

Agriculture

The USTN is implementing a rice-growing project in the Niger river valley. The scheme provides employment for workers who have lost their jobs as a result of retrenchment. The project includes housing, a school and a dispensary for workers' families. The government made the land available to the USTN, which allocated the plots and organized the workers into a cooperative. The project is currently under threat from the local population, which is claiming better compensation for the land.

Education

More than ten years ago the USTN created training schools for young people aged 20-25, whose families could not afford to educate them. The two-year course prepares them for office work and more than 1000 students enrol every year. There are already four schools and the federation plans to open four more in regions which are not yet served.

Health

Action is taken in response to epidemics and widespread health problems, such as poor eyesight. Unions in the health sector organize the free distribution of vaccines, medical consultations, surgical operations and the provision of spectacles.

5.2 Collaboration with government-led social development efforts

Unions participate in the conception and execution of government policy in public health, education and social development. The most notable example was the creation of the national social security system in 1965. The Caisse Nationale de Sécurité Sociale (CNSS) is administered by workers, employers and government. Until 1996 the Secretary-General of the USTN was president of the Executive Board of the CNSS. Collaboration with state institutions, however, depends on relations with the political authorities. In view of the tension between unions and the state, active collaboration between them has almost ceased during the last five years.

5.3 Interventions made in the general interest

Certain types of concession are granted by the government to beneficiaries supported by unions. These facilities are usually of an administrative nature, such as a permit, but they may also take the form of a land grant, as in the USTN rice-growing project.

In response to currency devaluations and salary cuts which hit the general population very hard, unions intervened to obtain price reductions on basic goods and housing rents. All union programmes include the defence of democracy and human rights, which necessarily involves them in the political struggle.

On the other hand, the democratization of union structures themselves has made little progress. Union life is very often confined to the activities of the leaders. Links with the rank-and-file workers are distant, despite the fact that their genuine participation in the movement is essential to the promotion of a democratic society.

5.4 Development cooperation

Like the government, unions depend on foreign partners for financial assistance and training. All unions have a special department responsible for strengthening existing cooperation, establishing new contacts and diversifying the development partners. The traditional partners are, of course, the international federations, but unions are forging more and more links with foreign governments, usually through their embassies. The strategy consists of four main elements:

- Appealing for solidarity and interunion cooperation in the request for funding.
- Dealing directly with development partners by drafting projects which are likely to be accepted by the funding agency to which they are submitted.
- Using the possibilities provided by agreements between the state and the development partners, such as World Bank facilities for reducing the social costs of adjustment.
- Applying for sponsorship. The appeal for class struggle and condemnation of Western imperialism is giving way to pragmatism in face of the need to gain financial support from the governments and state authorities of wealthier countries.

6. Union interventions in favour of women and youth

Women continue to be under-represented in union structures and activities as working women do not mobilize sufficiently to break the male monopoly of union leadership. Top unionists have become more aware of the need to involve women in their activities, however, particularly as many women's organizations, which were created to fight for democracy, are now competing with unions for new members.

6.1 Women workers

The USTN and the CNT have both created a department responsible for recruiting and involving more women in the union movement. The women's department has a network of links at local and regional level, which means that it participates actively in union affairs all over the country, although the four women in charge of the department have not taken on a wider management function. Under two international cooperation projects (ILO/DANIDA and PANAF) efforts are being made to organize women in the informal sector and to train them in workers' education.

6.2 Young people

Young people are even less involved than women in union activities, mainly because unions have no structures or departments to deal with their special concerns. One of the objectives of the ILO/DANIDA project is to benefit young people in the informal sector. The project provides literacy classes for them and facilitates access to credit. The union training schools mentioned in section 5.1 also assist young people of both sexes.

The unions have initiated a national plan of action to combat child labour, in the context of the ILO international programme known as IPEC. In view of the scale of the problem in West Africa, unions have created a non-governmental organization called *Fight against Child Labour*.

6.3 Relations with women's organizations and youth groups

The women's departments of the union federations have a working relationship with women's organizations and NGOs defending women's interests. They take part in each other's activities and contribute their own particular expertise.

Relations with youth groups are less formal, largely because of the lack of structures. The federations maintain solidarity with the Union des Scolaires Nigériens (USN), a students' union which is the only organized youth group in the country, and which represents more than 10,000 students at university, college and high school. In 1990 the trade unions drew up a common platform with the USN to fight for democracy and to defend Niger's educational system against the SAP.

6.4 Recruiting and training unionists

Unions make great efforts to provide members with workers' education. The USTN aims to create 250 study circles which will raise awareness among 2000 members. Women make up a quarter of the beneficiaries of training seminars and study tours, but few young people take part. Unions cannot maintain their independence without a sufficient income, and some are planning to create their own enterprises or cooperatives in order to raise revenue or provide services for their members in addition to workers' education.

6.5 Strategies on women and youth

The strategies adopted by unions in Niger are inspired by the resolutions taken at international conferences. They fall under six main headings: advancing the interests of women and young people; promoting equality between men and women; fighting discrimination against women; educating and training women and young people; strengthening relations with women's organizations; and promoting the union movement. It must be said that these points are more an expression of principle than of practice, in view of the lack of any clear policy on women and youth. Union leaders themselves need to be sensitized to gender issues before the status of women in the labour movement will be enhanced to any significant degree.

7. Summary and conclusions

In a context marked by structural adjustment programmes and the continuing impoverishment of many social groups, trade unions have to redouble their efforts to find redress for workers' grievances. This is becoming more difficult as the scope for action becomes more limited. Under such conditions, unions are obliged to join forces: they have to fight together to maintain an organizational framework, to improve the conditions of work and increase recognition of civil and political rights.

The political context is likely to determine union responses to globalization. This paper has identified the measures and strategies employed to safeguard workers' acquired rights and adapt to the new economic environment. The strategies described in section 2 relate to the following concerns:

- paying salaries, pensions and arrears;
- protecting jobs and reintegrating redundant workers;
- improving the conditions of work;
- ensuring social benefits;
- defending political and civil rights.

7.1 Strategies relating to traditional union demands

In the absence of any real social dialogue, unions resort to strikes: intermittent 48-hour strikes, strikes of indefinite length, and work stoppages because of 'incapacity'. Depending on the relations between unions, strikes may be general or sectoral. The authorities remain indifferent to this type of action, reacting neither to length nor type of strike.

Many unions hesitate to call a strike in view of the boomerang effect that generally occurs: non-payment of salaries, requisitions, arrests of strike leaders, selective layoffs and failure to mobilize the rank and file. But unions do not always accept this situation. Some have initiated "contingency strikes" and others use work stoppages.

Contingency strikes

These strikes aim to exploit the possibilities of a special event or circumstance. For example, before a World Bank or IMF mission to Niger, or during a political conflict, unions might threaten to take strike action if working conditions are not improved. The government is obliged to negotiate or to satisfy at least some of the union demands in order to reassure the financial institutions. When this type of strike occurs in education, industry or health, humanitarian groups immediately try to bring the social partners together in order to avoid the closure of schools or medical services, especially if no minimum service is guaranteed by the strikers.

Work stoppages

Another strategy for gaining the attention of employers and the general public is to stop work because of 'incapacity'. Officially there is no strike, simply a situation where it is impossible for workers to do the job in the absence of a decent salary or working conditions. The government generally yields in this situation, or partly gives way, because the suspension continues until at least some demands are granted.

The rare successes, apparent or real, of union strikes, are seldom the fruit of any careful preparation: they owe more to the political situation or to the nature of the opportunity than to a planned mass action. Already in 1990 the demand for democracy overtook USTN leaders, who had no coherent overall vision. The USTN had simply followed in the footsteps of academics and students whose protests against the SAP had set off a general political outcry.

Although unions continue to favour strike action they do not always take account of its scope or consequences. A number of social movements are so badly prepared that it seems that union leaders wish them to fail. This is one of the reasons why USTN strike calls get little support and why few people attend the meetings. A badly managed strike has repercussions on later strikes and on workers' morale.

Indefinite strikes generally get a bad press among unionists partly because of mismanagement, partly because they often have a negative effect on the strikers. This leads to demoralization and apathy among workers.

The legal approach

The limited results from strikes have led unions to turn to the courts as a way of achieving their traditional demands. They also use an administrative approach, notably through the Consultative Council of Public Sector Workers.

Unions hope that lawyers will listen to them and examine their complaints, if they cannot get a hearing from politicians or employers. This strategy has made it possible to address a number of contentious issues, as the judiciary has remained fairly independent.

Since a legitimate government was installed the unions have not hesitated to bring their disputes with employers before the courts. This is not only a way of recognizing the role of magistrates, but also a way of saving financial resources. In addition, it puts pressure on legislators to respect the laws they make. Through this approach unions are trying to adapt to the legitimate government, to explore the mechanisms open to them and to use these means to settle labour disputes. As a last resort, unions appeal to international organizations such as ILO in the case of violations of labour Conventions.

Active prevention

Unions are trying to adapt to globalization, knowing that privatization and layoffs cannot be avoided. The strategy of 'active prevention' means to anticipate privatization decisions, which are the cause of layoffs or loss of social advantages. The unions make a study of enterprises which are to be privatized to discover their exact situation. The information gained is presented in a memorandum to decision makers and the public, and all the possible ways of preserving jobs are set out. Efforts are made to avoid unjustified privatization, or the loss of a significant number of jobs.

In this way unions have managed to preserve all the jobs in some companies. In other companies they have negotiated agreements providing for 'voluntary redundancies' under conditions which are acceptable to workers.

7.2 Financial strategies

Union finances demonstrate that they have shown imagination in adapting to the new political and economic environment. The measures outlined above have allowed them to ensure the survival of their organizational framework, while maintaining a relative independence from employers. We should point out that under the Fourth Republic the CNT and certain unions were created at the instigation of the government in order to weaken the USTN. These newer union bodies enjoy better operating conditions than the USTN and the independent unions.

While unions have shown imagination, certain of the measures they have adopted give rise to some reservations. For example, if the check-off system promotes trade unionism, it also tends to make unions dependent on the government, which can paralyse their activities by refusing to apply the check-off. Even if the authorities agree to apply the system they may demand a truce or the postponement of a strike in exchange. This undermines union independence from the country's main employer.

The second reservation concerns the funds generated by trade union conferences. When a union is reduced to relying on conferences or congresses for finance, it is in trouble. Big meetings do not take place frequently and they do not generate a significant amount of money.

More fruitful are union initiatives to organize informal sector workers; this has great potential for improving union finances in view of the number of workers concerned. Nevertheless, investments are required in order to unionize this sector. Other praiseworthy initiatives include the introduction of special contributions from unions which are in a better financial situation; this is likely to strengthen solidarity between workers and unions. Another approach is to promote income-generating activities such as the sale of staple commodities, which will improve workers' standard of living and strengthen unionism.

7.3 Alliances with community organizations

Unions have made little effort to ally themselves with humanitarian associations, women's groups, political parties or cooperatives. Links with such organizations are very weak; sometimes there is even distrust and suspicion between them. There is thus a need for unions to develop strategies which will gain the support of such groups and mobilize them in favour of the workers' struggle.

7.4 Attracting new members

Strategies relating to women are mostly inspired by the recommendations of international conferences and by the ILO. Unions have shown little imagination here.

It is unfortunate that the unions do not invest sufficiently in attracting young people and looking after their interests. They have left this field open to the political parties. Unions need to extend their contacts with young people beyond the traditional links with students' associations.

As the image of unions is inextricably linked with the image of their leaders it is important for top unionists to be seen as models of integrity and rectitude. The absence of such qualities among many leaders influences employers' perceptions of the labour movement. It also influences rank-and-file workers and the general public. This affects the climate of negotiations and undermines efforts to mobilize unionists and partners in the community.

In sum, unions in Niger are poorly adapted to the new economic context of globalization in that their strategies are often traditional and inappropriate. Workers are therefore becoming defenceless against employers in a rapidly changing environment.

7.5 Outlook for the future

According to the most optimistic forecast, Niger will take at least ten years to recover from the multisectoral crises which have marked the last decade. Certainly, the Fourth Republic is no more, but much remains to be done to stimulate the economy and ensure the well-being of workers. The political creed of the Fifth Republic proclaims good governance, the stabilization of government finance and the mobilization of national resources, but election pledges have yet to be fulfilled in practice. There is a strong probability that living and working conditions will continue to deteriorate, particularly since the privatization programme begun under the previous government will be pursued with even greater zeal.

One of the ten poorest countries in the world, Niger can no longer count on her principal export, i.e. uranium, of which she is a major world producer. Owing to the collapse of the international markets Niger is now selling only 2000 tonnes of this mineral. The government has encouraged the production of cash crops, notably cotton (40,000 tonnes), but this has not achieved the expected results. (A neighbouring country, Mali, produces more than 500,000 tonnes). Oil has been discovered in the north-east of Niger, but no steps have been taken to exploit this new resource.

The privatization of public enterprises, which are a serious drain on the state, thus seems to be a way for the government to raise revenue and use its financial resources to better effect. This is particularly important in view of the foreign debt burden. In 1999 foreign debt exceeded 842,000 million FCFA (67 per cent in multilateral loans) while annual revenue was about 110,000 million FCFA. Financial constraints are formidable and the inflation rate, currently among the highest in the region at 4.5 per cent, could go up rapidly with the introduction of new tariffs in the UEMOA countries (Union Economique et Monétaire Ouest-Africaine).

Economic and financial prospects are sombre and Niger continues to depend heavily on other countries, even to keep the state running. The national budget includes significant contributions from abroad, both multilateral and bilateral. Since the new government took power public sector salaries have been paid with assistance from Belgium and France. For the last ten years the country has not formulated its own economic and financial policy, being effectively obliged to follow the recommendations of the international financial institutions. It is only out of courtesy that one speaks of the sovereign state of Niger today.

As it is required to apply structural adjustment measures which mean reducing the size of the public sector, the government will cease to be the biggest employer. The privatizations which have been announced, notably of Nigelec (electricity), SNE (water) and Sonitel (telecommunications), will be a heavy blow to employees in these sectors and to the union movement. Thousands more workers will swell the ranks of the unemployed. Job security, previously guaranteed in the public sector, will be a thing of the past and recruitment will be competitive. This means that unskilled workers will be the principal victims of the government withdrawal from state-owned enterprises. Older people and women will be disproportionately affected by compulsory retirement at the age of 50, or after 30 years' service. Young workers with more skills should benefit from this situation but the labour market is so constrained that many will remain unemployed. They will drift into the informal sector and the future will see more and more 'little jobs', and temporary and part-time work.

It is clear that the labour movement in Niger will be seriously weakened. The two existing federations will be undermined and new unions will emerge. In the best possible scenario these will be affiliated to the USTN or the CNT, unless they form a third federation consisting mainly of private sector unions. Given the sharpening of class conflict and the inglorious past of the two existing federations, there is reason to fear a strong deunionization of the world of work.

Private sector unions today are not very active in defending workers' rights, and new unions are likely to follow their example of conformity and passivity to avoid putting jobs at risk. Many workers are not psychologically prepared for the private sector, where they are at the mercy of an employer whose only goal is to accumulate wealth.

The struggle to preserve acquired social and political rights will continue to be the role of traditional unions in the public sector, notably those in education and health. The initiative for social and democratic reform will probably come from these unions, supported by their partners in the community and by youth organizations. But by accentuating social inequalities, rampant globalization may blunt all inclination to fight, and may even cause the most vulnerable workers to withdraw from the struggle.

This trend has already begun. The unions often fail to work together, although their goals are the same. At best they organize their efforts on an inter-union basis, as the federations have no impulse to fight and take no initiatives. With the current deepening economic crisis, and the growing number of unemployed people and part-time workers, the break-up of the union movement is probably irreversible. Its fragmentation is made more likely by the failure of many union leaders to project a positive image of militant unionism to workers and the general public.

Towards global social movement unionism? Trade union responses to globalization in South Africa

Andries Bezuidenhout

1. Traditional campaigns organized by the labour movement

1.1 Introduction

The rise of the independent trade union movement gave workers an opportunity to become involved in the democratization process and to take part in a parliamentary democracy for the first time in history. Institutional fora such as NEDLAC (National Economic, Development and Labour Council) made it possible to shape the transformation process in such as way that it takes a progressive form. This possibility was described as "radical reform" just before and after the 1994 elections (Adler and Webster, 1995).

However, since then the view that economic relations in South Africa can be socially regulated to bring about a more equitable society, has been influenced by the economic transition shaped by globalization. As in the rest of the world (UNDP, 1999) instead of a more equitable distribution of resources through social regulation, South Africa has moved towards increased reliance on market regulation. Instead of radical reform, Webster and Adler (1998) now describe this as a "double transition", based on a process of "bargained liberalization". The dominant discourse influencing policy makers changed from a "language of rights" to a "language of the market".

This section describes the impact of the trade union movement on the democratization process, as well as the impact of the return to economic orthodoxy on the labour movement. The discussion focuses on traditional trade union *campaigns*, but also comments on the *context* in which such campaigns took place. Section 2 focuses on more recent campaigns.

1.2 The rise of the labour movement

Labour movements in South Africa go through cycles of organization and disorganization. A number of unions emerged as social movements when industrialization was sparked by the discovery of gold and diamonds in the late 1800s. However, several of these movements disappeared again. In many cases, unions were not able to sustain themselves because of 'legal', as well as illegal forms of harassment by the Apartheid state. Structures were vulnerable, since leaders who openly associated with the liberation movements could be prosecuted under legislation designed to destabilize oppositional politics.

The first major labour movement to organize black workers emerged in the 1920s, in the form of the Industrial and Commercial Workers' Union (ICU). This general union, which achieved considerable success originally, later collapsed after failing to respond to massive growth by adapting its organizational structures. Pleas to break the general union down into smaller industrial unions were rejected. It was also plagued by internal corruption and bureaucratization (Simons and Simons, 1983, pp. 353-385).

Whereas the ICU expelled Communists from its ranks, the South African Congress of Trade Unions (SACTU) was openly aligned to the Congress movement and basically became a union movement in exile when many of its officials and office bearers were banned by the Apartheid government. By the 1960s, SACTU had disintegrated internally. However, from its new office in London, the exiled SACTU continued to play a role in the anti-Apartheid struggle. In 1990, it returned to South Africa and merged with the Congress of South African Trade Unions, COSATU (Roux, 1990).

Hence, the ICU collapsed because it was not able to adapt its structures to cope with a rapid expansion in membership. It was plagued by internal strife and corruption. On the other hand, even though the union federation was not officially banned, SACTU basically went into exile, since many of its leaders were banned, jailed and harassed by the Apartheid state machinery. Unionists learned from these experiences, and the labour movement which became strong after the 1970s was careful to build accountable workplace structures and to avoid open involvement in liberation politics.

As a result, South Africa is one of the few countries where trade unions have gained members in recent history. Of the different trade union federations, COSATU is currently the strongest, with an estimated membership of 1.7 million. This success can be traced to certain structural conditions coupled with effective forms of organization which took advantage of these conditions.

1.3 The rise of the "independent" trade unions

Ever since the Industrial Conciliation Act of 1924, black African workers were excluded from the legal definition of 'employee'. They were not allowed to strike legally, while white workers were able to bargain collectively for wages and conditions in Industrial Councils, which covered industries with sufficient employer/employee representation. By the late 1960s, South Africa was experiencing phenomenal economic growth, but the wages of African workers were kept relatively low. There were import-substitution industrialization policies, a considerable involvement of the state in the economy through public ownership of large corporations, and foreign exchange controls. A relatively high gold price coupled with cheap labour provided a secure tax base. However, the emergence of militant social movement unionism was a substantial challenge to this system.

The emergence of COSATU can be traced to the early 1970s. In January 1973, an estimated 100,000 workers went on strike: the strikes started in the Durban-Pinetown area and expanded across the country (Webster, 1995a, p. 1). They were significant in that they happened spontaneously, i.e. they were not organized by existing trade union structures. But after these strikes, workers started to organize themselves into unions, following the British model of workplace organization based on shop stewards. These new unions were referred to as 'independent trade unions', since they were seen as separate from existing unions dominated by white workers and the state (Maree, 1987, p. viii; Wood, 1999; Friedman, 1987).

Learning from previous experience, many union organizers were careful not to be openly associated with the liberation movement -- instead, they concentrated on building durable shopfloor structures based on shop stewards committees. At first, the movement struggled to survive but from the late 1970s on, membership rocketed. Unions began to develop an alternative collective bargaining strategy by ignoring the government-sanctioned system of formal exclusion and they started to sign recognition agreements with individual firms. These agreements were based on common law and resulted in the emergence of an alternative decentralized collective bargaining system. In 1979, there were five recognition agreements in place – by 1983 they had increased to 406 (Maree, 1987, p. 8). In April 1979 several unions formed the Federation of South African Trade Unions (FOSATU), with an original membership of around 20,000 (Buhlungu, 1999, p. 4).

Faced by this challenge, the Apartheid government set up the Wiehahn Commission of Enquiry in 1977. Based on the recommendations of the Commission, the government passed the Industrial Conciliation Amendment Act in 1979. African workers were included in the legal definition of 'employee' and were granted limited rights. The Wiehahn system envisioned incorporating the emerging trade unions in the centralized Industrial Council system, but instead, unions continued to expand their shopfloor structures. They used the legal space created by the new Act, specifically the legal concept of 'unfair labour practice', to successfully challenge employers in the Industrial Court. Only later, when they were much better organized on an industrial level, did unions take up collective bargaining on a sectoral level (Friedman, 1987).

From the 1950s when it was formed, the Industrial Council system was dominated by the Trade Union Council of South Africa (TUCSA), a loose federation of trade unions which mostly catered for white workers. However, when these unions were challenged by the newly emerging independent trade unions, they unsuccessfully attempted to accommodate the interests of black workers. Some of the affiliates, for instance, had separate branches for black and white members. By the early 1980s it became clear that TUCSA would not survive as a federation and in 1986 it was disbanded (Bendix, 1996, pp. 201-210).

In 1985, unions affiliated to FOSATU, together with several others including the National Union of Mineworkers (NUM), formed the Congress of South African Trade Unions (COSATU). COSATU brought together 33 unions representing a paid-up membership of 462,359 workers. This represented 33 per cent of workers who were members of registered trade unions (Buhlungu, 1999, p. 4). The new federation affirmed its commitment to the tradition of worker control. Structures were set up in accordance with this principle, where elected shop stewards played a central role. At its founding conference, COSATU committed the federation to the principles of the Freedom Charter, but did not affiliate with any political party or organization. In founding COSATU, five core principles were accepted:

- non-racialism;
- worker control;
- paid-up membership;
- international worker solidarity; and
- one industry, one union: one country, one federation.

In 1986, another significant new federation was formed when the Azanian Council of Trade Unions (AZACTU) and the Council of Unions of South Africa (CUSA), joined forces to form the National Council of Trade Unions (NACTU). The newly formed federation had an estimated membership of 200,000. Whereas COSATU adhered to the principle of non-racialism, many of the affiliated unions insisted on black leadership. Like COSATU, NACTU mostly organized blue-collar workers. Currently, NACTU has an estimated membership of 370,000 (Buhlungu, 1999, pp. 4-5; Bendix, 1996, pp. 211; 227-229).

From the mid-1980s onwards, the new independent trade unions started using the Industrial Council system to bargain with employers at sectoral level. In several industries, such as motor manufacturing, steel and engineering, clothing and textiles, Industrial Councils became central to unions' negotiating strategies. However, they continued to base their shopfloor structures on shop stewards committees. At factory and company level, they also continued to bargain collectively using recognition agreements. In effect, a dual collective bargaining system had developed, where negotiations took place at industry- as well as at company level. It should be noted, however, that these Industrial Councils were only established in industries where the union movement was strong and had sufficient representation. The significance of these fora for industrial relations as a whole in South Africa is sometimes overestimated, especially when the Councils are blamed for so-called rigidities in the labour market. Only 36.4 per cent of non-agricultural private sector employees are covered by Council agreements (ILO, 1999, p. 98).

During the 1980s, following changes to the legislative framework governing employment relations in 1979, the Apartheid government went some way towards allowing trade unions and employers to construct a bargaining framework within the legal parameters. However, towards the end of the 1980s, government became uncomfortable with the growing strength of COSATU. In 1988 it attempted to close down some of the legal space created for the union movement by amending the Labour Relations Act. The amendments changed (by codification) the definition of an 'unfair labour practice', and enabled employers to sue unions for damages caused by illegal strike action. This resulted in widespread protest from unions. Strike action forced employers to reconsider their position and negotiations between COSATU, NACTU and the South African Consultative Committee on Labour Affairs (SACCOLA), an employers' organization, resulted in an accord which condemned the changes to the Labour Relations Act. The government was forced to reconsider its position and accept that it would have to include organized labour in policy processes before changing the regulatory environment. The National Manpower Commission was established as a tripartite forum in which such negotiations could take place. This meant that the labour movement had become a national force to be reckoned with.

1.4 The transition: Political democratization

In 1989, F.W de Klerck took over from P.W. Botha as state President, and in early 1990 the government lifted the ban on all the major liberation movements. As a result, the American National Congress (ANC), the Nationalist Party government and several other political parties began negotiations on the nature of a post-Apartheid society. COSATU was closely involved in these negotiations, and established a formal alliance with the ANC and the South African Communist Party (SACP).

Simultaneously, another process of realignment was taking place. This eventually resulted in the formation of a new trade union federation whose membership surpassed that of NACTU when yet another new federation was formed in 1997. Many of the trade unions that were affiliated to the old Trade Union Council of South Africa (TUCSA) never formally joined a federation. The largest of these unions organized public sector workers, who were mainly white bureaucrats. When it became clear that the Nationalist Party would not be in government indefinitely, some of these unions began to see the need for a trade union federation that could protect the interests of their members in the public service. As a result, the Federation of South African Labour (FEDSAL) was formed. By 1994, FEDSAL had 230,000 members.

In 1997, however, FEDSAL merged with a number of other unions to form the Federation of Unions of South Africa (FEDUSA), and succeeded in expanding its membership among black employees. FEDUSA currently has a membership of 540,000.

The process of transition before the 1994 elections was peculiar in terms of policy making and governance. The country was technically still governed by the Nationalist Party, but as the ANC role in negotiations became stronger, the lack of government legitimacy to make decisions became quite stark. In 1991, for instance, the government changed the system of taxation on sales from a general sales tax (GST) to a value added tax (VAT). This affected the price of basic goods, with considerable economic implications for the poor. COSATU campaigned against the unilateral decision, and the government responded by setting up the National Economic Forum to consult on major economic decisions as part of the policy process. This forum, coupled with the National Manpower Commission, represented a shift towards a corporatist mode of policy making. During the 1990s, several other fora were set up to provide space for participation, not only for trade unions, but for stakeholders from civil society in general. These fora included the National Housing Forum and the National Electricity Forum. The government's lack of legitimacy to make decisions, coupled with a well-organized civil society in general, led to this increase in "participative democracy", albeit not formalized constitutionally.

The trade union movement, recognizing its growing role in the formulation of public policy, was mindful of the fact that it was based on fora which were fragile and temporary. Unions also realized that the gains made in terms of organizing workers were not legally entrenched as rights. Already at its 1989 National Congress, COSATU resolved to draw up a Workers' Charter to spell out certain basic rights which would enable trade unions to remain an independent force in society. In 1990, the issue received renewed attention. Both COSATU and NACTU took part in the process, which became known as the Workers' Rights Campaign. COSATU adopted a document spelling out workers' rights at a special congress in September 1993. The document recognized the gains made by the labour movement, such as participation in decision making at various levels, including plant-level collective bargaining based on recognition agreements, industry-wide participation in Industrial Councils, and national fora, such as the National Economic Forum and the National Manpower Commission. But to formalize these gains, the document made the following demands:

- First, that the new government should sign "the international labour law Conventions of the ILO concerning freedom of association, collective bargaining, workplace representation and the other Conventions dealing with fundamental rights".
- Second, that the country's new Bill of Rights should guarantee the right of workers to "join trade unions... strike on all social, political and economic issues... [and to] gain access to information from employers and the government".
- Third, that "the new constitution and law should ensure that civil society, including trade unions, is able to be actively involved in public policy making".
- Fourth, that labour legislation must be changed to provide a single statute to govern labour relations "for all workers throughout the economy", as well as legislation governing basic conditions of employment for the whole economy. It also argued that negotiations with trade unions should be mandatory, and that centralized collective bargaining arrangements should be instituted in every industry.

Also in 1993, while COSATU was campaigning for the entrenchment of basic labour rights in the country's Bill of Rights, the Nationalist Party policy makers were expressing concern about the trend towards centralization in industrial relations. Already then, the "language of rights" used by the labour movement was challenged by the "language of the market". These calls were legitimated again in 1996, when the new government abandoned a macroeconomic policy which prioritized the social regulation of economic relations.

While the ANC, the Nationalist Party, and other stakeholders were negotiating the nature of a future dispensation, COSATU, and the National Union of Metalworkers of South Africa (NUMSA) in particular, were busy formulating a strategy for social transformation in a post-Apartheid society. The strategy saw a central role for the state in the reconstruction of South African society. Gotz (2000) argues that this document was used by the ANC negotiators as a trade-off to convince the "left" to accept certain concessions made to the Nationalist Party in an attempt to break the deadlock in the negotiations. One must keep in mind the escalating levels of violence in the country and the concern of negotiators about an apocalyptic outcome to the process. The strategy was taken on board by the ANC as its election manifesto, and, after eight drafts, became known as the Reconstruction and Development Programme (RDP).

The RDP, even though considerably watered down and vague in terms of specific goals compared with the original document, maintained that the state should play a central role in the reconstruction process. Significantly, the labour movement had succeeded in shaping the agenda, at least on a formal level, of the ANC, its alliance partner. The ANC, in its turn, was able to use COSATU structures to campaign in the 1994 elections. At that time, it seemed possible that the labour movement, through its alliance with the ANC, but still maintaining its independence, could drive a programme of "radical reform" – using policy-making institutions and its strategic alliance with the strongest political party to drive a process of national reconstruction aimed at meeting basic needs.

In 1994, the ANC was elected as the majority party in the new Government of National Unity. During the first years after the elections, COSATU was able to achieve many of the goals set out in the Workers' Rights Campaign. First, the National Manpower Commission and the National Economic Forum were replaced by a new body, the National Economic, Development and Labour Council (NEDLAC). Second, through negotiations on a new constitution and mass campaigns, COSATU succeeded in entrenching several workers' rights in the Bill of Rights. These included the right to strike and to form trade unions. Third, the new government ratified several international labour Conventions. Fourth, a new Labour Relations Act was negotiated in NEDLAC, formalizing several campaigns of the late 1980s and the early 1990s. While not succeeding in demands for mandatory centralized collective bargaining, dispute resolution mechanisms were streamlined and certain organizational rights were operationalized. The Act provided for workplace fora which, although COSATU is still sceptical about their usefulness, provided access to information and a form of co-determination at workplace level.

1.5 Continuities: Economic orthodoxy

The philosophy of the RDP, coupled with the potential impact of reform in the labour relations environment based on "empowerment", provided a powerful alternative to the Nationalist Party's Normative Economic Model, which argued for a limited government role in economic and development policy. This alternative "language", as indicated, was a "language of rights". In 1993 a group of researchers, the Macroeconomic Research Group (MERG), attempted to translate this "language" into a "programme" based on a macroeconomic model. They used a neo-Keynesian approach, which implied a central role for the state in rectifying structural conditions created by the Apartheid economy. This programme was never taken up into the structures of the ANC, for various reasons (see Marais, 1998; Padayachee, 1998). At the level of formal policy the ANC had seemingly adopted a left-Keynesian stance, but already in 1993 it had made a number of concessions on economic policy. According to Webster and Adler (1998, p. 14), these concessions signalled a move to the right, well in advance of the formal adoption of liberal macroeconomic policies in 1996.

In late 1995, the Government of National Unity announced a programme of privatization. It was clear that an alternative language was developing, showing continuities with the Nationalist Party programme. In 1996, a business think tank, the South Africa Foundation (SAF), released a document which proposed to increase growth through a programme of economic liberalization. Significantly, it introduced the "language of flexibility", arguing that the South African labour market was rigid as a result of the Bargaining Council system and other regulations applied to the labour market. The release of this document was the first real challenge to the "language of rights" in the public domain. In the context of globalization, the government had to scale down "restrictive" practices and allow the market to determine the level of wages. The document argued that the labour market had to be more flexible (see Bezuidenhout and Kenny, 1999).

Even though arguments that the labour market was rigid had no empirical foundation, and still do not, the issue of labour market flexibility became a major public debate after 1996. Several studies, including some made by the ILO (Standing, 1996; ILO, 1999), showed the contrary – the labour market was extremely flexible. But the "language of flexibility" had now become a wider critique of the legitimacy of the labour movement's position in society.

Following a rapid depreciation in the value of the rand in 1996, Trevor Manuel, the newly appointed Minister of Finance, released a new macroeconomic strategy in Parliament, called Growth, Employment and Redistribution (GEAR). This strategy supported the broad approach proposed by the South Africa Foundation as favoured by the Nationalist Party in the early 1990s. It committed the government to speeding up privatization, to monetary liberalization, fiscal discipline, and a "flexible labour market", even though the chapter on the labour market was "brief and vague", in the words of Maria Ramos, Director-General of the Department of Finance.

Of course, COSATU reacted strongly to the government position that the new strategy was "non-negotiable". This is understandable, since the government is required by the NEDLAC Act to consult the social partners in NEDLAC before making policy decisions on the economy and labour. The federation was unable to use its position in NEDLAC or as an alliance partner of the ANC to shape the broad principles underlying the country's response to globalization. Instead, they are allowed to negotiate the details in NEDLAC, with the Chamber dealing with fiscal and financial policy becoming virtually defunct. "Radical reform" became a process of "bargained liberalization".

Instead of shaping South Africa's broad economic policy, COSATU had to focus on negotiating draft legislation, such as the Basic Conditions of Employment Act and the Employment Equity Act. These negotiations were influenced by the calls for "labour market flexibility", which had redefined the policy agenda towards the "language of the market". Apart from these negotiations, they were involved in monitoring trade negotiations, such as the agreement with the European Union, and attempts to keep the "social clause" on the agenda, with partial success (see Gostner, 1997).

1.6 Conclusion

The labour movement in South Africa took the shape of social movement unionism. From the early 1970s onwards, the independent trade union movement slowly opened up space for itself through campaigns linked to the broader anti-Apartheid struggle. South Africa was transformed from a labour repressive society based on racism to one in which basic labour and human rights are enshrined in the Constitution. In the 1990s, unions attempted to use their alliance with the new government to bring about a more egalitarian economic order. Instead, in 1996, the government announced a new approach in the form of GEAR, which embraced the concept of globalization. The state withdrew from economic restructuring to enable markets to operate "freely". The "language of the market" became dominant and closed down some of the space available for the labour movement to insist on including social concerns in economic policy.

Commentators still disagree on the extent to which globalization is affecting national sovereignty. In the South African context, Webster and Adler (1998, p. 1) propose that certain arguments exaggerate the power of globalization. They point out that all capital should not be equated with financial capital, and that "many firms are highly immobile and employers may not only be profit-maximizers, but also risk-avoiders interested in steady, long-term and sustainable profit". The global is shaped by the local, they argue, and South Africa has built the institutions in which a class compromise can take place to repeat the political compromise on an economic level. Central to this class-compromise is organized labour's ability to shape the outcomes.

It is clear that globalization, as an economic force or as an ideology, has fundamentally reshaped South Africa's approach to managing its economy. But this process took place in a context of political democratization – not only in terms of a parliamentary democracy based on constitutionalism, but also in terms of structures such as NEDLAC where policy can be shaped. But COSATU's position as part of a social movement has also been altered. The labour movement now has to defend gains made as a result of campaigns for labour rights and political democratization in the context of globalization. As indicated, Webster and Adler (1998) describe this as a process of "bargained liberalization". However, institutions where liberalization is negotiated can themselves come under pressure. Therefore, a narrow approach *exclusively* based on campaigns in the nation-state is no longer an option for progressive trade unions. In this context, section 2 provides an assessment of more recent union campaigns in response to globalization in South Africa.

2. New campaigns in the context of globalization

2.1 Introduction

In the new dispensation, the labour movement formalized many of its campaigns of the 1980s as gains. However, increased reliance on market regulation forced the labour movement, and specifically COSATU, to consider new campaigns. In fact, in 1996 the union federation established a "Commission of Enquiry" to assess the movement's position in the context of these changes. The Commission was chaired by Connie September, then second vice-president of COSATU, and became known as the *September Commission* when the final report was published in 1997. This report provides considerable insight into the thinking of trade union leaders in the context of the double transition.

This section draws on the September Commission report, as well as several surveys, interviews and other studies to describe how union campaigns have changed in South Africa in the context of globalization and the double transition. A central argument is that COSATU as a union federation is undergoing a transition of its own. This transition has to do with the fact that the federation has realized many of the objectives it fought for in the 1980s. In the context of a parliamentary democracy, the federation is losing many of its social movement characteristics and, even though economically located in the developing world, is moving into a position similar to many Western European and North American unions. This is linked with the fact that COSATU's gains are coming under threat as a result of competition for investment from neighbouring countries as well as Asia. Whereas COSATU used to draw on support from unions in the North, the federation now finds that it has to support the struggles of social movement unions in countries where basic human and labour rights are still denied by authoritarian regimes. Consequently, COSATU as a union federation will retain some of its social movement characteristics, while exhibiting some similarities with the "older" unions of the North.

2.2 Membership campaigns

Standing (1997a) argues that globalization leads to a segmentation of labour markets. This has to do with new opportunities opening up globally for skilled professionals, but also with the casualization of work at the 'lower' end of the labour market. No reliable data are available on the extent of casualization in South Africa, but a number of studies indicate rapid casualization in several industries including mining, retail, construction, transport and manufacturing (see Bezuidenhout and Kenny, 1999).

It has to be noted that this process of casualization is taking place in a labour market that is already historically segmented (Kenny and Webster, 1999). In addition, there is no comprehensive social security system that can alleviate the social impact of underemployment (Bezuidenhout and Kenny, 1999).

However, since the early 1970s, trade union membership as well as trade union density has increased as a result of successful membership campaigns. A total of 673,000 workers were members of trade unions in 1976. In 1998, the number had increased to 3.8 million, of whom more than 1.7 million were members of COSATU. Union density in the non-agricultural formal sector of the economy increased from 18 per cent in 1985 to 51 per cent in 1998.

According to Barrett (1993), this growth in membership can be attributed to the successful organization of three major sectors in the economy. Unions in the manufacturing sector currently account for 30.2 per cent of COSATU membership, the National Union of Mineworkers accounts for 14.9 per cent and public sector unions account for 36.4 per cent.

These three categories of union account for almost 82 per cent of all COSATU members. The remainder are unions organizing construction workers, agricultural and plantation workers, and workers in the service sector. Rapid growth in public sector union membership reflects large-scale restructuring in that sector. Where workers felt secure in their jobs in the past, retrenchments and outsourcing are contributing to insecurity. Another factor is the privatization of certain sectors. It should be noted here that FEDUSA, the second largest union federation, has a strong membership base among white-collar workers, mostly in the civil service and the public sector.

Membership campaigns have been successful in manufacturing and the public sector, where workers seem to have relatively stable jobs. However, unions have been less successful in 'vulnerable' sectors – particularly services, construction and agriculture. Included in the service sector is the large number of African women engaged as domestic workers. The inability of unions to organize 'vulnerable' sectors is reflected in the fact that men make up 71 per cent of union members, while women, who are mostly employed in the informal sector and casual jobs, only constitute 29 per cent of members.

However, 37 per cent of men in formal sector employment are union members against 32 per cent of women in the formal sector. This implies that women in formal employment are more readily organized than women in casual jobs and the informal sector (Naidoo, 1999, p. 18). Unions have also not been able to attract younger people. Only 7 per cent of workers between the ages of 15 and 24 have joined a trade union, against 35 per cent of those between 25 and 34. This may relate to the high levels of youth unemployment, but when one considers only formal employment, the proportion of young workers who are members of unions is still significantly lower than older workers.

The increased casualization of employment contracts also has the potential to erode the membership base of unions in well-organized sectors. The September Commission expressed concern about COSATU's record of not organizing the "growing layers of 'flexible' workers". It pointed out that, if the federation continued with no change, "subcontracting, casualizing [and] labour brokering [may] become more common... Ultimately COSATU could end up being based in a shrinking section of the working class, as happened to trade unions in a number of countries" (COSATU, 1997, p. 125). The Commission proposed six themes for organizing casual workers. These included an annual campaign to recruit vulnerable workers; the creation of advisory services; advocacy through statutory bodies such as bargaining councils and wage boards; educating union officials and shop stewards; centralized collective bargaining to institute minimum labour standards; and insisting that parastatals and the public services comply with minimum labour standards.

Apart from proposing strategies to unionize casual workers in relatively well-organized sectors, the September Commission also recommended certain strategies to organize 'vulnerable' workers in 'vulnerable' sectors.

On the recommendation of the September Commission, the Sixth National Congress of COSATU, held in 1997, resolved to start a process to form trans-industrial "super unions". This touches on one of the founding principles of COSATU, namely "one industry, one union". The 1997 resolution therefore adapted the COSATU model of industrial unionism to a form of trans-industrial unionism.

Since the 1997 National Congress, several unions have merged. However, these fusions did not involve unions operating in "vulnerable" sectors merging into strong industrial unions. Hence, the September Commission proposals for dealing with the casualization of work in well-organized sectors of the economy, such as manufacturing and mining, can be accommodated within existing union structures. The proposals focus on advocacy within existing regulatory frameworks, such as bargaining councils, wage boards and agreements between unions and individual firms. The introduction of advice centres for casual workers indicates a different approach to servicing a certain layer of employees. Unions will have to link up more closely with advice centres, community-based organizations and other civil bodies if they want to succeed in representing these workers. Another point is that union membership fees are subtracted from salaries by stop orders. This method of financing is based on the assumption that workers have a permanent and consistent flow of income, which is very often not the case with casual and/ or subcontract workers. Unions will therefore have to rethink their approach to signing up members and collecting union dues.

The fact that the September Commission put these issues on the agenda does not, however, mean that the labour movement is acting effectively to address them. As the Commission itself acknowledges, responses are generally piecemeal. Attempts to deal with casualization and workers in vulnerable sectors remain rhetorical to large extent.

2.3 Structure and finances of unions

Since the early 1990s, COSATU has undergone substantial structural changes, partly in response to the challenges posed by globalization, but also as a result of engagement in various national institutions, such as NEDLAC. In addition, the coming of parliamentary democracy opened other avenues for the labour movement to influence policy making. As a result, COSATU is losing some of its characteristics as a social movement union.

There has always been tension in trade unions between 'democracy' and 'efficiency'. This tension plays out on many levels - between members and officials, between members and elected representatives, and between the structures at different levels – local, regional and national (Buhlungu, 1999). In this context, the 'independent' trade union movement in South Africa is largely based on organization at workplace level based on shop stewards. The shop stewards have always been central to plant, local, regional and national structures. COSATU and its unions have maintained the principle that the number of representatives on executive committees who are shop stewards, i.e. actual wage workers, should be greater than the number of union officials, i.e. people employed by trade unions or federations. Shop stewards and officials are not allowed to take decisions on behalf of workers without proper mandates.

But the tradition of 'worker control' seems to have undergone changes in the past decade. These changes should be seen not only in the context of the labour movement's involvement in more structures, such as NEDLAC, but also in the context of the rapid growth of unions from the late 1980s until recently. The average size of a trade union affiliated to COSATU is just over 100,000 members, with structures spread geographically across the whole country. This massive growth had certain implications for trade union structures:

- The influx of a large number of new members put pressure on the existing traditions of worker control. Many new shop stewards were appointed, who did not necessarily share the collective memory of the post-1973 model of organization (Marie, 1992, p. 21). A survey conducted in 1991 found that 28 per cent of COSATU shop stewards were in their twenties. This implied that many were not experienced and did not share the "union traditions of democratic worker control" (Collins, 1994, p. 30).
- The increase in membership "necessitated complex nationally centralized structures". This resulted in a "greater division of labour and responsibilities between structures and among staff" (Marie, 1992, p. 21).
- A large membership body demands greater focus on servicing, which meant a shift from an organizing model of trade unionism towards a servicing model (Marie, 1992). Apart from more demands for effective servicing, shop stewards were required to attend more and more meetings at different levels. Many unions responded to these demands by reducing the frequency of branch meetings, to enable shop stewards to engage in regional and national structures (Collins, 1994, p. 31).
- To deal with the increased workload, the number of full-time shop stewards has been expanding, enabling elected representatives to play a more central role in the daily running of union matters. This practice has been criticised for removing shop stewards from the daily experience of the workers they are supposed to represent (Collins, 1994, pp. 33-34).

However, several surveys have found that members of unions affiliated to COSATU still regularly elect shop stewards, usually by secret ballot (Collins, 1994; Wood, 1999). A survey conducted in 1994 found that 84 per cent of shop stewards were elected by members, 13 per cent were appointed by union leaders, and 1 per cent were appointed by management. In a 1998 survey, the number of shop stewards elected by members increased to 92 per cent. Only 3 per cent of workers reported that shop stewards were appointed by leaders, with management appointments remaining constant at 1 per cent. These figures actually imply an expansion of shopfloor democracy in terms of the election of shop stewards. Indeed, 93 per cent of workers interviewed in 1998 pointed out that shop steward elections are held at least every three years (Wood, 1999, pp. 10-12). The 1999 COSATU National Congress mandated the federation to coordinate shop steward elections for all the affiliates on an annual basis. In future, these elections will take place at the same time, giving the election process a higher profile.

A major shift, which occurred from 1994 to 1998, is *how workers view the role of shop stewards*. In 1994, 26 per cent of workers felt that shop stewards "had the right to represent workers' interests as they saw fit, or that they had discretion within a broad mandate". In the 1998 survey, this number increased to 50 per cent. Wood argues that this could reflect the "increased complexity of the bargaining environment", where "industrial relations are increasingly institutionalized". The proportion of workers who felt that shop stewards should be dismissed when they failed to do what their constituencies desired remained constant at 93 per cent in both surveys. Wood concludes: "It is evident that an increasing number of workers are willing to trust shop stewards to engage with management on their behalf, as long as they report back from time to time"(1999, p. 13). However, 71 per cent of the workers interviewed in the 1998 survey said that they attended union meetings at least once a month. This number had declined from 77 per cent in 1994 (Wood, 1999, p. 9).

There also seemed to be a *generational shift* in terms of worker opinions on the role of shop stewards. Younger workers were more likely to give shop stewards a broad mandate, or treat them as a form of indirect democracy. The views of older workers, however, conformed much more to the militant form of direct participation based on worker control. The data confirm the view that the role of shop stewards as "simple bearers of the mandate" (Marie, 1992, p.23), is changing towards a role of active representation with more discretion.

Apart from changes in the relationship between members and shop stewards, there also seems to be a shift in the role of full-time union officials. This has to do with the complex challenges posed by rapid transformation. Unions tend to rely more on experts to respond to pressing deadlines, leading to what is described as 'bureaucratization' (see Buhlungu, 1997, p. 44). A new generation of officials "are coming in at a phase where there is an increasing tendency for officials to lead office bearers rather than the other way round" (Collins, 1994, p. 37). Concerns were also expressed about the 'brain drain' from COSATU. Experienced union leaders were lost to Parliament, the structures of the governing African National Congress and, ironically, big business and some of the unions' own new investment corporations. According to Baskin (1996, p. 15) COSATU lost about 80 of the 1,450 officials employed by affiliates in 1994 alone. In 1999, six of COSATU's four national office bearers left the labour movement, some to pursue careers as parliamentarians, and one as a provincial premier.

In the 1970s and 1980s, many unions had a policy of not paying their officials more than the highest paid workers in the industries which they organized (Buhlungu, 1997, p. 17). However, in response to the so called "brain drain" of union officials (Buhlungu, 1994), COSATU and its affiliates have been moving towards higher remuneration structures in an attempt to retain experienced officials. Standard union packages include benefits such as a car allowance, housing allowance, medical aid and provident funds (Buhlungu, 1997, p. 17).

A consequence may be that union officials move further away from the class position of their members. Internally, the movement has also seen an increased wage gap between officials at different levels. Packages are generally linked to grading systems. Buhlungu's survey also showed that 63.4 per cent of employed officials did not see themselves working in the union movement in five years' time. Furthermore, it indicated that a majority of [union] officials (57 per cent) had only been working in the union for four years or less.

This implies a careerist attitude among a large proportion of union officials, as well as inexperience resulting from rapid staff turnover. According to Buhlungu (1997), this means a process of "generational transformation" is taking place among trade union officials.

The above structural changes relate to individual unions. But COSATU has also consciously engaged in a process of organizational restructuring in order to "coordinate and reinforce the collective bargaining strategies of the affiliates" in the context of the "likelihood that collective bargaining will come under increasing pressure from employers under the guise of international competitiveness and 'globalization'"(COSATU, 1997, p. 192). These changes implied the setting up of new decision-making bodies and stronger implementation structures.

A new body, the Central Committee, was set up to enable the federation to speed up policy decisions. As the second highest decision-making structure, this body meets annually to consider policy matters. The first Central Committee meeting took place in June 1998. Apart from the annual meetings, a Central Executive Committee (CEC) was set up to meet twice a year with the national office bearers to consider policy matters.

The National Executive Committee, which in the past met only six times per year, was made smaller, and now meets once a month. This body considers operational and administrative issues and is responsible for driving the negotiations strategy of the federation. Also, instead of once every four years, the National Congress now meets once every three years.

2.4 Regional and global action

All three of the major trade union federations, COSATU, the Federation of Unions of South Africa (FEDUSA), and the National Council of Trade Unions (NACTU), are affiliated to the International Congress of Free Trade Unions (ICFTU). Several other unions are affiliated to the ICFTU international trade secretariats. In addition, both COSATU and NACTU are involved in the Organization for African Trade Union Unity (OATUU), as well as the Southern Africa Trade Union Coordinating Council (SATUCC).

Transnational involvement is not new to the South African labour movement. However, engagement with organized workers and bodies set up by or "for" them, has certainly not been unproblematic. It has been characterized by immense levels of solidarity at times, but also by suspicion and animosity. Significantly, the relationship between South African unions and global players, such as ICFTU and the World Federation of Trade Unions (WFTU) was shaped by the internal struggle against Apartheid, as well as by global Cold War politics. Southall (1995) argued that COSATU was able to draw on resources from unions in the North while maintaining its independence through a policy of non-alignment. However, now that COSATU has achieved many of the campaign goals of the 1980s, its position as a recipient of assistance is changing to one where it is forced to become more outward looking and to contribute to the struggles of other social movement unions in Southern Africa and Asia.

Following internal persecution by the Apartheid state in the 1950s and 1960s, the South African Congress of Trade Unions (SACTU) went into exile, along with several of the liberation movements. At that time it used its links with WFTU to lobby in the ILO against the representation of the Trade Union Council of South Africa (TUCSA), which was a racially based federation. Following this, and several other campaigns, South Africa was expelled from the ILO in 1963 (Southall, 1996, pp. 8-9).

When small industrial unions emerged after a wave of strikes in 1973, several trade unions from across the globe, mostly affiliated to ICFTU, offered assistance. ICFTU itself became more involved in assisting the emerging independent trade union movement. In 1974, it set up the Coordinating Committee for South Africa (COCOSA), which, according to Southall (1996, pp. 10-11) became involved in industrial action to boycott South African goods, assisting the emerging trade unions with legal costs, pressing transnational corporations to recognize South African trade unions, and channelling and coordinating financial assistance from ICFTU affiliates to South African trade unions (more than US$6.6 million from 1976 to 1984).

ICFTU and its affiliates provided funding to a broad spectrum of the emerging black unions - to FOSATU (later COSATU), unions affiliated to what became known as NACTU, and other independent unions (Fraser, 1991, p. 27). However, in the context of the Cold War, COSATU actively pursued an approach of non-alignment. Likewise, NACTU was not formally affiliated to ICFTU, even though its predecessor, CUSA was (Southall, 1996, pp. 10-11; Naidoo, 1991; Ngcukana, 1991). SACTU in exile was not only suspicious of ICFTU's role in South Africa, but was originally also hostile towards the emerging independent trade union movement. The Congress insisted that it was the sole representative of the South African working class abroad and that funding to South African unions had to be channelled through SACTU.

However, ICFTU and its affiliates maintained direct links with South African trade unions. In fact, South African trade unionists formed networks with many unionists abroad through attending short educational courses. Southall (1996, p. 15) argued that this resulted in "a formidable network of personal, sectoral and professional contacts which proved of inestimable value during particular industrial struggles or when unions became subject to political attack".

International solidarity became prominent especially in industries with globalized production, such as steel and motor manufacturing, and in industries that were particularly vulnerable to tariff cuts, such as clothing and textiles. In the case of the National Union of Textile Workers (NUTW) and the American Clothing and Textile Workers' Union (ACTWU), unionists had first established personal contacts through international meetings. ACTWU vice-president John Hudson (1991, p. 41) pointed out that his union members were particularly interested in NUTW because of "a desire to further contribute to the fight against Apartheid". Through their involvement, the unions supported each other on matters such as health and safety training, and exchanged research materials on companies operating in both countries. When NUTW merged with another union to form the South African Clothing and Textile Workers' Union (SACTWU), they also drew on the experience of ACTWU, which had gone through a merger previously. Hudson mentioned specifically that his union learned a lot from NUTW organizing strategies.

These "direct links" were sometimes successful in campaigns, and sometimes not. Southall (1996, pp. 15, 17) argued that South African unions formed closer links with trade unions generally affiliated to ICFTU more than WFTU, since they were linked through transnational corporations. Unions organizing in former Socialist countries could not offer the same level of assistance as their counterparts in the capitalist world. Towards the end of the 1980s, SACTU "quietly buried" its opposition to direct links, and in the context of the British anti-Apartheid movement, had a much more harmonious relationship with the TUC.

The picture changed considerably with the collapse of the Soviet Union, and with the lifting of bans on the ANC, the SACP, the Pan African Congress (PAC), and other liberation organizations in 1990. Politically, South Africa began negotiations on the nature of a post-Apartheid society. Internally, COSATU played an important role, now in formal alliance with the ANC and the SACP. In 1990, COSATU put the issue of international relations on its agenda. Jay Naidoo, then General Secretary of the federation, pointed out that this was for very specific reasons, mentioning "particularly the world restructuring of the economy, and the loosening of the political climate internationally with the formal ending of the Cold War and the collapse of Eastern European regimes". In this context, Naidoo felt that "workers are going to begin sharing common problems, particularly where there is an unbridled move to free market systems, where the lives and jobs of workers, the benefits they have gained, are being jeopardized" (Naidoo, 1991, p. 18).

COSATU began to re-evaluate its relationship with international bodies such as ICFTU and WFTU, holding its first meeting with the Executive Council of ICFTU in December 1990. COSATU also attempted to "normalize" its relationship with the American Federation of Labour - Council for Industrial Organizations (AFL-CIO), having already established strong links with affiliates of AFL-CIO.

On 15 March 1991, COSATU appointed its first international officer, in the person of Mcebisi Msizi, who had worked for the exiled union federation SACTU. At this time, COSATU also increased its activities in Africa generally, attending the congress of the Organization of African Trade Union Unity (OATUU) for the first time in 1990. Apart from establishing relations with OATUU, COSATU had also been building links with unions in the Southern African region, through the Southern African Trade Union Coordinating Committee (SATUCC). The federation was involved in setting up a social charter for workers' rights. Already in the 1980s NACTU had established links with OATUU and was actively involved in SATUCC. It affiliated to OATUU even before COSATU did so in 1991.

Where COSATU and NACTU traditionally drew on support from unions in the North, there was already a realization in the early 1990s that they had to engage with other unions in Africa, and Southern Africa in particular. South African unions, in the context of the Southern African region, increasingly occupy a position similar to the unions of Western Europe and the United States globally.

In the early 1990s, COSATU was also involved in other international activities, mainly through conferences with labour movements from elsewhere. They included the Indian Ocean Regional Initiative and joint conferences with the Italian General Confederation of Labour and the Workers' Centre of Brazil.

In February 1993, at a time of increased violence in South Africa, COSATU and NACTU hosted a delegation from ICFTU, which included unionists from the Scandinavian countries, Italy, Japan, the Netherlands, the United Kingdom, the United States and Zambia. The Coordinating Committee on South Africa (COCOSA) met in South Africa for the first time since it was founded in 1976. Representatives from the international trade secretariats were also present.

Towards the end of the 1990s trade unions became more aware of the need for global cooperation. Both NACTU and COSATU formally affiliated with ICFTU and its members. In 1998, FEDUSA also affiliated with ICFTU.

COSATU's involvement in OATUU and SATUCC led to more active campaigns in the region. COSATU's role led to the federation supporting the campaigns of other unions, rather than being supported. But individual unions have also been involved in transnational campaigns, especially in the clothing and textile industries. The result of a recent campaign is the *Maputo Declaration on the Textiles, Clothing and Leather Industries*, signed on 9 May 1999. Unions from Lesotho, Malawi, Mauritius, Mozambique, South Africa, Tanzania, Zambia and Zimbabwe met in Maputo to discuss the state of the industry in the region.

The participants identified common problems such as the erosion of labour standards, the impact of structural adjustment programmes on their economies, export processing zones eroding labour standards, the impact of tariff reductions as well as large-scale smuggling of goods, and the trading of second-hand clothing intended as donations. The Declaration called for more appropriate macroeconomic policies, the promotion of worker rights, links between trade and labour rights, a more careful consideration of the reduction of import tariffs on specific industries, and the integration of export processing zones into national economies.

The involvement of SACTWU in this initiative illustrates the point that, whereas it drew on international support for recognition struggles in the 1970s and the 1980s it now contributes to the struggle for basic rights of other unions in the region. The approach of the Maputo Declaration to trade unionism reflects COSATU's and its predecessors' model of unions controlled by workers and strong shop stewards committees, linked to broader campaigns for democratization, i.e. social movement unionism.

Currently, the 'new internationalism' is on COSATU's broader agenda, and the federation hosted several high profile conferences and congresses in South Africa in 1999. The first was the Seventh Ordinary Congress of OATUU, which was held in Johannesburg in September, and the second took place in October 1999, when COSATU hosted a conference of the Southern Initiative on Globalization and Trade Union Rights (SIGTUR). Unionists from Australia, India, Indonesia, Republic of Korea, Pakistan, Philippines and South Africa attended the conference. The third congress, that of the International Federation of Chemical, Energy, Mine and General Workers' Union (ICEM), was held in Durban from 3 to 5 November. Apart from these three high profile conferences, the general congress of ICFTU is scheduled to take place in Durban in 2000.

Towards the end of the 1990s all three major trade union federations in South Africa formally affiliated to ICFTU, and are attempting to shape the direction of the federation so that it represents the interests of unions in developing countries.

2.5 Collective action and institutional benefits

The institutional context in which collective action takes place in South Africa has changed considerably in the past decade. The changes build on historical arrangements while attempting to introduce, albeit unsuccessfully, a new institutional framework. The Labour Relations Act of 1995 envisioned three levels of collective bargaining, and it was expected that this structure would lead to a coordinated labour market (Klerck, 1998, p. 101).

National-level bargaining

Since the late 1980s, the labour movement has engaged in negotiations with government and organized business at national level. New institutions were formed to accommodate the process: first the National Manpower Commission and the National Economic Forum, and since 1994, the National Economic, Development and Labour Council (NEDLAC). The three major trade union federations, COSATU, FEDUSA and NACTU, all take part in NEDLAC.

NEDLAC consists of four chambers, i.e. the labour market chamber, the trade and industry chamber, the public finance and monetary policy chamber, and the development chamber. In the first three chambers, government, labour and business are represented. The fourth chamber, however, includes "civil" representatives as well as workers, employers and government (Webster, 1995b).

The NEDLAC Act establishes the objectives of the Council as follows. NEDLAC shall:

- strive to promote the goals of economic growth, participation in economic decision making and social equity;
- seek to reach consensus and conclude agreements on matters pertaining to economic and social policy;
- consider all proposed labour legislation relating to labour market policy before it is introduced in Parliament;
- consider all significant changes to social and economic policy before it is implemented or introduced in Parliament;
- encourage and promote the formulation of coordinated policy on social and economic matters (Gostner and Joffe, 1998, p. 133).

Hence, the process of political democratization opened up space for the labour movement to influence policy making. Also, its position in society is recognized through the formalization of workers' rights as human rights that are protected in the Bill of Rights enshrined in the Constitution. In the context of the double transition, however, commentators differ as to whether these institutions enable the labour movement to shape the direction of policy, or whether it merely "institutionalizes" the labour movement to accept the government's macroeconomic strategy.

Since 1996, the government's position that macroeconomic policy cannot be negotiated in NEDLAC has curtailed the extent to which the labour movement was able to use the Council to influence the national developmental policy framework. Instead, NEDLAC became an institution in which the implementation of liberalization could be negotiated.

Also, labour's participation in NEDLAC is hampered by a lack of capacity to engage consistently in complex negotiations around issues such as trade agreements. Gostner and Joffe (1998, pp. 144-146) argue that labour representatives have not succeeded in moving from a reactive mode of operation into a proactive mode. This does not only relate to the undermining role of the non-negotiability of the macroeconomic framework; it is also because labour has not succeeded in setting up functional structures, or a coherent framework of mandating. There are also difficulties in mobilizing workers around the very complex issues under negotiation.

Industry-level bargaining

Meso-level collective bargaining usually takes place in bargaining councils. These councils can be industry-wide, but some are also geographically determined. The functions of bargaining councils are to:

- negotiate collective bargaining agreements concerning wages, working conditions and other procedural issues;
- administer and enforce agreements,
- prevent and resolve disputes;
- promote and establish training and education schemes;
- establish and administer benefit schemes; and
- deal with requests for exemptions from agreements (Webster, 1999, p.6).

It is important to note that agreements on wages and conditions reached in bargaining councils can be extended by the Minister of Labour to non-parties in the industry or geographical region where the bargaining council is registered. Employers can apply for exemption where they consider the requirements as too onerous.

The extent of the move towards meso-level collective bargaining has been overstated. Only 32 per cent of non-agricultural employees are covered by bargaining council agreements. When the Chamber of Mines is included, this figure increases to 36.4 per cent of workers in the non-agricultural private sector. The inclusion of the Transnet bargaining council (the transport parastatal) and the public sector bargaining council artificially inflates the number of employees covered by bargaining council agreements.

It is also important to note that collective bargaining at industry level is based on voluntarism. The parties can only register bargaining councils if there is sufficient representation from both organized labour and organized employers, and if both parties agree.

The Labour Relations Act also provides for Statutory Councils, sometimes described as "trainee bargaining councils". These can execute the functions of a bargaining council, but wage agreements cannot be extended to non-parties. These councils can be established in industries where employers or employees have a representation of 30 per cent. The aim of this was to break the deadlock in negotiations on voluntary versus mandatory centralized collective bargaining (Webster, 1999, p. 7).

Bargaining councils have recently come under attack, especially in the framework of calls for labour market flexibility. The South Africa Foundation (1996) blamed labour market rigidities on the extension of bargaining council agreements to non-parties. However, it should be noted that only a third of private sector employees are covered by such agreements. Also, as indicated, firms can apply for exemption from bargaining council agreements. In 80 per cent of cases, these exemptions are granted (ILO, 1999). The South African Enterprise Labour Flexibility Survey found that larger companies – between 150 and 400 workers – generally apply for exemptions. Very few firms with less than 50 workers apply. This may imply that small business does not find bargaining council agreements restrictive. An alternative explanation may be that they simply ignore such agreements (Standing, 1997b).

Nevertheless, very few new bargaining councils are currently registered and it seems unlikely that a trend towards centralization will continue. In fact, a number of bargaining councils have been deregistered since 1995.

Plant-level collective bargaining

As pointed out in section 1, South Africa has developed a dual collective bargaining system, where wages and conditions are negotiated at industry-as well as at plant-level, the latter according to recognition agreements. Influenced by the German model of Works Councils coupled with centralized wage negotiations, the authors of the Labour Relations Act attempted to apply these principles. The LRA could not outlaw plant-level collective bargaining, but introduced a new concept, the workplace forum, in an attempt to facilitate a movement away from distributive collective bargaining towards integrative bargaining. It was hoped that these fora would provide for co-determination at the workplace and that bargaining over wages and conditions would gravitate towards the centre. The Labour Relations Act envisaged a transformation of adversarial industrial relations at the workplace into a regime of co-determination, where unions actively take part in efforts to improve productivity through their involvement in workplace fora.

However, since the LRA was adopted, only six such fora have been established (see Psoulis et al., 1999). Instead of this approach, there is evidence of a trend towards *lean production* based on the casualization of work and attempts to by-pass unions, instead of involving them in restructuring initiatives.

Webster (1999, p. 10) argues that "attempts at productivity increases have invariably been accompanied by job losses". He quotes a survey of 165 companies employing 315,000 employees which found that "company restructuring", rather than "economic downturn" is now the prime contributor to retrenchments. The accompanying movement towards the introduction of team work supported by remuneration structures linked to individual or team performance (respectively referred to as work process and wage flexibility), has been treated with scepticism by trade unions. In South Africa, the phrase "world-class manufacturing" is used quite often to describe the introduction of these practices (see Ewert, 1992; 1997). Instead of post-Fordism, evidence of restructuring initiatives in South Africa seems to point towards a movement towards 'neo-Fordism'. This entails only "a partial movement away from racial-Fordist regulatory practices" (Kraak, 1996, p. 42).

The September Commission described management strategies of retrenching, outsourcing or subcontracting as "seeking to by-pass the union by refusing to consult or engaging in meaningless consultation". According to the Commission, the dangers of these initiatives for organized labour include the "division of workers into 'insiders' and 'outsiders'", and the possibility that "union responses to restructuring may create ideological confusion among members and activists" (COSATU, 1997, pp. 96-97).

The Commission does, however, point out that in some cases unions have used the space created by restructuring initiatives to resist retrenchments and subcontracting, to win "the right to information", and to set up consultative fora. But, "in the majority of cases", unions have not engaged with these processes effectively. Even in cases where restructuring agreements are signed, unions find it difficult to actually use the gains to their advantage in practice (COSATU, 1997, pp. 97-98). Different reasons for this are mentioned. The first points to the perceived route taken by management; "most managers are more concerned to reduce costs and workers and weaken the unions, than to cooperate with unions or to upgrade the skills of their workers". Secondly the Commission acknowledges that unions lack clear vision and policy guidelines on restructuring, as well as the capacity to engage effectively (COSATU, 1997, p. 98).

Hence, in the context of the institutional environment for collective action, labour has partly succeeded in using NEDLAC to shape the nature of post-Apartheid South Africa. However, the labour movement's role in NEDLAC is constrained by a lack of capacity to shape debates, as well as the government stance on the non-negotiability of its macroeconomic strategy. NEDLAC does provide labour with an opportunity to engage in trade negotiations, and provides a platform to keep issues such as the social clause on the agenda.

In terms of industrial relations at a meso-level, it seems that the trend towards centralization has come to an end. Only 36 per cent of the non-agricultural private sector workforce is covered by bargaining council agreements and firm-level bargaining, according to recognition agreements, still forms the foundation of collective bargaining.

Trade unions have had little success in dealing with company-level restructuring and South Africa's version of "world-class manufacturing". They are still trying to find a response to the movement away from standardized contracts of employment and remuneration, towards individualized contracts and bonus systems, coupled with an increase in casualization. Unions may find themselves *defending* the gains made during campaigns in the 1980s and 1990s, and, in the process, will be forced to become more outward looking as companies seek cheap and docile labour elsewhere.

2.6 Collective action and social alliances

The social movement character of COSATU implied that it was in broad alliance with other social movements in its attempts to overthrow the Apartheid regime. However, these alliances also implied tensions and differences in opinion on what the struggle had to entail. Towards the end of the 1980s these tensions became less pronounced, and COSATU entered into a formal alliance with the ANC and the SACP.

During the 1990s, this alliance can be characterized as one of contradictions. On the one hand, it was a way for COSATU to increase its influence in the ANC, thereby maintaining an ANC with a "working-class bias". On the other hand, the alliance was repeatedly used to contain COSATU's militancy and to implement macroeconomic policies.

Various attempts were made from the mid-1990s onwards to define and redefine the role of the alliance in the context of this obvious contradiction. Opinions from COSATU members indicate continued support for remaining in the alliance, even though the level of support seems to be waning. Also, the ANC's overwhelming victory in the 1999 elections demonstrates that there is still support for the party.

In 1994, the survey asked COSATU members about their expectations on delivery from the government; expectations were relatively high. The 1998 survey asked COSATU members to rate the government's performance and workers seemed impressed with the level of delivery on issues such as clean water, electricity, and access to telephones. However, on housing, enough nutritional food and, notably, higher wages, opinions were more moderate to negative.

Buhlungu and Psoulis (1999, p. 11) explain the continued support among COSATU members for the alliance as an "enduring solidarity", based on the traditions and networks built up during the struggle against Apartheid. They also argue that the survey of COSATU members shows a pragmatic attitude among workers.

It should be noted that this pragmatism would imply different voting behaviour if workers, over the long term, do not view the ANC programme as acceptable. Thus, while solidarities seem to endure for now, the rift between the ruling party and the trade union movement may become more stark if current aggregate job losses continue.

Since the end of the anti-Apartheid struggle, many NGOs and community-based organizations have been demobilized, either as a result of funding being directed to other areas, or because of a view that the role of civil society has changed from resistance to cooperation with government. But in light of the magnitude of job losses, many groups have become more active again, notably progressive church groupings. Some of these have been instrumental in the campaign to cancel Third World debt, while others presented an independent voice against the casualization of work at the Jobs Summit held by NEDLAC in 1998.

COSATU has recently made an attempt to rekindle its links with civil society. In October 1999, following a resolution at its 1999 National Congress, the federation called a series of meetings on "deepening unemployment" with various other unions, NGOs, churches, sports organizations, research bodies and traditional leaders. While still formally committed to the alliance with the ANC, these meetings signal a realization in the labour movement that links with broader social movements are still important.

2.7 Unions and public opinion

Public opinion about the labour movement has changed considerably. COSATU is no longer involved in an anti-Apartheid struggle, and unions in South Africa are now accused of being a labour aristocracy, and sometimes a factor contributing to unemployment. However, "public opinion" is a concept that is often abused or used in a very uncritical way. Often, it is portrayed as a monolithic construct, without consideration of the different *interest groups*. The mass media play an important part in forming public opinion in general, but also in forming the image that policy makers have of "public opinion".

The mass media were controlled and censored in various ways during the Apartheid regime. Often the labour movement was vilified and on one occasion Jay Naidoo, then General Secretary of COSATU was described as the "devil incarnate". However, a vibrant alternative press, including the *South African Labour Bulletin*, existed alongside the mainstream press. The independent press provided readers with alternative perspectives on politics in general, and also on the labour movement.

In the 1980s, alongside the South African National Civics Organization (SANCO) and other exponents of mass democracy, the labour movement played a very visible role in campaigns against Apartheid. Obviously, as South Africa moved towards a constitutional democracy, this role, and people's views on the labour movement have changed. Whereas the early stages of transition were dominated by a "language of rights", this changed to a "language of the market" in the late 1990s. The shift was also reflected in the media. Especially since 1996, as net job losses in the formal economy have received increased attention, the "language of the market" has been expressed in the opinion that the South African labour market is rigid, and that the "high" cost of labour is a reason for high unemployment.

The ideology of globalization filtered through the mass media especially through the concept of labour market flexibility, which was generally treated in a very uncritical way (see Bezuidenhout and Kenny, 1999). Indeed, commenting on the way in which debates on labour market flexibility were conducted in South Africa, Guy Standing argued that in the 1990s "most governments are almost prisoners of international opinion... Economic policy is determined not only by realities, but by impressions that filter through a small community of commentators".

It is important to note that very little research has been done in South Africa about trade unions and public opinion. Steven Friedman, Director at the Centre for Policy Studies, pointed out in an interview that the only previous research project which tested public opinion on trade unions had been conducted after the elections in 1994. The research was based on focus group interviews which had only been conducted with black participants. As a result, it did not constitute a sample from which one could generalize about the whole population. At that stage, there had seemed to be general sympathy for trade unions. However, there was a variety of opinions, one of which held that the trade union movement had behaved irresponsibly and had been disadvantaging the unemployed.

Nine out of the 12 people interviewed in the context of the present study felt that attitudes towards the trade unions were changing. However, they disagreed as to how these attitudes were changing and in which direction. One person interviewed did not think that "opinions on the whole" had been changing. Two pointed out that there was no basis for such an assertion, arguing that it was necessary to define "the public".

Emerging organizations claiming to represent the unemployed have criticized trade unions for protecting a labour aristocracy. Two examples of these organizations are the Malamulela Social Movement for the Unemployed,[1] and the Unemployed Masses of South Africa (UMSA). These

---

[1] Malamulela means "saviour" in Sotho.

organizations' calls for labour market flexibility are often accompanied by xenophobia directed at immigrant workers in South Africa.

However, the labour movement engaged in a number of innovative campaigns to counter these claims and perceptions. When a Presidential Jobs Summit was held in 1998 to address the problem of unemployment, the three federations set up a job creation fund and called on their members to contribute a day's wage to the fund. An independent team of trustees was appointed to oversee job creation projects. The event received wide media coverage when President Nelson Mandela gave a day's wage as the first contribution. Unfortunately the collection of donations from members was not well organized, and the fund currently operates with finances considerably lower than expected.

A second campaign was for a coordinated social plan to alleviate the effect of job losses on communities and workers. The labour movement argued that there was a need for a coordinated approach from government, business, the labour movement and other organizations to set up retraining facilities, essential services and welfare to communities affected by increased levels of unemployment. The campaign has been partially successful in that government and business have agreed to set up a social plan.

A third campaign was protest action against the reduction of import tariffs, especially in industries such as clothing and textiles. The labour movement partly succeeded in diverting attention away from the labour market flexibility debate to the fact that the government was reducing import tariffs faster than agreed in multilateral agreements. During the campaign, SACTWU argued that government was responsible for introducing a coordinated industrial policy framework, including effective supply-side measures, before embarking on rapid tariff reduction.

Hence, impressionistic evidence points towards a more sophisticated approach to trade unions in some sectors of the "public", while opinion in other sectors may become more negative. There is an impression that the media support a "common sense view" that globalization is inevitable and a liberal programme naturally follows. However, the announcement by the state railway company that it would reduce its workforce by 29,000, coupled with the mining industry shedding 90,000 jobs in 1998 alone, refocused the unemployment debate towards an increased awareness of the social consequences of globalization. A sophisticated response to this, coupled with awareness of the fact that globalization as practised currently does not have a "human face", may change the language and redirect policy towards the *social regulation* of economic life.

2.8 A broader agenda for union action: Towards global social movement unionism?

It should be noted that the South African labour movement was instrumental in campaigns to end Apartheid. This campaign was based on durable shopfloor structures organized through shop stewards committees. Membership of the post-1973 trade unions rocketed, not only because they were able to address the real problems of their members in the workplace, but also because unions formed part of a *broader social movement of civil alliances.* Trade unions were assisted by unions abroad – especially those organizing workers in the same transnational corporations. The South African case is an example of how workers can use their collective power and alliances with other organizations to win campaigns against inhumane social structures. After 1990, many of these gains were established as rights under a new democratic dispensation.

However, the labour movement did not achieve its broader goal of transforming society economically. Instead, many of the gains are coming under pressure as a result of globalization. Global forces, coupled with local dynamics, have caused the labour movement to respond in various ways:

There is a realization that new membership campaigns will have to be taken seriously – casual workers and workers in "vulnerable sectors" will have to be organized into the labour movement. Otherwise, labour market segmentation may leave unions with a shrinking share of the working class, which could contribute to allegations that they represent a privileged minority. Proposed campaigns include special recruitment drives to organize casual workers and the setting up of advice centres. Usually, however, these campaigns remain rhetorical. Unions in general have not been able to recruit casual workers, or organize vulnerable sectors such as agriculture, construction and domestic service.

The South African labour movement has moved on from fighting for basic labour rights to maintaining these rights in the face of globalization. In the context of a parliamentary democracy, the social movement character of trade unions has become less pronounced. Also, unions have been growing and the traditional "organizing model" runs the risk of becoming a "servicing model" through bureaucratization. This is ironic as unions in the North are realizing the limits of a "servicing model" and focusing on organizing workers as part of broader social movements. There is evidence of a generational shift within COSATU, among both workers and officials. In order to respond to globalization, unions will have to maintain membership solidarity under conditions of increased individualization of labour relations and the need for coordinated centralized action and campaigns.

Democratization has led to several new possibilities for the labour movement to shape the outcome of social processes - institutions such as NEDLAC and bargaining councils are examples. However, it does seem that global competition may increase pressure to move away from centralized collective bargaining. A sophisticated response from trade unions is needed. This may include campaigns to draw attention to the "positive" aspects of such institutions, such as more coordinated approaches to education and skills development, and the formulation of industry-wide responses to increased competition. Also, unions will have to find creative ways of responding to company-level restructuring. But a company-level response is not adequate in itself. In the end, a collective "race to the bottom" will not contribute to sustainable competitiveness – therefore a global response is required, closely modelled on the South African unions' fight for recognition in the 1970s. But this time South African unions will have to act in solidarity with unions in Asia, South America and, specifically, Southern Africa.

Opinions differ on the nature of COSATU's alliance with the ANC. Considerable tensions arose when the ANC openly supported liberal macroeconomic policies. Should COSATU decide to part with the ANC, such a departure will have to be carefully orchestrated so as not to destroy the union movement itself. However, evidence points to waning, yet still significant support among COSATU members for the alliance with the ANC. Early attempts have been made by COSATU to rekindle its links with civil society, primarily around a campaign for increased levels of unemployment.

Public opinion has become a major source of contestation. Even though the public is "diverse", debates which are shaped by the media shape the policy agendas of government. The labour market flexibility debate has reshaped the agenda of "rights" towards a narrow "market" approach - a short-term approach which may have dire long-term consequences for the reproduction of the South African labour force. Some unions have found sophisticated ways of dealing with the media, but public sector strikes, which may affect services to ordinary people, will have to be accompanied by active media campaigns.

This also goes for campaigns of global solidarity. Campaigns in this regard include setting up a union-funded Job Creation Fund, campaigns around the impact of rapid trade liberalization on employment, and attempts to alleviate the impact of job losses on workers and communities through a social plan. The South African labour movement has used various campaign modalities to draw attention to the negative impact of globalization. Unions have been unable to deal with work intensification and casualization, both key consequences of globalization. It is here that unions will be forced to become more outward looking, and to link up with unions and social movements globally.

Opportunities are many, but capacity is lacking at this stage. A key challenge for COSATU is to revitalize and strengthen its social movement characteristics, especially those of worker control and links with civil society. Like national campaigns, global campaigns depend on the active support of members, building on a consciousness of the importance of solidarity. Global social movement unionism provides a model for this, and is based on some of the traditions that the South African labour movement shares with labour movements elsewhere.

References

Adler, G.; Webster, E. 1995. "Challenging transition theory: The labour movement, radical reform and transition to democracy in South Africa", in *Politics and Society*, No. 23(1).

Barrett, J. 1993. "New strategies to organise difficult sectors", in *South African Labour Bulletin*, Vol. 17, No. 6, pp. 45-50.

Baskin, J. 1996. "Unions at the cross-roads: Can they make the transition?" in *South African Labour Bulletin*, Vol. 20, No. 1, pp. 8-16.

Bendix, S. 1996. *Industrial relations in the new South Africa*. 3rd edition (Cape Town, Juta).

Bezuidenhout, A. 1999. *"Restore profitability or we pull the trigger": The politics of productivity in the South African gold mining industry in the 1990s*. Paper presented at the Annual Congress of the South African Sociological Association, Saldanha Bay.

—; Kenny, B. 1999. *The language of flexibility and the flexibility of language: Post-Apartheid South African labour market debates*. Paper presented at the Annual Congress of the South African Sociological Association, Saldanha Bay.

Buhlungu, S. 1994. "The big brain drain: Union officials in the 1990s", in *South African Labour Bulletin*, Vol. 18, No. 3, pp. 26-32.

—. 1997. *Working for the union: A profile of union officials in COSATU*. Labour Studies Research Report No. 8 (Sociology of Work Unit, University of the Witwatersrand).

—. 1999. *Gaining influence but losing power? Labour under democracy and globalization in South Africa*. Paper presented at the Annual Congress of the South African Sociological Association, Saldanha Bay.

—; Psoulis, C. 1999. *Enduring solidarities: Accounting for the continuity of support for the Alliance amongst COSATU members*. Paper presented at the Annual Congress of the South African Sociological Association, Saldanha Bay.

Collins, D. 1994. "Worker control", in *South African Labour Bulletin*, Vol. 18, No. 3, pp. 33-42.

Congress of South African Trade Unions (COSATU). 1997. *Report of the September Commission of Enquiry into the Future of the Trade Unions* (Johannesburg) (Online: http://www.COSATU.org.za/congress/septcomm.htm).

Ewert, J. 1999. "Restructuring industry on the factory floor: Neo-Fordist tendencies at Western Cape firms", in *South African Sociological Review*, Vol. 5, No. 1, pp. 1-22.

—. 1997. "Training for 'world-class manufacturing': Rhetoric and reality in the South African engineering industry", in *South African Journal of Labour Relations*, Vol. 22, No. 2, pp. 25-41.

Fraser, D. 1991. "The ICFTU in South Africa: Coming on strong." (Interview by D. Pillay) in *South African Labour Bulletin*, Vol. 15, No. 7, pp. 27-31.

Friedman, S. 1987. *Building tomorrow today: African workers in trade unions 1970-1984* (Johannesburg, Ravan).

Gostner, K. 1997. *Organised labour and globalization: A case of David and Goliath?* MA research report (Department of Sociology, University of the Witwatersrand).

—; Joffe, A. 1998. "Negotiating the future: Labour's role in NEDLAC", in *Law, Democracy and Development*, No. 2, pp. 131-151.

Gotz, G. 2000. "Shoot anything that flies, claim anything that falls: Labour and the changing definition of the Reconstruction and Development Programme", in Adler, G.; Webster, E. (eds.) *Trade unions and democratization in South Africa, 1985-1997* (London, Macmillan).

Hudson, J. 1991. "The practice of solidarity", in *South African Labour Bulletin*, Vol. 15, No. 7, pp. 40-43.

International Labour Office (ILO). 1999. *Studies on the social dimensions of globalization: South Africa* (Geneva, ILO).

Kenny, B.; Bezuidenhout, A. 1999. "Fighting subcontracting: Legal protections and negotiating strategies", in *South African Labour Bulletin*, Vol. 23, No. 3, pp. 39-46.

—; Webster, E. 1999. "Eroding the core: Flexibility and the resegmentation of the South African labour market", in *Critical Sociology*, Vol. 23, No. 3, pp. 216-243.

Klerck, G. 1998. "Between corporatism and neo-liberalism? Collective bargaining and South Africa's new Labour Relations Act", in *African Sociological Review*, Vol. 2, No. 1, pp. 85-113.

Kraak, A. 1996. Transforming South Africa's economy: From racial Fordism to neo-Fordism? in *Economic and Industrial Democracy*, No. 17, pp. 39-74.

Marais, H. 1998. *South Africa: Limits to change, The political economy of transformation* (London and New York, Zed Books).

Maree, J. 1987. *The independent trade unions, 1974-1984* (Johannesburg, Ravan).

Marie, B. 1992. "COSATU faces crisis: 'Quick fix' methods and organizational contradictions", in *South African Labour Bulletin*, Vol. 16, No. 5, pp. 20-26.

Naidoo, J. 1991. "More that unites than divides" (Interview with C. Mather and K. Von Holdt) in *South African Labour Bulletin*, Vol. 15, No. 7, pp. 16-21.

Naidoo, R. (ed.). 1999. *Unions in transition: COSATU into the new millennium* (Johannesburg, Naledi).

Ngcukana, C. 1991. "Rooting out dependency" (Interview with C. Mather and K. Von Holdt) in *South African Labour Bulletin*, Vol. 15, No. (7), pp. 22-26.

Normative Economic Model (NEM). 1993. *The restructuring of the South African economy: A normative model approach* (Pretoria, Central Economic Advisory Service and Government Printers).

Padayachee, V. 1998. "Progressive academic economists and the challenge of development in South Africa's decade of liberation", in *Review of African Political Economy*, No. 77, pp. 430-431.

Psoulis, C.; Moleme, K.; Spratt, J.; Ryan, E. 1999. *Workplace forums: What is their future?* Labour Studies Research Report No. 9 (Johannesburg, University of the Witwatersrand, Sociology of Work Unit).

Roux, R. 1990. "SACTU: End of an era", in *South African Labour Bulletin*, Vol. 14, No. 8, pp. 47-51.

Simons, J.; Simons, R. 1983. *Class and colour in South Africa* (London, International Defence Aid).

South Africa Foundation (SAF). 1996. *Growth for all: An economic strategy for South Africa* (Johannesburg).

Southall, R. 1995. *Imperialism or solidarity? International labour and South African trade unions* (Cape Town, UCT Press).

—. 1996. *International labour and South African trade unions*, Labour Studies Research Report No. 7 (University of the Witwatersrand, Sociology of Work Unit).

Standing, G. 1996. "Tackling the jobless", in *Mail* and *Guardian*, 26 Nov.

—. 1997a. "Globalization, labour flexibility and insecurity: The era of market regulation", in *European Journal of Industrial Relations*, Vol. 3, No. 1, pp. 7-37.

—. 1997b. *Labour market dynamics in South African industrial firms: The South African labour flexibility survey.* Unpublished paper (Pretoria: Conference on Labour Markets and Enterprise Performance in South Africa, Reserve Bank).

—; Sender, J.; Weeks, J. 1996. *Restructuring the labour market: The South African challenge. An ILO country review* (Geneva, International Labour Office).

United Nations Development Programme (UNDP). 1999. *Globalization with a human face: Human Development Report* (New York, UNDP).

Webster, E. 1995b. "NEDLAC – Corporatism of a special type?", in *South African Labour Bulletin*, Vol. 19, No. 2, pp. 40-45.

—. 1999. *ILO research project on the contribution of collective bargaining to employment protection and to competitiveness: The case of South Africa* (Johannesburg, Sociology of Work Unit).

—; Adler, G. 1998. *Towards a class compromise in South Africa's 'double transition': Bargained liberalization and the consolidation of democracy.* Paper presented at the 14th World Congress of Sociology, Montreal, Canada. 26 July - 1 Aug.

Wood, G. 1999. *Shopfloor democracy in the Congress of South African trade unions in the late 1990s.* Paper presented at the Annual Congress of the South African Sociological Association, Saldanha Bay.